# LOVE, MARRIAGE, and JEWISH FAMILIES

## HBI SERIES ON JEWISH WOMEN

Shulamit Reinharz, *General Editor*
Sylvia Barack Fishman, *Associate Editor*

The HBI Series on Jewish Women, created by the Hadassah-Brandeis Institute, publishes a wide range of books by and about Jewish women in diverse contexts and time periods. Of interest to scholars and the educated public, the HBI Series on Jewish Women fills major gaps in Jewish Studies and in Women and Gender Studies as well as their intersection.

The HBI Series on Jewish Women is supported by a generous gift from Dr. Laura S. Schor.

For the complete list of books that are available in this series, please see www.upne.com

Sylvia Barack Fishman, editor, *Love, Marriage, and Jewish Families: Paradoxes of a Social Revolution*
Cynthia Kaplan Shamash, *The Strangers We Became: Lessons in Exile from One of Iraq's Last Jews*
Marcia Falk, *The Days Between: Blessings, Poems, and Directions of the Heart for the Jewish High Holiday Season*
Inbar Raveh, *Feminist Rereadings of Rabbinic Literature*
Laura Silver, *The Book of Knish: In Search of the Jewish Soul Food*
Sharon R. Siegel, *A Jewish Ceremony for Newborn Girls: The Torah's Covenant Affirmed*
Laura S. Schor, *The Best School in Jerusalem: Annie Landau's School for Girls, 1900–1960*
Federica K. Clementi, *Holocaust Mothers and Daughters: Family, History, and Trauma*
Elana Maryles Sztokman and Chaya Rosenfeld Gorsetman, *Educating in the Divine Image: Gender Issues in Orthodox Jewish Day Schools*
Ilana Szobel, *A Poetics of Trauma: The Work of Dahlia Ravikovitch*
Susan M. Weiss and Netty C. Gross-Horowitz, *Marriage and Divorce in the Jewish State: Israel's Civil War*
Ronit Irshai, *Fertility and Jewish Law: Feminist Perspectives on Orthodox Responsa Literature*
Elana Maryles Sztokman, *The Men's Section: Orthodox Jewish Men in an Egalitarian World*
Sharon Faye Koren, *Forsaken: The Menstruant in Medieval Jewish Mysticism*
Sonja M. Hedgepeth and Rochelle G. Saidel, editors, *Sexual Violence against Jewish Women during the Holocaust*
Julia R. Lieberman, editor, *Sephardi Family Life in the Early Modern Diaspora*
Derek Rubin, editor, *Promised Lands: New Jewish American Fiction on Longing and Belonging*
Carol K. Ingall, editor, *The Women Who Reconstructed American Jewish Education: 1910–1965*
Gaby Brimmer and Elena Poniatowska, *Gaby Brimmer: An Autobiography in Three Voices*
Harriet Hartman and Moshe Hartman, *Gender and American Jews: Patterns in Work, Education, and Family in Contemporary Life*
Dvora E. Weisberg, *Levirate Marriage and the Family in Ancient Judaism*
Ellen M. Umansky and Dianne Ashton, editors, *Four Centuries of Jewish Women's Spirituality: A Sourcebook*
Carole S. Kessner, *Marie Syrkin: Values Beyond the Self*
Ruth Kark, Margalit Shilo, and Galit Hasan-Rokem, editors, *Jewish Women in Pre-State Israel: Life History, Politics, and Culture*

# LOVE, MARRIAGE, and JEWISH FAMILIES

## Paradoxes of a Social Revolution

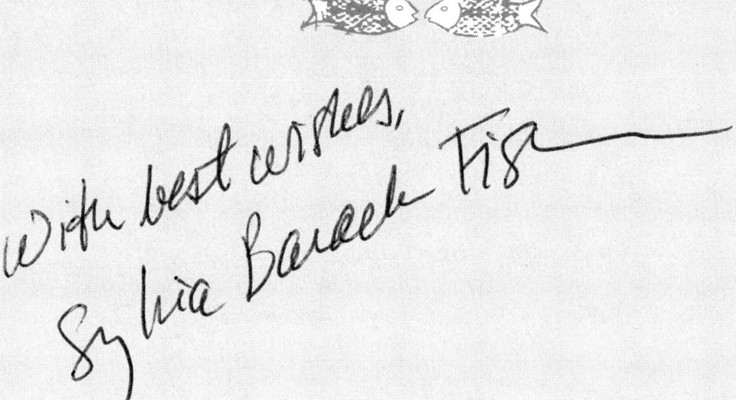


SYLVIA BARACK FISHMAN, EDITOR

BRANDEIS UNIVERSITY PRESS
*Waltham, Massachusetts*

Brandeis University Press
An imprint of University Press of New England
www.upne.com

Manufactured in the United States of America
Designed by Vicki Kuskowski
Typeset in Granjon LT Std by Westchester Publishing Service



Library of Congress Cataloging-in-Publication Data
Love, marriage, and Jewish families : paradoxes of a social revolution / Sylvia Barack Fishman, editor.
pages cm. — (HBI series on Jewish women)
Includes bibliographical references and index.
ISBN 978-1-61168-859-7 (cloth : alk. paper) — ISBN 978-1-61168-860-3 (pbk. : alk. paper) — ISBN 978-1-61168-861-0 (ebook)
1. Jewish families. 2. Marriage—Religious aspects. 3. Families—Religious aspects. 4. Jewish way of life. 5. Jews—Social conditions—21st century. 6. Jews—Social life and customs—21st century.
I. Fishman, Sylvia Barack, 1942– editor.
HQ525.J4L68 2015
306.85'089924—dc23

5 4 3 2 1

For my grandchildren,

Joshua Samuel,

Ari Shai,

Leor Barak,

Netanel Nehemiah,

Ayelet Rina,

Yonina Leah

*Tzetzaei tzetzaeinu*

# CONTENTS

# FOREWORD

The HBI (Hadassah-Brandeis Institute) Series on Jewish Women is pleased to present this volume, edited and with an Introduction by the HBI co-director, Sylvia Barack Fishman. The Introduction and thirteen essays that comprise *Love, Marriage and Jewish Families* are fascinating and illustrate the continuous morphing of family forms among generations and contexts. Take for example the 1960s Broadway musical, "Fiddler on the Roof," which reworks Sholom Aleichem's depiction of the changing Jewish family in the Russian Pale of Settlement in the early twentieth century. Golde, the play's middle-aged wife and mother, responds to her husband's question, "Do you Love Me?" with an answer that would not pass muster today. "For twenty-five years I've washed your clothes, cooked your meals, cleaned your house, given you children, milked your cow . . ." But Tevye—observing his daughters opting for love over duty—wants more than Golde's dutiful performance of household chores; he wants love and he wants her to express it.

Nowadays, love seems to be what everyone wants, including Jews. As modern society has focused on individualism, on each person considering herself or himself a unique person and not just a member of a group, that individuality requires and deserves the unique devotion to the individual that we call love. How love emerges (or doesn't) in or before a relationship develops remains a mystery. Some people call it "chemistry." And for those people who do not experience it, life can become frustrating—or not.

Given the new requirement that one must find the perfect partner to match oneself as a unique individual, it is not surprising that "single Americans make up more than half the adult population," 50.2 percent, up from 37 percent in 1976 when the government started keeping track, according to Bureau of Labor statistics as reported in *Bloomberg* (Miller, 2014). This figure reflects a decrease in family-based and intergenerational households. As the chapters in this book demonstrate, singles comprise a larger segment of the American *Jewish* community than in past generations, as well. Nevertheless, the majority (not the totality) of highly educated, affluent Americans—the group to which most American

Jews belong—do marry eventually, and according to the most recent research, the majority of these marriages do not end in divorce. At the same time, the percentage of Jews cohabiting also has risen. Marriage is no longer the only love relation of choice.

As is widely understood among educators watching enrollments diminish in Jewish educational settings, younger American Jews have fewer children now than their counterparts did in the past. For people who worry about the negative environmental impact of a growing population, the decline in the birth rate may be good news. But for Jews who are concerned with the shifting demographics of the Jewish population, decline in family size is a major challenge and makes Jewish continuity a precarious proposition. Some of this decrease in family size reflects conscious choice. In other cases, Jews need assistance in having children for various medical or social reasons. To mitigate this handicap, in the winter 2014–2015 issue of *Lilith* magazine, founding editor Susan Weidman Schneider proposed the creation of a Jewish national fund to assist American women who lack the means for expensive reproductive technology and childcare thereafter. Israeli women already benefit from generous reproductive technology assistance—a major cultural difference between that country and the United States. Nevertheless, Israeli and American, married and single, heterosexual and LGBTQ Jews sometimes pursue parenthood through the use of modern reproductive technology.

As the analyses in these chapters inform us, Israeli Jews tend to marry somewhat earlier than their American counterparts and to have more children than American Jews. Thus, it is not Jewishness alone that creates norms for family size, but Jewishness in the culture of the specific country in which Jewish people live. It is also interesting to note that the average secular Israeli has more children than the average American Modern Orthodox Jew, indicating that the degree of observance may be less significant in determining family size than the at-large culture in which the individuals live.

These findings of sophisticated researchers and statisticians are mirrored in the popular culture of the United States and Israel. Television series in both countries portray individuals who live alone or with one or more "friends." The Jewish comedian Jerry Seinfeld, whose eponymous television show enjoyed an enormous run (1989–1998), focused his show on four people: the single Jerry himself, a single close male friend, a single male neighbor, and a single ex-girlfriend. In the nine years that *Seinfeld* was on the air, none of these characters developed a lasting relationship with a potential partner.

The Israeli television series *Srugim* is similarly wildly popular. As Willa Paskin wrote for Slate on June 30, 2014:

> *Srugim* takes as its starting point the generation of [Israeli] Modern Orthodox Jews who are simultaneously (meticulously) observant and also, genuinely, contemporary. (The [show's] title means *knitted*, and refers to the stitching of a style of yarmulke, as well the characters' full integration into Israeli society). It begins with its characters going on a familiar series of bad dates—the blind date, the speed date, the date that devolves into a fight about salaries—clichés that, as with everything about *Srugim,* are lightly reinvigorated by religion. The closet case, sleeping with an ex, losing one's virginity, trying to advance one's career, weekly dinners with friends: *Srugim* puts all of these recognizable [themes] in a new cultural context. It is comfort food you've never tasted before. Eat up.

Although we've titled this volume *Love, Marriage and Jewish Families*, the chapters here also devote attention to sex and sexuality. Many observers have discussed a contemporary disconnect between sexual activity and love; there is often a similar disconnect between sexual activity and marriage. Some American Jews participate in casual sexual activity beginning in their early teen years and continuing through their twenties and thirties. However, the contributors here also show that this disconnect is not typical in the ultra-Orthodox or Haredi community, where sexual activity is confined to marriage.

The chapters grouped in part 1, "Love, Sexuality, and Personal Choice," include discussions of delayed marriage in the United States and in Israel, and of gay and lesbian Jewish families in Israel, providing major insights into these life choices and populations, respectively. Part 2, "Family Transformations," reflects the HBI's emphasis on comparative analysis rather than pat generalizations when discussing the attitudes and behaviors of Jews. In these chapters, readers will discover the commonalities and differences between American and Israeli Jewish women and men in their personal and family goals. Part 3, "Marriage and the Law," explores topics concerning Jewish and civic law that are regularly analyzed by the HBI's Project on Gender, Culture, Religion, and the Law, a division of the HBI headed by one of the contributors, Lisa Fishbayn Joffe.

Mimicking Isaac Newton's Third Law of Motion (for every action, there is an equal and opposite reaction), sociologists have long recognized that for every social change, there is a counterforce pushing against the change. In the social realm, unlike in physics, we do not expect the reaction to be equal in power, but still, pushback is to be anticipated. Thus this volume ends with a two-essay section titled "Backlash and Reaction." This section reveals how the Israeli Haredi community wrestles with changing concepts of maleness and femaleness, and with masculine and feminine virtue and beauty. Culture and the arts, particularly the films of Haredi and Modern Orthodox students at the Jerusalem-based film school Ma'aleh, also delve deeply into these topics. Similarly, Reina Rutlinger-Reiner's *The Audacity of Holiness,* published by the HBI and available in digital format from the Brandeis Institutional Repository, shows how Israeli Orthodox women and men have created theatrical performances about their challenges with sensitive topics of sex, love, marriage, and the law.

The HBI's mission statement calls for "developing new ideas about Jews and gender," and certainly this volume does exactly that. I congratulate all the authors on their stellar contributions.

Shulamit Reinharz
Director, Hadassah-Brandeis Institute

# ACKNOWLEDGMENTS

This book began its journey toward publication as a cooperative research venture of the Hadassah Brandeis Institute (HBI) and the Van Leer Jerusalem Institute (VLJI). I am immensely grateful to HBI and VLJI for supporting and helping me organize an international workshop and an international conference in two successive winters, 2012 and 2013, that invited a broad range of papers and artistic works exploring "new understandings of gender, love, and the Jewish family." The presentations documented and analyzed the sweeping social changes in which we all, consciously or inadvertently, participate. I am especially grateful to VLJI's Dafna Schreiber and Rabbi Naftali Rothenberg, and to HBI's Shulamit Reinharz and Lisa Fishbayn Joffe, who contributed to the workshop and conference and afterwards helped me conceptualize the critical topics for this volume.

The scholars who bring their pioneering analyses to *Love, Marriage, and Jewish Families: Paradoxes of a Social Revolution* deserve admiration for their systematic scientific discussions of complex, powerful topics. It has been a joy and inspiration to build this volume with them. I am grateful to artist Andi Arnovitz, whose beautiful works on the cover and in the pages of this book reflect and illuminate disturbing issues in contemporary life.

My framing of *Love, Marriage, and Jewish Families* was informed by colleagues at diverse institutions in the course of research projects and academic events. Steven M. Cohen, with whom my current research on aspects of the new Jewish family proceeds, continues to share invaluable insights. I am glad to acknowledge the ongoing enrichment of conversations with Len Saxe of Brandeis University's Cohen Center for Modern Jewish Studies and with Rabbi Yitz Greenberg, Jack Wertheimer, Harriet Hartman, Tova Hartman, Margalit Shilo, Riv-Ellen Prell, Adam Ferziger, and Steven Bayme. It is my pleasure to thank faculty colleagues in the Near Eastern and Judaic Studies Department (NEJS) at Brandeis University, whose interest and support helped make it possible for this project to continue.

Related issues of some aspects of this book have been explored in other publications. I am grateful to colleagues who helped me think through additional dimensions of these multifaceted topics in articles such as "Gender in American Jewish Life," in the *American Jewish Year Book 2014*, edited by Arnold Dashefky and Ira Sheskin; Avinoam Bar-Yosef and Shlomo Fischer of the Jewish People Policy Institute (JPPI), who enabled me to contribute to several important JPPI annual assessments; Lynn Levy and Saul Andron, who created a special family issue for the *Journal of Jewish Communal Service.*

NEJS administrators Joanne Arnish and Jean Manion and HBI administrator Nancy Leonard lent invaluable practical assistance at various stages of the project; my special thanks go to NEJS graduate research assistants Rachel S. Bernstein and Kendra Yarbor. Both NEJS and HBI provided helpful research grants. At Brandeis University Press, executive editor Phyllis D. Deutsch was, as always, a smart, tireless, and skilled comrade-in-arms; at University Press of New England, managing editor Amanda Dupuis steered the manuscript to print.

It's always a privilege and a joy to conclude an acknowledgments section with thanks to my family, whose support for my work is palpable and energizing. This book is dedicated to my grandchildren, *tzetzaei tzetzaeinu,* delightful and very interesting human beings growing with astonishing rapidity toward adult concerns. Their parents—both by birth and by marriage my cherished children—are role models and happy exemplars of the wonders of the contemporary Jewish family. Not least, Phil, my *ben zug*—we both know how lucky we are.

# LOVE, MARRIAGE, and JEWISH FAMILIES

# INTRODUCTION

## Paradoxes of a Social Revolution

Sylvia Barack Fishman

"LOVE," "MARRIAGE," AND "FAMILY," are fluid concepts.[1] Legal, economic, social, and religious attitudes vary significantly in different times and places, and discrete societies construct divergent normative gender roles, sexual interactions, and family arrangements. Many today regard the 1950s affection-based Western nuclear family as the "conventional" model of family life, but social scientists have argued for decades that the companionate marriage based on emotional satisfaction and romantic love was itself a significant departure from earlier historical formulations.[2] Today, that nuclear model has declined, and concepts of marriage have undergone "a transition from the companionate marriage to what we might call the *individualized marriage*." Economist Andrew Cherlin explains that spouses may not be interested in "fulfilling socially valued roles such as the good parent or the loyal and supportive spouse," and "personal choice and self-development loom large in people's construction of their marital careers."[3]

Concepts of gender, sex, intimacy, and love, and the role of children in familial constellations, have also undergone extraordinary, overlapping transformations in many Western societies over the past few decades.[4] In open Western societies family styles are diverse, cultural boundaries appear porous and eroded, and social protocols and religious hierarchies are often ignored.[5] Erotic, marital, and familial expectations differ from community to community. However, in some traditional contemporary communities, marriage continues even today to be used as it was in many historical societies—as a vehicle for political, economic, social, and/or religious arrangements, with less emphasis placed on companionate and individualistic emotional factors.

### Changing Jewish Families around the World

*Love, Marriage, and Jewish Families: Paradoxes of a Social Revolution* views these profound social changes within their larger contexts in the United States and

Israel, the countries with the two largest Jewish communities. The thirteen chapters collected in this volume by social scientists, historians, and legal scholars break new ground, focus primarily on younger Jews, and paint a transnational panorama by examining a broad spectrum of American and Israeli Jewish life, from secular and unaffiliated to devoutly religiously observant. Each chapter examines specific societies and spheres of social change in Israel or the United States, and spotlights distinctive subgroups. Indeed, Jewish communities internationally each have their own individual profile; nevertheless, important commonalities emerge in areas such as attitudinal and demographic change, Jewish legal approaches, and conservative religious resistance to change.

There is a critical need now for both the general picture and the particulars these chapters provide because as yet little comprehensive research has been published: "Family scientists have done little in the area of theory development,"[6] sociologist Farrell J. Webb comments. Regarding Jewish families, there has been much written and spoken about limited topics, especially intermarriage, but not much systematic analysis published on the sweeping, intersecting changes—and their implications—in our understandings of gender and sexuality, love and marriage, and family formation.[7] Together, the chapters of this book cast a wide disciplinary net, documenting and analyzing the Jewish dimensions of overarching critical questions: (1) What are the personal and social gains—and losses—emerging from the transformations we are witnessing? (2) How have they affected family formation and functioning from social and legal standpoints? (3) What is the nature of the personal and institutional anxiety about and backlash against these changes? This introduction begins the book's discussion and frames the following chapters by exploring changes in sexual mores and material, economic expectations—love and money—that undergirded, galvanized, and nurtured the social revolution in question and its paradoxical responses.

## Jewish Families and "Sexual Liberation"

One didn't have to live in America to believe in the sentiment expressed in the song. "Love and marriage go together like a horse and carriage," crooned by Frank Sinatra in 1955, articulating post–World War II family centeredness and heteronormativity at its most frontal. "This I tell you brother, you can't have one—you can't have none—you can't have one without the other," he sang, evoking a smooth progression from sexual attraction and love to marriage and fertility, and also articulating societal disapproval of any attempts to separate sexuality from marriage. Through the middle of the twentieth century most Western societies displayed cultural norms that linked individualistic love and marriage as an institution. Significantly, Paula Hyman showed that Jewish families in prior eras may have exhibited some modern companionate qualities.[8] But in the mid-1950s distinctive American and Israeli social, religious, and cultural factors invested this common familism with somewhat different symbolic meanings: in Israel references to romance, marriage, and fertility were often overtly or implicitly enriched by their value as a posthumous victory over Hitler and a boost for Jewish demographics in the Jewish State, while in America even for Jews the cultural contexts tended to emphasize personal happiness and nuclear familial togetherness.

In the 1950s and early 1960s American Jews, like their gentile counterparts, were influenced by societal approval of earlier marriage and larger families. Half of American Jewish women married by the time they were 21, and they gave birth, overall, to an average of about three children. Near-universal Jewish marriage and above-replacement fertility were supported not only by traditional Jewish familism but also (and perhaps preeminently) by American societal expectations about gender and sexuality. Middle-class American Jews shared American bourgeois gender-role construction circa 1955; in a double standard that derived from widespread Judeo-Christian religious prescriptions and was reinforced by literature, films, and popular culture, women were expected to ensure that sexual activity was connected to marriage and reproduction. Unmarried females were encouraged to be sexually appealing but virginal, while premarital sexual initiation and activity was an accepted American male rite of passage. As Herman Wouk described in his 1955 novel *Marjorie Morningstar*: "Twentieth century or not, good Jewish girls were supposed to be virgins when they got married. . . . For that matter, good Christian girls were supposed to be virgins too; that was why brides wore white."[9]

The tension between an unmarried woman's need to radiate "sex appeal" while retaining "good girl" inexperience led to what Wouk characterized as a "rigidly graduated" continuum of behavioral standards. Men were expected to cajole and persuade; women were expected to resist and dole out sexual favors carefully and incrementally, with the goal of gradually enticing men into engagement and marriage. Both men and women understood what "good girls" did and didn't do. Doris Day movies were indoctrinating American women on how to navigate between the Scylla of promiscuity and the Charybdis of frigidity, with consequences that affected men too. As Wouk's Noel Airman lamented: "I don't have a chance [at sex] without that wedding ring."[10] Societies created sanctions and demanded a price for transgressive behavior—at least from the women. While many men and women defied the societal norms, sexually active middle-class women who were "caught" by unwanted premarital pregnancies were typically subjected to a choice between quick marriages, difficult-to-arrange secret abortions, or exile somewhere far away where they could gestate and then give a child up for adoption.

Conservative, Reform, and even Modern Orthodox Jews, for the most part, devoted little educational attention to admonishing teenagers and single young adults on sexual matters. Few schools or sermons instructed singles on rabbinical strictures against having physical contact; indeed, some Modern Orthodox synagogues sponsored social events with ballroom dancing. Rabbis seldom preached against women singing on the presumption that women's voices were sexually arousing (*kol b'isha ervah*). With the exception of the then small and mostly immigrant population of Haredi (ultra-Orthodox) Jews, Jewish religious authorities in the 1950s and early 1960s relied on the expectation that middle-class Jewish singles would be shaped by and would conform to well-articulated external social standards. And, as Michael Broyde argues, as long as American gentile society required reasonably modest dress among its girls and women, American Orthodox Jews left the subject of modest female wardrobe to situational standards as well,[11] and minimal emphasis was placed on the details of female modesty (*tzniut*) outside of Haredi circles.

Societal attitudes toward sexuality, love, and marriage changed in the mid-1960s and early 1970s, when 1950s middle-class conformity, gender-role clarity, and family centeredness were disrupted by intersecting forces. In an era of complex and widespread social and political unrest, precipitated by the Vietnam War and the American civil rights movement, some young Americans accused their elders of hypocritical external adherence to bourgeois proprieties and neglect of authenticity and the inner life. Some experimented with "mind-expanding" drugs and communal living.

Even for the majority who did not move far afield of middle-class norms, critiques of conventional marriage and family life were in the air. Many men were influenced by the "*Playboy*" philosophy that urged men to enjoy their freedom fully before capitulating to the demands of marriage and family, as Barbara Ehrenreich suggests.[12] Women too began to view marriage skeptically, following Betty Friedan's *The Feminine Mystique* (1963).[13] Ever broader waves of feminist commentary on women's lives and choices raised the consciousness of America's middle-class women, warning them that they lacked economic and psychological preparation to function independently and to fulfill their own needs. Just as the *Playboy* philosophy argued for sexual pleasure as a private matter, uncomplicated by societal expectations, feminist voices asserted that women's sexuality should not be supervised by religious or political leaders or potential husbands. Significantly, Jewish women were prominent among the leaders and active laity of American second-wave feminism.

Not least, changes in personal behavior, along with male and female "liberation" movements, were fueled by increasing availability of birth control, especially the pill. While no generation invents sexuality, and liberal sexual mores have cycled in and out of fashion in numerous historical eras, the *de facto* biological separation between sexual activity and reproduction in 1970s America precipitated sweeping societal reevaluations of middle-class sexual mores and had a profound impact on the life choices of individual men and women. Anthropologist Lionel Tiger asserts that beginning in the 1970s when usage of the pill became widespread, separating sexual activity from pregnancy, men became "alienated from the means of reproduction," fatherhood, and family responsibilities.[14] Memoirs and interviews with Americans who were single in the 1970s and 1980s, as well as articles and fiction coming out of that period, reveal that sexual activity was a given for most women and men by the time they reached their early twenties,[15] especially in the years before common knowledge about a spectrum of sexually transmitted diseases.

The relationship between love, heterosexual marriage, and parenthood ceased to be inextricably "united socially, morally, and legally," challenging the "sense of order and predictability" that had been associated with conventional "organized domestic life."[16] Among other changes, the liberation of men and women to pursue sexual relationships independent from the quest for marriage and family eroded differences between "male" and "female" expectations in the protocols of courtship. As Laura Gardner remembers Brandeis University in the 1950s and early 1960s, parietal dormitory rules were based on the assumption that "female students were 'gals' who needed 24/7 supervision. Male students were supposed to help the women follow the rules." Even fathers and brothers were barred from women's dorm rooms. Brandeis students rebelled against these rules in "the parietal protest of 1964," as sexual mores began to change and as the American culture of protest began to heat up. In succeeding years, college campuses moved toward their current casual freedoms. Conventional courtship dating for singles, and idealized notions of the gallant male and cherished female that went with the 1950s "co-ed" dating scene, largely declined, and egalitarian behavior increased.[17]

In more recent decades, the pattern of pairing off into stable romantic dating partners has become less frequent in American college settings. According to recent journalistic accounts, college men and women tend to attend concerts or parties in loose groups of friends, rather than with "dates." For some, sexual needs are satisfied through spontaneous ad hoc liaisons. Serious dating relationships tend to begin later in life, during graduate or professional training or later. Tellingly the phrase "date night" as used in popular American culture today refers not necessarily to singles but rather to frantically busy, somewhat older married couples trying to set aside personal time for romantic interactions together.

## Economics and Changes in Courtship and Marriage

Economic factors played an extremely important—and not always sufficiently acknowledged—role in changing attitudes and behaviors toward sexuality and courtship. In the 1960s and 1970s the gap decreased between men's and women's educational levels and earning potential for well-educated middle- and upper-middle-class Americans (the socioeconomic groups among whom American Jews were increasingly found). Women with effective birth control not only had more control over their personal lives but also could make reliable commitments to careers. Economic pressure made those careers desirable not only for those women who preferred to be labor-force participants, but also for their families. These intersecting trends undermined the social rationale for men to be the exclusive initiators of dating relationships and to pay expenses for women who were increasingly their economic peers.

That interaction between economics and romance extended to family formation as well. Coontz comments that one "pillar supporting the stable marriages of the postwar era was the fact that most women could not earn a living wage on their own. Fifty years ago, the average college-educated woman earned less than the average high-school-educated man." Both men and women expected men to be the primary wage earners when families were formed, and as late as 1977 "two-thirds of Americans believed that the ideal family arrangement was for the husband to earn the money and the wife to stay home."[18] In the 1950s college attendance actually enhanced marital prospects because the four years of college served as a virtual marriage market. "For men, going to college was the way to get a good job. For women, it was the way to get a good husband," Coontz succinctly summarizes. Few Jewish women were in the labor force permanently after graduation; instead they worked for a few years, married, had children, and became homemakers, partially because middle-class women "understood the likelihood of social censure if they pursued" their own careers.[19] Over the past two decades, in contrast, women's aspirations for high levels of career achievement have become socially approved in most Jewish and non-Jewish American bourgeois communities. Such ambitions, much more than education alone, may contribute to later romantic commitments and marriage, as singles postpone family formation until after they have completed defined education and career benchmarks.[20]

## Chaste Courtships in a Sexual World

As sexual mores were liberalized both in Israel and in the United States, the concept and practice of dating, and the stylized gendered roles that went with dating, remained paradoxically salient for religiously oriented youth, such as evangelical Christian college students and "Promise Keepers,"[21] and American Modern Orthodox singles. In Israel also, the ethos of male gallantry toward females became more and more the province of Modern Orthodox or Religious Zionist single adults, as Ari Engelberg points out (chapter 2 in this volume). However, in other ways, without a broader societal framework of behavioral rules, dating posed a challenge to many religious assumptions about appropriate premarital behavior. Some Modern Orthodox singles continued to maintain the common American middle-class pattern of expressing limited physical affection but avoiding sexual intercourse in premarital dating situations. Others took advantage of the popularized liberalization and became sexually active like their non-Orthodox peers. The phenomenon of the "*tefillin date*"—when a single Orthodox man brings phylacteries with him because he assumes he will be spending the night with his date and will still be at her home when it is time to pray in the morning—was already a topic of conversation in the 1960s.

In contrast to such patterns of liberalization, increasing numbers of Orthodox Jews both in Israel and the United States responded to more relaxed sexual standards in their secularized surroundings by pushing back; they became stricter, eschewing premarital physical affection and avoiding any physical contact with the opposite sex before marriage, a prescription described in Jewish religious legal language as *shomer negiah* (guarding against touching). Strict adherence to the avoidance of physical contact before marriage was and is a normative expectation in Haredi communities, including both Hasidic communities and non-Hasidic Yeshivish ultra-Orthodox communities. Those communities were relatively small in the 1950s but grew substantially in the 1970s and 1980s, especially in American and Israeli communities that were home to prominent *yeshivot* (pl. Hebrew, *yeshiva*), rabbinical seminaries. Within Haredi communities, couples are typically matched up for the purpose of marriage in their late teens through official matchmakers, subject to financial and logistical negotiations between the parents of the two families. "Dating" for Haredi singles is usually limited to a few meetings in public places such as hotel lobbies, or in chaperoned home settings, so that the young man and woman can acquire some minimal familiarity with the potential spouse. Thus, for Haredi singles—who are typically below voting age—both temptation and opportunity for premarital physical contact are virtually nonexistent.

A dramatically different situation from the Haredi world surrounds U.S. and Israeli Modern Orthodox singles, who have educational and occupational patterns virtually identical to those of non-Orthodox Jews and plenty of opportunity for secluded interactions with members of the opposite sex. Modern Orthodox schools responded to the liberalization of sexual mores by emphasizing chaste courtships. Beginning in the 1970s the concept of *shomer negiah* acquired an unprecedented new prominence in Modern Orthodox circles. As Jewish historian and communal professional Steven Bayme and sociologist Samuel Heilman have each commented, these restrictions are almost certainly more closely observed today than they were fifty years ago.[22]

It was at the fraught moment in the mid-1960s when sexual activity became more overt in non-Orthodox culture and thus more threatening in Orthodox minds that renowned Modern Orthodox theologian Rabbi Irving "Yitz" Greenberg expressed some of his developing thoughts on the subjects of sexual mores in an interview that was transcribed onto the pages of Yeshiva University's *The Commentator* (April 28, 1966). In that interview, Greenberg discussed "Orthodoxy, YU, Viet Nam, and Sex," according to the newspaper headline, and most of the article was devoted to the first three topics. Greenberg's thoughts on sexuality, although only three paragraphs long, were articulated in language that for many readers could have been—and was—considered provocative. Greenberg had previously dealt with Orthodox responses to the liberalization of sexual mores at a Yavneh convention in 1964 and in his Yeshiva University class, titled Ethical Thought in the 19th Century, but this was the first time his ideas on sexuality had appeared in print for a broader reading audience. Rabbinic authorities were directly accused of unresponsiveness or worse in a statement at the end of the second paragraph: "Sex has come to be considered as a secular activity only because the *Poskim* [rabbinic authorities] have abdicated their responsibility in examining its true meaning." At fault, according to Greenberg, were rabbinic leaders who simply repeated laws that stemmed from defunct sociological assumptions and who neglected to give contemporary Jews religious guidance.

His example of such unrealistic prescriptions was the prohibition against unmarried men and women touching each other: "The prohibition of *negiah* is based upon a technical *halacha* [Jewish law]—that a girl is in a state of *nidah* [sexual unavailability] until she performs *t'vilah* [immersion] in the *mikvah* [ritual bath]," Greenberg asserted, explaining that the reason unmarried girls were forbidden by medieval rabbis to immerse in the mikvah was the rabbis' fear about "the looseness of morals of many, who, having gone to the mikvah would feel free to do anything."[23] Rather than persisting in this medieval view, Greenberg declared that "sex is a religious activity, it is the expression of relationship and caring for the other, we abuse it by ignoring it." He urged contemporary Orthodox rabbinic authorities to create laws that reflected peoples' real religious choices, and he proposed a structure for those choices grounded in "the depth" of the interpersonal "encounter":

> Today the Poskim should recognize that there is nothing wrong with sex per se, and should promulgate a new value system and corresponding new *halachot* about sex. The basis of the new value system should be the concept that experiencing a woman as a *tzelem Elokim* [image of God] is a mitzvah, just as much as praying in *Shul* [synagogue]. The Poskim should teach people that the depth of one's sexual relationship should reflect the depth of his encounter. . . . This new approach to sex, even with its problems, would be much better than our present suppression of such a deep and meaningful activity. Indeed, I believe that more people would end up observing, for they would see relevance and rationale in the new halachic categories.[24]

Greenberg in *The Commentator* was challenging Orthodox authorities to create religious guidelines for sexuality that would be meaningful and appropriate in a profoundly changed social milieu. Clearly he struck a sensitive point—written responses by Modern Orthodox rabbis and thinkers to his challenge were immediate, strong, and negative.[25] Fascinatingly, Greenberg's much lengthier comments on other salient subjects attracted few published responses. While the details of the harsh responses to Greenberg are outside the purview of this introduction, they had a chilling effect: for years after the interchange, few Orthodox leaders ventured public statements on the creation of a Modern Orthodox sexual ethic.

The Modern Orthodox struggle with liberalized Western attitudes toward premarital sexuality continued over the decades, as singlehood increasingly became an extended life stage for a substantial minority of Orthodox Jews. Testimony to seriousness about physical abstinence was articulated at a 2005 Yeshiva University Orthodox Forum conference called Men and Women Inside and Outside of Marriage. A panel of four young Modern Orthodox singles described the dating situation they observed around them: many of the Modern Orthodox singles they knew were so worried about "being *over* [transgressing] on shomer negiah" that when they were attracted to each other, but did not feel ready to make a permanent life commitment, they broke off the relationship with that person when their feelings got too intense to resist. Middle-aged academics and several prominent Modern Orthodox rabbinic scholars (including some who had attacked Greenberg forty years earlier) attending the conference were shocked to hear that obsessions about restrictions on premarital touching—much of it inculcated in their own educational institutions—were actually interfering with the development of affectionate and potentially serious lifelong relationships among Modern Orthodox singles.

Some scholars believe that general ignorance about sexuality and anxiety about transgressing the behavioral restrictions prescribed within Jewish family law may also have an inhibiting effect on married sexuality in Orthodox, especially some Haredi, societies. For example, a vivid episode from Samuel Heilman's masterful ethnography of Haredi Jews, *Defenders of the Faith*, describes the startling obliviousness of some Haredi yeshiva boys about the "facts of life" before marriage. Having never been exposed to the physical realities of basic biology, some young men Heilman interviewed found the idea of sexual intercourse outlandish and repulsive; in the most extreme cases these negative attitudes interfered with the consummation of their physical relationships.[26]

For the majority of Haredi couples, of course, premarital ignorance does not prevent religiously mandated marital sexual activity; in the memorable words of writer Cynthia Ozick's narrator in "The Pagan Rabbi," observing ultra-Orthodox fecundity, "Jews are not Puritans." In contrast to Heilman's glimpse into possible emotional and erotic impoverishment within some Haredi families, professor of Jewish culture Naomi Seidman argues that Haredi societies actually have richly emotional environments, as they create alternative strategies to meet some of the emotional needs of their men and women outside of the nuclear family through the "complementary" warmth provided by the "homosocial structures" replete in Haredi communities. Synagogues and study halls for the men and separate designated spaces for women provided, Seidman suggests, "a ramified, single-sex socio-religious culture that supplemented, indeed sometimes supplanted, the mixed-sex spaces of home and marketplace."[27]

Concerned that Modern Orthodox Jews with Western educations may also share religiously produced negative, ignorant, or fearful attitudes, a cadre of Orthodox scholars and activists in the field of sex education have turned their attention to married as well as unmarried Orthodox practitioners. One participant in the Yeshiva University singles' panel, Jennie Rosenfeld (since married, and recently appointed as the first Orthodox communal spiritual leader in the Israeli settlement of Efrat, near Jerusalem[28]), copublished *The Newlywed's Guide to Physical Intimacy.*[29] This slender volume, written with respect for Jewish law, features graphic physical clarity about all aspects of sexual expression and includes an envelope with pen and ink drawings. In addition to Rosenfeld, some other Orthodox professionals dealing with issues of Orthodox women's health, intimacy, and sexuality who have gained recent prominence include Rabba Sarah Hurwitz (who made headlines as the first American Orthodox female rabbi ordained at Yeshiva

Maharat), American counselor Batsheva Marcus (dubbed "the Orthodox sex guru" by the *New York Times*),[30] and Naomi Marmon Grumet, director of Eden, an Israeli agency that trains Orthodox counselors for brides, grooms, and newlyweds, among other projects.

## Delays in Dating, Marriage, and Parenthood

Although the lives of Israeli and American Jews in their twenties and thirties differ pointedly, there are commonalities regarding dating and marriage—but many differences regarding parenthood. Daniel Parmer and Ari Engleberg (chapters 1 and 2 in this volume) document the fact that both in Israel and in the United States the years of singlehood are extended, and marriage often takes place later than it did several decades ago—although contributing factors differ. In Israel, obligatory military or "national service" occupies most non-Haredi youth in their late teens and early twenties, often followed by extended travel for rest and recuperation, and post–high school education is acquired only after army service and travel are completed. As a result, many Israeli young people postpone marriage for several years after the army. However, despite somewhat later marriage, Israel remains a strongly pronatalist society. Like the Israeli society around them, *hiloni* or self-described secular couples are far more pronatalist than their American counterparts; even hiloni couples aspire to having between three and four children, and give birth to almost three children per family (2.8), as illustrated by Sergio DellaPergola (chapter 5 this volume).

Extended singlehood and later marriage in America, by contrast, are associated with a marked decline in fertility rates. As anthropologist Riv-Ellen Prell points out, a recent Pew study of American attitudes reveals that "younger Americans do not *value* marriage"—that is, they do not see marriage as a top priority for society or for themselves.[31] In the United States, even men and women who eventually marry often delay the five social characteristics of adulthood: completed education, financial independence, marriage, parenthood, and independent living arrangements. The majority of unmarried Jewish adults in their twenties and beyond are sexually active, and many cohabit for at least some period in their lives. Some younger adults move back into parental homes, reversing patterns of past decades—and further postponing adult status.[32] Almost three-quarters (74%) of American Jewish men and 43 percent of American Jewish women age 25–34 are not married, according to the Pew Foundation research study *A Portrait of Jewish Americans* (2013).[33] The portion of Jews never married by age 34 in the Pew study has risen even in comparison to data recorded by the National Jewish Population Survey 2000–01 (NJPS 2000–01), when more than half of men and almost a third of women were unmarried at that age.[34] Today, Jewish men achieve a 90 percent ever-married rate only at age 45, and Jewish women when they are over age 50.[35] These results are striking in comparison to earlier periods when American Jews achieved nearly "universal marriage" well before age 30.

Moreover, American Jewish personal aspirations regarding children are often not matched by realistic decisions regarding fertility, Michelle Shain argues in this volume (chapter 6). Among younger American Jews today, the number of children born is not above a replacement level, defined by demographers as 2.1 children per woman. Younger non-Orthodox American Jews have an average of 1.7 children per woman. Harriet Hartman suggests that a social norm of lower fertility may have been in place among American Jews for decades, since NJPS 2000–01 showed an average of 1.6–1.7 children for Jews ages 35–54.[36]

These differences between the number of children considered normative among contemporary well-educated American Jews versus both their Israeli peers and earlier generations of American Jews illustrate the powerful effect of social norms and social contagion[37]—the effect of the behaviors of the people around us. Such social pressure has an impact even in Israel, where Tel Aviv journalist Dana Kessler wryly comments about her "30-something friends": "There are two opposing attitudes when it comes to kids. . . . In some social circles having a baby is super trendy," but people in other circles are extremely vocal about their conviction "that wishing to reproduce is a mistake."[38]

"Single mothers by choice," well-educated Jewish women in their thirties and forties, have also increased both in Israel and in the United States.[39] Women's reproductive capacities diminish at earlier ages than those of men. According to recent figures, between 3 percent and 5 percent of women in their twenties experience infertility. A woman's chance of experiencing infertility when she is between the ages of 30 and 34 is 8 percent, climbing to 15 percent at ages 35–39, 32 percent at ages 40–44, and 69 percent at ages 45–49.[40] More women are turning to strategies such as freezing their eggs,[41] or to giving birth to children as single mothers, rather than waiting for a partner.[42] Among those women deciding to give birth to and raise children outside of the context of marriage, as Tehilla Blumenthal emphasizes in this volume (chapter 7), are many who are religiously observant, especially in Israel. Indeed it is their religious pronatalist values that give them strong incentives to go through the sometimes difficult process. "Reproducing Jews" is an easier project when the government foots the bill, as anthropologist Susan Martha Kahn observes.[43] The relative prevalence of IVF technology in Israel is partially due to the fact that the Israeli government pays for eight attempts toward pregnancy, whereas prospective parents in the United States must pay privately. Since many of the women who choose motherhood as singles are in their late thirties, when infertility may also be an issue, the economics of fertility treatments are quite salient.

Medically assisted reproduction, adoption, and the use of surrogates or other types of personal "outsourcing" are also important strategies for the increasing numbers of gay and lesbian Jewish partnerships in which children are desired. But medical fertility technology introduces important moral concerns, as many have noted, and societies are affected profoundly by new issues around fertility, infertility, and reproductive technology. Both civic and religious law, for example, are challenged by new concepts of parenthood: who is the legal and religious "mother" when one person donates material genetic material (the ovum or egg) for an in vitro fertilization, another gestates the embryo, and a third woman pays for these procedures? Which expenditures to enhance fertility are moral—and which are questionable? Israeli American artist Andi Arnovitz captures the cuteness of the much-longed-for newborn infant, along with the commercialization of childbirth that is one undesirable side effect of technology, in her artistic installation, reproduced in this volume (page 121), "The Commerce of Fertility."

While many later-starting would-be parents struggle with unwanted infertility and Western societies encounter low fertility and an aging population, familism faces challenges from another direction: both learned journals and popular periodicals and media question the rationale for marital and parental sacrifices. Journalistic accounts such as Anne-Marie Slaughter's "Why Women Still Can't Have It All" are much read and discussed.[44] Some women are fearful that they will have to make choices between meaningful and satisfying work, loving spousal relationships, and parenthood during the years when conception and gestation are easiest. They decide to pursue their careers first, and marriage and children later. Similarly, many men—including many Jewish men—postpone commitments because they are fearful of having their personal freedoms abridged by commitments to a spouse and children. In addition, many men feel particularly sensitive about the financial responsibility of supporting a family, even in this age of two-paycheck households. While women often describe delaying childbearing because of career considerations, many men are "particularly worried about the financial burden of parenthood," according to Michelle Shain's interviews (chapter 6 in this volume). Similarly, some gender theorists and social scientists cast a jaundiced eye on early marriage. Particularly salient observations are offered by the National Marriage Project at Rutgers' National Marriage Project, which asserts that "today, getting married at 19 or 22 is not a steppingstone to independent adulthood; it's an obstacle."[45]

Others question the project of motherhood altogether, fearing that motherhood functions both as a symbol of male oppression and as a kind of entrapment, diminishing women's ability to fulfill themselves and control their own lives and destinies.[46] A portrayal of motherhood as an instrument of patriarchal oppression has emerged once more among some feminist writers, such as Elisabeth Badinter, whose *The Conflict: How Modern Motherhood Undermines the Status of Women* reintroduces a radical viewpoint voiced decades ago by second-wave feminists such as Gloria Steinem and Shulamit Firestone.[47] Steinem argued in 1987 that the origin and purpose of marriage was a means "to restrict the freedom of the mother—at least long enough to determine paternity." Men promoted religious and social restrictions of female sexuality so that they might control "the most basic means of production—the means of reproduction."[48] Some writers in this circle find the very physicality of the process of gestation and lactation repellent. Firestone (who grew up in a large Orthodox family in St. Louis, Missouri) describes gestation and childbirth as primitive, brutal processes.[49] Such antinatalist theories have practical implications. As nurse and author Margaret Sandlewski explains, some "feminist writing has emphasized the continuing medicalization of childbearing and motherhood and the male expropriation of reproductive power from womanhood, furthering female subordination." Such interpretations contain little "that suggests real empathy with infertile women."[50]

Nevertheless, judging from the interview data in the studies by Parmer, Shain, and Bernstein (chapters 1, 6, and 8 in this volume), many younger Jewish women and men believe that parenthood is one of the great defining experiences of human adulthood, and they aspire to that condition—someday. Yet antifamily rhetoric overtly and implicitly influences the women and men making family decisions. Societal conceptions of "families" are transformed by plummeting fertility; what a "family" looks like to us is influenced by what the families around us look like in communities where, as American columnist Ross Douthat warns, "there's been a broader cultural shift away from a child-centric understanding of romance and marriage"[51]

## Marriages with Shared Responsibilities

In Israel, it has been common for decades for women to work outside the home for pay, due to economic pressures perhaps more than ideology. However, according to anecdotal reports in Israel, feminist-inspired blurring of male and female expectations in marriage regarding childcare and household responsibilities is not as widespread as in the United States, partially because of the physical and psychological impact of the demands of army and reserves (*miluim*) service for husbands and sons. Moreover, unlike the "third shift" of facilitating Jewishness that creates extra tasks for American Jewish spouses, as Rachel Bernstein evocatively argues (chapter 8 in this volume), in Israel being Jewish seldom adds an additional layer of work to family life. In Israel, unlike America, Shabbat and Jewish holidays define even the secular calendar year, and children learn Hebrew and are inculcated with Jewish culture without religious observances and without being shepherded to Hebrew school.

In the United States the old pattern of the bourgeois family, in which the father is the primary or even the sole breadwinner and the mother devotes herself to children, household, and good works in the community—and to driving Hebrew school car pools—has been in sharp decline for decades. Many American Jewish women work in meaningful careers, and not merely for a paycheck, and most mothers work outside the home for pay, even when they have children under age six in the household. Increasingly, these American families are distinguished for their homogamy or spousal parity—that is, husbands and wives have very similar levels of educational achievement and occupational prestige—and often very similar salaries. Contemporary American families, especially those high on the educational, occupational, and socioeconomic ladder, are undergoing "an unfinished revolution."[52] There is an expectation for many American Jews, discussed by Bernstein and Fishman (chapter 8 in this volume), that within these "partnership marriages" the childcare and various tasks of familyhood will be divided, as will the additional American tasks of maintaining Jewishness within the family, adding more layers of complexity and negotiations.

Some have predicted that such reconstructions of gender roles are doomed to failure because they contradict "human nature." A spate of recent popular books draws on theories of evolutionary biology to "prove" that male and female gender roles and mating goals are conditioned by primitive psychological factors, unchanged since the stone age.[53] Psychologist Steven Pinker, for example, insists in his *The Blank Slate* on hard-wired male–female binaries, and he scorns the feminist notion that culture inscribes most social-psychological gender differences.[54] However, recent research shows that men and women today—like those of earlier historical eras—respond to changing socioeconomic conditions by adjusting their expectations and behaviors regarding courtship and marriage. In the current economic climate, the superior earning power of prospective spouses is a consideration for both men and women. According to recent studies, well-educated men today seek out similarly well-educated women, rather than selecting mates primarily for youth and putative fertility. As Rosalind Barnett and Caryl Rivers put it, "the more education a woman has the more marriageable she is."[55]

In pronounced contrast to the assertions of Carol Gilligan and her followers that women are hard-wired for empathy and compassion—and thus better parenting[56]—sociologist Barbara Risman has found that actively parenting married fathers and single fathers demonstrate parenting skills similar to those of mothers.[57] A national study of the changing American workforce found that working mothers spent slightly less time with their children and working fathers slightly more on workdays than they had in the past; on non-workdays both mothers and fathers spent increased time with children, with the increase among fathers slightly greater than among mothers.[58] These marriages of homogamously well-educated dual-earner couples are far more stable than those of unequally or poorly educated Americans—who are also less likely to marry overall. In homogamous marriages, parenthood often precipitates negotiation and cooperative management—developing in fathers parenting skills that once were assumed to be embedded in female psychology.

Increasing levels of spousal homogamy and cooperative couplings can be regarded as "good news" for some demonstrable, objective reasons. Several recent studies show that the combination of the characteristics of these marriages—namely, two careers of somewhat equal status, relatively high household income, and an approach to child care and household tasks that make them the responsibility of both partners—are conducive to personal happiness and sense of well-being. Economists Betsey Stevenson and Justin Wolfers assert that their "basic principles of Lovenomics" show that couples who "work alike" professionally, outsource as many domestic chores as possible, and have children are good for the "economics of coupledom."[59] Themselves life partners and the parents of two children, Stevenson and Wolfers have argued that, contrary to the Easterlin Paradox that claims increased income does not increase happiness, their research finds that "the relationship between well-being and income is roughly linear."[60] And a new study by economists John Helliwell and Shawn Grover demonstrates that "people have the capacity to increase their happiness levels" by committing themselves to a partner and "finding support in long-term relationships," according to Claire Cain Miller.[61]

As this introduction notes, partnership marriages have low rates of divorce and a strong record of spousal homogamy. However, compared to American Jewish marriages of the past—and compared to Israeli marriages—these "successful" marriages are sometimes paradoxically unsuccessful in enabling Jewish women to give birth to the number of children they had hoped to have. The very delays in marriage that are statistically related to marital durability and viability are also often related to unwanted fertility problems.

A potentially interesting model is provided by the numerous Modern Orthodox American two-career families with children who illustrate in their quotidian lives how to manage (albeit no doubt variously and imperfectly) the Jewish juggling act. Among all wings of American Judaism, Modern Orthodox couples exhibited the greatest degree of spousal homogamy, the Hartmans found working with NJPS 2000–01 data.[62] The *Pew Portrait* (2013) similarly revealed that, compared to couples in other wings of Judaism, Modern Orthodox Jews had the highest levels of secular education and occupational achievement and the highest household income level, startling facts taken together with their relatively high fertility rates.[63] The lifestyle that has become the norm in the American Modern Orthodox community generally features somewhat earlier marriage, typically when partners are in their twenties, than non-Orthodox Jews, high educational achievement and prestigious careers, and numbers of Jewishly educated children in excess of a demographic replacement level.

## The Jewish LGBTQ Nation

Jonathan Krasner's chapter on American Jewish homosexual gay, lesbian, bisexual, transgender, and queer (LGBTQ) Jews with children (chapter 3 in this volume), reveals that Jewish communal acceptance drew many of his subjects closer to Jews and Judaism, and was influential within intermarried LGBTQ Jewish households as well. American Jews have a demonstrable ideological and political history of advocating for greater inclusiveness regarding gay, lesbian, and transgender Jews. The Pew *Portrait*, for example, reported that 82 percent of America's Jews say homosexuality "should be accepted by society": that percentage increases to 89 percent of Jews age 18 to 49, and 89 percent of Jewish college graduates.[64] Today, about 7 percent of American Jews identify as LGBTQ, a recent study by Steven M. Cohen, Caryn Aviv, and Ari Kelman shows. The same study reported that 31 percent of self-reported LGBTQ Jews are married or partnered, and another 9 percent are raising their own children.[65]

Jewish LGBTQ Jews who marry or sacralize their partnerships are often interested in creating Jewish families with children. Their values and lifestyles in many ways present a Jewish version of a 2008 cover article in the *New York Times Magazine*, "The Newlywed Gays! Life among Young Men Who Are Married (to Men) in Massachusetts Could not Be More Normal." With a memorable cover photo picturing a smiling, deliberately stereotypically clean-cut male couple barbecuing broccoli and steak in their suburban backyard under the bluest of skies, the article by Benoit Denizet Lewis asserted that young gay men are "yearning for companionship and security." Commenting that demographic studies have shown lesbian women already have a track record of permanent partnerships, long-term cohabitation, marriage when possible, and raising children, Benoit argues that many young gay men today "profess to want what they've long seen espoused by mainstream American culture: a long-term relationship and the chance to start a family."[66]

Partnerships, marriages, and families of LGBTQ Jews are increasingly acknowledged by and incorporated into American Jewish institutions. The Reconstructionist movement and the Reform movement's Central Conference of American Rabbis (CCAR) approved the marriages of LGBT Jews in the mid-to-late 1990s. The Conservative movement's Rabbinical Assembly (RA) Committee on Jewish Law and Standards affirmed in 2006 that marriages between two Jewish men or two Jewish women "have the same sense of holiness and joy as that expressed in heterosexual marriages." Two formal ceremonies to sacralize such marriages were proposed by that committee in 2012. These Conservative-authored same-sex wedding ceremonies are based on traditional Jewish wedding ceremonies but omit some of the language and blessings, and these ceremonies are not called *Qiddushin*,[67] the ancient ceremony consecrating the contract whereby a Jewish bridegroom acquires a bride. This liberalism about homosexual family units, however, is not widespread within Orthodox institutions; in Krasner's study, not surprisingly, "those families who attempted to find a home within the Orthodox community generally had a more negative experience."[68]

Similarly, Irit Koren's study, "Gays and Lesbians in Israel—an Overview" (chapter 4 in this volume), finds that LGBTQ Jewish Israelis often create long-term relationships, raise children, and are able to find more or less comfortable social circles, especially in Tel Aviv. However, Israeli LGBTQ families struggle with issues of family and children when they must interact with official institutions—which are often influenced by Orthodox attitudes and sometimes see LGBTQ familism as provocative behavior rather than as an embrace of Jewish family values.

## Gay and Lesbian Orthodox Jews

The increased prominence of observant homosexual Jews poses a challenge to Orthodox authorities. The official stance of most streams within Orthodoxy is that open LGBTQ behavior is contrary to biblical and Jewish law. Male homosexual acts are widely understood by most Orthodox rabbinical authorities—and many Orthodox Jews—to be prohibited by biblical law. Female homosexual acts are strongly discouraged in Talmudic discussions. Many Orthodox rabbis have even recently articulated the idea that homosexuality is a "choice," and thus can be avoided through will power, motivation, and medication—despite overwhelming scientific evidence to the contrary. However, other Orthodox voices have urged a more realistic and compassionate approach. In recent years several programs and events held under Modern Orthodox auspices have made it clear that

Orthodox practitioners feel more connected to their gay coreligionists than might be surmised from official platforms. Such programs include a controversial 2009 panel discussion at the Yeshiva University Tolerance Club and Wurzweiler School of Social Work, which reportedly attracted eight hundred people,[69] and several enthusiastically received panels at conferences of the Jewish Orthodox Feminist Alliance (JOFA).

Many Orthodox minds were opened and changed by the 2001 film *Trembling Before God*, which vividly portrays the heart-wrenching struggles of gay and lesbian Jews to reconcile—or at least juxtapose—their homosexual and Orthodox lives. That film, produced by Sandi Simcha Dubowski, put real faces and souls to what had been for many Orthodox leaders an abstract and somewhat alienating issue. The process of making the Orthodox homosexual issue feel immediate through personalization was furthered by Orthodox gay Rabbi Steven Greenberg in his 2004 book *Wrestling with Man and God: Homosexuality in the Jewish Tradition*. Perhaps symbolically, that book precipitated a review in the *Edah Journal* by Asher Lopatin, now the director of Yeshivat Chovevei Torah, who is widely perceived as being "liberal" or "open" Orthodox; Rabbi Lopatin concluded that the book is a "brilliant work of creativity and research," but which could not yet "enter the Orthodox bookshelf" because it does not include sufficiently traditional Orthodox thinkers and their attitudes.[70]

In Israel, Tova Hartman and Irit Koren authored the study "Between 'Being' and 'Doing': Conflict and Coherence in the Identity Formation of Gay Orthodox Jews." They came to the conclusion that true resolution of gay and Orthodox identities is often impossible, but that that fact ceases to matter for many:

> Instead of abandoning the valuative framework that rejects their sexual identity, or vice versa, the Orthodox gay men and women we interviewed allowed their religiosity to push them to understand their homosexuality as an integral element of their religious destiny, which in turn has required them to delve into it all the more profoundly. . . . This evolving relationship between these two mutually exclusive, highly defining aspects of identity . . . in turn serves as a source of inspiration, consolation, and strength.[71]

Thus, when Yitz Greenberg was asked to write an imaginary letter to an imaginary homosexual son, which was published in *Moment Magazine* in 2011, the issue of Orthodox homosexuals was already on the American Orthodox radar screen. Unlike some rabbis—even outside of Orthodoxy—who didn't gain compassion until they themselves had a homosexual child, Rabbi Greenberg's letter was sober and realistic, as well as loving and compassionate. First he stipulated that a declaration of homosexuality should only be made by a "mature" person who had "considered" fully the implications of his "decision." Greenberg then articulated what I would argue are his first principles or holy commandments regarding sexual activity. In this letter to an imaginary son he includes a statement about nonmarital sexuality framed within ethical and cosmological beliefs that are central to his worldview and to his profound belief in sexuality as sacred expression. I have bolded that section below:

> My heart goes out to you. As you were raised as an Orthodox Jew, you already know that since the time of the Torah, homosexuality has been condemned in our community, especially in more traditional circles. While treatment is improving, I fear that you will face much rejection and hostility, and I wish that I could prevent it or protect you. Nevertheless, if you live your life this way, I would hope that you would apply the Torah's other guidelines for sexuality to your own practice. **Sex should not be casual or promiscuous. It should never be exploitative or abusive. Sexuality should express relationship and love; the deeper the sexuality, the deeper the relationship that it should express. You should try for the Jewish ideal, which remains family and creating/nurturing life via children (by conception or adoption).** This is a great joy and a fulfillment in life. Your mother and I love you very much as a total person. This feeling has not changed with your announcement.[72]

In the 2013 international JOFA conference several enthusiastically received panels further explored Orthodox homosexuality. Among other speakers, Rabbi Steven Greenberg discussed the various issues that arise as he and his (male) partner raise their religiously observant children.

## Social, Political, and Religious Pushback to Change

Changes in sexual, social, and familial values and behaviors are frequently regarded as disruptive and dangerous by conservative societies and their political and religious leaders. Some respond by putting old rules and hierarchies back in place—or inventing new ones to limit women's personal autonomy and mobility and to marginalize women from the public square; some promulgate prescriptions for the way women are to dress and be educated.[73] These attempts to control chaos by controlling women go back to ancient human cultures, suggests Andi Arnovitz's "Cover Her Up," a sardonic artistic riff on Durer's etching of Adam and Eve in the Garden of Eden, which is reprinted in this volume (285). Arnovitz pictures Adam enjoying a close-to-prelapsarian state of freedom, encumbered only by one strategic leaf, but Eve is plastered over head to toe—closed off, immobilized, and silenced—by foliage.

Economic factors are a significant dimension of social, political, and religious pushback to changes in gender roles and family formation. The often-invoked rabbinic expectation that a woman would prefer to be married to any man at all, no matter how flawed, rather than to be unmarried, is partially an economic observation. That is, when the economic and social price of being unmarried is unbearably high, women may tolerate an unappealing marital prospect, marriage at inappropriate times in their lives, or marriages that are difficult to achieve or maintain. However, when the negative economic and social consequences of unmarriage are reduced, the price of marriage itself appears more onerous.

Social economist Robert Cherry works out elaborate mathematical economic models to show how economic factors can drive the desirability or undesirability of marriage for particular social groups. As women earn more and men earn less, the price of marriage can seem off-putting to both men and women. Women's enfranchisement and economic independence can thus be realistically perceived as contributing to late marriage and to declining rates of marriage overall. This is one reason that social conservatives speaking from either religious or political realms often oppose the expansion of women's opportunities. In the United States, conservative politicians from former vice president Dan Quayle onward have linked the prominence of successful working women—who can support themselves, and can choose to have babies without benefit of marriage—to the decline of conventional families.[74]

Evidence from historical and some contemporary societies and from some foundational religious texts, including classical Jewish texts, offer prooftexts illustrating the widespread control of men over women—especially over women's sexual and reproductive activities—in patriarchal communities.[75]

Religious leaders in conservative milieus often discourage women from working outside the home. Where women are the primary wage-earners in families—as often in Haredi communities—other measures are employed to ensure women's compliance with expected family and social behavior. For example, women's workplaces are carefully supervised, especially as regards Internet access.[76] Opposing loss of traditional gendered lifestyles (as well as diminishment of their own power) some Haredi rabbis have ruled that women should not pursue higher secular education or drive cars, and that they should strictly avoid taking on public roles in religious or political arenas.

Another reactionary strategy is to place ever-increasing emphasis on female modesty. As David Jacobson argues, patriarchal religious-societal prescriptions for female modesty are an expression of social determinations of "who owns or controls one's body, especially when it comes to women: is it the individual herself or the community, through enforced practices of honor, virginity, veiling, and marriage?"[77] In Israel many have described events such as the restriction of women to the back of Jerusalem buses, ripping women's faces from public posters and advertisements, and the silencing of singing female soldiers in the Israeli army as a kind of "war on women." As one observer noted, "Silencing and blotting out is what we do to Haman—not to Jewish women!"

Some recent rabbinic demands for women's modesty are obsessively detailed: the prominent Israeli Rabbi Shlomo Aviner, for example, published a long list of stringent standards for girls and women,[78] such as buying clothing several sizes too large, so that when they turn to the side no female form is visible in profile, and wearing only dark neutrals rather than colors that would attract attention, such as red. Aviner also stipulates that heavy visible stockings should be placed on girls' legs from the age of three onward (to prevent male onlookers from imagining that they are seeing a toddler's naked limbs). Such demands for "modesty" paradoxically sexualizes young girls, insists artist Andi Arnovitz. Protesting and making palpable such perversity, Arnovitz created an artwork in the form of a sheer black negligee "onsie" sized for an infant girl, with three black lace pasties sewn strategically over the areas that would be erogenous zones in a grown woman; that artwork comprises an accusation against those Haredi males who perceive eros ubiquitously, and—rather than educating their boys and men to restrain and control their own impulses—strive to avoid male erotic stimulation by constricting female lives.

Interestingly, some Orthodox women do not experience escalating demands for their physical modesty as oppressive. Recent sociological research examines the reasons why some girls and women embrace and internalize such obligations. First, an item of clothing, such as a head covering, is often "a sign of belonging to a community." Second, it is a visible symbol of a change of status, such as becoming a married woman.[79] Third, instead of adopting an article of clothing in exactly the way that has been stipulated, which has the effect of erasing individualism in wardrobes, some Haredi women ratchet the prescriptions up a notch, using their individualism by inventing innovative new expressions of "modesty" beyond those required by the rabbis of their communities and eagerly separating themselves from the world of men. Indeed, female modesty as a religious value has been so thoroughly internalized by pious Jewish women that some have often gone beyond the directives of male clergy, taking upon themselves voluminous shape-hiding cloaks,[80] and in a few cases even burqas.

Rabbi Danya Ruttenberg challenges Orthodoxy to create innovative new "formulations of *tzniut*," elaborating: "In this formulation, the internal, rather than external aspects of *tzniut* are emphasized. Living in relationship to God and to the deep well of one's own spiritual power is at the forefront. . . . It is with this love that we serve God."[81] Lea Taragin-Zeller (chapter 13 in this volume) shows how some Haredi women unknowingly anticipated Rabbi Ruttenberg's concern: Taragin-Zeller describes Haredi young women creating an unlikely hybrid concept: escalating manifestations of female modesty as an expression of a woman's intimate relationship with her Creator.

As Yoel Finkelman (chapter 12 in this volume) shows, within Haredi societies responses have included adaptation (sometimes unwitting) to changing values, as well as backlash. However, the influences affecting men and women are asymmetrical, Finkelman insists. Just as men can walk through an Orthodox synagogue women's section but women cannot walk through the men's section, girls and women are rigorously excluded from male environments and activities. Men are not relegated exclusively to the males-only synagogue and the study hall, but are increasingly encouraged in Haredi texts written by and for Haredi men to spend time with their children and in other quasi-domestic activities. Finkelman argues that such prescriptions demonstrate transformed conceptions of masculinity. Once again, research shows the influence of changing attitudes and mores in the outside world upon insular Haredi definitions of maleness and femaleness—and the relationship between men and women.

## Paradoxical Adaptations on Both Sides of the Equation

Shifting sexual mores and related material and economic changes, discussed above, helped enable new understandings of love, marriage, and Jewish families in the United States and Israel. Together they contributed to the transformations in marital status among Jews in their twenties, thirties, and forties that are analyzed in this volume's chapters, including singlehood as an expanded stage of life, often with cohabitation; declining fertility and debates about parenthood; parenthood among groups previously considered unlikely to raise Jewish children, such as single mothers and gay and lesbian Jews; new visibility and roles of the Jewish LGBTQ nation, including homosexual religiously observant Jews; and the mainstream prominence of "partnership" two-career families aiming for egalitarian relationships. The chapters also explore responses to these transformations, including innovative civic and Jewish legal approaches and—paradoxically—Haredi resistance, reinforcement of traditional boundaries, and some appropriation of those transformations. This introduction proposes that the same phenomena that galvanized overt transformations within more liberal segments of American and Israeli Jewish societies also paradoxically precipitated pushback within more insular groups.

Some of the extraordinary transformations in attitudes, behavior, and the surrounding culture that this book analyzes challenge what we might call "Jewish family values." Despite these challenges, many aspects of traditional Jewish families have enduring appeal. Elements of traditionalism are embedded in the remarkable flowering of partnership marriages in many American Jewish communities, which appear to be unusually stable. Some respondents in my earlier studies suggested that the inconveniences as well as the joys of family life, the presence of family members in one's personal space, and the necessity of attending to intimately connected others on a quotidian basis broaden one's moral horizons.[82] That doesn't make family life easy or simple: Rachel S. Bernstein and I show (chapter 8 in this volume) that juggling competing priorities is an ongoing challenge and sometimes a source of conflict for spouses in partnership marriages. But journalist Michael Winerip asserts in "A Man's View on 'Having It All'" that such struggles are immensely worthwhile and meaningful, drawing upon his own experiences in a two-career family with four children. In contrast to the pervasive individualistic American ethos, Winerip extolls contemporary families in which both fathers and mothers are deeply committed, making sacrifices so that they can "be there" for each other and for their children:

> I had to be selective about the reporting positions I took, and I earned that freedom by working so hard there was no question I was working so hard. My balancing act didn't feel hard because I love what I do. I'd put in a few hours, wake the four, make lunches and get them on the bus. Then I'd work until they came home, oversee activities, cook dinner, and monitor homework. When they became teenagers—a hormonal storm a parent absolutely must tend to in person—I'd enforce curfews, police the drinking, eyeball the friends.[83]

Committed life partnerships are a good choice of marital status for many—but not all—people. As Claire Cain Miller emphasizes, "social scientists have long known that married people tend to be happier," especially when they can "find a spouse who is also . . . a best friend." According to recent studies, the nearly homogamous couplings that are disproportionately characteristic of marriages in the American Jewish community are especially frequent among Jews where "the roles of men and women have become more similar," creating relationships in which spouses are "companions and confidants." Economist John Helliwell explains: "The biggest benefits come in high-stress environments . . . because they have a shared load and shared friendship."[84]

Powerful evidence of traditionalism may also be seen among Jews in their twenties, thirties, and forties with less conventional family profiles. Traditional "Jewish family values" are often a factor for Jewish women and men determined to achieve parenthood even when confronted by the physical challenges of infertility or in the absence of spouses or life partners. One may observe striking Jewish commitments among many married or partnered gay and lesbian Jewish couples. However, it is important to recognize the decline of traditional familism among this cohort as well: some—with or without children—do not wish to marry; some live alone by preference; some select cohabiting rather than married status; some—married or unmarried—are not interested in raising children; and among those who once aspired to marriage and/or children, some are ultimately not able to realize their earlier goals. In addition, within each decade of age, those people who report that they were "ever married," divorced, or widowed, and their families, comprise increasing communal proportions, groups not within the purview of this volume but highly important to the broad picture of households in American and Israeli Jewish societies.

Changes in understandings of love, marriage, and Jewish families are significant not only to individual Jews involved in those issues but also to the Jewish community. "It is clear that the 'Jewish family' is not something *separate* from Jewish history or Judaism," anthropologist Jonathan Boyarin suggests; indeed, "Jewishness in its many forms is, broadly speaking, inconceivable without Jewish families."[85] Perhaps some would argue with Boyarin's premise, but there is no doubt that family formation is critical to Jewishness today. In America, studies from the National Jewish Population Surveys of 1990 and 2000–01 to the Pew Center's *A Portrait of Jewish Americans* (2013) to various recent Jewish metropolitan reports, repeatedly demonstrate that delays in—and absence of—marriage and childrearing not only erode the numerical size of the next generation of Jews but are also associated with weakened Jewish connections of many younger Jews.[86] Taking on the responsibilities of Jewish family life—in all its contemporary diversity—often makes Jewishness, as an ethnicity, religion, and culture, powerfully salient to Jewish individuals, sometimes in ways that surprise them.[87] In Jewish societies both in Israel and America, Jewish engagement is tied to engagement with other Jews and to the most intimate decisions of personal lives—personal lives that have undergone profound transformations over the past four decades.

## NOTES

1. Aspects of subjects discussed in the introduction to *Love, Marriage, and Jewish Families Today* are presented with a different focus in Sylvia Barack Fishman, "Gender in American Jewish Life," in *American Jewish Year Book 2014*, eds. Arnold Dashefsky and Ira Sheskin (New York: Springer Publishing, 2014). A more detailed presentation of demographic issues touched on in this introduction can be found in Sylvia Barack Fishman, "Identity and Transmissibility in an Open World: The Marshall Sklare Award Lecture," in *Contemporary Jewry* (June 2015); Sylvia Barack Fishman, "Liberal/ Conservative False Binary for Today's American Jewish Families," *Mosaic* (August 2013); and Sylvia Barack Fishman and Steven M. Cohen, "The Transmission of Jewish Identity: Major Variations and their Policy Implications," *JPPI Annual Assessment* (June 2015).
2. E. W. Burgess and H. L. Locke, *The Family: From Institution to Companionship* (New York: American Book, 1945); Stephanie Coontz, *The Way We Never Were: American Families and the Nostalgia Trap* (New York: Basic Books, 1992).
3. Andrew Cherlin, "The Deinstitutionalization of American Marriage," *Journal of Marriage and Family* 66 (November 2004): 848–61, esp. 851–53.
4. Kristi Williams, "Has the Future of Marriage Arrived? A Contemporary Examination of Gender, Marriage, and Psychological Well-Being," *Journal of Health and Social Behavior* 44 (2003): 470–87.
5. Paul R. Amato and Alan Booth, *A Generation at Risk: Growing Up in an Era of Family Upheaval* (Cambridge, MA: Harvard University Press, 1997).
6. Farrell J. Webb, "The New Demographics of Families," in *Sourcebook of Family Theory & Research*, eds. Bengtson, Acock, Allen, Dilworth-Anderson, and Klein (London: Sage Publications, 2005), 101.
7. Two intriguing recent works are Mark Pagel, *Wired for Culture: Origins of the Human Social Mind* (New York: W. W. Norton, 2012); and Steven Pinker, *The Blank Slate: The Modern Denial of Human Nature* (New York: Penguin Books, 2002).
8. Paula Hyman, "Introduction: Perspectives on the Evolving Jewish Family," in *The Jewish Family: Myth and Reality*, eds. Steven M. Cohen and Paula Hyman, eds. (New York: Holmes and Meier, 1986), 180.
9. Herman Wouk, *Marjorie Morningstar* (New York: Simon and Schuster, 1955), 228–30.
10. Ibid.
11. Michael Broyde, "Hair Covering and Jewish Law: Biblical and Objective or Rabbinical and Subjective," *Tradition* 42, no. 3 (Fall 2009): 97–179.
12. Barbara Ehrenreich, *The Hearts of Men: American Dreams and the Flight from Commitment* (Garden City, NY: Doubleday, 1984).
13. Betty Friedan, *The Feminine Mystique* (New York: Norton, 1963).
14. Lionel Tiger, *The Decline of Males: The First Look at an Unexpected New World for Men and Women* (New York: St. Martin's Griffin, 2000), 162.
15. Carol Tavris and Susan Sadd, *The Redbook Report on Female Sexuality* (New York: Delacourt Press, 1977).
16. Steven L. Nock, "The Divorce of Marriage and Parenthood," *Journal of Family Therapy* 22 (2000): 245–63.
17. Laura Gardner, "Rules of Engagement," *Brandeis Magazine* (Summer 2014): 21–15.
18. Stephanie Coontz, "The New Instability: Women Expect More, While Men Can Provide Less," *New York Times*, July 27, SR 1, 7.

19. Stephanie Coontz, *A Strange Stirring: The Feminine Mystique and American Women at the Dawn of the 1960s* (New York: Basic Books, 2011), 108.
20. Parmer, "Marriage and Non-Marriage," chapter 1 in this volume.
21. Ken Abraham, *Who Are the Promise Keepers? Understanding the Christian Men's Movement* (New York: Doubleday, 1997); Dane S. Claussen, ed., *Standing on the Promises: The Promise Keepers and the Revival of Manhood* (Cleveland, OH: Pilgrim Press, 1999).
22. Steven Bayme, "Dr. Irving Greenberg: A Biographical Introduction," *Continuity and Change: A Festschrift in Honor of Yitz Greenberg's 75th Birthday* (Lanham, MD: University Press of America, 2011), 2. Samuel Heilman, *Symposium on Modern Orthodoxy Responds to Changing Sexual Mores* (Oxford, UK: June 24, 2014).
23. "Dr. Greenberg Discusses Orthodoxy, YU, Viet Nam, and Sex," *The Commentator*, Thursday, April 26, 1966, 6–10.
24. Ibid.
25. Letter to the editor, "Greenberg Clarifies and Defends His Views," *The Commentator*, Thursday May 12, 1966, 8–9.
26. Samuel Heilman, *Defenders of the Faith: Inside Ultra-Orthodox Jewry* (New York: Schocken Books, 1992), 322–32.
27. Naomi Seidman, "The Erotics of Sexual Segregation," in *The Passionate Torah: Sex and Judaism*, ed. Danya Ruttenberg (New York: New York University Press, 2009), 107–15, esp. 111.
28. Jeremy Sharon, "Orthodox woman appointed to serve a communal spiritual leader in Efrat," *Jerusalem Post*, January 20, 2015.
29. Jennie Rosenfeld and David S. Ribner, *The Newlywed's Guide to Physical Intimacy* (Jerusalem: Gefen Publishing House, 2011).
30. Daniel Bergner, "The Orthodox Sex Guru," *The New York Times Magazine*, January 22, 2015.
31. Riv-Ellen Prell, "The (Un)Importance of Jewish Difference," *Mosaic Magazine*, November 17, 2014.
32. Katherine S. Newman, *The Accordion Family: Boomerang Kids, Anxious Parents, and the Private Toll of Global Competition* (Boston: Beacon Press, 2012).
33. Luis Lugo, Alan Cooperman, Gregory Smith et. al., *A Portrait of Jewish Americans: Findings from a Pew Research Center Survey of U.S. Jews* (October 1, 2013). Cited in Parmer, "Marriage and Non-Marriage," table 2, "Marital Status of American Jewish Adults by Age and Gender"; Pew results repercentaged. See chapter 1 in this volume.
34. The National Jewish Population Survey 2000–01 was conducted by the United Jewish Communities (UJC), Lawrence Kotler-Berkowitz, and others. In total, 5,148 respondents were interviewed. See www.jewishdatabank.org for more information and to download the data.
35. Harriet Hartman and Moshe Hartman, *Gender and American Jews: Patterns in Work, Education, and Family in Contemporary Jewish Life* (Waltham, MA: Brandeis University Press, 2009), 29.
36. Harriet Hartman, The Intersection of Gender and Religion in the Demography of Today's American Jewish Families, Brandeis University Seminar on Creating and Maintaining Jewish Families, March 2007.
37. Nicholas A. Christakis and James H. Fowler, *Connected: How Your Friends' Friends' Friends Affect Everything You Feel, Think, and Do* (Boston: Little Brown and Company, 2009).

38. Dana Kessler, "The Great Baby Divide," *Tablet*, May 10, 2013.
39. Natalie Angier, "The Changing America Family," *New York Times*, November 25, 2013.
40. Sara Rosenthal, *The Fertility Sourcebook* (New York: McGraw-Hill Professional, 2002).
41. Elissa Gootman, "So Eager for Grandchildren They're Paying the Egg-Freezing Clinic," *New York Times*, May 14, 2012.
42. Jason Deparle and Sabrina Tavernise, "Unwed Mothers Now a Majority before Age of 30: New Threshold in U.S., Most Rapid Growth Has Been Among White Women in 20s," *New York Times*, February 18, 2012.
43. Susan Martha Kahn, *Reproducing Jews: A Cultural Account of Assisted Conception in Israel* (Durham, NC: Duke University Press, 2000).
44. Anne-Marie Slaughter, "Why Women Still Can't Have It All," *The Atlantic Monthly*, July/August 2012.
45. B. D. Whitehead, "Forget Sex in the City—Women Want Romance in Their Lives," *Washington Post*, February 9, 2003.
46. Sarah Blaffer Hrdy, *Mother Nature: Maternal Instincts and How They Shape the Human Species* (New York: Ballantine, 1999). Hrdy asserts that it is "typical of the entire Primate order" that "high-status male primates" are "intent on controlling when, where, and how females belonging to his group reproduced."
47. Elisabeth Badinter, *The Conflict: How Modern Motherhood Undermines the Status of Women* (New York: Metropolitan, 2012).
48. Gloria Steinem, "Humanism and the Second Wave of Feminism," *Humanist* (May/June 1987): 11–15, 49.
49. Shulamith Firestone, *The Dialectic of Sex* (New York: Morrow, 1971).
50. Margaret Sandelowski, "Fault Lines: Infertility and Imperiled Sisterhood," *Feminist Studies* 16, no. 1 (Spring 1990): 33–51.
51. Ross Douthat, "More Babies, Please," *New York Times*, December 2, 2012, 11.
52. Kathleen Gerson, *An Unfinished Revolution: How a New Generation Is Reshaping Family, Work, and Gender* (New York: Oxford University Press, 2010).
53. Robert Wright, "Feminists, Meet Mr. Darwin," *The New Republic*, November 28, 1994, 34.
54. Steven Pinker, *The Blank Slate: the Modern Denial of Human Nature* (New York: Penguin Books, 2002), 342.
55. Rosalind Barnett and Caryl Rivers, *Same Difference: How Gender Myths Are Hurting Our Relationships, Our Children, and Our Jobs* (Basic Books: New York, 2004), 79.
56. Carol Gilligan, *In a Different Voice: Psychological theory and women's development* (Cambridge: Harvard University Press, 1982).
57. B. J. Risman and D. Johnson-Sumerford, "Doing It Fairly: A Study of Postgender Marriages," *Journal of Marriage and the Family* 60 (1998) 23–40.
58. T. Bond, E. Galinsky, and J. Swanberg, *The National Study of the Changing Workforce* (New York: Family and Work Institute, 1998).
59. Motoko Rich, "A Couple's Basic Principles of Lovenomics 101," *New York Times*, February 11, 2012.
60. Betsey Stevenson and Justin Wolfers, "Subjective Well-Being and Income: Is There Any Evidence of Satiation," NBER working paper 18992 (Cambridge, MA: National Bureau of Economic Research, April 2013), www.brookings.edu/research/papers/2013/04/subjective-well-being-income.
61. Claire Cain Miller, "Study Finds More Reasons to Get and Stay Married," *New York Times*, January 8, 2015.

62. Hartman and Hartman, "Gender and American Jews," 88–89.
63. Pew Research Center, *A Portrait of Jewish Americans* (Washington, DC: Pew Research Center, 2013), 43.
64. Ibid., 101.
65. Steven M. Cohen, Carol Aviv, and Ari Kelman, "Gay, Jewish, or Both? Sexual Orientation and Jewish Engagement," *Journal of Jewish Communal Service* 84:154–66.
66. Benoit Denizet-Lewis, "Young Gay Rites: Why Would Gay Men in Their 20s Rush to the Altar?" *The New York Times Magazine*, April 27, 2008; the cover art featured the text, "The Newlywed Gays! Life among young men who are married (to men) in Massachusetts could not be more normal. Strange."
67. Ben Sales, "Conservative Rabbinic Group Issues Guidelines for Same-Sex Wedding Rituals," *JTA*, June 4, 2012.
68. Ibid.
69. On December 22, 2009, YU Tolerance Club and Wurzweiler School of Social Work hosted an event titled "Being Gay in the Orthodox World: A Conversation with Members of the YU Community," moderated by Rabbi Yosef Blau.
70. Asher Lopatin, "What Makes a Book Orthodox? *Wrestling with God and Men* by Steven Greenberg (Madison: University of Wisconsin Press, 2004)," *The Edah Journal* 4, no 2 (2005).
71. Tova Hartman Halbertal with Irit Koren, "Between 'Being' and 'Doing': Conflict and Coherence in the Identity Formation of Gay Orthodox Jews," in *Identity and Story: Creating Self in Narrative*, ed. Dan P. McAdams, Ruthellen Josselson and Amia Lieblich (Washington DC: American Psychological Association, 2006), 37–61.
72. Yitz Greenberg, "A Rabbi's Advice: How to Respond to Your Gay Child," *Moment Magazine*, November 16, 2011.
73. Richard W. Stevenson, "Social Issues Return to Dominant Role in National Debate," *New York Times*, February 5, 2012; and Charles M. Blow, "Santorum and the Sexual Revolution: At War with the 1960s," *New York Times*, March 3, 2012.
74. Robert Cherry, "Rational Choice and the Price of Marriage," *Feminist Economics* 4, no. 1 (1998): 27–49.
75. Men are given responsibility for and authority over women's sexual and reproductive activities in the Hebrew Bible, for example, where female children belong to the father, who transfers ownership to a bridegroom following prescribed protocols. The Talmudic Tractate *Qiddushin* stipulates that a woman may only achieve the status of emancipation—of being responsible for herself, *konah et atzmah* (literally, she "buys" herself)—through three methods: being divorced by her husband, becoming a widow through a husband's death, or simply outlasting her father and being a grown woman when he dies.
76. Rivka Neriya Ben-Shahar, "Haredi (Ultra-Orthodox) Women and Mass Media in Israel: Exposure Patterns and Reading Strategies" [Hebrew] (PhD diss., Hebrew University, Jerusalem, 2008).
77. David Jacobson, *Of Virgins and Martyrs: Women and Sexuality in Global Conflict* (Baltimore: Johns Hopkins University Press, 2013), 2.
78. Shlomo M. Brody, "Ask the Rabbi: Do Norms of Modest Attire Change?" *The Jerusalem Post*, January 10, 2013.
79. Valeria Siegelshifer and Tova Hartman, "From Tichels to Hair Bands: Modern Orthodox Women and the Practice of Head Covering," *Women's Studies International Forum* 34 (2011): 349–59, esp. 350.

80. Sima Zalcberg Block, "Shouldering the Burden of Redemption: How the 'Fashion' of Wearing Capes Developed in Ultra-Orthodox Society," *Nashim: A Journal of Jewish Women's Studies and Gender Issues, Special issue on Gender and Jewish Identity* 22 (Fall 2011): 32–55.
81. Danya Ruttenberg, "Toward a New Tzniut," in *The Passionate Torah: Sex and Judaism*, ed. Danya Ruttenberg (New York: New York University Press, 2009), 203–11.
82. Sylvia Barack Fishman with Rachel S. Bernstein and Emily Sigalow, "Reimagining Jewishness: Younger American Jewish Leaders, Entrepreneurs, and Artists in Cultural Context," in *The New Jewish Leaders: Reshaping the American Jewish Landscape*, ed. Jack Wertheimer (Waltham, MA: Brandeis University Press, 2011), 159–213.
83. Michael Winerip, "A Man's View on 'Having It All,'" *New York Times*, March 24, 2013, 11.
84. Cited in Miller, "Study Finds."
85. Jonathan Boyarin, *Jewish Families* (New Brunswick, NJ: Rutgers University Press, 2013), 29.
86. Pew, *Portrait of Jewish Americans*, 35–37.
87. Sylvia Barack Fishman, *Double or Nothing? Jewish Families and Mixed Marriage* (Waltham, MA: Brandeis University Press, 2004) cites numerous interviews in which both Jews and Christian-raised parents reflected that they didn't realize how much religion mattered to them until they gave birth to their first child and began to deal with lifecycle markers and religious calendar years.

# 1

# Love, Sexuality, and Personal Choice

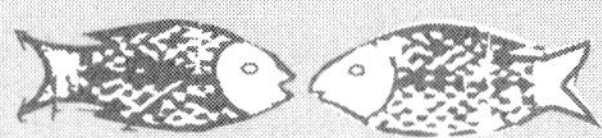

# 1

## What's Love Got to Do with It?

### *Marriage and Non-Marriage among Younger American Jews*

Daniel Parmer

TO PARAPHRASE MARK TWAIN, reports of the death of marriage have been greatly exaggerated. To be sure, there are plenty of signs pointing to the demise of the institution. Fewer Americans get married today than in the past; when they do, it is at a later age, for shorter periods, and remarriage is less likely.[1] If recent trends continue, the erosion of marriage is a foregone conclusion. Yet the counter-narrative suggests that marriage continues to be highly significant and valued among the majority of Americans. The tension between these narratives is illustrated in a recent Pew Research Center study on marriage and the family. On one hand, the study reports that nearly 40 percent of Americans say marriage is becoming obsolete. Only 52 percent of all Americans 18 and older are currently married. On the other hand, despite these and other signs of ambivalence, marriage remains deeply ingrained in the population of the United States. Most—over 90 percent—of all Americans will get married at some point in their life. The same Pew study that offers a pessimistic prognosis on marriage also reports that a majority of young Americans (67 percent) say they are upbeat about the future of marriage and that they intend to marry at some point in their life.[2]

This chapter examines the development of recent trends in marriage among American Jews and offers new evidence to support the counter-narrative claim that marriage remains a relevant and highly desirable form of family formation amid a changing landscape.

Many readers will recall *Newsweek*'s 1986 cover depicting a graph and the ominous warning that a single college-educated woman was "more likely to be killed by a terrorist" than marry.[3] The 1980s saw a flurry of academic and institutional activity to try to understand changes then becoming apparent in the American (and American Jewish) family sparked, in part, by the social and cultural revolution of the 1960s and 1970s. Reading through this literature gives one the sense that although interest in the topic has ebbed and flowed over the decades, today's trends are neither recent nor unprecedented. Writing in Sklare's 1982 edited volume *Understanding American Jewry*, Sheila Kamerman describes trends in the Jewish family and family policies:

> There are fewer families with children and those families with children have fewer of them; there has been a rapid growth in the number and percentage of two-earner families and of single-parent, working-mother families (usually a consequence of divorce); Jewish children born in the last quarter of the twentieth century are more likely to experience living in a one-parent family, in a reconstituted family, in a family with working parents, in a family with one parent who was not born Jewish. Despite all this, individuals are likely to get married, have children, and continue to assert that a happy family life is the single most important factor in contributing to their own sense of well-being."[4]

Calvin Goldscheider likewise noted in the early 1980s, "for the first time in recent American Jewish history significant proportions of men and women aged 20–35 are not marrying. The increasing proportions of the never married adds to the growing number of nonmarried, divorced, and separated Jewish men and women."[5] Data from the 1970 National Jewish Population Survey (NJPS) as well as local community studies such as the 1975 Boston Jewish community survey provided solid evidence that dramatic shifts had occurred in the Jewish family.[6] By the end of the decade several scholars joined the chorus lamenting changes in the Jewish family and young Jewish Americans in particular. Steven M. Cohen summarized these trends, declaring, "fewer young Jews than young non-Jews were married in the 1970s, and they were less likely to be married than young Jews in the 1960s,"[7] and Sylvia Barack Fishman wrote that "in terms of marital status the contemporary American Jewish community resembles the contemporary non-Jewish community far more than it resembles the American Jewish community of 20 years ago."[8]

It would seem that qualitatively, little has changed in Jewish family life since the 1980s (a later-marrying pattern emerged in the Depression in the 1930s but then receded in the years after World War II[9]). However, there are some novel changes in family life, marriage, and partnering today. For example, the number of American Jews that remain single at all age groups has increased, the number of couples that cohabit before—or in the place of—marriage has increased, and the number of American Jews who identify as secular or nonreligious has increased. These trends are shared by Americans more broadly, reflecting the deep integration of American Jewry in larger society.

While their lives illustrate these widespread trends, American Jews nevertheless maintain a certain distinctiveness compared with the broader society. To echo Goldscheider, it is remarkable that the American Jewish family remains relatively traditional, considering the radical social transformations of American Jewry over the past century.[10] For example, most Jewish young adults today view marriage as a positive milestone that they expect to reach and indeed approximately nine in ten Jews will marry at some point in their lives.[11] The processes that underlie the distinctive features of American Jews may best be understood via "cultural resiliency." Where culture is defined as "the transmission of shared values, beliefs, skills, and adaptive behaviors between generations and through shared participation in settings and situations,"[12] cultural resilience is the mechanism by which an individual's cultural background can help facilitate the process of overcoming adversity (i.e., assimilation).[13]

This chapter makes three contributions to the literature on marriage and non-marriage among American Jews. First, the chapter provides an analysis of trends in family formation and marital status among American Jews using recent data. Even as American Jews have fully integrated in society, competing cultural models of American individualism and traditionalism underscore features of distinctiveness among American Jews compared with Americans more broadly. Second, the work presents a theoretical framing of marital trends that contextualizes the position of American Jews in this new sociological milieu. Third, original research conducted as part of a broader study of marriage among Jewish young adults is examined.[14] This final piece offers insight into the *how* and *why* of marriage as opposed to the *what* that has characterized much of the literature to date.

## American Jews: A Part and Apart

Over the past century, marriage has transformed from primarily a social institution in the nineteenth and twentieth centuries to what sociologist Ernest Burgess called "companionate" marriage—marriage characterized not by patriarchal relationships, but by egalitarian relationships bonded by love, friendship, and common interests.[15] Andrew Cherlin, professor of sociology and public policy, goes further, arguing that Burgess's companionate marriage peaked in the 1950s, and marriage has since become "individualized marriage" based primarily on individuals' personal self-growth and happiness.[16] Indeed, as will be reflected in the qualitative analysis below, most Jewish young adults today are planted firmly in this third understanding of marriage. These changes in marriage have led to two perspectives on the trajectory of marriage in the United States: the marital-decline perspective and the marital-resilience perspective.[17] Although both perspectives present merit, the evidence presented here suggests that marriage remains a vital and resilient institution. This perspective posits that the following hallmarks of marriage are preserved: the institution of marriage is not necessarily in decline and the ideal of marriage is viewed positively, Americans have not become excessively self-absorbed, changes in marriage and family life have had few negative consequences for society, and those changes have strengthened rather than undermined our quality of relationships, especially for women and sexual minorities.[18]

Answers to many of the most fundamental questions about marriage among American Jews remain elusive—What does marriage look like today? Do American Jews and non-Jews differ? Historically, the US government collects "vital statistics" on the public through the US Census, through the Survey of Income and Program Participation (SIPP), and more recently through the National Survey of Family Growth (NSFG); however, the government is restricted from collecting information on religious identity. Furthermore, for many religious groups—especially low-incidence religious groups (those ranging between 1 percent and 10 percent of the population) data must come from an external source.[19]

The following section provides a statistical portrait of marriage among American Jews and their non-Jewish counterparts in the United States. Data from the 2013 Pew survey of American Jewry is used to provide the basic contours of marriage among Jewish adults today.[20] Prior to this, NJPS 2000–01 was the most comprehensive portrait of American Jewry.[21] Comparison of trends in marriage over time is made using these and other data (1970 and 1990 NJPS).[22] Data on the general non-Hispanic white population is also provided for comparison using official statistics.

## Marriage and Non-Marriage in the United States

Today marriage is often portrayed as a weakened and declining institution in sharp contrast to depictions of family life of the 1950s, a decade that typically evokes nostalgia of strong family values and near-universal acceptance of marriage at a young age. However, the 1950s present an anomaly in the marital history of Americans dating back to the late 1800s. Without diminishing the extent of change evident today, it is important to emphasize that the use of the 1950s as a baseline for change is misleading. The fact is that marriage rates in 2010 look more similar to those from the period between 1890 and 1940 than those from the 1950s.[23] Still, with marriage rates exhibiting decline for over half a century, present reality cannot be ignored. Between 1970 to 2010 the marriage rate of non-Hispanic white adults dropped from 74 percent to 56 percent.

Conversely, the rate of never-married adults has increased dramatically over time. Looking at trends in the SIPP data from 1986 to 2009, Elliot et. al. show that, especially for non-Hispanic white women aged 25–29 and 30–34, the rates have nearly doubled, increasing from 24 percent to 43.3 percent and from 11.3 percent to 22.9 percent respectively. Yet, as noted before, the increase in the never married during their twenties and thirties signifies a delay in marriage rather than a rejection. By age 40, approximately 90 percent of women will have been married.[24]

Similarly, the rate of cohabitation has steadily increased—especially among younger Americans. The NSFG reports 48 percent of women interviewed in 2006–2010 cohabited as a first union compared with 34 percent a decade earlier. Of these, 40 percent of premarital cohabitations transitioned to marriage within three years, while 32 percent remained intact (unmarried) and 27 percent dissolved. Cohabitation is typically formed in one of two ways. For the majority, cohabitation represents a transitional step toward marriage in the form of dating or engagement. For others, cohabitation is formed as an alternative to marriage. Unfortunately, no comparably detailed data are available for American Jews.[25] However, as others have noted, "transitions to marriage are more likely for cohabiting women with higher levels of education and income than for cohabiting women of lower socioeconomic status."[26]

## American Jews: A Portrait

What is known about the size and characteristics of American Jews comes primarily from analyses of the decennial National Jewish Population Survey (NJPS) completed in 1970, 1990, and 2000–01. The Jewish Federation of North America (formerly UJC) elected not to sponsor an NJPS 2010. In its absence the Pew Research Center carried out a national survey of American Jewry in 2013. Figure 1.1 compares the rate of Jewish adults currently married with that of the non-Hispanic white adult population between 1970 and 2010–2013. If the rate continues to decline, it is likely that the proportion of adults currently married will fall below 50 percent by 2020.

Table 1.1 shows changes in the percentage of adults currently married by age and gender. The most dramatic change since 1990 appears among those 25 to 34 years old as the rate of currently married adults nearly halves. By age 35 to 44, the marriage rate peaks with percentages comparable to those found over the past two decades. The evidence presented here confirms what has been noted elsewhere; marriage among American Jews is being delayed rather than rejected.[27]

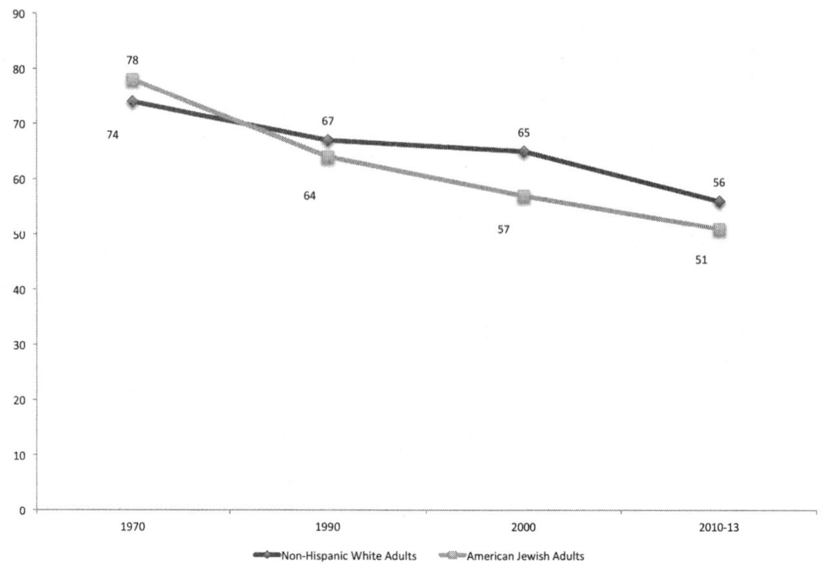


FIGURE 1.1: Percent currently married, 1970 to 2010–2013. *Source*: American Jews NJPS 1970, 1990, 2000–01; Pew, *Portrait of Jewish Americans* (2013); US Census 1970, 1990, 2000, 2010

Table 1.1. Rate of currently married American Jewish Adults by age and gender: 1990–2013

| | 18–24 (%) | 25–34 (%) | 35–44 (%) | 45–54 (%) | 55–64 (%) | 65+ (%) |
|---|---|---|---|---|---|---|
| MEN | | | | | | |
| 1990 (NJPS) currently married | 2 | 46 | 73 | 77 | 87 | 82 |
| 2000–01 (NJPS) currently married | 9 | 46 | 67 | 73 | 70 | 76 |
| 2013 (Pew) currently married | 2 | 24 | 75 | 65 | 70 | 72 |
| WOMEN | | | | | | |
| 1990 (NJPS) currently married | 12 | 62 | 74 | 75 | 77 | 57 |
| 2000–01 (NJPS) currently married | 18 | 56 | 70 | 72 | 65 | 54 |
| 2013 (Pew) currently married | 7 | 37 | 75 | 53 | 65 | 40 |

SOURCE: NJPS 1990, Table 5.2, "Marital Status of American Jews Percentages by Age and Gender." Adapted from Fishman, *Jewish Life and American Culture*, 119. Copyright 2000 by State University of New York. NJPS 2000–01, Table 3.1, "Marital Status by Age and Gender." Adapted from Hartman and Hartman, *Gender and American Jews*, 29. Copyright 2009 by Brandeis University Press. Pew, *Portrait of Jewish Americans* (Feb. 20–June 13, 2013). Age. Results repercentaged to exclude nonresponse.

Table 1.2. Marital status of American Jewish Adults by age and gender

| | 18–24 (%) | 25–34 (%) | 35–44 (%) | 45–54 (%) | 55–64 (%) | 65+ (%) |
|---|---|---|---|---|---|---|
| MEN | | | | | | |
| Currently married | 2 | 24 | 75 | 65 | 70 | 72 |
| Living with a partner | 4 | 14 | 3 | 5 | 7 | 5 |
| Divorced/Separated | 0 | 4 | 4 | 19 | 13 | 9 |
| Widowed | 0 | 0 | 0 | 1 | 2 | 9 |
| Never been married | 94 | 58 | 18 | 10 | 9 | 5 |
| Ever married | 2 | 28 | 79 | 85 | 84 | 90 |
| WOMEN | | | | | | |
| Currently married | 7 | 37 | 75 | 52 | 65 | 40 |
| Living with a partner | 7 | 15 | 11 | 5 | 3 | 2 |
| Divorced/Separated | 3 | 4 | 8 | 23 | 18 | 15 |
| Widowed | 0 | * | * | 4 | 5 | 40 |
| Never been married | 84 | 43 | 5 | 15 | 9 | 3 |
| Ever married | 10 | 41 | 84 | 80 | 88 | 95 |

SOURCE: Pew, *Portrait of Jewish Americans* (Feb. 20–June 13, 2013). Age. Results repercentaged to exclude nonresponse.

Perhaps most revealing is the drop in current marriage rates among adults ages 45 to 54 according to the Pew 2013 estimates (table 1.2). Compared with previous decades, this age group typically peaks; however, the decline may represent fewer adults re-marrying after experiencing marital dissolution.[28] If one looks at the "ever married" rate for this age group, 85 percent of men and 80 percent of women age 45 to 54 have been married at least once before. Furthermore, 19 percent of men and 23 percent of women age 45 to 54 reports being divorced or separated.

Differences between Jewish men and women also persist as more women marry at a younger age compared with men (table 1.2). By age 35 to 44 the gender gap all but disappears among the currently married; however, differences remain among other categories of marital status. For example, by age 35 to 44 Jewish women are nearly four times more likely than Jewish men to report that they are living with a partner. And women are two times as likely as men to report that they are divorced or widowed, a result that can likely be attributed to the higher rates of marriage at a young age compared with men. Increasingly, Americans who choose to marry are sharply divided by class (as race often intersects with

Table 1.3. Marital status of American Jewish Adults by education: 2013

| | HIGH SCHOOL OR LESS | SOME COLLEGE | COLLEGE DEGREE OR HIGHER |
|---|---|---|---|
| Currently married (%) | 36 | 44 | 59 |
| Living with a partner (%) | 6 | 5 | 8 |
| Divorced/Separated (%) | 15 | 11 | 10 |
| Widowed (%) | 13 | 9 | 4 |
| Never been married (%) | 29 | 32 | 21 |

SOURCE: Pew, *Portrait of Jewish Americans* (Feb. 20–June 13, 2013). Age. Results repercentaged to exclude nonresponse.

class, they are racially divided as well). In the past, those with less education were more likely to be married.[29] Today, the opposite is true; Americans with a four-year college degree or higher are more likely than those without to be married. Authors of the Pew study on marriage and the family suggest that while most Americans desire marriage, those without a college education view financial security as a prerequisite for marriage, and with lower earning potentials than their college educated peers, it takes them much longer—if ever—to achieve that level of financial security.[30]

Educational attainment is critical to understanding why American Jews, as a group, look different compared with Americans broadly and even non-Hispanic whites more generally. Indeed, Harriet and Moshe Hartman argue that even compared with college-educated non-Hispanic whites, American Jews differ. They marry later, are less likely to divorce, are less likely to remarry, and have fewer children.[31] Since most Jews attain at least a four-year college degree, this educational homogamy is higher among Jews than their non-Jewish peers. Others have also found that the impact of education in the marriage market has become increasingly significant.[32] Table 1.3 shows the marital status of American Jews in 2013 by level of education. Among those with a college degree or higher, 59 percent reported that they are currently married.

It is also important to note that the American Jewish community is not homogenous. Divisions within the Jewish community often fall along denominational lines. In their analysis of NJPS 2000–01 data, Harriet and Moshe Hartman found differences by denominational affiliation but concluded, "when Jewish identity and behavior are controlled for, few differences persist except among Orthodox women. When Jewish identity and behavior are controlled for, denomination ceased being a significant predictor of age at first marriage or at age of first child."[33] Table 1.4 shows the marital status of Jewish adults by denominational affiliation in 2013. The greatest differences occur within the unaffiliated,

Table 1.4. Marital status of American Jewish Adults by denomination: 2013

| | ORTHODOX (%) | CONSERVATIVE (%) | REFORM (%) | UNAFFILIATED (%) |
|---|---|---|---|---|
| Currently married | 69 | 55 | 52 | 44 |
| Living with a partner | 1 | 8 | 6 | 8 |
| Divorced/Separated | 8 | 11 | 12 | 11 |
| Widowed | 3 | 8 | 9 | 3 |
| Never been married | 18 | 18 | 22 | 35 |
| Ever married | 81 | 74 | 72 | 57 |

SOURCE: Pew, *Portrait of Jewish Americans* (Feb. 20–June 13, 2013). Age. Results repercentaged to exclude nonresponse.

with 35 percent reporting that they have never married compared with just 22 percent of Reform Jews and 18 percent of both Conservative and Orthodox Jews.

## The Data

Existing data on marital status or attitudes toward dating or marital preference provide only the contours of partnering and marriage patterns among American Jews. To more fully understand these issues the present work analyzes qualitative data collected from a sample of Jewish young adults. Data come from a target population of applicants to the *Taglit*-Birthright Israel program. Because the applicant pool is so large, most Jewish young adults are represented in the sample.[34]

A small subsample was selected from the New England region. Participants were contacted and interviewed between September 2012 and May 2013. Interviews covered background information, how participants were raised, their social networks from childhood to the present, their past and current relationships, and their connection to and engagement in the Jewish community. Interviews were conducted with individuals that were currently married, single (never married as well as divorced), and currently in a relationship, including those who were dating, cohabiting, and engaged. Participants included men and women as well as those who identified as gay or lesbian.

The following discussion is based on findings from twenty-seven interviews designed and analyzed using content analysis and reason analysis. Content analysis enables identification of patterns and themes that develop across individual interviews. Reason analysis is useful when determining *how* individuals make the decisions they do. Charles Kadushin writes, "If one wants to know how an action came to be—what steps were taken and what the key choices were; what the actor thought he was doing and how he felt about it; what influences were present and what triggered the action; and finally, what outcomes the actor expected—then no technique other than reason analysis can be used."[35]

Data from the interviews yield a rich portrait of Jewish young adults' attitudes toward and behaviors during dating, relationships, cohabitation, and marriage. The following section explores key dimensions of these themes. In particular, three aspects of Jewish young adults' attitudes and behaviors toward marriage are analyzed: near-universal acceptance and desirability of marriage, meaning in marriage, and delay of marriage.

## The Desirability of Marriage

Compared with the US population more broadly and non-Hispanic whites in particular, American Jews manifest distinctiveness on a variety of measures. Similar to other ethnic or religious minorities, American Jews exist between competing cultural models of American individualism and traditionalism. One explanation, as discussed earlier, posits that the group maintains distinctiveness through the processes of cultural resilience.

The Jewish young adults who participated in the research articulated this bifurcated tension in terms of marital decisions. Virtually all respondents expressed a strong desire to marry and have children. They viewed this as a natural course of events stemming from their own Jewish upbringing and experience. One participant, David, a young professional living in a Boston suburb who is married and has one child appeared exasperated by the decision of some to veer from this "normalized" trajectory:

> I've never understood why people wouldn't get married. If you're all in together—I feel like people are trying to rebel against something by doing that. I don't know. Maybe I'm just too normalized, but I don't understand, if you want to have kids with somebody and you want to live together, society sort of expects you to get married, and so you have to have a reason why you wouldn't want to, I guess.

On the other hand, Jewish young adults are quick to assert American individualism, sharing an acceptance of a broad range of lifestyles and life choices. Research participants, regardless of background characteristics, affirmed that all individuals have a right to live as they choose and that there was little difference between a long-term committed relationship and a marriage. Yet virtually all participants expressed a strong personal desire to marry and that having children within marriage was highly desirable. Some, like Susan, a young single woman who grew up in southern New Hampshire, expressed this internal conflict during the interview:

> I get this kind of contention between things I feel strongly and passionately about and being really open-minded about things. But then also kind of, things that I would want for myself. I think I would want to [get married]. Yeah, I think I would want to be married. But I wouldn't have to rush into that right away. I feel like just a committed relationship is the most important thing.

Many Jewish young adults articulated that although they were open to the idea of committed relationships outside the institutional framework of marriage, the decision to have children should be made only after marriage has occurred. Data from the 2013 Pew survey of American Jewry reveal that between 5 percent and 11 percent of single, never married respondents (men and women of all ages) report the presence of children. This number stands in stark contrast to Americans more broadly. Recent findings show that more than half of births to women under 30 in the general population happen outside of marriage.[36] From Susan again:

> I think I would really handle marriage in that kind of way, being really thoughtful and not rushing into it [just] because I feel like it's the next step or what should be done. . . . So I think it is really possible to achieve those other things without marriage involved, but I think I would want to be married, and I would want to have that kind of unity in terms of starting a family.

Even among those interviewed who expressed a minority opinion of relative ambivalence toward marriage, most still felt a personal draw to it. Sharon, a young professional who grew up in a Conservative household and presently lives with her boyfriend in a long-term relationship described her views this way:

> It's hard to say what the difference is between marriage and between just a long-term committed relationship where you're living together. I don't think that it changes much in the day-to-day, which makes me kind of wonder why people are so scared of it, aside from the fact that it's ostensibly a lifetime commitment. But yeah, I guess in the bigger picture it is kind of representative of a larger commitment.

Sharon is typical of young adults who are comfortable with the idea of delaying marriage into their thirties and engaging in long-term cohabiting relationships that can last for several years. But their ambivalence toward marriage is expressed primarily as an attitude of acceptance of alternate forms of cohabitation outside of marriage rather than a rejection of marriage altogether, as Sharon clarified:

> I'm not the kind of kid who was dreaming of my perfect wedding from the day I was born. I have no idea what dress I want or anything. But I definitely want that next step. I definitely wouldn't want to have a kid without being married, for the technical reasons—the taxes and all that—but also for the traditional reasons. I don't care about a lot of traditions that much, but in terms of life milestones, I really do want the more traditional path. It's funny, on one hand I'd be very uncomfortable with that—with being in a long-term relationship with no hope of marriage. But on the other hand, where I'm really happy with my boyfriend, I'm a little bit afraid of bringing up the talk at any point. If at this point he said, "I never want to get married," I'm like, "Do we have to break up?" What do I do now, because that's not compatible with my long-term goals.

Sharon's response raises some important questions about why individuals remain in committed relationships for several years before marrying. It also highlights the anxiety felt by many cohabiting couples. For young Jewish adults, the overall trend is clear: marriage remains highly desirable, most feel that marriage should precede children, and most will marry at some point in their life, despite trends of increased cohabitation before marriage and marital delay.

## What's Love Got to Do with It?

If most Jewish young adults desire to marry, it is critical to understand why. Understanding how young adults define marriage in their lives is important, as this definition shapes the way they view their partner and their role and commitment to their spouse in marriage. It also highlights an interesting contrast with previous generations. Earlier generations may be better characterized by Cherlin's earliest model of marriage, one dominated by expectations of conformity and entering a social as well as an individual contract. Generations closer to the participants more typically took part in companionate marriage, where mutual affection and companionship took center stage and the social role of marriage began to wane. Today, young adults view marriage as an expression of their own individual self-growth. It is one of the few transitions that marks their entrance to adulthood.

To gauge how young Jewish adults feel about marriage and how they personally define it, research participants were asked an open-ended question about what marriage means to them. Just three participants suggested that marriage equated with love. This is not to say that individuals who marry don't find love important, or that they don't love their spouse; rather, the idea that love is a primary filter by which they understand marriage was absent or perhaps it was assumed to be a part of the courtship period.

Instead, nearly all participants responded to the question by describing marriage as a partnership, a team, or as a commitment that they forged. These young adults spoke of marriage in the same way a young entrepreneur might talk about a start-up company. The task of marriage involved finding an equal partner who complemented the skills and strengths of the individual and added value to the team. In 1966, a study of American Jewish wives identified a similar theme, but as Lawrence Fuchs writes in *Beyond Patriarchy*, "several of them talked of their marriages as partnerships, but they meant something quite different from what many contemporary Jewish women mean by the same term."[37] Partnership, according to these women, meant that husbands and wives had complementary rather than shared roles. One of the Jewish wives in the mid-1960s study remarked, "Ours is a partnership. I run the home; he runs the office."[38] In today's relationship dynamic, each partner expects the other to contribute to both office and home, though, as several participants remarked, traditional gender roles are easy to fall in to.

Although few participants equated marriage with love, many observed that marriage was about more than love. Marc, a law student in Boston, offered that marriage is "more than just about love—it's about a commitment to a person." Echoing the sentiment that marriage is about "more than love," Rachel, a modern Orthodox mother of two described her view of marriage:

> Marriage, I think, is a union between two people. It doesn't necessarily have to be between love or money or all those different things, but I think it creates a strong family unit and trust and a partnership throughout life with a companion . . . I think that there's a great partnership that can come from marriage, divide tasks and conquer.

These views were repeated by several participants regardless of gender or sexual orientation. For example, Jessica, a young woman living in Connecticut with her same-sex spouse suggested "that in a very practical sense it's a union between two people that creates stability and certainty that aids in childrearing." She continued:

> But I also think that it's about being able to rely on someone else, no matter what. It's almost like a commitment—it's more than love because if it was about love, then you wouldn't try to keep loving that person, and if it fizzled, you would not really care about it either way.

The responses provide further evidence to support the argument that young adults today reside in the third phase of marriage described by Cherlin. Whereas

Burgess and Locke's assessment that marriage had transformed from an institutional obligation to an expression of mutual affection and companionship reflected the experience of earlier generations, today's young adults reflect the second transformation of marriage, from companionate to individualized marriage. It is important to note that mutual dependencies—being able to count on one's partner—remain an important element of individualized marriages.

Many respondents described marriage as a type of relationship that fosters self-growth (meeting goals, growing as a person). One young woman described marriage as having "someone to spend the rest of your life with; someone who can be a partner in your life and have the same goals, and want to help you want to reach your own goals and help them reach their goals." Likewise, Hannah, a married woman from western Massachusetts said:

> When we got married, I really felt like it was all about joining. Now I feel like it's this commitment of support that we have for each other, but we're in this phase in our lives now that it's really about our growth—our own personal, professional, spiritual growth, and growing our children, and maintaining the commitment and support for each other through that, like for each other in our separate goals.

This perspective that marriage should provide opportunities for each individual as well as for the couple and the family as a whole was shared among the married and unmarried alike. Miriam, a young single woman, viewed marriage as a team endeavor, describing it as having two components, an independent and joint aspect. Of the individual, Miriam said:

> It's two independent people's lives coming together and still having their own independent lives and pursuits, but also now creating a . . . some pursuit together in life. So I think the independent part of it is very important for a successful marriage, but that team approach as well in living life is that new creation that they have together. I think that marriage is a time where each individual partner can help stimulate and challenge and help that other partner succeed in their own individual pursuits with, whether it is just by support, whether it is by helping them make decisions on their own life path and also being supportive or actually in some way stimulating and challenging them and inspiring them in some way.

This idea of joining to create something new but maintaining separateness in which each individual can grow became a familiar trope throughout the interviews.

Whether there are any implications for the cleavage between different generations' understanding of marriage remains untested. It may be that an approach that emphasizes partnership and team building is more conducive to stability and long-term commitment. It is certainly the case that most participants viewed marriage positively and were hopeful that marriage would be a "forever" commitment in their own lives. Alternatively it may be that the lack of institutionalization and social expectations for marriage will further the trend of high divorce rates. Indeed, just two respondents described marriage in terms of a social contract with vows made before their community, emphasizing a sort of social obligation.

## The Unmarried: Marriage Delayed not Rejected

As the profile of American Jewry described earlier confirms, the majority of American Jews get married at some point in their life. Compared with the general population they marry later on average; however, delay in marriage should not be confused with rejection of marriage. Participants described several reasons for delaying marriage. For example, both men and women discussed their education and career as contributors. Others delayed marriage because there was less pressure to marry before a certain age, an indication that participants believe alternative attitudes toward long-term relationships, unmarried cohabitation, and delayed childbirth are acceptable. Although the majority of participants viewed marriage as distinct from long-term relationships, this did not prevent them from dating or engaging in committed relationships, but they were inclined to put off the decision to marry until they were "ready." This tactic seems to contribute to a tension between individualism and traditionalism. By waiting, young people keep open the perceived opportunities available to them as single or unmarried adults.

Based on the evidence presented, young adults today are firmly stationed in Cherlin's third phase or model of marriage, characterized by self-growth. The delay in marriage and rise in cohabitation are part of an extended adolescence or "emerging adulthood" as described by research psychologist Jeffrey Arnett. One of the principle characteristics guiding the behavior of emerging adults is that it is a period of self-growth. The roles and responsibilities of adulthood that previous generations adopted at a much earlier age are delayed, extending the period of college and post-college young adulthood. As Arnett explains, "staying unmarried allows emerging adults to keep their options open, not just in terms of whom they might marry but in terms of whom they might become and what they might decide to do with their lives."[39] Since this period of self-discovery does not preclude dating or relationships, young adults feel they may test the waters with a partner while exploring themselves.[40]

For some study participants, delaying marriage was necessary to focus on education or a career. Amy, a 28-year-old Boston-area resident, spoke of her desire to cement her career before turning attention to her personal life, saying, "I don't have timelines or anything, a five-year plan . . . My career is kind of coming together, so I'm feeling like that area of my life is coming together, so I'm thinking more about personal life." Another young woman remembered conversations she had with her mother and the impact it had on her own decisions:

> My mom was a very big advocate for going to college and establishing yourself. Right after high school I wanted to take a year off and volunteer before I went to college, and my mom was like, "Absolutely not." And I think because she dropped out of college after two years and got married, she was adamant that you go to college, you establish yourself.

However, as participants spoke of the reasons marriage is delayed, a division between men and women emerged. Both men and women viewed education and careers as driving forces in the delay to marry; however, women were particularly sensitive to the historical implications of gender roles in marriage. Women spoke with a greater sense of urgency than men did of the need to complete their education—often graduate school—or establish themselves in a career before thinking of marriage. Women also spoke of the tension between their desire for achievement and material stability and their desire to marry and have children, driven often by their concern about their biological clocks. Many assumed the likelihood of completing a post-college degree or establishing a career would diminish if they married or had children. When describing the timing of marriage, men also attributed differences between the sexes to women's—but not their own—biological clocks.

In contrast with women's concerns, some men spoke of "sowing their oats" before marriage. To be sure, several men remarked that they wanted to be financially secure and able to support a family before proposing marriage. However, both men and women noted that men were more likely to have fun before thinking seriously about marriage. One young man, who spoke strongly in favor of marriage, discussed the reason he waited until the present to think about marriage:

> I would feel some lingering wish to sort of have had my chance to go be crazy and do whatever I wanted and sleep with more women, and I feel like I've gotten that now. I can meet the person that I'm going to be with and settle down with them and not live with this wish that I got my rocks off more often before that.

A second young man who is currently married suggested that when he was younger, marriage was far removed from his mind. Asked about whether he thought he would someday be married, he responded, "Yeah, I figured eventually. But it was so far off. It was like death. It's so far off that it's not something I need to think about. It's just, let's have fun and see where it goes."

The majority of interviewees, however, simply saw the delay to marry as a generational norm. Some noted that it stemmed from an increased acceptance of cohabitation, the lack of stigma associated with unmarried coupling, and increased opportunities to engage in self-growth. Historical data on marital status inform us that these trends developed and increased over several decades. The difference today is that acceptance of previously marginalized attitudes has reached a tipping point.

## Cohabitation: Try Before You Buy

Between 1970 and the present, the number of unmarried couples living in cohabiting households increased more than fivefold.[41] For many young adults today, living with a romantic partner is commonplace. Cohabitation, as described earlier, typically takes one of two forms: as an intermediate step toward marriage or as an alternative to marriage. The majority of Jewish young adults practice the former form, although they maintain that they are little different from those who choose the latter. Yet the distinction is important, as a bevy of research suggests that cohabiting couples who later marry are at higher risk of divorce compared with those who marry without cohabitation or cohabit for a short period (typically an interim period between engagement and marriage).[42] Recent research argues that the key factor is not necessarily the act of cohabitation but the intent of commitment in a cohabiting relationship. That is, divorce is more likely when there is not already a commitment to marriage in place, such as being engaged or having made plans to become engaged.[43]

Although the trend toward increasing cohabitation has developed over several decades, many young adults were unaware of this growing pattern and talked about the phenomenon as one devised by their generation. Margaret, a young woman living with her boyfriend in Cambridge, Massachusetts, spoke of her experience:

> I definitely think that living together is an important part of the equation at this point. It's kind of a new thing for this generation, especially . . . I guess the kind of ideal timeline, now that I've had these several experiences, would be more like date a couple years, live together a couple years, be engaged a couple years, like, blossom a year or two in each stage.

The goal of cohabitation for many interview participants was not to claim an alternative to marriage, but to test the marriage waters without entering the level of commitment that marks marriage. The rise of the so-called starter or trial marriage, which made headlines during the 1990s,[44] seems to have been supplanted by increasing numbers of adults choosing to cohabit as attitudes toward cohabitation have reached wide acceptance. Furthermore, as attitudes have relaxed, many view cohabitation as a viable alternative since the exit rules are loose and largely unregulated compared with marriage (i.e., compared to the rules that govern divorce).

The majority of respondents reported little distinction between a long-term cohabiting relationship and marriage, even if they found personal meaning or satisfaction in marriage. These views are reflected in research demonstrating that non-Hispanic whites and college-educated individuals are more likely to marry even as rates of cohabitation have increased over all groups. Moreover, for American Jews marriage is viewed as a cultural norm even as the path to marriage has changed. Asked about the difference between marriage and long-term committed relationships, Amy, a young professional residing in southern Connecticut commented:

> No, I don't think there is, as long . . . as long as I feel like we both are monogamous and very much committed to the growth of the relationship. Now, I don't know—I would be very curious why we wouldn't get married. I guess I would feel a little bit less secure that he or I would want to just run more quickly and abandon the relationship during the difficult times.

This blurred distinction between cohabitation and marriage suggests that while most Jewish young adults find marriage personally meaningful and attractive, there is little stigma against unmarried coupling. Indeed, many proposed that differences exist only in the institutional structures that have been built around marriage—legal rights such as property and ownership, tax benefits, custody rights, and so on—so that marriage is more desirable insofar as it affords access to these benefits.

The long-term implications of greater acceptance of cohabitation and the tendency for couples to remain unmarried for longer periods are inconclusive. As research develops on the topic, it may be that the role of acceptance of these behaviors in society and thus the extension of traditional support systems may have more influence on marital stability than the behaviors themselves. There are also calls to regulate the entrance and exit rules of cohabitation so that individuals are extended many of the same protections and benefits permitted the legally married.

## Conclusion: Choosing to Say I Do

Observing the state of marriage among contemporary American Jews, both statistical and especially qualitative evidence provided in this study's interviews points to a changing but still vibrant future of the institution. It is unlikely that the trends witnessed over the past half century will reverse; marriage is likely to represent just one option in a growing marketplace of possible family formations. Yet for many Jews the decision to marry reinforces their Jewish identity through the connection and continuity they feel with their ancestors and tradition. Furthermore, the positive feelings toward marriage expressed by Jewish young adults contribute to their proclivity to marry. This increased desire to marry acts as a signal to potential partners that they embody certain desirable traits in the marriage market.

The Jewish community's interest in *whom* one marries has dominated Jewish communal life for several decades, much more than *when* and *how* Jews marry. Prior research demonstrates that it's not just who stands under the *chuppah* (the traditional wedding canopy) that impacts the decision to participate in Jewish life and raise children Jewish.[45] Young adults today are choosing to marry, but these decisions are being made later in life and in the context of greater acceptance of alternate expressions of commitment and family life.

Recognizing that the majority of Jews find value in the traditional model of marriage amidst an expanding marketplace of family formations is an important first step to developing programs and policies to support and encourage these individuals. It is also important to understand that most Jews are likely to marry and believe that marriage should precede children. Yet the financial burden associated with marriage and childrearing (as well as delayed or missed career opportunities) should be at the center of this discussion. Moreover, as many of the study participants remarked, these decisions affect both women and men, suggesting that programs should target both genders while remaining sensitive to the persistent gender discrimination felt largely by women.

Several of the findings presented here carry implications for the American Jewish community. For example, the emphasis on self-growth in marriage is often characterized by the lengthening of the "emerging adulthood" phase into the thirties. As Jewish young adults pursue advanced degrees and establish careers before marriage, many focus on how marriage will benefit them further. Another issue is that this lengthening of time between entering adulthood and marriage increases both the chance that individuals will have multiple serious relationships before marriage and the chance that their marriage will be preceded by a long-term cohabiting relationship. One challenge facing the Jewish community is to understand how to engage this group and to welcome them and their partners in meaningful ways.

Finally, while delay of marriage may carry certain benefits, such as greater financial stability, home ownership, and emotional maturity, it also presents various risks. As the interviews suggest, marriage is still seen by most Jews as a critical precondition to children. The implications of having children later in life are complicated by increased risk to health and lower levels of fertility than study participants might have wished. Issues that remain unexplored here relate to parents of school-age children who are also caring for aging adults (i.e., the sandwich generation). The future of marriage as an institution within the Jewish community is likely to remain vibrant and strong. However, whether it looks similar to the marriages of the past is open to debate.

## NOTES

1. Paul R. Amato, *Alone Together: How Marriage in America Is Changing* (Cambridge, MA: Harvard University Press, 2007); Andrew J. Cherlin, *The Marriage-Go-Round: The State of Marriage and the Family in America Today* (New York: Knopf, 2009).
2. Paul Taylor et al., "The Decline of Marriage and Rise of New Families" (New York: Pew Research Center, 2010), 122.
3. Eloise Salholz, "The Marriage Crunch," *Newsweek* 22 (June 2, 1986).
4. Sheila B. Kamerman, "Jews and Other People: An Agenda for Research on Families and Family Policy," in *Understanding American Jewry*, ed. Marshal Sklare (New Brunswick, NJ: Transaction Books, 1982), 146–62.
5. Calvin Goldscheider, "Demography of Jewish Americans: Research Findings, Issues, and Challenges," in *Understanding American Jewry*, ed. Marshal Sklare (New Brunswick, NJ: Transaction Books, 1982), 1–55.
6. Floyd A. Fowler, "A Study of the Jewish Population of Greater Boston, 1975" (Boston, MA: Combined Jewish Philanthropies of Greater Boston, 1975); Fred Massarik, "Demographic Highlights: Facts for Planning," in *National Jewish Population Survey 1971*, ed. C. o. J. Federations (New York: Council of Jewish Federations, 1973).
7. Steven M. Cohen, "The American Jewish Family Today," in *American Jewish Year Book*, vol. 82, eds. Morris Fine, Milton Himmelfarb, and David Singer (New York: American Jewish Committee and Jewish Publication Society, 1982), 136–54.
8. Sylvia Barack Fishman, "Marginal No More: Jewish and Single in the 1980s," *Journal of Jewish Communal Service* 65, no. 4 (1989): 4.
9. See for example Sidney E. Goldstein's work *Meaning of Marriage and Foundations of the Family: A Jewish Interpretation* (New York: Bloch, 1942). Goldstein, chairman of the Jewish Institute on Marriage and the Family, lamented the growth of the unmarried and the decline of marriage among American Jews, warning, "men and women, especially young people, will come to interpret marriage in nothing more than scientific and secular terms."
10. Goldscheider, "Demography of Jewish Americans."
11. Luis Lugo, Alan Cooperman, and Gregory A. Smith, *A Portrait of Jewish Americans: Findings from a Pew Research Center Survey of U.S. Jews* (Washington, DC: Pew Research Center's Religion and Public Life Project, 2013).

12. See also Robert T. Carter, *The Influence of Race and Racial Identity in Psychotherapy: Toward a Racially Inclusive Model* (New York: John Wiley and Sons, 1995); Celia J. Falicov, "Training to Think Culturally: A Multidimensional Comparative Framework," *Family Process* 34, no. 4 (1995).
13. Caroline S. Clauss-Ehlers, "Re-inventing Resilience: A Model of 'Culturally-Focused Resilient Adaptation,'" in *Community Planning to Foster Resilience in Children*, eds. Caroline S. Clauss-Ehlers and Mark D. Weist (New York: Springer, 2004), 28.
14. Data presented in this chapter was collected as part of the author's doctoral dissertation (forthcoming) titled "Determinants of Marriage among Jewish Young Adults: The Role of Religion, Homogeneity, and Social Networks in the Marriage Market."
15. Ernest W. Burgess and Harvey J. Locke, *The Family* (New York: American Book Company, 1945).
16. Andrew J. Cherlin, "The Deinstitutionalization of American Marriage," *Journal of Marriage and Family* 66, no. 4 (2004): 848–61; Cherlin, *The Marriage-Go-Round*.
17. Amato, *Alone Together*.
18. Ibid.; Judith Stacey, *In the Name of the Family: Rethinking Family Values in the Postmodern Age* (Boston: Beacon Press, 1996).
19. Even where religious affiliation is collected, the question is typically formulated to capture only those who identify as Jewish by religion. Recent estimates put the percent of those identifying as Jewish by religion at approximately 80 percent, suggesting that 20 percent of the Jewish population would be missed by these surveys. Furthermore, the number of Jewish respondents is so small that subgroup analysis is impossible.
20. While raw data from the Pew study was unavailable at the time of writing, Pew Research Center provided several additional analyses for this chapter.
21. Data on American Jews in 2000 presented in this chapter come primarily from the analyses of gender and American Jews prepared by Harriet and Moishe Hartman (2009) using the NJPS 2000–01 data. The Hartmans provide one of the most serious and sophisticated analyses of marriage using the NJPS 2000–01 data to date, notwithstanding the limitations of the data itself. Furthermore, use of the data presented in their analysis provides greater consistency and accuracy across the literature.
22. Readers should use appropriate caution when making inferences based on comparison across data sources due to sampling and methodological differences.
23. Stephanie Coontz, *Marriage, a History: From Obedience to Intimacy, or How Love Conquered Marriage* (New York: Viking, 2005); Diana B. Elliott et al., "Historical Marriage Trends from 1980–2010: A Focus on Race Differences" (paper presented at the annual meeting of the Population Association of America, San Francisco, CA, 2012); Elizabeth Peters and Claire M. Kamp Dush, *Marriage and Family: Perspectives and Complexities* (New York: Columbia University Press, 2009).
24. Rose M. Kreider and Renee Ellis, *Number, Timing, and Duration of Marriages and Divorces: 2009 Current Population Reports* (Washington, DC: US Census Bureau, 2011).
25. The 2013 Pew study of American Jewry does not ask respondents about current living arrangements or whether they had cohabited prior to marriage. Furthermore, the Pew study does not ask about marital history, and a percentage of those responding "living with a partner" may have been previously married. Thus, while data on current marital status is available, it is impossible to calculate the rate of "ever married." Where the rate of ever married is presented using the Pew data, it should be read as a conservative estimate, as some portion of those currently living with a partner were previously married.

26. Casey E. Copen, Kimberly Daniels, and William D. Mosher, *First Premarital Cohabitation in the United States: 2006–2010 National Survey of Family Growth National Health Statistics Reports* (Washington, DC: National Center for Health Statistics, 2013).
27. Sylvia Barack Fishman, *Jewish Life and American Culture* (Albany: State University of New York, 2000); Harriet Hartman and Moshe Hartman, *Gender and American Jews: Patterns in Work, Education, and Family in Contemporary Life* (Waltham, MA: Brandeis University Press, 2009).
28. Cherlin, *The Marriage-Go-Round.*
29. Coontz, *Marriage, a History.*
30. Taylor et al., *Decline of Marriage*, 122.
31. Hartman and Hartman, *Gender and American Jews.*
32. Hans-Peter Blossfeld and Andreas Timm, *Who Marries Whom?: Educational Systems as Marriage Markets in Modern Societies* (Boston: Kluwer Academic, 2003).
33. Hartman and Hartman, *Gender and American Jews.*
34. Respondent characteristics cover the spectrum of Jewish background and engagement, from secular Jews with no Jewish background to Orthodox Jews. Still, on the whole the sample leans toward the somewhat more engaged.
35. Charles Kadushin, "Reason Analysis," in *International Encyclopedia of the Social Sciences*, ed. David L. Sills (New York: MacMillan, 1968), 338–43.
36. Elizabeth Wildsmith, Nicole R. Steward-Streng, and Jennifer Manlove, *Childbearing Outside of Marriage: Estimates and Trends in the United States* (Washington, DC: Child Trends, 2011); the rates are substantially lower among whites and the college educated. It is estimated that 92 percent of college-educated women are married when they give birth.
37. Lawrence H. Fuchs, *Beyond Patriarchy: Jewish Fathers and Families* (Waltham, MA: Brandeis University Press, 2000).
38. Gwen G. Schwartz and Barbara Wyden, *The Jewish Wife* (New York: P. H. Wyden, 1969).
39. Jeffrey J. Arnett, *Emerging Adulthood: The Winding Road from the Late Teens through the Twenties* (New York: Oxford University Press, 2004).
40. Steven M. Cohen and Ari Y. Kelman, *Uncoupled: How Our Singles Are Reshaping Jewish Engagement* (New York: Jewish Identity Project of Reboot Andrea and Charles Bronfman Philanthropies, 2008).
41. Lynne M. Casper and Suzanne M. Bianchi, *Continuity and Change in the American Family* (Thousand Oaks, CA: Sage Publications, 2002).
42. R. Kelly Raley and Elizabeth Wildsmith, "Cohabitation and Children's Family Instability," *Journal of Marriage and Family* 66, no. 1 (2004): 210–19; Fiona Steele, Constantinos Kallis, and Heather Joshi, "The Formation and Outcomes of Cohabiting and Marital Partnerships in Early Adulthood: The Role of Previous Partnership Experience," *Journal of the Royal Statistical Society*, series A, *Statistics in Society* 169, no. 4 (2006): 757–79.
43. Wendy D. Manning and Jessica A. Cohen, "Premarital Cohabitation and Marital Dissolution: An Examination of Recent Marriages," *Journal of Marriage and Family* 74, no. 2 (2012): 377–87.
44. See, for example, "'Starter' Marriages: So Early, So Brief," *New York Times*, July 7, 1994.
45. Fern Chertok, Benjamin Phillips, and Leonard Saxe, *It's Not Just Who Stands Under the Chuppah: Intermarriage and Engagement* (Waltham, MA: Cohen Center for Modern Jewish Studies, Brandeis University; Steinhardt Social Research Institute, 2008).

# 2

# Caught in the Middle

## *Gender, Dating, and Singlehood among Religious Zionist Jews*

Ari Engelberg

ISRAELI JEWISH SOCIETY is divided along religious lines in important ways that affect gender roles, dating practices, marriage, and singlehood, among many other aspects of life. The four central socioreligious groups are the Hiloni (secular), the Masorati (traditional), Dati (non-ultra-Orthodox religious or Religious Zionist), and the Haredi (ultra-Orthodox Israeli Jews, who themselves have subdivisions). Historically, the largely secular Socialist Zionist pioneers were the backbone of the Zionist enterprise, while the ultra-Orthodox rejected Zionism. The Religious Zionists can be described as traveling a middle road between ultra-Orthodox and secular Israeli Judaism. Unlike Haredim they enlist in the army, earn academic degrees, participate in the workforce, and enjoy leisure-culture products that Haredim view as forbidden. However, like Haredim many live in "enclave" communities and have intricate dress codes that may be less conspicuous than those of the ultra-Orthodox but are recognizable to the initiated. Many men continue to devote many hours to the study of Talmud. These patterns are inculcated educationally as well as socially: secular Israelis, Religious Zionists, and the ultra-Orthodox have separate school systems and quite distinct formal and informal socialization processes.

Most Religious Zionists do not view traveling a middle road as compromising; rather they consider themselves to be living out the Torah-true religious identity that, to their mind, necessitates the realization of the sanctity of the Zionist enterprise and an integration of modernity and tradition. They are in fact distinct from both Israeli Haredim and American Modern Orthodoxy.[1] Nationalism, rather than other aspects of modernity such as acculturation to secular society—so significant to American Modern Orthodoxy—is the central component that defines their religious identity.[2] As a result, some branches of Religious Zionism are stricter in many religious observances than American Modern Orthodox.

This chapter discusses the impact of fluctuations in gender relations upon what is known by Israeli Religious Zionists as "the singles problem." This phrase refers to the growing number of young men and women who remain single into their late twenties and beyond,[3] the early twenties being the prior normative age for marriage and still a desideratum for many Orthodox Jews. Gender and romantic relations in Religious Zionism are currently in a state of flux. During the twentieth century, the movement achieved a successful integration of religion and modernity, which includes a gender-based separation of spheres and a neo-Victorian courtship process in which romantic love plays a central role. However, twenty-first-century late modernity seems to be catching many Religious Zionists by surprise, shaking the foundations of gender relations and raising new questions, such as how to deal with homosexuality,[4] with single mothers by choice,[5] and with prolonged singlehood.

This chapter focuses on the "older" singles dating scene where men and women meet and attempt to bridge the gender divide. I show that young women have internalized some aspects of late-modern youth culture and feminist ideology, more so than their male counterparts. This is both because some cultural changes improve their status relative to that of the men and because their religious marginalization allows them greater exposure to outside influences. As a result, frictions regarding gender issues during the dating process are ubiquitous.

The original findings presented in this chapter are drawn from (1) my analytical overview of rabbinical writings and orally transmitted teachings on this subject, (2) my ethnographic observations of religious singles events, and (3) in-depth interviews that I conducted among singles living in different locations in Israel and representing various levels of belief and adherence with twenty-two women and twenty-three men who are single, or who had been single for longer than average before marrying, and five marriage brokers and activists. Unless otherwise cited, quotations are taken from these interviews. The interviewees' names have been altered and identifying information omitted to preserve their anonymity. Interviews were conducted in Hebrew; the excerpts quoted were translated by me. I also draw upon recent relevant published research.

## Religious Zionist Gender Ideology

Many Orthodox Jews, including Israeli Religious Zionists view liberal secular Western society as morally depraved due to the lax sexual norms that characterize it. Pre-marital sex, homosexuality, and even simply overindulgence in sexuality are considered by the Orthodox as sins that draw the individual away from the spiritual realm and engross him in the material (*gashmi*) world. The separation of the sexes in various public and private spheres is viewed as essential to maintain a chaste society. In fact, this issue is so salient that the degree of gender separation in any given Orthodox subgroup is a central indicator of its location on the social spectrum of religious strictness. Alongside the policy of gender separation, a "feminist religious revolution" has taken place in non-Haredi Orthodoxy over the last decades. In traditional Jewish society before the twentieth century, girls received very little institutional education of any sort. Sarah Schneirer led to a change in the field of Orthodox women's education when she initiated the Bais Yaakov Network (of schools) in the 1920s. The goal was to keep girls within the fold by including traditional Jewish learning in their curriculum while maintaining a difference between the content and style of their studies and those of the boys studying in yeshiva. Beginning in the United States in the latter half of the twentieth century and entering Israel via American immigrants in the 1980s, the Torah-studies-for-women revolution went a few steps further, championing female Jewish scholarship. This revolution has been accepted or accommodated to varying degrees in the Israeli non-Haredi Orthodox educational system (but rejected by Haredi society).[6] Most religious Zionists concede that women should receive more Jewish education than they did in the past, but oppose changes in liturgy and ritual.[7]

Although Religious Zionist men and women participate in contemporary Israeli society in many ways, gender essentialism remains a central value imparted in the socialization process. According to Rapoport, Garb, and Penso, who observed classes in a religious Zionist girls school, the central message there is that men and women were created differently and therefore have different missions.[8] In Orthodox guidebooks to marriage, feminism is often critiqued for what is described as its attempt to blur God-given gender differences, while nevertheless allowing that it has had some accomplishments. Authors of these books advise readers to strive for marital cooperation as opposed to egalitarianism.[9] As mentioned above, gender issues such as single mothers and religious participation of women continue to stand at the center of public attention

The Religious Zionist socialization process is structured, among other things, by the gender ideology described above. Most parents send their children to gender-segregated schools, but many of those same children attend coed youth movements. After high school, boys attend men-only higher yeshivas, many of which offer programs that combine military service and Torah studies. They come into close contact with members of the opposite sex only at the next stage of the socialization process when they are discharged and enroll in academic institutions, but even then some of the more strictly religious prefer single-sex colleges to avoid illicit temptations, while those who seek to become Torah scholars remain in yeshiva. The socialization process of girls follows a parallel trajectory. Most Religious Zionist female high school graduates volunteer for a year or two of National Service. Some do enlist, but usually they serve in partially insular military units that shield them to some extent from intense and unsupervised contact with secular society, men, and military vulgarity. Many young women also study for a year in post-high-school-level theological institutions known as *midrashot* before acquiring an academic education. The next stage of their socialization process is parallel to that of the men; some attend universities open to the general public, while others prefer gender-segregated religious academic institutions.

## Dating Norms Today and in Historical Perspective

Dating norms in Israeli society are sharply divided along religious identity lines, although all groups have been affected by modernity compared to norms in the nineteenth century. In Eastern European traditional Jewish society, for example, marriages in which both partners were younger than 14 were not uncommon, and there was of course no dating.[10] Contemporary Haredim marry in their late teens and early twenties, and typically most go out on at least a few dates and have some say in the decision-making process regarding the marriage. Nevertheless, boys and girls meet only after careful scrutiny of potential partners by the parents.[11] In contrast, Israeli secular society's dating norms are quite similar to Western countries.

Religious Zionist dating patterns are linked to its in-between gender separation policy. As with Haredim, dating begins in the late teens or early twenties and is marriage oriented, but it is not controlled by parents and matchmakers (though they may play a role).[12] On average, dating lasts for a few months during which the couple is expected to refrain from sexual contact of any sort (a dictum that is upheld to varying degrees by couples), after which they are expected to reach a decision. Unlike Haredim and like couples in Western societies, however, there is a clear, if unstated, social expectation that to marry the couple should be "in love."[13]

Viewed from a historical perspective, Religious Zionist dating has many modern characteristics.[14] To an extent not always appreciated, contemporary Religious Zionist courtship norms that encourage romantic love but oppose premarital sex are quite similar to Israeli and American dating norms from the 1950s. However, since the sexual revolution of the 1960s and the feminist movement's achievements that won more independence for women, in the non-Orthodox population the age of marriage has risen, and most middle- and upper-middle-class youth no longer wed during or soon after college. This has led to the formation of a new stage of the lifecycle that researchers have named "young adulthood," "emerging adulthood," or "youthhood." This stage is characterized by independent living in downtown sections of large cities where close-knit social networks are formed. Members of these networks seek romantic and sexual, as well as other, experiences and are in no rush to settle down and establish families.[15]

A related though not identical phenomenon is the transformation of attitudes toward dating and romantic relationships. As Anthony Giddens explains, while Victorian and mid-twentieth century courtship encouraged "falling in love," this love was often based upon very little real knowledge of the beloved, since the couple often did not spend substantial time together or get to know each other, and cohabitation was not common. In fact, this lack of knowledge was a factor in the lovers' abilities to project upon their beloved gender-specific ideal characteristics.[16] Even after marriage, sharing one's deepest feelings and secrets was not a common expectation of couples. Typical late-modern relationships, on the other hand, are influenced by the therapeutic discourse, the feminist movement's achievements, and the sexual revolution, and they are characterized by partners' expectations to achieve high levels of emotional as well as sexual intimacy.[17] Jamieson has critiqued Giddens for his assumption that such late-modern relationships are egalitarian when in fact equality remains an unachieved goal. She claims that the efforts to achieve emotional intimacy in relationships are shouldered mainly by women,[18] an assertion that resonates with the findings of the present work. Jamieson's claims are supported by other researchers who have found that women shoulder an unfair portion of the emotional division of labor within heterosexual relationships.[19]

Given the centrality of family values in Orthodoxy and the observance of *halakhah* (Jewish religious law), it is not surprising that prolonged singlehood and the related new stage of the lifecycle are viewed by Religious Zionist society as problematic. Like their secular counterparts, many Orthodox young adults remain single after completing their academic studies and move into rented apartments located in downtown Jerusalem and Tel Aviv neighborhoods that are known to be singles haunts. No longer in their parents' home or under the watchful eye of educational institutions and authorities, their societal supervision is relaxed at precisely the same time that they are exposed to the temptations of the big-city life and late-modern youth culture.

This circumstance sometimes leads to transgressions of religious rules regarding gender separation and sexual conduct as well as Orthodox cultural norms. In Orthodox yeshivas boys are encouraged not to fraternize with girls at all, but in singles haunts fraternization is commonplace. More liberal singles hold dance parties that are quite similar to those of their secular counterparts; such events do not take place in mainstream married society. Outright religious transgressions occur as well among singles. The most prominent are transgressions of laws forbidding any physical contact for the sake of obtaining sexual pleasure among dating couples. The extent of these transgressions depends of course upon the couple; some only pet, others go further, and some remain chaste.[20] The numbers of those belonging to the latter group diminish as singles get older. All in all, singles can be described as inching nearer to secular youth-culture lifestyle and away from Orthodox standards with regard to leisure, culture, and gender relations.[21]

Moreover, communal life is family based; although singles can in theory participate in religious communal life on their own, most choose not to. This leads to reduced involvement in synagogue life and absence from prayer services. Together these experiences add up, for most singles, to a feeling of decline in their religious observance.[22]

## Gender Relations and Religious Zionist Dating: Evidence from the Field

Religious Zionist men and women are tugged at by opposing forces, wishing to participate in contemporary life and opportunities and at the same time wishing to be loyal to their understandings of authentic Judaism. It is within this complex context that singles go on dates where they meet a member of the opposite sex with whom they hope to start a family and thus return to the yellow brick road of socialization from which they strayed by dint of remaining single past the conventional age. Many of my interviewees viewed gender relations as a factor that has led to difficulties in their attempts to find a suitable partner for marriage. The issues they brought up can be divided into two general categories: (1) disparate visions of men and women regarding gender roles after marriage and the related issue of male discomfort regarding women with careers, and (2) differing attitudes regarding love and relationships.

### Gender Role Disagreements and Relationship Formation

Bilha Admanit examined the attitudes of adolescent Religious Zionist girls and boys regarding three aspects of women's status in the family: (1) the gender division of labor, (2) attitudes toward the question of combining motherhood and a career, and (3) "active religiosity" on the part of women. She found that on all counts girls held significantly more egalitarian beliefs than those of their male cohort, and although the level of religiosity influenced beliefs regarding egalitarianism (the more religious a respondent, the less likely s/he was to hold egalitarian beliefs), Admanit reports that "the most religious of girls [still] aspire to more egalitarianism than the least religious of boys."[23]

My findings are in tune with those of Admanit. In my interviews, women were much more likely than men to bring up fears that their career goals would make them unappealing to prospective dates and husbands. Their perceptions were borne out by the fact that more strictly Orthodox men were in fact more patriarchal in their attitudes. Shai is a 40-year-old single man who works in the field of education and is one of the more stringently religious interviewees. He, for example, is *shomer negia*, meaning that he avoids all physical contact with women before marriage. During the interview he brought up the subject of disagreements regarding gender roles that he had encountered while dating:

> There are certain recurrent patterns . . . The whole thing with women's status, how she views her role in the family, what she should do, what our relationship should be like and her attitude to her career . . . I had more than a few dates in which the women were unwilling to give up their career for the sake of the family . . . A girl who chooses to be a doctoral candidate or a computer programmer . . . I don't want to change her. "If that is what you want then thank you very much, I don't see my future home like that, that you'll be coming back at 8 p.m. or at 6 p.m. and our relationship will be on wheels."[24] You don't try to change her and she doesn't want to change, so the relationship ends.

Shai is expressing concern regarding his date's willingness to invest time in their future home, but implicitly he seems to be concerned regarding her (relatively) high status as well. After all, a doctoral candidate may be able to spend more time at home than a social worker. Shalom is a 30-year-old single man who was raised and continues to reside in a socially peripheral city (unlike most singles that migrate to Jerusalem or to the Tel Aviv region).[25] A professional career man himself, he was even clearer than Shai about his expectations regarding the gender division of labor after marriage:

> Let's begin by saying that I will be very happy if the woman goes to work . . . so that she feels she is actualizing herself . . . I'd be happy for her to work around four and a half hours a day so that she spends more time at home than I do . . . and yes, as far as housework is concerned she should do more than me. I'm talking about washing dishes, things like that that are related to the home. What I will give in return is the upkeep of the

> home, like taking care of the car, fixing stuff. I don't mind washing dishes and doing the laundry every now and then, I don't want her to have a breakdown or something like that, but generally speaking those will be her responsibilities.

Both of these interviewees are aware of the feminist discourse and address "the woman's need to actualize herself" but nevertheless draw clear boundaries that delineate well-defined gender roles and set limits to their future wives' actualization. In all, more women than men addressed the issue of women's high professional status as a factor that deters men.

Yafit—a strictly religious single university professor in her mid-thirties who, like Shai, is *shomer negia*—said, "I think my profession ruins a lot [of relationships] for me 'cause boys are scared of the doctorate; it doesn't make them feel good. The very fact that I enjoy it and talk about it; it's not just something that I do in the morning and then at night do something else. Boys really don't like that." Yafit highlights the high status of her profession as problematic, and this is borne out by the statements of Shai, quoted above. A similar point was made by Naama, a 28-year-old single academic who combines feminist awareness with a deep religious commitment. She spoke to me about women's liberation but is at the same time strict in her observance of religious rules forbidding premarital sexual contacts and has a deep personal relationship with God (though unlike Yafit she sometimes wears trousers, not only skirts or dresses). She too thought that Religious Zionist men she dated were wary of "over-educated," ambitious women:

> I get along well with secular boys who are more open and accepting . . . I think religious boys are still very threatened. It's like, "It's really nice that you're getting a degree, but maybe you'll be a teacher? That would fit in better with our lifestyle." They're threatened by the fact that I have an opinion, that I know what I want, that I'm strong, that I'm assertive. It means that he won't run our relationship; we'll run it together.

Naama's narrative focuses upon the link between female education and empowerment. She is convinced that her graduate degree and career aspirations will lead to her having more say in her marital relationship, and that this fact has given pause to some of the men that she has dated. Interestingly, "over-education" of women is an issue that more conservative Religious Zionist rabbis also address when attempting to solve "the singles problem." Rabbi Elnekaveh, the Sephardic rabbi of Gush Katif before Israeli disengagement from the Gaza strip, composed a prayer for singles that was recited in a special prayer service that he led at the Western Wall. The prayer includes a surprisingly candid plea for single women to be spared "over-education" that may ruin their chances of finding a suitable husband.

The narratives of some of my interviewees regarding educational achievements are remarkably similar to those of American college women interviewed by Komarovsky in the 1940s.[26] Her interviewees reported receiving conflicting messages about their studies: while some family members encouraged them to excel, others expressed concern that if they were too smart they would chase away men; they received similar messages from their dates.[27] Later research conducted in the 1980s and 1990s in the United States found the gaps between men and women regarding the desirability of women developing a career to have considerably diminished.[28] The affinities between these seemingly far-flung cases may be explained as a result of certain structural similarities. Both mid-twentieth-century middle-class American society and current Israeli Religious Zionists held or hold cherished "family values," in both it was assumed that men and women have unique characteristics and complementary roles, and both were challenged by feminist concepts. As a result, young women in both cultures were or are pulled in opposing directions.[29]

## Gender Segregation as an Obstacle to Romantic Relationships

Changing gender roles and their impact on the Religious Zionist courtship process are sometimes explored in Israeli popular culture. In the popular Israeli TV drama series *Srugim* that focused on the lives of Religious Zionist singles, Reut (actor Sharon Fauster), an accountant employed by a large firm, repeatedly encountered problems when dating due to her high status and salary. One of the criticisms laid out by religiously observant viewers of the series was that it besmirched Religious Zionist men; the focus of such critiques was not Reut's dates who were threatened by her success, but rather the escapades of another star of the show, Nati (Ehud Knoler), a smug ladies' man, who in the first season seemed never to be content with whomever he happened to be dating and was always on the prowl. (In later seasons his character transforms.) Nati's flaws are similar to those enumerated by some female interviewees who claimed that their dates were emotionally obtuse. Nati's flaws—and my interviewees' complaints—are also congruent with criticisms of "normative" male behavior leveled by second-wave feminists.[30]

However, my interviewees ascribed these shortcomings of Orthodox men to experiential sources beyond millennia of patriarchy, especially the long years of gender segregation during the socialization process. The claim that gender separation has a negative impact upon the dating process challenges a central tenant of the Religious Zionist socialization system. Regarding gender separation in Religious Zionist schools, it should be emphasized that boys and girls are not only schooled separately but have different curricula as well. Boys in yeshiva high schools study the Talmud in a traditional mode for half a day every day. Girls study much less Talmud and instead are exposed to other religious studies and to a more diverse secular curriculum. After graduating high school, most men devote a few years to religious studies in secluded yeshivas, while women serving in national service are more exposed to secular culture. In university, most Religious Zionist men choose to study "practical" fields, such as law and economics, while most women study various therapeutic and educational disciplines that necessitate more exposure to psychology and humanistic disciplines.

Pua, a matchmaker and activist who leads workshops for religious singles, shared with me her thoughts on the results of the different curriculums at the high school level:

> The boys' education closes them. I'm talking in very general terms, because Himelfarb isn't the same as Horev,[31] and Har Hamor isn't the same as the Gush,[32] but part of the boys' education is very fundamentalist—I don't mean religiously. The boys study Jewish philosophy while the girls study literature; the boys study Talmud while the girls study psychology and communication. My daughter combines *Torah im derech eretz*.[33] She goes to the theater and to the movies, reads literature, did her matriculation exams in media studies, and is open[-minded]. Some of the boys are more constrained—not more religious but more closed, less worldly.

It is also worth noting, as described above, that gender essentialism is an educational message that the Religious Zionist educational system imparts to students, and it is a central Orthodox line of defense against secular-liberal and radical feminist ideologies.[34] So gender differences are cultivated in both practice, via segregation, and through formal messages. Complaints about their dates' low emotional intelligence were more common among female interviewees than complaints about classical feminist issues of the type discussed in the previous section; often, interviewees linked these complaints to gender separation during the socialization process.

Neta is a 30-something single professional. She found that she has a difficult time forming deep emotional relationships with the religious men she dates because they are not conversant with feelings and emotions: "I go out with all kind of guys; I can't talk to them about life, about insights, about people." Neta spent a few months abroad in Denmark, during which time she lived with locals and secular Israeli ex-patriots. This kind of travel is highly unusual among fellow singles. The time she spent in Denmark allowed her to compare the secular (and gentile) men she encountered there with the Religious Zionist men she was familiar with:

> Their [yeshiva graduates'] inspiration (*she'er ruach*) is only with regard to rational issues. An emotional connection with guys? Believe me, I've been out with many *hesder* boys[35]—it wasn't there. And they also see girls as an "other." Young secular men are less likely to see us that way. I really felt that in Denmark, they treated me more like a human being. Of course I am also a girl. Here, in Israel, it's a combination of chauvinism, religion, the army, I don't know . . . I'm [only] a girl!

In Neta's narrative two reasons for her difficulties in forming close relationships with Religious Zionist men can be identified: their lack of emotional intelligence, a characterization that resonates with widespread masculine stereotypes, and their tendency to objectify women, which she attributes to chauvinism and the influence of religion and the army. Both of these attributes may be exacerbated by the gender separation policy.

Another highly articulate interviewee who linked gender separation and objectification in her narrative was Tamar, a 30-year-old career woman in the creative sector. The focus of her narrative was the singles scene and what she views as the sexual objectification of women by single Religious Zionist men. She begins by describing the men who followed the preferred social script by marrying "on time": "This is how it goes: some are really religious (*dosim*) and marry young. They're good kids; they marry the first girl they meet on a date when they're 22. They don't know any better, so they continue to love her for the rest of their lives." She then goes on to describe the men who remain single: "If he stays a virgin till the age of 40, something is wrong with him. He develops all kinds of inhibitions; this is not somebody I would want to be with." Of course it should be noted that other, more stringently religious women are interested in precisely such men and consider more libertine men to have succumbed to temptations. At any rate Tamar prefers men who have not remained chaste, but she finds them to be problematic in other ways:

> There are many boys who studied in *hesder* and were on the right track . . . Now that they're living on their own and are not supervised by teachers or rabbis, they're living on an island of young men and women. They're late bloomers; they touched a girl for the first time at the age of 27, their attitude is that of a sexual party; they're degenerate! . . . The sudden freedom that they found causes them to lose their senses . . . They don't view

> a girl as a friend, only as a woman. They didn't study with her in yeshiva or serve with her in the army.

Note Tamar's reference to "the right track"—the Religious Zionist yellow-brick road. Regarding the issue at hand, Tamar asserts that gender segregation while studying in yeshiva and serving in the army is responsible for the objectification of women by yeshiva graduates. The subsequent transition from the gender-segregated yeshiva environment to the open late-modern youth culture prominent in singles haunts adds the sexual edge to this objectification. Following this transition, some yeshiva graduates (who in religious terms, and sometimes their own as well, have "fallen") attempt to make up for lost time, while most single women remain as marriage oriented as ever. Tamar is insistent upon the difference between religious and secular men, or at least some secular men, regarding this issue: "Secular guys like the guy I met are much more value laden (*erci*) in their attitude to women, because he did grow up with her, studied with her for high-school matriculation exams, went to the scouts with her.[36] He sees her as a friend." Tamar is convinced that the gender-segregated socialization process is to blame for the Religious Zionist men's attitudes.

A few of the male interviewees also spoke about how gender separation leads to difficulties in communicating with the opposite sex, though their underlying message was, naturally, different. Yoni, an academic and writer who married in his late thirties, claimed that gender-segregated education was responsible for the "singles problem." When I questioned him as to why the ultra-Orthodox, who also have segregated institutions, don't have similar problems, he responded:

> Because we [men and women] speak different languages, there is a lot of trauma . . . Many of the difficulties in forming relationships are because we can't communicate with the opposite sex. Communication. But listen, the ultra-Orthodox are more structured; [they] come from separate worlds, and their relationships will be like that as well. It's all very structured there among the ultra-Orthodox or the *hardal*.[37] Here, on the other hand, you're educating towards a middle path. We're very exposed, and we come with sexual fantasies and a Western worldview, and on the other hand *halachik* (Jewish legal) limitations of the ultra-Orthodox world, and that leads to dissonance which explains prolonged singlehood.

Yoni describes Religious Zionist men and women as speaking different languages. The importance he attributes to interpersonal communication skills, and his reference to sexuality as a salient aspect of relationships, are indicative of the influence of late-modern ideas regarding relationships described above.[38]

Itzick is a 40-year-old engineer who is more on the quiet side. He lives with his aging mother in a socially peripheral town near Tel Aviv. He did not follow the educational path of the elite by attending a post-high-school-level yeshiva. Instead he enlisted to serve in a military position that enabled him to acquire a civilian profession. Like Yoni, he too considers his lack of acquaintance with girls while growing up to be one of the causes of his continued singlehood. He feels that he learned much from female society, after he finally encountered it as an older single:

> I think women have a richer and more varied emotional world; men's emotional world is narrower. You can tell girls about what's going on with you, but guys less. It's also fun hanging out with them, I missed out on that during my youth . . . When I began going to singles get-togethers . . . I changed, opened up to people, connected. You become less closed off. I think the religious man is a closed man because he spends all his time with men . . . maybe if that had happened to me earlier I would have been married by now.

Itzick and Yoni are quite different characters, but both narratives regarding gender separation can be understood as connected to the shift of Religious Zionist youth society toward a late-modern model in which young men and women live in rented apartments in downtown areas and maintain close friendships. Romantic relationships in such societies are based upon intimate knowledge of the partner, as described by Giddens, and for this a common language is necessary. Unlike the female interviewees quoted above, these two men don't describe women as victims of the gender gap, but they do view the emotional impoverishment they experience as a result of that gap as an obstacle in their attempts to form relationships. As Yoni emphasizes though, it is only an obstacle because they are attempting to straddle two lifestyles and value systems; after all, gender segregation does not impede the Haredi semi-arranged marriage system.

To a striking extent, the reports of Religious Zionist women echo those of women in the broader Israeli and American societies, but they have some unique aspects. As was mentioned above, research conducted in various Western societies has shown that complaints regarding men's ability to be emotionally intimate are common among women,[39] and the results of the present research may be seen as simply supporting these findings—that women seek emotional intimacy more than men, and that this leads in some cases to marital (or premarital) strife. Interestingly, though, female interviewees in the present research insisted that attributes such as lack of emotional intelligence and a tendency to objectify women are peculiar to Religious Zionist men. While these women may simply be projecting their wishes onto secular society that they view as more liberal, it is reasonable to presume that gender segregation during the socialization process coupled with the essentialist gender ideology that is taught in Religious Zionist schools does indeed widen the gap between women's and men's sensibilities and attitudes, and thus exacerbates gender-specific attributes that may make it more difficult to form successful romantic relationships.

Although this issue kept coming up in my interviews with singles, the question of whether gender separation is responsible for singlehood is not addressed by the movement's rabbis. In the only Religious Zionist book to date devoted to the issue of singlehood, an anthology that includes articles by rabbis, educators, and social workers, the rabbis ignore the issue of gender segregation during the socialization process altogether, but some of the other writers do discuss it; pertinently, most of the contributors to this discussion are women. Yehudit Gorfine, the editor of the volume, writes: "The separate education enabled us to fortify the character of the boys and the girls but also led youngsters to exhibit a lack of patience towards the needs of the opposite sex."[40] Sarah Eliash, the principal of an *ulpana*,[41] also claimed that the gap between the socialization process of boys and girls leads to later difficulties since "while girls are seeking to be friends with their partner, boys are not looking for a friend."[42] Even these writers, who are critical of gender segregation during the socialization process, do not favor coed education. Instead they propose to establish educational programs, especially for boys, which will prepare them for marital "partnership."

## A Conflict That Will Continue

The central argument of this article is that Religious Zionist gender relations, as they express themselves in the "older" singles dating scene, reflect the gradual shift of society from modernity to late-modernity, a shift that entails changes in gender and romantic relations. These changes express themselves in a variety of forms in the dating relationships of the interviewees, but two stood out: (1) disagreements regarding gender roles and (2) difficulties in communicating across the gender divide.

Regarding the first of these—there is a gap between the attitudes of some male interviewees, *especially* the more strictly religious ones, and female interviewees, *including* the more strictly religious ones, regarding the post-marital gender division of labor. The disagreements however, are not limited to the division of labor and instead include differing ideas about men and women's roles. Naturally, such gaps lead to difficulties in forming relationships across the gender divide. This finding is consistent with the findings of the survey conducted among adolescents discussed above. Interestingly, this issue is hardly addresses by Religious Zionist authorities seeking to solve "the singles problem."

The second issue is not related to overt, declarative stands regarding gender relations and is therefore more subtle. It is related to the ongoing evolution of the self in modernity. As Jamieson demonstrates, in the beginning of the twentieth century, couples did not expect to experience "disclosing intimacy," to share their innermost secrets and childhood memories with each other. In late-modernity this has become a common expectation especially among women. This change can be attributed to various factors including the psychotherapeutic discourse with its emphasis on introspection and communication, and the ongoing process of individualization.[43]

It is here that Religious Zionism's middle position in Israeli society is most conspicuous. In collective societies with arranged marriages, same-sex friendships tend to be more intimate than marital relationships, which are more functional.[44] In Haredi society, which has some collectivist elements, couples do not expect to achieve intimate feelings before their marriage.[45] For its part, Religious Zionist society rejects the sexual standards of secular society but is deeply influenced by its intact attitudes toward romantic love. Like the secular, they are part of late-modern society; they partake in the IT economy and consume pop-culture products. On the other hand, gender separation expands the gender gap, and so it is not surprising that some singles have difficulties forming late-modern intimate relationships.

A comparison may be made between the current transition from modernity to late-modernity and the processes that took place in nineteenth-century Eastern Europe when traditional Jewish society first encountered modernity and the *haskala* (Jewish enlightenment) movement. Iris Parush describes how, paradoxically, the marginality of women in nineteenth-century Jewish Eastern European society accrued them some advantages. They were excluded from what that society considered to be the most prestigious activity—studying holy texts—and given more leeway in their cultural contacts with the gentile world, allowing them to read novels and study foreign languages. This drew them closer to haskala movement ideals; romantic novels were especially influential in leading readers to develop an aversion to the traditional matchmaking process and to the yeshiva boys whom they were meant, by others, to marry.[46]

In current Religious Zionist society, men's Torah studies continue to be more highly prized. Thus, men spend more time studying Talmud and are more secluded from external influences, while women's marginality allows them greater exposure. As a result, a gap forms between the sensibilities of single men and women in today's Religious Zionist society, one that is admittedly not as wide as the gap described by Parush but nevertheless a recurring feature characterizing traditional and later Orthodox Judaism's struggle with outside secular influences. All this may lead one to conclude that Religious Zionism is simply lagging behind secular society, but my data shows that Religious Zionists in Israel are unlikely simply to catch up belatedly with current liberal attitudes toward gender, marriage, and sex. Resistance to liberal Western beliefs regarding sexuality as well as other issues is at the heart of Orthodox ideology. Nevertheless, Religious Zionists are also not likely to adopt the clear-cut gender definitions and family expectations of Haredi society.

Orthodoxy's long-term reactions to these developments have yet to play themselves out. What is clear is that the developments described in this article and others in this volume cannot simply be ignored. Their conflicts and struggles provide a fascinating symbol of, and a window into, the tensions between historical Jewish attitudes and the broad array of contemporary choices regarding gender, love, and the Jewish family.

## NOTES

1. Some researchers, especially those belonging to therapeutic disciplines, do refer to Religious Zionists as "Modern Orthodox" when publishing in English, but in fact the term Modern Orthodox is used by Religious Zionists themselves only to denote the liberal left wing of Religious Zionism, see Hanan Moses, "From Religious Zionism to Post-Modern Religiosity" [Hebrew] (PhD dissertation, Bar Ilan University, 2009).
2. Aryei Fishman, "Modern Orthodox Judaism: A Study in Ambivalence," *Social Compass* 42, no. 1 (1995): 89–95; Charles Liebman, "Religious trends among American and Israeli Jews," in *Terms of Survival: The Jewish World Since 1945*, ed. Robert S. Wistrich (London: Routledge, 1995), 299–319.
3. The Social Survey's of the Israeli Central Bureau of Statistics indicate a steady but dramatic rise in the percentage of singles among the "religious." It should be noted that Israeli Jews refer to RZs simply as "religious," while the ultra-Orthodox are known as "Haredi."
4. See Koren, chapter 4 in this volume.
5. For the most part, Religious Zionist single motherhood by choice is a result of prolonged singlehood, see Blumenthal, chapter 7 in this volume.
6. See Tamar El-Or, *Next Year I'll Know More: Literacy and Identity among Young Orthodox Women in Israel* (Detroit: Wayne State University Press, 2002).
7. Asher Cohen, "The Knitted Kippah and What Is Beneath it: Plural Identities in Religious Zionism" [Hebrew], *Akdamot* 15 (2004): 9–30.
8. Tamar Rapoport, Yoni Garb, and Anat Penso, "Religious Socialization and Female Subjectivity: Religious-Zionist Adolescent Girls in Israel," *Sociology of Education* 68, no. 1 (1995): 48–61.
9. Nurit Novis-Deutsch and Ari Engelberg, "Meaning Making Under the Sacred Canopy: The Role of Orthodox Jewish Marriage Guidebooks," *Interdisciplinary Journal of Research on Religion* 8 (2012): article 6.

10. Immanuel Etkes, "Marriage and Torah Study among the *Lomdim* in Lithuania," in *The Jewish Family: Metaphor and Memory*, ed. David Kraemer (New York: Oxford University Press, 1989), 153–78.
11. Modernity has in fact enhanced the scrutinizing process, see David Lehmann and Batya Siebzehner, "Power, Boundaries and Institutions: Marriage in Ultra-Orthodox Judaism," *European Journal of Sociology* 50 (2009): 273–308.
12. Ofra Shalev, Nehami Baum, and Haya Itzhaky, "Mate Selection and Marriage Decision in Bicultural Society: Modern Orthodox Society in Israel," *Marriage & Family Review* 48, no. 2 (2012): 210–26.
13. Ari Engelberg, "Seeking a 'Pure Relationship'? Israeli Religious-Zionist Singles Looking for Love and Marriage," *Religion* 41, no. 3 (2011): 431–48.
14. On the link between modernity and romantic-love-based marriage, see Lawrence Stone, *The Family, Sex and Marriage in England 1500–1800* (New York: Harper and Row, 1979).
15. Michelle du Bois-Reymond, "I Don't Want to Commit Myself Yet: Young People's Life Concepts,'" *Journal of Youth Studies* 1, no. 1 (1998): 63–79; Sue Heath, "Peer-Shared Households, Quasi-Communes and Neo-Tribes," *Current Sociology* 52, no. 2 (2004): 161–79.
16. Anthony Giddens, *The Transformation of Intimacy: Sexuality, Love, and Eroticism in Modern Societies* (Cambridge, MA: Polity Press, 1992).
17. Lynn Jamieson, *Intimacy: Personal Relationships in Modern Societies* (Cambridge, MA: Polity Press, 1998).
18. Lynn Jamieson, "Intimacy Transformed? A Critical Look at the 'Pure Relationship,'" *Sociology* 33, no. 3 (1999): 477–94.
19. See for example Jean Duncombe and Dennis Marsden, "Love and Intimacy: The Gender Division of Emotion and Emotion Work," *Sociology* 27, no. 2 (1993): 221–24; Gabriele Schäfer, "Romantic Love in Heterosexual Relationships: Women's Experiences," *Journal of Social Sciences* 16, no. 3 (2008): 187–97.
20. This is of course related to the couples' religious views, but there is not always direct correlation. I interviewed a liberal-minded single who was a virgin in his early thirties while others who ostensibly support strict observance of the halakhah have had sexual relations with various partners.
21. Ari Engelberg, "Israeli Religious Zionist Singles in Late-Modern Society," *Israeli Studies Review* 28, no. 2 (2013): 1–17.
22. Ibid.
23. Bilha Admanit, "Her Family, His Family: Attitudes of Religious Female and Male Adolescents Regarding Woman's Place in the Family, as a Function of One's Level of Religiosity, Family's Ethnic Background and Pro-Tolerance Aspects of the Educational Context," (PhD diss., Hebrew University of Jerusalem, 2010).
24. Hebrew expression meaning "unstable."
25. In Israel the term periphery is used to denote both geographical locations and a low socioeconomic status; often there is correlation between the two.
26. Komarovsky's analytical concepts are considered outdated by current feminist researchers, but the validity of her data has never been questioned.
27. Mira Komarovsky, "Cultural Contradictions and Sex Roles," *American Journal of Sociology* 52 (1946): 182–89.
28. Amy Peake and Karen L. Harris, "Young Adults' Attitudes toward Multiple Role Planning the Influence of Gender, Career Traditionality and Marriage Plans," *Journal of Vocational Behavior* 60 (2002): 405–21.

29. I thank my advisor, Professor Harvey Goldberg, for this insight.
30. See for example Sandra L. Bartky, *Femininity and Domination: Studies in the Phenomenology of Oppression* (New York: Routledge, 1990).
31. Himelfarb and Horev are well-known Jerusalem Religious Zionist boys' high schools.
32. Har Hamor and Gush are well known post-high-school-level Religious Zionist yeshivas that signify the opposing edges of that religious spectrum.
33. Literally, Torah and the way of the world. This verse has many interpretations.
34. See for example Yuval Cherlow, "Changes in Gender Definitions and Their Impact on Establishing Families" [Hebrew], in *Please God by You*, ed. Yehudit Gorfine (Rosh Pina: Marot, 2002), 114–36.
35. Hesder yeshivas allow students to combine yeshiva studies and military service in a program that lasts for five years. In the past almost all Religious Zionist men joined Hesder programs rather than enlisting for regular army service; now many Religious Zionist youth attend *mechinot* that offer shorter learning stints, but Hesder yeshivas remain popular as well.
36. Earlier in the interview she mentioned having had a relationship with a secular man.
37. Religiously stringent Religious Zionists.
38. Giddens, *Transformation of Intimacy.*
39. Jamieson, "Intimacy"; Duncombe and Marsden, "Love and Intimacy"; Schäfer, "Romantic Love Heterosexual Relationships."
40. Yehudit Gorfine, "introduction" [Hebrew], in *Please God by You*, ed. Yehudit Gorfine (Rosh Pina: Marot, 2002), 8–11.
41. Religious Zionist girls' high schools that devote more time to religious studies, have dorms, and are considered more prestigious than regular religious high schools for girls; not to be confused with *ulpan*—schools for Hebrew as a second language.
42. Sarah Eliash, "Differences between Male and Female Graduates of the Religious Education System" [Hebrew], in *Please God by You*, ed. Yehudit Gorfine (Rosh Pina: Marot, 2002), 152.
43. Giddens, *Transformation of Intimacy*; Eva Illouz, *Saving the Modern Soul: Therapy, Emotions, and the Culture of Self-Help* (Berkeley: University of California Press, 2007); Jamieson, "Intimacy."
44. William R. Jankowiak and Edward F. Fischer, "A Cross-Cultural Perspective on Romantic Love," *Ethnology* 31, no. 2 (1992): 149–55.
45. They may not expect such high levels of intimacy after marriage either, but this issue has yet to be investigated.
46. Iris Parush, *Reading Jewish Women: Marginality and Modernization in Nineteenth-Century Eastern European Jewish Society* (Waltham, MA: Brandeis University Press, 2004).

# 3

## "We All Still Have to Potty Train"

### *Same-Sex Couple Families and the American Jewish Community*

Jonathan Krasner

ANDREW AND SCOTT,[1] a gay couple who live in a metropolitan-area suburb with their eight-year-old adopted son, are part of the twenty-first-century face of American Judaism. Andrew is a high school teacher in his thirties raised in a Reform Jewish family on the West Coast. Scott, who manages a nonprofit organization, grew up in the South; his family attended a Catholic church, and he was active in a Christian youth group. Today, they raise their son exclusively Jewish and send him to a local Conservative Jewish day school. Yet Scott never converted to Judaism, and the family decorates a Christmas tree in their home every December.

Andrew and Scott were participants in a qualitative study of same-sex parents who were raising their children as Jews. The findings of this study illuminated both the ways in which gay and lesbian American Jewish families were similar to heterosexual families and the ways in which they differed. The experiences of same-sex couples raising their children as Jews mirror those of lesbian and gay parents more generally, particularly in relation to decision-making about becoming parents and negotiating a heteronormative society. While decisions about childcare and housework were often made on the basis of practical consideration and personal preference, the couples in this study of Jewish families—like similar studies of non-Jewish families—sometimes embraced a division of labor that reinforced conventional gender stereotypes. Nevertheless, many divided child-care responsibilities more evenly than their heterosexual counterparts.

Exploring the extent to which same-sex couples with children perceive the Jewish community to be welcoming of them and their children, this study found that the American Jewish community has become more accepting of homosexuality, same-sex marriage, and gay parenting. However, Orthodox environments often maintained significant barriers. A welcoming or unwelcoming community was an important factor influencing the relative success or failure of these parents' endeavors to integrate Jewish culture and religious practices into their family lives: welcoming communities together with supportive families and friends played a profoundly important role in deepening the family's Jewish connections. Decisions about the religious and cultural upbringing of children in same-sex parent families where only one parent was Jewish were often moved toward Jewish commitments because Jews and Judaism were perceived as being more receptive toward lesbian, gay, bisexual, transgender, and queer (LGBTQ) individuals and their families than other religious traditions in which non-Jewish spouses had been raised. Some perceived a sympathetic connection between gayness and Jewishness. Nevertheless, the study also shows that Jewish outreach to gay and lesbian families in which one spouse is not a born Jew frequently affects the couple's decisions around child-rearing.

In her study of gay adoptive fathers, Abbie E. Goldberg concluded that "sexual orientation is only one—albeit one very important—influence on their parenting decisions and trajectories," and that economic status—what she termed "financial privilege"—significantly affected decision-making related to adoption. It influenced whether couples pursued adoption or surrogacy, and whether adoptive parents opted for the private domestic, private international, or public domestic routes.[2] Other research indicates that biological, social, legal, and geographical considerations, as well as endemic societal heterosexism, and internalized homophobia, also play a role in shaping how individuals and couples make choices.[3]

Far less research has been published on the relative impact of religion and culture on decision-making. Religious attitudes can impact the extent to which individuals support the parenting aspirations of gay and lesbian family members.[4] There is also some intriguing research on the extent to which lesbian adoptive parents, in particular, may be more open to transracial adoption than the general population.[5] Nevertheless, one recent review of the available research identified the constellation of questions regarding the impact of race and ethnicity on gay and lesbian parenting as among the "key content gaps in existing research."[6]

An important goal of this study was to explore the relative importance of Jewishness in influencing choices about the decision to parent. To minimize the potential for answers to be influenced by the interviewer, subjects were asked in the most general terms to narrate their road to parenting before specific questions were broached about the influence of Judaism on family life. Respondents expressed many of the same attitudes and concerns as parents in other studies, perspectives that bore little obvious connection to Judaism. For example, their reasons for choosing a particular route to parenthood were often influenced by such factors as cost, average length of the process, legal considerations, fertility (in the case of women), the relative importance of having a biological connection to their child, and, in the case of adoption, preferences about race, age, or gender.

## Jewish Gay and Lesbian Families in America

The phenomenon of same-sex parenting, exceedingly rare in North America before the 1970s, increased markedly, particularly in cosmopolitan urban centers, by 2013. The United States Census Bureau's 2011 American Community Survey estimated 605,472 same-sex households in the country. Of these, 168,092 reported being married.[7] As this book goes to press, the court ruled in *Obergefell v. Hodges* (2015) that the US Constitution guarantees the fundamental right to marry to same-sex couples, thereby legalizing same-sex marriage throughout the United States and its territories. One expects that the number of such marriages will increase substantially. States on the West Coast and in the Northeast and Southwest, as well as Florida, Minnesota, and Hawaii, tended to have a higher percentage of same-sex couples than the country as a whole. Overall, 16 percent of same-sex couples (22% of female couples and 10% of male couples) reported having biological, step, or adopted children in their homes.[8] The 2011 Census in Canada reported 64,575 "same-sex couple families," including 21,015 married couples and 43,560 same-sex common-law couples. Of these, 9.4 percent (16.5% of female couples and 3.4% of male couples) had children in their homes.[9]

Similarly, the visibility of LGBTQ people, including same-sex couple families has increased within the Jewish community. A 2009 study conducted by Steven M. Cohen, Caryn Aviv, and Ari Kelman found that 7 percent of American Jews self-identified as lesbian, gay, or bisexual. About 31 percent reported being married or living with long-term partners, and 9 percent were raising their own children in their homes.[10] The Jewish Community Study of New York, 2011, found that 5.1 percent of respondents self-identified as LGBTQ, of which 34.8 percent were married or living with a partner, and 14.4 percent were raising children.[11]

The rise of same-sex couple parenting has coincided with a growing tolerance of homosexuality and same-sex marriage within general society. In March 2013, according to a study by the Pew Research Center, 57 percent of Americans agreed that homosexuality should be accepted by society, a 10 percent increase since 2003. The same survey found that 49 percent approved of allowing same-sex couples to legally marry, and 66 percent believed that same-sex couples should have the same legal rights as heterosexual couples. Significantly, 64 percent agreed that same-sex couples would be as good parents as heterosexual couples. This figure also jumped ten percentage points in the past decade. The Pew numbers may be conservative, at least in regard to same-sex marriage. A slightly differently worded question on same-sex marriage in a March 2013 Washington Post/ABC News poll found that 58 percent of respondents believed that same-sex marriage should be legal.[12]

The American Jewish community is even more accepting of homosexuality and same-sex marriage than the general population. Only the Orthodox movement does not ordain openly gay rabbis or sanction same-sex religious marriage. The Reform movement's rabbinical conference voted to allow rabbis to officiate at same-sex marriage and commitment ceremonies in 2000, while the Conservative movement issued officiation guidelines for same-sex marriage ceremonies in 2012. The Pew Research Center's 2013 Survey of American Jews found that 82 percent believed that homosexuality should be accepted by society, consistent with findings that American Jews are more liberal on political and social issues than the general American public. As with Americans more generally, Jews under 30 are even more accepting of homosexuality than their parents.[13] Similarly, a 2012–2013 Pew study found that 76 percent of Jews were in favor of allowing same-sex couples to legally marry, as opposed to 34 percent of Protestants and 53 percent of Catholics. Among non-Jews only those who indicated no religious preference—the so-called "nones"—expressed a level of support for gay marriage (74%) that approached that of the Jewish community.[14]

Despite the generally liberal attitude of American Jews and the non-Orthodox movements toward homosexuality and same-sex marriage, synagogue policies that affect LGBTQ Jews vary considerably. A 2009 study of synagogues found that while 73 percent of rabbis believed that their congregations did a good or excellent job making gays and lesbians feel comfortable, only 31 percent of Conservative and 49 percent of Reform rabbis reported that their synagogues were actively welcoming "to a great extent." Further, 24 percent of rabbis, including most Orthodox rabbis, reported that their congregations were minimally welcoming or not at all welcoming of gays and lesbians. Behind these general statistics, the survey found that roughly 70 percent of Reform and 35 percent of Conservative congregations would consider hiring an openly gay or lesbian rabbi. Congregational leaders reported a greater openness to hiring an openly gay and lesbian educator than an intermarried educator. At the same time, only about 50 percent of Reform rabbis and 20 percent of Conservative rabbis indicated a willingness to officiate at a same-sex marriage ceremony, and very few synagogues included language explicitly inclusive to gays and lesbians and "non-traditional" or "alternative" families in their mission statements. The majority of congregations also reported offering no programming specifically targeted to gay and lesbian congregants. The study did not explore the policies of congregational religious schools in relation to the children in same-sex parent families or the extent to which religious school curricula explore issues related to Judaism and sexual orientation.[15]

One question that deserves further study is the extent to which parenting affects LGBTQ Jews' levels of Jewish engagement and community identification. Surveys have consistently found a positive correlation between parenting and Jewish engagement among heterosexuals. Whether or not LGBT Jews exhibit similar behavior patterns is unknown. Data from the Jewish Community Study of New York (2011) for example, are inconclusive due to the sample size. In general, LGBTQ Jews scored lower on a Jewish engagement index than heterosexual Jews, but the differences were more pronounced among singles than those who were partnered. Even in this case, while the findings are suggestive, the sample size is too small to draw any conclusions.[16]

As same-sex couples increasingly embrace parenthood, researchers have progressively focused their attention on gay and lesbian parents and their children. Indeed, the growth of research coupled with the increased interest in same-sex parent families on the part of policymakers, lawyers, educators, health-care professionals, and others, has to date warranted the publication of two book-length syntheses and analyses of scholarship,[17] as well as multiple article-length reviews.[18] However, this proliferation of research has barely touched the Jewish community. To date, there has been no published study on same-sex parent families who are raising their children as Jews. It is hoped that the present study will begin to fill in this lacuna.

## Methodology

This study adopted a qualitative research approach, which was especially well suited for exploring the thought processes behind decision-making. Ninety individuals, including 44 couples, were interviewed between April and August 2013. Subjects ranged in age from their late twenties to early seventies, with 38 percent between 30 and 39 and 42 percent between 40 and 49. The subjects were somewhat better educated and more affluent than the Jewish population as a whole. For example, all but one of the subjects were college graduates (compared to 58% of Jews in the 2013 Pew Report), and 43 percent reported household incomes of more than $150,000 per year (compared to 25% in Pew). The differences reflect in part the absence of ultra-Orthodox Jews in the study, and the clustering of subjects around the prime earning years. To some extent, they also reflect demographic peculiarities of the LJBT Jewish population.[19] In 2009, Cohen, Aviv, and Kelman found that very few Jews over 60, and few Orthodox Jews, identified as gay, lesbian, or bisexual. They also found that lesbian and gay Jews tended to be better educated than the Jewish population as a whole.[20] Since this study was limited to couples who were raising children as Jews, interview subjects were in some respects more Jewishly identified than the LGBTQ Jewish population as a whole.[21] Subjects were more likely than LGBTQ Jews more generally to belong to a synagogue, contribute to a UJA/Federation campaign, and socialize with mostly Jewish friends. Indeed, in all of these areas, the subjects more closely resembled heterosexual Jews. For the same reason, there were fewer interfaith couple families included in the sample than might be expected in the general population. According to Cohen, Aviv, and Kelman, nearly nine out of ten gay and lesbian Jews in committed relationships reported that their partners or spouses were not Jewish.[22] Randal Schnoor and Morton Weinfeld found a comparable rate of interfaith relationships among gay and lesbian Jews in Canada.[23] Nevertheless, about half of the couples who participated in the study included a non-Jewish partner, and another 10 percent included a partner who converted to Judaism from another faith. Although efforts were made to obtain a diverse sample, we make no claim that it is representative or that the results can be generalized to the broader population. The data collected is highly suggestive, but painting a statistically valid portrait of same-sex couple families raising Jewish children must await further research. However, the study does much to advance our understanding of the attitudes and behaviors of this population.

## The Decision to Become Parents

For many couples, Judaism came to the fore at critical junctures on their road to parenthood, including donor choice in the case of lesbian couples choosing artificial insemination, and the choice of both egg donors and the gestational carriers in the case of gay male couples opting for surrogacy. A few lesbian couples, like Anne and Beth, both in their early thirties, took a fatalistic approach to the process of donor selection. "I've seen a lot of people stressed so, so hard in that process, and we really didn't," Anne explained. "Whoever our children ended up being, whoever they came out being, they were going to be our children. So it didn't really matter so much." But they were the exceptions.

Far more commonly, lesbian couples identified a list of preferred characteristics in a donor. Jewish background was among the most oft-cited criteria, second only to a clean medical history. Carolyn, a business owner in her mid-fifties, and Donna, a police officer in her mid-sixties, recalled being swayed by the "Jewish values" in the essay of the donor they chose. "He said that he saw it as a mitzvah because he also donated blood as well as sperm," Carolyn explained. "He sort of thought it was part of his job to help the world in this way. We liked the sentiment, so we went for it."

Emily and Fern, in their mid-forties, also prioritized Jewish background when they chose a donor. They explained that they were looking for someone who felt familiar to them and who appeared to share their values. The man they chose shared their socioeconomic profile and attended similarly competitive universities. But what ultimately won the couple over was their sense that under different circumstances the donor could have been a close friend. "On an intellectual level, I know that the image we have of him is as much our own creation as reality," Fern conceded. "But in my gut I feel a bond." They were not the only ones for whom a somewhat ethereal sense of connection ended up playing a decisive role in their ultimate choice.

Not everyone indicating a preference for a Jewish donor ended up choosing a Jew. Many sperm banks have few Jewish donors. Donation criteria at many sperm banks are narrow and specific, including limits on age and height, and competitive education requirements. Some banks only accept donors who have had exclusively female sexual partners. They also typically conduct a thorough screening process that involves sperm analysis, STD and infectious-disease screening, blood and urine tests, and a physical examination.[24] When confronted with a limited pool of Jewish donors, some couples ended up choosing a non-Jew because the Jewish donors did not meet other significant criteria. Bonnie and Alyssa initially gravitated toward a Jewish donor but picked a non-Jew who presented a stronger health history. Other couples similarly identified a preference for a Jewish donor but prioritized other characteristics, such as physical features, intelligence, and musical or artistic ability. As with lesbian couples in the general population who choose to parent through donor insemination,[25] some attempted to match the physical features and cultural background of the donor to the non-biological mother.

Only five lesbian couples chose known donors. Others briefly considered but ultimately abandoned the idea due to legal considerations, a reluctance to share parenting with another person or couple, or a concern for personality conflicts down the road. Those who opted for a known donor most often expressed the view that it would be healthier for the child to know the identity of his or her biological father. Some were also hoping that the biological father would serve as a male influence in the child's life. In one case, a single lesbian mother was looking to share parenting responsibilities with a gay male couple. In four out of five cases the donor identified as Jewish.

Finding a Jewish donor was particularly important to Gina, who was looking to coparent. The biological father and his husband not only share custody of their child with Gina, but also Sabbath dinners and Jewish holiday celebrations. A Jewish donor was considered similarly essential by Hannah, a consultant to nonprofits, and her partner, Ilana, a lawyer. While they did not wish to share custody of their children with the biological father, they wanted him to be a presence in their children's lives. They chose an individual who shared their love of Judaism and lived his Jewish and humanistic values.

Gay male couples who pursued surrogacy were somewhat less likely to prioritize Jewish background when choosing an egg donor and a gestational carrier. As with sperm donors, Jewish egg donors are difficult to find and Jewish carriers are even more rare. From the perspective of *halakhah* (traditional Jewish law), there is some disagreement about whether maternity is determined genetically or fixed at the time of birth, although most decisors come down on the side of the birthmother.[26] But only the most traditional subjects mentioned halakhic considerations among the factors that they considered when choosing a donor and surrogate. Indeed, those who prioritized Jewish background tended to be more concerned about the identity of the donor than the carrier. Perhaps this is a function of the contemporary appreciation for the role of genetics in shaping emotional disposition and social behavior.

Like Emily and Fern, men who placed an importance on Jewish background often seemed to be craving familiarity, someone to whom they could relate. Bert, a doctor, recalled scanning through a catalog of prospective egg donors: "Out of this book there was this one woman who I just thought . . . I liked her, and I always thought this would actually be the kind of woman my brother would date, and then the fact that she was Jewish kind of sealed the deal for me."

Interestingly, the two Israeli-born subjects, one male and one female, and a female subject born in Latin America, spoke about Jewishness in terms that were more tribal than the Americans. Gal, a financial analyst, who was born and raised in Israel before moving to the United States to attend university, decided to use the agency A Jewish Blessing, which only worked with Jewish egg donors. Clarifying his reasons for seeking out a Jewish egg donor, he explained that "I really had a feeling of kind of like a continuation of the Jewish people." Gal added that "there were a lot of women [in the donor database] that were Jewish by conversion, or their dad was Jewish but their mother was not. And [my husband and I] thought that if we want a Jewish egg donor, we should really take a Jewish egg donor that is not by conversion or anything." He and his husband Ross, a non-Jewish, American-born financial manager, ultimately chose a Jewish Israeli donor. Interestingly, Gal's strong identification with Judaism as an ethnicity or nationality did not dissuade him from marrying a practicing Episcopalian.

Michal, a scientist who grew up in Latin America, but who now lives with her wife in the United States, also wanted a donor who was "a hundred percent Jewish and identified as such." When asked to elaborate, she explained that, for her, "genetics" was paramount. She wanted children who were culturally akin to herself, who "looked Jewish," by which she seemed to mean Ashkenazi. While she attributed her attitude to her scientific background, her explanation seemed to focus as much if not more on the metaphysical and, some might say, the racial: "For me I think of the facial expressions that tell me that we belong . . . it's a cultural thing. . . . [a] cultural attachment to your people."

Tellingly, Michal's wife, Janet, an American-born business executive, admitted to being somewhat uncomfortable with her own emphasis on "pedigree." For her, the "Jewish identity" of the donor was very important:

> I felt a little weird about it because I remember friends of ours were going through [alternative insemination] at the same time we were, and [they] were not concerned about this at all. In fact, they didn't pick a Jewish donor because they said, "Well, what difference does it make? [The child] will be raised Jewish so it doesn't make a difference." And I felt a little self-conscious about it because I'm, like, what am I doing, breeding a purebred dog here?

Ultimately, she explained their decision by stating that a fully Jewish donor "provided some security . . . because they were not strangers to me and Michal—that they weren't Scandinavian Eskimos living in the Tundra. . . . If he was one hundred percent Jewish, I think I felt like I knew him more, or at least I could pick him more." Janet's comment and others underscore the discomfort that many subjects felt with the donor-selection procedure. The sense of familiarity gained by choosing a Jewish donor helped many to overcome their overall uneasiness and abiding feeling that the process was unnatural.

Those couples, both male and female, who pursued adoption were less likely to raise the issue of Jewishness in relationship to their transition to parenthood. None insisted that their adopted children be Jewish at birth. This may in part be a function of the rarity of available Jewish children in both the domestic and international adoption systems. But it may also reflect the fact that those who opt for adoption are, as a matter of course, willing to tolerate a fairly limited degree of control over the genetic and cultural background of their children. To be sure, individuals engaged in domestic adoption routinely screen prospective birthmothers (and, often times, birthfathers) on the basis of race and factors such as reported health history and drug and alcohol use during pregnancy. But, in general, those seeking a genetic connection to their child will not find adoption an attractive family-planning option. Max, a lawyer in his mid-thirties, spoke for many adoptive parents in the study when he wondered aloud about why couples opting for surrogacy were "making such a big deal about genes." For him and his husband, Barry, a software developer, also in his mid-thirties, genetics was "not that relevant. Our family is created by the values we teach and that's why they're our kids; they don't need to have a genetic link to us."

Revealingly, one of the few subjects who struggled with the question of Jewish background in relationship to her adopted children initially opted for alternative insemination and only settled on adoption after three years of trying unsuccessfully to conceive. Karen, a business manager, acknowledged that although she was not conscious of it at the time, she was initially "stuck" on the idea that "we had to have a biological Jewish child" because her wife, Lorna, was a Jew by choice. "Looking back, it all makes sense. It's like, of course I wanted to give birth so that I could have a 'legit' Jewish kid." In retrospect, she contended that her fears were misplaced: "The comedy in all of this is like you would not see two more Jewish children than our children [even though] their birth mothers were not Jewish."

Karen and Lorna opted to have their children converted to Judaism as part of the adoption process, a step that was taken by other similarly traditional couples. *Halakhah* treats adoptive parents as agents of the biological parents and mandates that an adopted child born to a non-Jewish mother must undergo conversion, including immersion in a ritual bath, or *mikveh*, conferring of a Hebrew name, and, for boys, ritual circumcision.[27] For others, a ritual circumcision ceremony for a boy and a baby-naming ceremony for a girl doubled as a conversion ceremony. Many Reform and Reconstructionist rabbis have dispensed with the requirement of *mikveh*. It was not always clear from the interviews whether or not couples made choices about conversion in consultation with a rabbi. A few subjects were nonplussed when interviewers broached the topic of conversion, apparently unaware that in the case of an adopted child even the most liberal Jewish movements accept the religious identity of the birthparents as determinative. Other subjects were indifferent to the requirements of Jewish law in this instance, contending that, in their view, Jewish identity was a function of upbringing. One subject, Max, the lawyer, reacted adamantly when an interviewer asked whether his adopted daughter had undergone a conversion:

> It's a baby! I think it's, like, taking the view of a genetic link to Judaism way too far. She was going to be Jewish because we were going to raise her Jewish. The only people who would ever question if she was Jewish

> would be Orthodox Jews, and they would never accept her Jewishness anyway. We are two guys and were never going have an Orthodox conversion [for our daughter]. So it's like, what's the point? She's Jewish, because we think she's Jewish and everyone in our life thinks she is Jewish. Enough!

Adoptive couples often raised Jewish identity in relation to their deliberations about transracial adoption. A few studies suggest that gay and lesbian couples may be more open to transracial adoption than their heterosexual counterparts.[28] Indeed, two male couples in the study indicated that most of their gay friends who adopted domestically had African American children. "I always, always pictured us having our child for some reason being African American," explained Kurt, an actor. "I guess that's the way that a lot of gay families look nowadays." For Kurt and his husband, Josh, a lawyer, there was no apparent relationship between the race of their adopted child and their determination to raise him or her as Jewish. Other couples, however, did factor Jewish identity into their decision about whether to adopt transracially. When Max and Barry considered their comfort level with adopting a black child, they gave a lot of thought to the Jewish environment into which they would be bringing him or her. "A big thing we thought about was making sure that we could find a synagogue that would have people of different races and just an openness to diversity—and not just an ethnic view of Judaism, but really were part of a faith community [where] we accept everyone and just [are] really making sure that whatever color of skin our child had they feel accepted by the Jewish community," Max explained. Similarly, Ben and Mike asserted that adopting a child from Guatemala posed little problem for them as a Jewish family living in South Florida. "For [our son] it's very easy," Ben said. "He fits right in." According to one estimate, there are about 13,500 Latin American Jewish adults residing in Miami-Dade, Broward, and Palm Beach counties.[29]

For Lorna and Karen, an interracial couple, once they gave up on alternative insemination, adopting African American children was almost a foregone conclusion. "Being African American but also being educated and having come from a family where education was extremely important, I sort of always had the sense that in this country there are a lot of poor kids of color who could really use some good homes," Lorna said. "And I really felt like I could sort of give them that. So yeah, that was something that's been very important to me. . . . In terms of trying to repair the world, it's a very tangible thing that I feel like I've done with my life." Lorna's use of the idiom "repair the world" underscored that she viewed the adoption of underprivileged African American children through the lens of *tikkun olam*, the contemporary Jewish term for social justice. At the same time, however, she was conscious that in her Jewish community the children would be racially anomalous. "It was very important for me because we decided to raise the kids Jewish and because they are black, that they were very educated in terms of their Judaism," explained Lorna, who converted to Judaism as an adult. "It's very important for me that they speak Hebrew and that they feel extremely comfortable in synagogues, because these are all things that I'm still in many ways grappling with [as a Jew by choice]. . . . I think it's very important to me that they absolutely feel an ownership of the Jewish religion and Jewish culture."

## Finding a Supportive Environment

Lorna and Karen's desire to immerse their children in Judaism led them to select Jewish day school from among their educational options—this despite the fact that theirs is the only interracial family and one of only a few same-sex couple families in the school, and the kids the only African Americans there. "It has been an education for the [Jewish] community," Lorna reflected. "Honestly, had it not been for our family, most of the kids in the school would have never spoken to a black person, much less a black kid. So in that sense it's been, I think, mutually beneficial." Still, she acknowledged the social challenges her children faced both as African Americans and as the children of lesbians. As far as Lorna was aware, they had not met with overt discrimination. But she noticed that her older child went out of her way when speaking with her friends on the playground to avoid mentioning that she had two mothers, referring to them instead with gender-neutral terminology. So far, she and Karen have chosen to "take a step back" and let her daughter navigate the situation on her own. Nevertheless, Lorna was concerned that "at times she has seemed almost embarrassed," even while reassuring herself that "it's probably pretty typical."

In finding a welcoming environment at both their Conservative synagogue and the community day school, Lorna and Karen's experience was fairly typical. The majority of subjects found the Jewish community to be tolerant and in many cases explicitly welcoming. Even so, a few commented that at times there was a residue of awkwardness in their social interactions in synagogues and other Jewish institutions. Jason and José, both in their early thirties, felt at ease in their Conservative synagogue but noted that older members, in particular, sometimes inadvertently telegraphed a mild discomfort in social interactions by "trying too hard." Both recognized the good intentions that prompted the social awkwardness. In a similar vein, Josh, the lawyer, noted that he and his family were often enlisted as poster children for diversity. "We just know that whenever we go to an event there is going to be picture of our family, and it's going to show up in the brochure . . . because they like the diversity, which we're fine with. We're not put off by it because we understand how that works." He added that he preferred that the Jewish community be "a little awkwardly too welcoming" than cold or hostile. A few subjects observed that they had witnessed signs of a more general cultural shift toward greater tolerance and acceptance within their own communities. Likewise, the liberalization of non-Orthodox policies toward homosexuals in recent years reverberated on the local level. One Midwestern couple noted that they had resigned from their Conservative synagogue a decade ago because it refused to recognize their marriage and joined a Reform temple instead, but that the synagogue had since reversed its policy. Another couple, in Northern California, volunteered that they would have left their Conservative congregation in 2007 had the rabbi not liberalized synagogue policies in the wake of the decision by the movement's Committee on Jewish Law and Standards to allow individual rabbis latitude on whether to officiate at same-sex weddings.

The increasing visibility of openly gay and lesbian clergy, school directors, and teachers, some of whom were married and had children, was inspiring to some couples. They believed that the elevation of LGBTQ people as Jewish role models—much like the approbation of women rabbis a generation earlier—made a powerful statement, particularly to their children. "It is the Jewish community basically telling our kids that their family is normal," Mandy, a carpenter, stated. She and her wife, Diane, a saleswoman, and their son, attend a Reform congregation that until a few years ago was led by a gay rabbi with children.

Same-sex couple families were still confronted by the heteronormative nature of Jewish society, which some experienced as heterosexism. Stories abounded along the lines of a day school teacher who did not consider how a Mother's Day card assignment might affect a child with two dads, or a Jewish preschool form that asked for the names of the "mother" and "father" rather than "parent." One mother complained that a religious school teacher seemed ill-equipped to respond when a classmate asked her daughter why she had two moms and no dad. But many claimed that they and their children experienced more egregious indignities when navigating general society. In general, subjects found clergy, teachers, and Jewish communal workers to be well meaning and sometimes even inspiring in their efforts to be welcoming and sensitive. Orna, a health-care consultant in her late forties, recalled how her daughter became very distressed when her religious school class was studying the section of Leviticus (18:23 and 20:13) that condemns intercourse between men as *toeva* (typically translated as "an abomination"). The next time the family went to services, the daughter insisted on staying afterward to speak with the rabbi. "The rabbi was great in talking about how the Torah was written in a particular time and place, and different people have different beliefs, and that's why you're in this community that has a different belief than that," Orna said, characterizing the rabbi and the religious school director as "incredibly supportive," even as her daughter remained troubled. "I do think in time this is going be an area for [my daughter] to learn about," Orna acknowledged; "she said she doesn't want to be Jewish when she is grown up. And it's like, you know what? I'm giving you the opportunity to learn so that later you can decide how you want to live your life. So it's interesting."

Not surprisingly, perhaps, those families who attempted to find a home within the Orthodox community generally had a more negative experience. Mike and Ben left their Orthodox synagogue after they adopted their son. "We couldn't go to our Orthodox shul with [our son], and be coparents so we needed to leave. . . . It wasn't our choice. Even now I think that ideally we would be more comfortable in an Orthodox setting, but it just wasn't for our kids," Mike lamented. "They wanted one of us to be uncle, one of us to be dad. They refused to help with [our son's] conversion. They refused to allow us to have any type of *simcha* [celebration] there for [his] arrival." Judy and Joan had a similar experience; when Judy inquired about membership at the local Orthodox synagogue, the rabbi warned her that the couple would be asked to leave if they were honest with congregants about the nature of their relationship. They quickly decided that even if they put aside the issue of self-respect, being closeted with children was simply not an option. Mike and Ben also pulled their son out of the local day school because they were the only same-sex couple family. The decision was clearly gut-wrenching for them. "We both went to Jewish day schools our whole lives," Ben explained. "We're leaving to show [our son] that there are other families like us, that he shouldn't be the only one." Mike interjected: "It is a very hard decision. If we lived in a place like New York, he would still be in day school, because we would be able to find a day school that has that diversity."

If Mike and Ben's schooling decision was voluntary, the children of two other couples in the study were denied admission to Orthodox day schools because of their families' composition. In one case, the principal of the school was apologetic but candidly explained that his school was concerned about preserving its bona fides within the Orthodox world. Accepting the child, he feared, would be interpreted as condoning the parents' relationship. The couple eventually enrolled their child in a community day school and, a few years later, in a different Modern Orthodox school. A second couple, Manny and Patrick, were shocked when a Modern Orthodox high school rejected their one of their sons. When the boys were born, Manny recalled, "I was sure the kids were going to be bullied, ostracized, shunned" in the Jewish community, "and I must tell you that until two years ago, which was when [the twins] were going into high school, I never had one incident with anybody: Conservative, Reform, Orthodox, Hasidic." Manny's mother's family was close to a Hasidic grand rabbi, a relationship that Manny and Patrick participated in until the grand rabbi's death. The couple obtained a *segulah* (kabbalistic talisman) from the grand rabbi for the birthmother of their third child, when she was experiencing complications during her pregnancy. Manny, Patrick, and the children were guests on multiple occasions in the grand rabbi's home, and sometimes prayed in his synagogue. "He was really so open-minded and supportive," Manny reminisced.

The couple's experience abruptly changed, however, when one of their sons, who attended a Conservative elementary day school, decided to apply to the Modern Orthodox high school. The admissions director repeatedly obfuscated until it became clear that the school had no intention of enrolling their son. The well-connected couple enlisted the help of multiple community members with standing, including the federation director. Ultimately, however, their son ended up attending a Jewish community high school (not affiliated with any particular wing of Judaism) along with his brother. Looking back on the experience, Manny and Patrick blamed the Orthodox school's administration rather than the community as a whole. The men currently send their youngest child to a Chabad elementary school and have not encountered any overt discrimination. While it may seem inexplicable that the family would get a warmer reception from some Hasidic sects than from a Modern Orthodox institution, it is possible that the latter felt under greater pressure to patrol its boundaries precisely because its members were more engaged with the secular world. It is also notable that both Chabad and the late grand rabbi's Hasidic sect were committed to Jewish outreach. As with the day school that rejected the child of the first couple, it is also conceivable that the Modern Orthodox school acted out of insecurity and a perceived need to protect its right flank.

Even in more liberal Jewish settings, gay and lesbian couples sometimes felt the need to advocate for their families. For example, Pam and Roberta, a couple in their mid-thirties, recalled that their suburban Conservative synagogue only became more liberal on same-sex issues under pressure from the growing number of gay and lesbian congregants. In particular, they credited a gay male couple who engaged in a form of Jewish civil disobedience in response to perceived discrimination. When the couple's requests for an *aliyah* (Torah blessing honor) to commemorate a lifecycle milestone were rebuffed, they began standing during the Torah reading whenever a heterosexual couple was called up to Torah to mark a celebration. Gradually, others, including the synagogue president joined in their silent protest, and in short order the policy was changed.

More recently, a new rabbi who was generally far more supportive of gay equality, and even performed Pam and Roberta's wedding, hesitated when a group of gay congregants, including Pam and Roberta, suggested that the synagogue sponsor a gay pride Shabbat ice cream social. Roberta and the rabbi began a protracted negotiation over the wording on a flyer that initially left the couple flummoxed. "The rabbi finally said, 'Well, I'm not sure we want to say that [the synagogue] celebrates gay-pride month.' And I kind of was like—all the color, I could feel like all the blood drain out of my face. And I said, 'What do you mean you don't want to celebrate it?'" At first, Roberta and Pam were ready to cancel their membership. "My mother finally said to me something like, 'Don't you let her push you out of your synagogue! This is your community. . . . She's just the rabbi. You push back, and if you want to make a change then you make that change.'" Ultimately, they and the rabbi reached a modus vivendi.

## Jewish Identification and Involvement in Jewish Life

Pam and Roberta's investment in celebrating gay pride in their synagogue was a function of their level of engagement in congregational life. While the couple admitted that with three young children at home, they found weekly Sabbath service attendance unrealistic, the synagogue was the locus of much of their social and volunteer activity. They also viewed synagogue involvement as an important ingredient in strengthening their children's Jewish identities.

In an effort to ascertain the relative priority of Judaism and Jewishness in subjects' family lives, interviewers asked three separate questions. First, subjects were asked to narrate how they integrated Judaism and Jewish activities into their children's lives and whether their approach had changed over time. Next they were asked how important it was to them, relative to other priorities, that their children developed a strong and positive Jewish identity. Finally, they were queried about how they would react if, in the future, their children decided to abandon Judaism. As might be expected, the range of responses to the first question was broad, both in terms of variety and level of intensity. Among the Jewish interview subjects, there were those for whom the primary means of engagement was cultural, and others who focused on the intellectual. For some, God and spirituality were paramount, while others were avowed secularists. There were subjects who used halakhah as a measuring rod, and others who, to paraphrase Rabbi Mordecai Kaplan, believed tradition should get a vote but not a veto. There were subjects who identified primarily with Prophetic Judaism and the message of *tikkun olam*, and those who spoke the language of Jewish peoplehood. Some were regular synagogue-goers while others had not stepped foot in a synagogue in decades. A few described their engagement with Judaism and Jewish culture as minimal. Among the non-Jews there was also a great degree of variation, with some actively engaged in the Jewish lives of their partners and children and others indifferent. Four subjects attended church on a regular basis, and an additional eleven attended once or twice a year, usually on Christmas and Easter. Some described their Christian identity as "cultural" rather than "religious," and a few considered themselves Jews in everything but name. There were also two individuals who did not formally convert to Judaism but nevertheless identified as Jews.

Interestingly, despite this spectacular diversity, Jewish-born subjects overwhelmingly asserted that the Jewish identity of their children was an important or somewhat important priority. Those who elaborated on their reasoning cited a variety of factors, some of which were very personal. Two subjects viewed it as their "responsibility" as children of Holocaust survivors to contribute to the perpetuation of the Jewish people. "For a while I think I wanted kids so that my dad would have grandchildren," one subject confided. Similarly, a few others spoke in general terms about the "sacrifice" of previous generations. Six said they viewed Judaism as a source of values and a road map for how to live a meaningful life. One subject spoke about her deep connection to the state of Israel and of wanting to pass that bond to her children. A few expressed the view that a strong cultural and/or religious identity would help their children to feel more confident and connected. Five subjects, some referencing their own negative experiences in Jewish supplementary school, said that it was important to them that their children have positive, "happy" associations with Jewishness. "What we want [our son] to do is to love it," emphasized Sharona, a Jewish professional in her early thirties. "We don't want it to be like, 'Ugh, I have to go temple again.'"

Most Jewish-born subjects also acknowledged that they would feel "sad," "hurt," or even "devastated" if one of their children decided down the road to abandon Judaism. Tali, a teacher in her late twenties, was fairly typical in her response: "I don't know if it's something that I can even imagine . . . Look, it's not the kind of thing where I would say, oh, you're disowned, like that to me is anathema. Like, I could never imagine doing that to my kids. But it would be very painful to me. Of course, they would always be my kids and I would always love them, but that would be hard." If Tali was almost unable to fathom such a scenario, her wife, Violet, a social worker in her late-thirties, viewed it as within the realm of possibility and adopted a more philosophical approach: "I would understand their need to separate themselves from the upbringing that they've had and to explore who they are and create their own sense of self and identity separate from who we've told them we are as a family. I would have to imagine I would struggle, but that I would understand why, and come to accept them for who they are and how they make their decisions." A few other subjects similarly allowed that they would be accepting of their children's choices so as long as they grew up to be a good and moral individuals.

To be sure, when asked where Jewish identity fit in their list of priorities, many privileged concerns such as health, education, and happiness, but only two Jewish born subjects expressed an utter lack of concern. In at least one of those cases, the subject's response seemed to be colored by a strained relationship with her parents. Beth considered the Jewish environment in her home growing up to be coercive and did not want to "force Judaism down [her children's] throats." One subject believed that his strong feelings about the value of Jewish continuity seemed hypocritical in light of his family's relative lack of Jewish observance. "Talking about importance is kind of easy," Gal acknowledged. "It gets more complicated when the question becomes, What is the price that you are willing to pay? What are the sacrifices that you are willing to make?"

Jews-by-choice had a more complex set of responses to these questions. Some were as adamant in their views as the Jews by birth. But more often they referenced their own faith journeys and argued that they could not begrudge their children the same freedom of choice. "I think if they find a religious framework to live their life in, to be really useful for them, then I hope they have it," exclaimed Wynona, who was raised as a non-practicing Episcopalian and converted to Judaism about six years into her relationship with her Jewish-born wife. Similarly, when Roberta, a Jew by birth, allowed that she would be dismayed if her child married a non-Jew, her wife Pam robustly dissented: "I would feel like a complete hypocrite if I said that. So I don't have that feeling at all. I would rather that they fall in love with and marry someone who takes good care of them." Significantly, most related to Judaism primarily as a religion rather than a culture. One convert dismissed the culture as "the cosmetic parts of being Jewish," and said that it held little personal appeal. Whereas some Jews by birth asserted that even if their children became atheists they would still be Jews, Jews by choice more often equated identity with belief system. Thus they tended to frame the issue entirely in individual rather than communal terms.

Not surprisingly, non-Jewish partners were even less likely to view their children's hypothetical abandonment of Judaism as a disappointment. This sometimes resulted in stark differences in perspective between the Jewish and non-Jewish partners. For example, when their nine-year-old son announced that he was not Jewish and believed in Jesus, Alyssa, a Jewish-born nurse, and her wife, Bonnie, a software developer and lapsed Catholic, had very different reactions. "It was kind of like someone taking a knife and stabbing it in my heart," Alyssa recalled, without a hint of theatricality in her voice. "And I don't see it as that much of a loss because I guess I don't identify as Jewish," Bonnie chimed in.

She added: "I think they'll all end up having [Judaism] be part of who they are. And whether they go to temple or not, to me it's not that important." On the other end of the spectrum, Donna, the policewoman who was also raised as a Catholic, viewed her daughter's Jewish identity as central to her overall character development. "I really do believe that [Judaism]—even if she doesn't go to synagogue all the time—gives her some values that she lives every day."

Where there was widespread agreement across religious lines was that worse than a child's abandonment of Judaism would be his or her embrace of fundamentalism of any religious stripe. "I think if either of our kids ever became radical anything, that would be almost more disconcerting to me than anything else," Carlie, a 35-year-old teacher, stated. Kurt, the actor, agreed: "I hope [our daughter] doesn't become some crazy born-again Evangelical or something. Then we might have problems." Given the hyper-polarization in contemporary American society, these reactions hardly seem exceptional. One recent study compared a pair of surveys from 1960 and 2010 that asked respondents whether they would be "displeased" if their child married someone outside of their political party. While only 5 percent of respondents had answered affirmatively in 1960, the figure rose to 40 percent in 2010.[30] But same-sex couples were particularly alarmed by the prospect of their children becoming fundamentalists because they imagined that the decision would entail a personal rejection of their family. Pam articulated the matter succinctly: "I couldn't care less what their religion is as long as it isn't a religion that excluded me from their lives."

Some couples were pleasantly surprised that their children were more attached to Judaism than they might have predicted. Dena, a 49-year-old lawyer in the Northeast, credited her children's interest in Judaism for making it a priority for the entire family. Dena's wife, Ellie, a stay-at-home parent who was raised as a Catholic, is currently taking Judaism courses and is contemplating conversion, while Dena, a Jew by birth who was not observant before having children, studies classical Jewish texts with a rabbi. Dena explained that their son had been in the public school for a few years, but whenever the family would drive past the local Jewish day school he would say, "I want to go to that school. Isn't that where the Jewish kids go?" Ellie, a strong believer in the societal benefits of public education, was initially resistant. But the couple finally relented, and now their younger child attends the day school.

Dena explained that her son's feelings of otherness in public school contributed to his desire to attend the day school. She attributed part of his sense of alienation to being the only Jew in his class, and added that having two moms similarly marked him as different. She also acknowledged that he was a bit of an iconoclast, "a quirky kid." For all of these reasons, the day school ended up being a better fit for him. Emily and Fern told a somewhat similar story about the decision-making process around schooling for their eldest child. While they were attracted their city's day school because they valued Jewish knowledge, they reluctantly decided to enroll their son in public school because the location of the day school meant attending would entail a long commute. They ultimately changed their mind at their son's behest. When they asked their son to explain his rationale, it suddenly made sense: "I just don't want to be different anymore," he told them.

These two couples' stories of how and why their children came to attend day school illustrates the difficulty in treating gayness independently of other factors when focusing on same-sex parent families. While the fact of being a same-sex couple affected both couples' decision-making about schooling, the structure of their family was rarely, if ever, considered in isolation. Moreover, the way in which their gayness was processed by their kids was very much a reflection of the children's psychosocial makeup.

Certain patterns emerge from the data, but it is difficult to generalize about the factors that predisposed same-sex couple families in this study to be more or less involved in Jewish life. Although certain commonalities ran through many of the stories, each family was navigating a unique set of circumstances. Most of Jewish subjects (81%) claimed that being Jewish was either important or extremely important to them, and an even higher percentage (97%) asserted that they were proud of their Jewish identity. More than two-thirds agreed that the Jewish community was hospitable to LGBTQ people. About half of the Jewish subjects agreed that synagogue services were "not interesting to me," but only about one-quarter claimed that Jewish organizations were "remote and irrelevant to me." Not surprisingly, those interfaith families who were synagogue members tended to be more involved in Jewish life (even outside of their congregation) than those who were not. However, the stories that these couples shared underscored the folly of generalizing about whether synagogue membership was symptomatic of a preexisting commitment or a spur to greater engagement.

Regardless of whether both partners were Jewish, a prerequisite for Jewish family engagement was a strong Jewish commitment by at least one partner and the lack of opposition by the other. But two other factors were strongly correlated with Jewish engagement: welcoming Jewish institutions and an existing support system of family and/or friends. Fran grew up in a synagogue-going Conservative family but adamantly rejected organized Jewish life after watching in horror as a friend was publicly humiliated for being gay in her childhood congregation. Today, she and her wife, Gail, a non-practicing Catholic, are raising their young son as a cultural Jew. Gail asserted that she values many of Fran's Jewish traditions more than her own Irish Catholic customs and rituals, but Fran remains deeply ambivalent about Judaism and the family is entirely disconnected from Jewish institutions and community. In contrast, a close relationship with a synagogue and its rabbi was decisive in Mandy and Nora's Jewish trajectory. Not only was the community embracing of them as a lesbian couple, its members also provided emotional and spiritual support when they were dealing with the sickness and death of loved ones. The synagogue rabbi ended up officiating at their wedding and the Jewish ritual ceremonies celebrating their children's births. Nora was quick to point out that the sense of connection that she feels toward the synagogue does not necessarily translate to the Jewish community at large, which she finds somewhat colder and stand-offish. And while Mandy insisted that the couple's children be raised as Jews, both women acknowledged that, without the temple, it is unclear whether they would have shown sustained follow-through or whether the content of their children's Jewish identity would be substantive.

Parents and in-laws, siblings and other relatives provided a common first line of support for many couples in their efforts to imbue their children with strong and positive Jewish identities. Even when they did not live in close proximity, family members, particularly grandparents, were often intimately involved in role-modeling and Jewish meaning-making. Indeed, for many, Judaism was almost synonymous with family. When Jewish subjects were asked to rate several factors in terms of their importance to their sense of being Jewish—including antisemitism, the family, God, the Holocaust, the holidays, Israel, Jewish culture, Jewish law, the Jewish people, the Sabbath, and Torah—the family was far and away the most popular. In all, 81 percent of respondents viewed the family as "extremely important." The closest contenders, the Jewish people, Jewish culture, and the holidays, all scored in the low 50s. Intentional family—that is, friends and surrogate grandparents—was also vital in the Jewish lives of many of the families.

## Interfaith Families

Sometimes a commitment to raise the children as Jews coupled with a welcoming congregation provided insufficient scaffolding if it was not combined with a Jewish social and support system, such as Jewish family and friendship circles. When Alyssa announced to her non-Jewish wife, Bonnie, that she wanted to raise their children as Jews, Bonnie's response was benign indifference: "If she wanted to be the one getting them out of bed on Sunday, that's fine; I wasn't going stand in her way. But I also wasn't going to convert or participate in everything." A decade later, Alyssa was trying her keep her kids in religious school and to celebrate Jewish holidays with festive meals. But she admitted that she was struggling under the pressure of carrying the responsibility on her own. She acknowledged that the Jewish community, in particular their temple and Jewish preschool, was "far more welcoming to Bonnie and me, and certainly [to] our sexuality," than she initially imagined. Nevertheless, she emphasized, "It's been a real challenge, a real, real struggle, to get our kids engaged." Over time, Bonnie has softened her detachment. She occasionally attends services with Alyssa and even pitches in with the Sunday school drop-offs and pick-ups. Nevertheless, Alyssa attributed her difficulties to lack of family support. Her parents are deceased, and her siblings live far away. "I think that in watching other families and their connections with their grandparents, it's something that I feel kind of is a loss for my children, that I think it can be a huge positive influence. I wish I had more . . . adult support, whether grandparents, aunts, uncles that were also consistently participating and carrying on that tradition. And I feel like I don't have that, and that I'm kind of it."

It is fair to conclude that if Alyssa were experiencing the project of raising the children as Jews as a joint endeavor with her partner, she might feel the absence of family support less keenly. The dilemmas that same-sex interfaith couples experience around religion and childrearing are in many respects identical to those documented in studies of heterosexuals.[31] Interfaith couples in the present study had discussed the religious identity of their future children before embarking on the adoption or assisted-reproduction processes. In some cases, the Jewish partner reported being surprised by the depth of their convictions. Once the children were born, religion-related issues tended to bubble to the surface around lifecycle events, like birth and b'nai mitzvah ceremonies, as well as decisions about religious education. In addition, the winter holidays, in particular, became an annual invitation to revisit and either affirm longstanding agreements or consider accommodations. Sylvia Barack Fishman's finding that holiday observances are "a process rather than a static condition in mixed-married households" certainly held true among these interfaith gay couples.[32]

The similarity of experience between same-sex and heterosexual couples in negotiating interfaith relationships and childrearing was, in the words of one subject, "a no-brainer," but it comes as a revelation to some who work with interfaith couples. Ellie and her wife, Dena, decided to enroll in a Union of Reform Judaism course for interfaith couples planning to have children. At first, the facilitator was concerned that as a lesbian couple they would upset the course dynamic. "You know, this isn't a class where you can come and talk about homosexuality," she reportedly told them. Uncertain about whether to be amused or offended, they decided to give the course a chance and assured the facilitator that they were only interested in speaking about having children as an interfaith couple. They described the course as "intense" and rewarding. They also noted a change in attitude on the part of the facilitator. Once she realized that the issues facing interfaith couples transcended the gender and sexual orientation of the partners, she became an advocate for inclusion and began advertising the course in gay media outlets.

Some found that when they were planning their wedding it was far easier to find a rabbi who was willing to perform a same-sex ceremony than an interfaith wedding. Their experiences corresponded with those described in a 2013 *New York Times* article and the anecdotal information provided to the reporter by Idit Klein, the national director of Keshet, an advocacy organization for LGBTQ Jews.[33] One couple in the present study, Gaia and Jo, both in their early forties, decided to join the temple of the rabbi who officiated at their marriage. "Outreach is part of his mission," Jo explained, adding that "knowing that I'm valued rather than just tolerated makes a world of difference in terms of my level of enthusiasm." Anne and Beth similarly asserted that even though there was only one other same-sex couple family in their congregation, the prevalence of interfaith couples created an environment of acceptance. Significantly for Anne, it was not sufficient for the temple to be welcoming of her as a non-Jewish spouse. She valued her temple because she did not feel intimidated asking questions. Presently, she attends religious school with her girls and is learning to read Hebrew. "That's kind of how we always planned it," she says. "I didn't convert, but it was always the plan to learn with them as they grow."

Not surprisingly, interfaith couples who were synagogue members reported a far higher degree of both religious and cultural Jewish family engagement than those who were not. However, synagogue membership was not necessarily an indication of a single religious tradition in the home, nor did it preclude some deliberate religious syncretism, such as Hanukkah decorations on the Christmas tree or chocolate Easter eggs on the Passover seder plate. Some families took pride in the ways they were blending Jewish and Christian traditions with their children. Leanne, a Protestant minister and her Jewish-born wife, Moira, described a nightly bedtime ritual where members of the family gathered together to share what they were thankful for followed by a joint recitation of the first two lines of the Shema in both Hebrew and English. Beth and Anne look forward to annual joint Hanukkah and Christmas celebrations at Anne's (non-Jewish) parents' house. "[Our holiday celebrations] get really intertwined," Beth explained, adding, "and we like it that way."

On the other end of the spectrum, Ross, the foundation grants manager, found little appeal in "some sort of mixture thing where you blend the holidays. There's nothing wrong with that, but I just didn't see the point in it." Ross regularly attends an Episcopal church and expressed no desire to convert to Judaism. "This will sound strange, but [my husband] Gal wanted [our twins] to be raised Jewish, and I was totally more than fine with that." Gal explained that the two found that they shared a connection that transcended their particular religious traditions: "I actually found that we had more in common than [I had] with a lot of my friends. We both had a spiritual practice; I could relate to him." They decided that they were more likely to pass that sense of religious commitment to their children if they were raised in a single tradition. Explaining their rationale, they used words like "integrity" and "seriousness" that seemed to belie, or at the very least complicate, Ross's contention that he found nothing inherently objectionable to blending Jewish and Christian traditions. Even so, the decision came with mixed feelings. "I do end up saying what seems like a strange sentence, which is like, 'My children are Jewish,' which is not like a normal . . . I feel like I have these two little people who are connected to me more than any other people, and yet it's true that they're kind of members of a group that I'm technically not a member of. And I don't know what will happen with that as time goes on, if that will be stranger or not strange at all or what."

Ross's receptivity to raising the children as Jews stemmed in part from his appreciation that Judaism was an ethnicity as well as a religion. As a white Protestant he felt that his children would benefit in American society from not being "generic." At the same time, however, the recognition became a disincentive to conversion. In fact, the couple was married by a rabbi and belong to a synagogue, which Ross attends a few times a year. Indeed, Ross mentioned that when his mother became sick and ultimately died, the rabbi and the synagogue community were far more demonstratively caring than his priest and Episcopal congregation. He has also recently felt somewhat alienated from his church due to what he characterized as a "vocal anti-Israel minority." Although travel to Israel was highly unusual among the non-Jewish interviewees, Ross has traveled to Israel on multiple occasions to visit Gal's family. Travel to Israel was highly unusual among the non-Jewish interviewees. Only one other non-Jewish respondent reported visiting Israel.

Yet, in spite of this Jewish connectedness, Ross has ruled out conversion as an option, at least for now. Other non-Jewish subjects, like Donna, Leanne, and Jo contemplated conversion but decided against it either because the process was deemed too onerous or because they were afraid that their parents might view it as a rejection. Jewish subjects who were adamant about raising their children as Jews were far more reticent when it came to religious demands on their partners. They regarded the religious identity of their spouses as a matter of personal conviction and did not view conversion as a necessary step to raising Jewish children.

Interfaith couples in this study in many ways resembled the heterosexual couples in other studies, but sexual orientation frequently played a significant role in decision-making about children's religious identity. First, a significant minority of non-Jewish subjects stated that their religion's negative attitudes toward homosexuality made them more receptive to their Jewish partner's arguments in favor of raising their children as Jews. This was particularly common among those who were raised Catholic or within an evangelical Protestant denomination, but also among a couple of mainline Protestants. Nina, a visual artist, raised little objection when her wife, Ophelia, an author, insisted that their son be raised as Jewish. "My father was a Presbyterian minister. So I grew up with a lot of religion," Nina explained. "It was important to me that [our son] be raised in some kind of faith tradition. But, in fact, it would have been very hard for me to raise him as a Christian. It would have been a problem. So it was very convenient that Ophelia wanted to raise him as a Jew."

Some non-Jewish partners were predisposed to support raising their children as Jews because they perceived a sympathetic connection between gayness and Jewishness. Jamie, a graduate student who was raised with elements of both the Catholic and Baptist traditions, began dating his partner Bert while he was in the midst of the surrogacy process. Once he recovered from the initial surprise—"I've never gotten that before on a first date," he quipped—Bert's intention to raise the child as Jewish posed no problem for Jamie. "I consider myself more spiritual than anything else," he said.

> In terms of raising [their daughter] Jewish, it really didn't matter to me. I've always kind of identified with the Jewish religion. I've never understood why they've been so persecuted for so long. It felt very similar to being gay. So there's always kind of an identification with that in some way. I think I really liked that Bert was going to raise her Jewish because I think it is a really special history and heritage, and I think it makes her really special.

## Gender Relations

A third area of difference involved gender relations. As Paula Hyman demonstrated, Victorian gender roles were rapidly internalized by late-nineteenth and early-twentieth-century Jews, including Eastern European immigrants, in Western Europe and North America. With the advent of second-wave feminism and the widespread entry of women into to the workforce, those roles have to some extent been broken down.[34] But the US Labor Department's 2011 American Time Use Survey confirms that while men on average are devoting more time to childcare and household chores than they were a generation ago, these responsibilities continue to fall predominately on women.[35] In her study of intermarried heterosexual couples, Jennifer Thompson found that in those families where a decision was made to raise the children solely within the Jewish faith, the mother typically took on the responsibilities of creating a Jewish home and inculcating Judaism, regardless of her own religious convictions and identification. Thompson argued that those who privileged what she termed "ethnic famialism" over "universalist individualism" tended to lean more heavily on conventional gender roles in which the woman assumed responsibility for children's cultural, religious, and spiritual development.[36] Lesbian and gay couples have long been viewed by scholars as "family outlaws" who "live outside the traditional gender system and are therefore free to construct parental roles and labor arrangements that do not reflect and perpetuate the gender order."[37] Recent studies have complicated this perspective, revealing that while same-sex couples' approach to the division of labor tends to be more flexible and "proactively constructed," they are "by no means fully insulated from dominant institutional understandings of marital and parenting roles."[38] Thus, while decisions about childcare and housework are more typically divided on the basis of preference or a variety of practical considerations, same-sex couples often perpetuate gender stereotypes related to breadwinners and caregivers.[39]

Nevertheless, same-sex couples tend to share childcare responsibilities more evenly than heterosexual couples.[40] There was some evidence of this dynamic among couples with a more polarized division of labor, although it was by no means universal. Thus, Barry, who by virtue of his less demanding and more flexible job in the high-tech sector spends more time with his young daughter than his husband, Max, worries that friends and co-workers might question his masculinity. But José in Florida, the sole breadwinner in his marriage, whose husband Jason cares for their twins, casually referred to himself as "a little flamer" when recounting how he felt repressed due to the "heterosexist," "machismo culture" of the Jewish overnight camp he attended as a child. Moreover, there was little observable connection between traditional gender stereotypes and responsibility for religious and cultural upbringing of children. For example, subjects seldom spoke about domestic ritual observance, synagogue attendance, or assuming responsibility for the logistics of religious school attendance using gender-coded language. Parental involvement was more typically dictated by interest and considerations such as work schedules, although in cases where one parent acted as the primary caregiver, he or she was more likely to be primarily responsible for heritage transmission. Ten subjects (11%) reported that they were stay-at-home parents, while another thirteen (14%) reported working part-time. In some cases the parent who was deemed more Jewishly knowledgeable assumed primary responsibility for orchestrating holiday observances and taking children to synagogue and religious school. In others, as with Anne and Beth, inexperienced parents used their children's Jewish education as an opportunity to expand their own knowledge base and develop a greater degree of ritual and linguistic competency.

Finally, many female couples expressed discomfort around *brit milah*, or ritual circumcision. At least four of the interfaith female couples in the study chose not to circumcise their sons (the exact number is uncertain as interviewers did not directly ask about this ritual). As Naomi Schaefer Riley observed, it is hardly unusual for birth ceremonies to become flashpoints for conflict for interfaith couples.[41] Circumcision, in particular, can be contentious if one of the partners comes from a culture where the ritual is uncommon. While this was not the case for the interview subjects in this study, some objected to circumcision on ethical, medical, or aesthetic grounds. Reflecting their own squeamishness with the process, some Jewish women were at a loss to defend the practice liturgically when their non-Jewish partners raised objections. Others had their own qualms about the ritual and were more than willing to assent to their partners' wishes.

For Penny and her wife, Zoë, a couple in their mid-thirties, the decision not to circumcise their son came after much deliberation. Zoë, who is not Jewish and spent her childhood steeped in Eastern religious traditions, was opposed to circumcision from the outset, and the intensity of her feelings caused Penny to take a second look at a ritual that she had not much considered. "A lot of times she's given me a totally new lens on whatever Jewish ritual," Penny observed, "just because she doesn't take for granted that it has to be done." Once Penny began doing her own research, she found that the medical community was more divided on the efficacy of circumcision than she had believed, and she discovered a growing body of evidence that infants as young as eight days old feel pain. Speaking in the language of the sovereign self,[42] Penny explained: "I think for me it was more the fact that I didn't feel comfortable performing unnecessary or irreversible surgery on my newborn just because that's what we've done for thousands of years. Because now that I'm an adult and I'm making my own decisions, I don't do hardly anything because we've been doing it for thousands of years. The rituals that we do are because they're meaningful to us."

Even when both parents agreed not to ritually circumcise their son, the choice often generated conflict between the couple and the family of the Jewish partner. When Penny shared the couple's decision not to circumcise their son with her Orthodox parents, they were livid. The road to their acceptance of Penny's sexuality and her relationship with Zoë had been long and rocky. Penny's father had refused to attend the couple's wedding, and both parents insisted that she keep her orientation and relationship a secret in their community to avoid jeopardizing their other children's marriage prospects. The expectation of being grandparents had considerably softened them, and Penny's Syrian father even asked her to name a child for him.[43] With the decision not to circumcise her son, Penny was endangering their tenuous relationship. "At first he was just shell shocked . . . And then once he got over the shock, he started just lobbying hard. I think he said, 'If I have ever done anything for you, you will do this for me,' which is a pretty big statement to make about something that nobody is ever going find out about." Penny and Zoë briefly considered relenting in return for Penny's parents paying their children's tuition at a progressive synagogue preschool, but Penny says, "we ultimately decided we were unwilling to sacrifice my kid's foreskin" for a "bribe." As it turned out, Penny's parents were unwilling to forfeit a relationship with their grandchildren over principle. "They are very involved grandparents when they come to visit," Penny reports. "And I'm sure every time they change the diaper they get so mad."

Even endogamous female couples sometimes struggled with *brit milah*. Rollin and Shira, a young couple, recalled their son's ritual circumcision as one of the most disturbing events in their lives together. "That was horrible," Rollin exclaimed. Shira quickly chimed in: "Yeah, I hope I never have to do that again. Other than when we've had to like deal with mice in the house, I think that was the only other time we both were like, 'I wish there was a man in this relationship to make this decision.' It didn't feel right as two women deciding, like, 'I don't know if we should cut that off or not!' " When Janet and Michal decided to ritually circumcise their son they found a *mohel* (ritual circumciser) who was also a pediatric surgeon and was willing to give the baby an injection to ease the pain. Even so, neither mother could bring herself to watch the ritual.

## Conclusions

As the interviewer was about to thank Josh for his participation in the study, he said,

> People would be surprised at how typical family life is regardless of how many and who the parents are. In the end, we all still have to potty train. And we all still have to teach right from wrong and give swimming les-

> sons and bike-riding lessons and all that stuff. And the kid doesn't know the difference. They still need to learn all these things. And the parents, whoever they might be, are the only ones who can teach them. So in the end, [a same-sex couple family] may seem subversive or counter cultural . . . [but] we're the family that we are, and we're the family that we know, and we live and exist in that family everyday and that's all that we can do."

He added that "it feels exceedingly normal to be the family that we are. And we don't wake up every day thinking, 'Gosh, I'm so unique and really breaking down barriers every day.' There's too much else going on to sit around and think about that—the ground you're breaking."

Josh's observation was driven home repeatedly and consistently by the interview subjects. Same-sex couples sounded remarkably (or unremarkably) like their heterosexual counterparts when discussing matters profound and mundane related to childrearing. While their status as a same-sex couple factored into decision-making about such matters as synagogue affiliation, their children's religious education, and how they divided household responsibilities, it was seldom considered in isolation.

Other equally significant points emerge from the data. First, the decision to raise Jewish children had an important influence on choices that the couple made as they determined their route to parenthood. Whether they chose adoption, surrogacy, or alternative insemination, prospective parents were mindful of how the child would be perceived in their community. They were also mindful of how their choices would potentially affect emotional bonding with their child. The paths that they chose were also diverse and sometimes distinctive, reflecting their own circumstances and dispositions. For example, some viewed a biological connection to their child as critical to fostering a sense of Jewish connectedness, while others were moved by Jewish values. Still others were focused on the traditional legal definition of Jewishness. What most had in common was a desire for familiarity while navigating a process that often felt awkward, disconnected, and even unnatural.

Second, a welcoming and embracing community, coupled with a support system comprising friends and family played a significant, if not decisive, role in facilitating and buttressing same-sex couple families' Jewish involvement. In the twenty-first century, the decision to raise children as Jews, whether in the context of an endogamous or interfaith relationship is a choice. Thus, the impetus to nurture Jewishness in a family's children must begin with the convictions of at least one of the parents. There were subjects in endogamous relationships whose decision-making process about their children's religious identity was initially reflexive or passive. Ultimately, however, they too were confronted with choices about matters ranging from lifecycle ceremonies to education that had a major impact on the substance and content of their children's Jewish connections. When both parents' visions were aligned, they served to reinforce one another's, particularly during times of adversity, and they became one another's most vital basis of support. Nonetheless, subjects in this study looked to a variety of individuals and institutions to share the responsibilities and to enhance the sense of meaning that underlay the enterprise of raising children as Jews in the Jewish community.

Third, while the Jewish community has become more accepting of homosexuality, same-sex marriage, and gay parenting, Orthodox and religiously traditional same-sex couple families continue to face adversity and significant barriers to communal integration. Among the most poignant moments in the interviews came when couples described how they were met with rejection when they tried to join Orthodox synagogues or enroll their children in Orthodox Jewish day schools. Likewise, Orthodox subjects often shared gut-wrenching coming-out stories and prolonged periods of alienation from religiously traditional family members, sometimes gradually eased by only the most tenuous of reconciliations. These stories should not obscure the distance that segments of the Orthodox community have traveled on the issue of homosexuality over the past twenty years in response to medical and psychological research, changes in secular culture and law, and a greater awareness of and empathy for the LGBTQ Jews in their midst. Moreover, as Patrick and Manny discovered, pockets of tolerance and compassion can sometimes be found in seemingly unlikely places, particularly when the gay or lesbian "other" is revealed to be insider.

Fourth, on a Jewish communal policy-making level, the prevalence of interfaith relationships among gay and lesbian Jews makes interfaith outreach critical to the retention of LGBTQ Jews and their children. By virtue of their commitment to raise their children as Jews, the interfaith couples who participated in this study were predisposed to Jewish engagement, whether on a religious or cultural level. While the parameters of Jewishness varied from couple to couple, they shared a basic sympathy for Jewish tradition and practice. When proverbial doors were opened for them, they were inclined to look inside. Consider Andrew and Scott, the couple described at the beginning of this article. It never occurred to them to send their child to day school. But, when they were encouraged by friends to check the school out, they were won over by the warm and accepting atmosphere, and the unambiguous message that they not only would they be embraced as a same-sex couple family, but that Scott would be welcome as a non-Jewish parent.

It would be imprudent to generalize from the interview subjects to the wider population. Nevertheless, comparing the level of Jewish engagement of synagogue members in the study to non-synagogue members yields striking results. Interfaith couples who were members of synagogues almost universally enrolled their children in a religious school or day school. They were also more likely to enroll their young children in P. J. Library (a free Jewish book- and DVD-of-the-month program for children) and to report that "some" or "most" of their friends were Jewish. While it requires more study to determine whether there is a causal relationship between synagogue membership and these other markers of engagement, it seems fair to conclude, as Cohen and others do elsewhere,[44] that such Jewish commitments are mutually reinforcing.

Finally, like other American Jews, gay and lesbian Jewish parents feel empowered to make their own decisions in matters of religion and childrearing. They are unwilling to countenance a conflict between their gay and Jewish identities. Even the most observant subjects did not frame their gayness as a challenge to their aspirations in the realms of Judaism or parenting. Whereas a generation or two ago many LGBTQ Jews viewed their sexual and religious identities as irreconcilable,[45] the Jewish subjects in this study placed the onus on the Jewish community to accept them as they are or, as in the case of Patrick and Manny, not to penalize their children for their parents' decision to live openly and unapologetically as a gay couple. No doubt this attitude is partially a function of the ascendancy of the sovereign self as documented by Steven Cohen and Arnold Eisen.[46] It is also symptomatic of what Sylvia Barack Fishman termed coalescence, "a pervasive process through which American Jews [instinctively] merge American and Jewish ideas, incorporating American liberal values . . . into their understanding of Jewish identity."[47] But, it is also likely connected to the condition of parenthood. As Jonah, a 47-year-old teacher from the Boston area, observed, "Parenting focuses the mind and forces you to let go of petty concerns. And on the flip side of the coin, I find that as a parent I have a lot less tolerance for other people's hang ups . . . I can't worry if other people disapprove of my sexuality and our decision to raise a family. Life is too short and I'm too busy." One suspects that these sentiments will resonate with many parents regardless of religion, gender, or sexual orientation.

## NOTES

The author is grateful to his wonderful research assistants, Ryan Daniels and Yael Rooks-Rapport, and thanks Dr. Steven M. Cohen for his invaluable assistance in running data on LGBT Jews from the Jewish Community Study of New York: 2011. He also expresses his deep appreciation to the Hebrew Union College-Jewish Institute of Religion and, particularly, Provost Rabbi Michael Marmur, Ph.D., for providing funding for this research.

1. All names of subjects in this article are pseudonyms.
2. Abbie Goldberg, *Gay Dads: Transitions to Adoptive Fatherhood* (New York: New York University Press, 2012), 61.
3. Amy Agigian, *Baby Steps: How Lesbian Alternative Insemination Is Changing the World* (Middletown, CT: Wesleyan University Press, 2004); Jennifer Chabot and Barbara Ames, "It Wasn't 'Let's Get Pregnant and Go Do It': Decision-Making in Lesbian Couples Planning Motherhood via Donor Insemination," *Family Relations* 53 (2004): 348–56; Gerald Mallon, *Gay Men Choosing Parenthood* (New York: Columbia University Press, 2004); Abbie Goldberg, "The Transition to Parenthood for Lesbian Couples," *Journal of GLBT Family Studies* 2 (2006): 13–42; Adital Ben-Ari and Tali Livni, "Motherhood Is Not a Given Thing: Experiences and Constructed Meanings of Biological and Non-Biological Lesbian Mothers," *Sex Roles* 54 (2006): 521–31; Abbie Goldberg, "Lesbian and Heterosexual Preadoptive Couples' Openness to Transracial Adoption," *American Journal of Orthopsychiatry* 79 (2009): 103–17; Stephen Hicks, "Queer Genealogies: Tales of Conformity and Rebellion Amongst Lesbian and Gay Foster Carers and Adopters," *Qualitative Social Work: Research & Practice* 4 (2005):293–308; Dana Berkowitz and William Marsiglio, "A Socio-Historical Analysis of Gay Men's Procreative Consciousness," *Journal of GLBT Family Studies* 3 (2007): 157–90; Abbie Goldberg and Katherine Allen, *LGBT-Parent Families Innovations in Research and Implications for Practice* (New York: Springer, 2013).
4. Abbie Goldberg, *Gay Dads*, 137–38, 152–53.
5. Lynn Shelley-Sireci and Claudia Ciano-Boyce, "Becoming Lesbian Adoptive Parents: An Exploratory Study of Lesbian Adoptive, Lesbian Birth, and Heterosexual Adoptive Parents," *Adoption Quarterly* 6 (2002): 33–43; Abbie Goldberg, "Lesbian and Heterosexual Preadoptive Couples' Openness to Transracial Adoption."
6. Abbie Goldberg, *Lesbian and Gay Parents and Their Children*, 180–83.
7. Same-sex marriage was legal in six states when the data was collected. By November 20, 2013, same-sex marriage had been legalized in sixteen states.
8. U.S. Census Bureau, *Frequently Asked Questions about Same-Sex Couple Households* (Washington, DC: US Census Bureau, Fertility and Family Statistics, August 2013), www.census.gov/hhes/samesex/files/SScplfactsheet_final.pdf.
9. Statistics Canada, *Portrait of Families and Living Arrangements in Canada* (Ottawa: Minister of Industry, 2011), www12.statcan.ca/census-recensement/2011/as-sa/98-312-x/98-312-x2011001-eng.cfm.
10. Steven M. Cohen, Caryn Aviv, and Ari Kelman, "Gay, Jewish, or Both? Sexual Orientation and Jewish Engagement," *Journal of Jewish Communal Service* 84 (2009): 154–66.
11. Steven M. Cohen, Jack Ukeles, and Ron Miller, *Jewish Community Study of New York: 2011 Comprehensive Report* (New York: UJA-Federation of New York, 2012).
12. Pew Research Center, *Growing Support for Gay Marriage: Changed Minds and Changing Demographics* (Washington, DC: Pew Research Center, 2013), www.people-press.org/2013/03/20/growing-support-for-gay-marriage-changed-minds-and-changing-demographics.
13. Pew Research Center, *A Portrait of Jewish Americans* (Washington, DC: Pew Research Center, 2013), www.pewforum.org/2013/10/01/chapter-6-social-and-political-views.
14. Pew, "Same-Sex Marriage Detailed Tables," in *Growing Support*, www.people-press.org/files/legacy-detailed_tables/Gay%20marriage%20detailed%20tables.pdf.

15. Caryn Aviv, Steven M. Cohen, and Judith Veinstein, "Welcoming Synagogues Project: Preliminary Results from the 2009 Synagogue Survey on Diversity and LGBT Inclusion" (Los Angeles: Institute for Judaism and Sexual Orientation, and Jewish Mosaic: The National Center for Sexual and Gender Diversity, 2009).
16. The cross-tabulations were run and shared with me by Steven M. Cohen, who emphasized that there are not enough cases to make reliable statements about subcategories (such as LGBT Jews with children at home) within the LGBT sample. See Cohen, Ukeles, and Miller, *Jewish Community Study of New York* for an explanation of how the Jewish engagement index was created.
17. Abbie Goldberg, *Lesbian and Gay Parents and Their Children: Research on the Family Lifecycle* (Washington, DC: American Psychological Association, 2010); Abbie Goldberg and Katherine Allen, *LGBT-Parent Families: Innovations in Research and Implications for Practice* (New York: Springer, 2013).
18. See, for example, Julie Mooney-Somers, Susan Golombok, "Children of Lesbian Mothers: From the 1970s to the New Millennium," *Sexual and Relationship Therapy* 15 (2000): 121–26; Charlotte Patterson, "Family Relationships of Lesbians and Gay Men," *Journal of Marriage and Family* 62 (2000): 1052–69; Judith Stacey and Timothy Biblarz, "(How) Does the Sexual Orientation of Parents Matter?" *American Sociological Review* 66 (2001):159–83.
19. An interview protocol was designed and administered by the author and two research assistants, although interviewers were encouraged to ask follow-up questions as warranted. Couples could choose whether to be interviewed separately or together, and most chose the latter. Couples who chose to be interviewed separately were typically motivated by childcare and work-schedule considerations. In cases where couples were interviewed together, interviews were often concluded in a little less than two hours, but ranged between approximately 75 and 150 minutes. Single interviews typically lasted about 70 minutes, but ranged between 45 and 90 minutes. Subjects were found through a combination of snowball sampling and online advertising on a variety of social networking sites. Sixty-six subjects identified as female, twenty-three as male, and one listed their gender as "other." The gender breakdown was consistent with the higher rates of childrearing among lesbian couple families. None of the subjects were raising children born into a previous heterosexual marriage. Nineteen single and couple interviews were conducted via Skype and twelve were conducted in person. The remaining interviews were conducted over the phone. All of the interviews were recorded and transcribed verbatim. In an initial round of interviews, subjects were enlisted from the so-called Amtrak corridor (between Boston and Washington, DC). A second round recruited subjects primarily from the West, Southeast, and the Upper Midwest. In total, twenty-eight subjects resided in the Central Atlantic region, twenty in New England, twenty in the West, ten in the Southeast, and twelve in the Upper Midwest and Canada.
20. Cohen, Aviv, and Kelman, "Gay, Jewish, or Both?"
21. Of the subjects that identified themselves as Jewish, 34% considered themselves to be Reform, 19% Conservative, 17% Reconstructionist, 5% Orthodox, and 3% Renewal. The remaining 22% were unaffiliated. The 2011 New York study LGBT sample, which included respondents who identified as non-Jewish, found that 3.7% identified as Orthodox, 10% as Conservative, 25.8% as Reform, and 1.1% as Reconstructionist. The remainder were unaffiliated, professed no religion, or identified with another faith tradition (data shared with the author by study coauthor Steven M. Cohen).
22. Cohen, Aviv, and Kelman, "Gay, Jewish, or Both?"

23. Randal Schnoor and Morton Weinfeld, "Seeking a Mate: Inter-Group Partnerships among Gay Jewish Men," *Canadian Ethnic Studies* 37 (2005): 21–39.
24. See for example the basic requirements for sperm donors on the websites of the California Cryobank (www.spermbank.com/how-it-works/sperm-donor-requirements) and the New England Cryogenic Center (www.necryogenic.com/become-a-donor.php).
25. Jennifer Chabot and Barbara Ames, "It Wasn't 'Let's Get Pregnant and Go Do It.'"
26. Michael Broyde, "The Establishment of Maternity and Paternity in Jewish and American Law," *National Jewish Law Review* 3 (1988): 117–52; David Golinkin, "What Does Jewish Law Have to Say about Surrogacy?" *Responsa in a Moment* 7 (2012).
27. Michael Broyde, "The Establishment of Maternity and Paternity"; Shelley Kapnek Rosenberg, *Adoption and the Jewish Family: Contemporary Perspectives* (Philadelphia, PA: Jewish Publication Society, 1998).
28. Gary Gates, Lee Badgett, Jennifer Macomber, and Kate Chambers, *Adoption and Foster Care by Gay and Lesbian Parents in the United States* (Washington, DC: Urban Institute, 2007). Abbie Goldberg, "Lesbian and Heterosexual Preadoptive Couples' Openness."
29. Ira Sheskin, "The Jewish Demography of Florida," Berman Jewish Policy Archive, 2011, www.bjpa.org/Publications/details.cfm?PublicationID=13566.
30. Shanto Iyengar, Gaurav Sood, and Yphtach Lelkes, "Affect, not Ideology: A Social Identity Perspective on Polarization," *Public Opinion Quarterly* 76 (2012).
31. On heterosexual interfaith marriage see Sylvia Barack Fishman, *Double or Nothing? Jewish Families and Mixed Marriage* (Hanover, NH: Brandeis University Press, 2008); Naomi Schaefer Riley, *'Til Faith Do Us Part: How Interfaith Marriage Is Transforming America* (New York: Oxford University Press, 2013); Jennifer Thompson, *Jewish on Their Own Terms: How Intermarried Couples are Changing American Judaism* (New Brunswick, NJ: Rutgers University Press, 2013); Keren McGinity, *Still Jewish: A History of Women and Intermarriage in America* (New York: New York University Press, 2009).
32. Barack Fishman, *Double or Nothing?*, 73.
33. Samuel Freedman, "For Interfaith Gay Couples Just One Obstacle Is Cleared," *New York Times*, November 1, 2013, A17.
34. Paula Hyman, *Gender and Assimilation in Modern Jewish History: Roles and Representations of Women* (Seattle: University of Washington Press, 1995).
35. US Bureau of Labor Statistics, *Married Parents' Use of Time, 2003–2006* (Washington, DC: US Department of Labor, 2008), www.bls.gov/news.release/atus2.nr0.htm.
36. Thompson, *Jewish on Their Own Terms.*
37. Abbie Goldberg, *Lesbian and Gay Parents and Their Children*, 99.
38. Susan Dalton and Denise Bielby, "That's Our Kind of Constellation: Lesbian Mothers Negotiate Institutionalized Understandings of Gender within the Family," *Gender and Society* 14 (2000): 36–61.
39. Christopher Carrington, *No Place Like Home: Relationships and Family Life among Lesbians and Gay Men* (Chicago: University of Chicago Press, 2002).
40. Raymond Chan, Risa Brooks, Barbara Raboy, and Charlotte Patterson, "Division of Labor among Lesbian and Heterosexual Parents: Associations with Children's Adjustments," *Journal of Family Psychology* 12 (1998): 402–19.
41. Riley, *'Til Faith Do Us Part*, 86–88.
42. The term was popularized in the Jewish context by Steven M. Cohen and Arnold Eisen in *The Jew Within: Self, Family and Community in America* (Bloomington: Indiana University Press, 2000).

43. Syrian Jews traditionally name their firstborn sons for the paternal grandfather, even if he is not deceased. As a maternal grandfather, Penny's father was making a somewhat unusual request, a point that Hannah raised with him in the course of their circumcision argument.
44. Steven M. Cohen, *A Tale of Two Jewries: The "Inconvenient Truth" for American Jews* (New York: Jewish Life Network/Steinhardt Foundation, 2006); Steven M. Cohen, Jack Ukeles, and Ron Miller, *Jewish Community Study of New York*.
45. Moshe Shokeid, *A Gay Synagogue in New York* (New York: Columbia University Press, 2002).
46. Cohen and Eisen, *The Jew Within*.
47. Sylvia Barack Fishman, *Jewish Life and American Culture* (Albany: State University of New York Press, 2000), 1.

# 4

## Gays and Lesbians in Israel

*An Overview*

Irit Koren

HOMOSEXUALS IN ISRAEL occupy a position that is fascinating for many reasons, not least because their lives and experience provide a microcosm for observing a challenge that engages all of Israel—negotiating the fine line between the religious guidelines for behavior espoused by traditional Jewish societies and modern democratic values that protect individual freedom of choice. Israel is the only democratic country in the Middle East, but it is also one of the few modern countries in which religion and the state are still legally intertwined. This mixture creates distinctive complexity on many social issues, a complexity that is acutely reflected in the status of gay and lesbian individuals and communities. This chapter examines the issue of gays and lesbians in Israel, focusing on four issues that reflect the uniqueness of Israeli society, culture, and politics. To accurately portray public attitudes toward issues of gay families, which have undergone tremendous changes in the last few years, I draw primarily on academic studies supplemented with newspaper articles, television shows, published research, Internet sites, and other popular-culture references.

My study finds that Israel has made significant progress toward instituting personal freedoms for gay and lesbian citizens, which makes Israel more similar to liberal, humanist countries in the West than to its neighbors. However, Israel has not completely disentangled marriage and family life for gay and lesbian communities from religious and fundamentalist forces that exert pressure for exclusionary laws and social norms. In this regard, Israel is different from many Western democracies in that rabbinic decisors have government standing regarding certain personal status issues, such as marriage and parental status (see Susan Weiss, chapter 11 in this volume).

The history of gay and lesbian Jews in Israel falls into two distinct social-historical eras. The first era, from the establishment of the state until the 1980s, can be characterized as the "age of absence." During these years homosexuals and lesbians had no overt presence in the public arena, including the media, the education system, legislation, etc. The second era, from the beginning of the 1990s until the present, saw the start of the "age of presence." During this time the gay and lesbian community achieved impressive representation in all areas of society—political, social, the media, and the arts.[1]

Israel has made enormous cultural and legislative strides in the past twenty years. However, these changes have had surprisingly little effect on the gay and lesbian community. Changes in their public presence seem not to have increased the sense of well-being for either youth or adults. The uneasiness gays and lesbians feel is reflected in the difficulty many experience in coming out to society in general and to their families in particular. One possible explanation for this phenomenon is the gap that exists between Israel's liberal cultural and legislative accomplishments and the general conservatism that still characterizes Israeli society with respect to homosexuality. This conservatism manifests in the social struggle over accepting gays and lesbians as full members of the Jewish community,[2] as this essay will demonstrate.

I examine the situation of gays and lesbians in Israel by looking at four significant issues in the lives of Israelis:

(1) Laws and the legislative institution

(2) Homosexual family life and child bearing

(3) Homosexuals and religion and religious homosexuals

(4) Homosexuals and the Israeli army

These issues might seem somewhat arbitrary. However, I believe that they can help shed light on the complicated, unique factors that Israeli gay and lesbian people must address.

## Laws and the Legislative Institution

Israel does not have a constitution, as many other Western countries do. However, it has basic laws that serve as the foundation of its legal system. One of these laws forbid "unnatural" sexual intercourse between any two people. Although the instruction was general, public and legislative discourse created a connection between "unnatural" sexual intercourse and same-sex intercourse, and the punishment for this crime was up to ten years in prison. The law forbidding unnatural intercourse remained in place,[3] and it was not eliminated until 1988.[4] From this first dramatic legislative shift stemmed many other changes. Beginning in the early 1990s Israel made major alterations to its laws to accommodate the gay and lesbian population and give it more rights and equality—for example, the 1991 law that forbade discrimination by employers on the basis of sexual orientation. However, many of these relatively liberal laws were passed because of individual lawsuits, rather than as a result of an official public policy aimed at giving gays and lesbians equal rights in the realm of sexuality and family life.[5]

Most of the laws that were passed confer acknowledgment and economic rights on the significant other in a gay or lesbian couple, for example with respect to division of property or the transfer of financial benefits from the state to a significant other when one half of a same-sex couple who works for the IDF or the state dies. One of the most significant court cases produced the law of Danilevitz, passed in 1994, which required the Israeli airline El-Al to give the partner of a gay male flight attendant the same flight rights that partners of straight couples received. Other laws acknowledge the significant other as the guardian of the partner's biological child, allow the significant other to adopt the partner's biological child, and protect people in single-sex couples from violent partners.[6]

These laws are impressive from a legal point of view, and they contribute significantly to the liberalism of daily life in Israel. However, the state retains many conservative approaches toward same-sex marriage. In Israel, there is no civil marriage or divorce; one can be married only by a religious institution. For Jews, this institution is the Israeli Rabbinate, which does not acknowledge gay and lesbian marriages. Because of a lawsuit filed in 2007, Israel does currently recognize gay civil marriages that are performed outside the country.[7] In other cases, gay and lesbian couples have official common-law status, which means that laws affecting heterosexual couples apply to them as well in matters of divorce or separation.[8]

There are also many areas in which the law still discriminates against gays and lesbians. For example, Israel does not allow same-sex couples to use surrogacy to have a child, whereas heterosexual couples may do so. This particular law affects mainly male homosexual couples, since lesbians can conceive a child using sperm donation. I believe that this particular form of discrimination is especially significant in a country that values family life and views a couple, whether heterosexual or gay, as a family unit only when children are part of the picture.

## Gay Family Life

The unique situation of Israeli gays and lesbians with respect to family life stems from a combination of two factors. The first is Israel's pronatalism, which extends to the homosexual community. Second, as mentioned earlier, religion and the state are intertwined, such that Israeli society and laws perform a delicate dance between modernity and tradition. These two factors affect the character of the country as a whole and the situation of gays and lesbians in particular. In Israel today there are eighteen thousand single-sex couples. Among lesbian couples more than twenty-five hundred (25%) raise children together, and among the gay couples a few hundred (7%) raise children, and these numbers are growing. Some even describe the gay family as a unique subculture developing in Israel, specifically in Tel Aviv. According to different estimates, in no other country in the world do so many gays and lesbians have children.[9]

The gay and lesbian community has a strong presence, especially in Tel-Aviv, which became a magnet for gays and lesbians because of both the tolerance shown by the city and the services it provides this community.[10] In Tel Aviv one can witness a baby-friendly homosexual scene that reflects the baby boom within the larger Israeli homosexual community in the last few years. Since 2008 the number of Israeli men who have children through a surrogacy process in the United States or India has constantly increased. However, after the baby is born, only the biological father is recognized as a parent; the spouse must start a tedious process of adoption that takes several years. Moreover, most homosexual couples who start this process usually want more than one child, because "[in] Israel, one is not even enough," as Ron Poole Dayan, a gay father of three who married his spouse in Canada, declared.[11] Thus the couple faces a legal struggle that will last many years to get the state to recognize their parenthood regardless of who the biological father is. In addition, they must undertake a struggle for the children's Jewish identity to be recognized. Although these children are born to Jewish Israeli men, the issue of their Jewish identity is complicated, since according to Orthodox doctrine Judaism is transmitted through the mother, and that is the doctrine followed by the state.

## The Jewish Identity of Children Born to Gay Couples

One might think that a baby born to a gay or lesbian Jewish couple would automatically be Jewish as well. However, this is not the case in Israel. A gay Jewish couple who want to raise children together must spend an enormous amount of money and jump through a great many complicated bureaucratic hoops to have a child. Nor does this stressful process end once they bring the baby to Israel, for the mother is usually not Jewish, and therefore the Rabbinate does not acknowledge the Jewishness of the child. Even if the mother is Jewish, the Rabbinate has a problem accepting the Jewishness of a child raised by a gay couple. To make matters even more complicated, there is a *halakhic* argument over the question "What makes a child Jewish?" Is it the identity of the egg donor or the identity of the surrogate mother? The notion today is that even if the egg donor is halakhically Jewish (according to Orthodox *halakhah*) and the surrogate mother who carries the baby in her womb is not Jewish, the child is not Jewish.

Of course, the problem of converting a non-Jewish child who is the product either of a non-Jewish egg donation or gestation by a non-Jewish surrogate mother is shared by all couples in Israel who use medically assisted technology, heterosexual and homosexual. However, a heterosexual couple who adopt a non-Jewish child abroad has the choice to convert the child on condition that they declare they are living according to Jewish law and will give the child a religious education (a problem in itself for couples who are not religious).[12] For a homosexual couple, however, this option is not available. The Rabbinate conversion board does not accept homosexual couples and therefore will not convert babies who will be brought up by such a couple. Nor would it help to have the baby converted through the Reform or Conservative movement, since the Orthodox Rabbinate does not recognize these conversions and thus the child would not be recognized by the state as Jewish. Some couples consider this a problem because such children will experience discrimination throughout their lives: the boys will not count as members of an Orthodox *minyan* (religious quorum of ten men required for prayer); both girls and boys might have trouble getting into a religious school; both girls and boys will probably have trouble later on getting married in a religious service in Israel—the only marriage ceremony the state recognizes; and chances are that these children eventually will not be buried in a Jewish cemetery. These are only some of the problems they may encounter. Couples also seek the approval of the Orthodox Rabbinate for the sake of their parents—the children's grandparents—who might be Orthodox or traditional. One gay father expressed this feeling by saying, "I do want my children to be able to go to synagogue with my father." [13]

Some rabbis may suggest that these couples consider not telling the truth about their situation, or creating coparenting arrangements instead of surrogacy. That is, a couple of gay men might team up with a Jewish woman to create a "fictive family" to enable their children to be recognized as Jewish. Another suggested solution is to approach the Rabbinate as a single parent rather than a gay couple. However, these suggestions are not relevant for most gay couples, who do not want to live under false pretenses. As a consequence, most couples don't convert their children, who remain registered as Israelis with "no religion."[14]

## Homosexuals and Religion and Religious Homosexuals

While most gay and lesbian couples in Israel are not religious, living as a homosexual in Israel forces one, whether religious or not, to interact at some level with the traditional religious elements that characterize the state. For religious gays and lesbians in Israel, those interactions are both intense and complex. This subgroup of the Israeli homosexual community lives with a double identity, with each part of their identity contradicting the other. Moreover, they experience a dual marginality: as religious people in the gay community and as gay people in the religious community.[15]

For a religious gay person, especially a man, creating a coherent, reconciled identity as a homosexual Orthodox Jew poses fundamental challenges. Among the central challenges is the commitment to upholding a tradition that condemns and punishes homosexuality. For men, the source of the prohibition against homosexual intercourse is the Bible, specifically the book of Leviticus 18:22: "Do not lie with a male as one lies with a woman." This prohibition is repeated in Leviticus 20:13: "If a man lies with a male as one lies with a woman, the two of them have done an abhorrent thing; they shall be put to death—their bloodguilt is upon them." The Bible does not consider "homosexuals" as a category; rather it focuses on the forbidden act—male penetration. The emphasis is on the "doing," not on the "being." For women, there is no direct prohibition in the Bible. The direct prohibition for female homosexual acts first appears in the Talmud (and thus is considered less severe than a prohibition originating in the Bible). The Talmud (Tract. Yevamot, 1) says that women who are *mesolelot* are forbidden for the priesthood. That is, they are not allowed to marry a priest, since they are not considered complete virgins. The commentators argue about the meaning of the word mesolelot and conclude that it refers to sexual intercourse in which women rub their intimate parts against each other. It seems that the distinction often seen today—that homophobia about male homosexuality is much stronger than homophobia about lesbianism—is reflected in the canonical texts, which regard male homosexuality more seriously and punish it more severely than female homosexuality.

It is important to understand the central role these texts and their interpretations play in the lives of all Orthodox Jews, and specifically gay Jews.[16] To make peace with their gay identity, some religious gays and lesbians engage in a complex process of interpreting biblical law, as well as the vast rabbinic literature that interprets and elaborates on the biblical precepts. The fact that the Bible explicitly prohibits male intercourse but does not explicitly mention same-sex female intercourse explains why religious gay men must put more effort into trying to solve the contradiction between their sexual orientation and the Jewish sources compared to lesbian women, who focus more on family and social aspects of this issue.[17]

Although the religious legal issues posed by halakhah remain, this community has gone through a tremendous social change in the last decade. When my book *Altering the Closet* (in Hebrew, "A Closet within a Closet") was published in 2003, there was no acknowledgment of the LGBT population from the religious establishment and very few support groups for the community. Since then many support groups for both men and women have been created. One such group is Hod (glory), for religious homosexuals. Hod's website defines itself as "the first independent website written by Orthodox Jewish gay men, for Orthodox Jewish gay men, that is not affiliated with any organization or political movement." The forum is for religious men who are part "of the religious community, and who wish to remain part of it." The group claims that they wish to keep both their religious and gay identities, and that their aim is to "lead to a more tolerant dialogue in our society."

Another organization for religious gays is Havruta (study partners),[18] which "offers a social and support network for religious LGBT people in Israel." This organization actively works to "inform and educate the religious public about LGBT issues in their communities." They claim that because of their work, some religious leaders and rabbis are now speaking publicly about LGBT issues. The third large organization is KAMOHA (like You, an allusion to liturgical language), which is considered more strictly religious. This organization has established a fascinating project called ANACHNU (literally, "we"),[19] "a match-making project, the first of its kind, that matches Torah-observant gays with Torah-observant lesbians, and vice versa. In this project, all of the cards are open, and without the lies, half-truths, and 'mistakes,' because both participants know very well the nature of the prospective spouse's orientation." Rabbi Arelah Harel founded this project, whose goal is to help Orthodox gay and lesbian Jews establish a family.

There is only one exclusively religious female organization, called Bat-Kol ("echo," or "daughter of the voice"), which was established in 2005. Bat-Kol holds meetings regularly and offers a variety of social activities for religious lesbians. These meetings provide a social framework as well as support and encouragement. Bat-Kol's activities also provide educational resources geared toward the full integration of lesbians in the religious community."[20]

Rabbis in Israel hold different attitudes on this issue. Some leading rabbis such as Rav Aviner deny the phenomenon of religious gays. (See the introduction to this volume for Rav Aviner's stringencies regarding female modest clothing.) He writes on Internet sites and elsewhere that "there is no such thing as a religious Ho" (he will not even spell the whole word "homosexual").[21] Aviner believes and promotes the notion that homosexuality is an expression of human beings' inclination toward evil and a condition that can be cured. He advises people who consult him to get treatment in a project he founded called Atzat Nefesh (advice or guidance for the soul). It is run by volunteers who attempt to help gay men become straight via conversion therapy.

Nonetheless, I believe that because of the strength of the support groups for religious gays and lesbians, and the wide use of the Internet that enables many gays and lesbians to address their questions and issues to rabbis anonymously, increasing numbers of rabbis are responding to this community more seriously and sensitively than Aviner. These tolerant rabbis realize that the presence and integration of LGBT people into religious communities are serious social phenomena that cannot be ignored any longer.[22] One prominent rabbi who has been responding positively is Rav Yuval Sherlo, who encourages gay men to stay in their religious community and promotes their acceptance by the community, although he does not allow homosexual sexual intercourse.[23] In addition to the emergence of moderate rabbinical voices inside the religious community, the gay religious community has also made advances on the social front. A few gay-friendly synagogues have been established in Tel Aviv, including Yachad (together), a liberal orthodox modern community, and Yakar (precious),[24] a community that accepts any person as he or she is. The Orthodox gay organizations, the synagogues, and the liberal rabbis reflect, in my opinion, a real shift in the more liberal segments of Modern Orthodox communities in Israel.

## Homosexuals and the Israeli Army

Finally, it is important to consider the issue of homosexuality and the Israeli army, an institution that is central part of Israeli culture and society. Army service in Israel makes Israeli adolescence quite different from that in many Western countries. Forced military conscription defines a clear end point to Jewish adolescence. Although single women (though not married women) are recruited into the army just like men, this fact has not changed the predominant male character of the army in any significant way.[25] (In the first decades of the IDF, women served in the women's force and had different roles, opportunities for advancement, and military experiences than did men.[26]) In addition to a very clear differentiation between the genders, army culture is also based on gender stereotypes and clear hierarchies between women and men. The combination of different gender roles, the sexist environment, and gender power relations creates essentialist gender perceptions that reproduce gender hierarchies.[27] Even though the Israeli army has made significant policy changes in the roles of women in the army since the mid-nineties, change on the ground is slow. Officially, 90 percent of types of positions in the army are open to women, but only 67 percent are actually filled by women. Moreover, women constitute only 3 percent of the combat force, and only 4.4 percent of women reach high ranks in the army hierarchy.[28]

It is easy to conclude that the Israeli army has been and still is characterized by a sexist, male, macho culture. This culture is threatened not only by the entrance of women into typical male roles but also by males who do not fit the stereotypical male army image. Still, for both males and females in Israeli society, entrance into the army is a rite of passage marking entry into adulthood.[29] Youth who enter the army are socialized politically and civilly, and it matures them psychologically.[30] Soldiers work within a unique subculture that intertwines army life with manhood. While the explicit goal of the combat unit is to transform the individual from a civilian to a soldier, the symbolic goal is to transform the teenager into a man.[31] Thus, entering the army can be especially challenging for gay men, since their manhood is seen as different. Sion shows in her research how through humor and curses unconventional manhood, specifically homosexuality, are stigmatized. The act of male penetration is viewed as an injury to male pride,[32] so that gay men, who are assumed to engage in such sexual acts, become a threat to the male identity of the Israeli soldier.

In 1983 a command was issued declaring that gays could be assigned only to certain units in the army because they could create a security risk. In addition, army diagnosticians were told to consider homosexuality a sexual deviation. They were instructed that when they suspected a soldier was gay, they had to consider whether he was well enough adjusted to serve in a combat unit.[33] This meant that every commander who knew that one of his soldiers was homosexual had to refer him to the army mental-health clinic and report him to the field officers. One argument for this policy was that assigning a homosexual to a combat unit could create dissention among soldiers who felt differently about this issue, which would result in violence in the unit, decreasing morale and thereby efficiency.[34]

This stance was reviewed only in 1993, after Uzi Even, a well-known professor of chemistry and high-ranking army officer, stood before the Knesset and described the discrimination he suffered in the army due to his sexual orientation. The result was a new fiat forbidding any discrimination on the basis of sexual orientation in the IDF recruiting process. Since 1998 any discrimination against any soldier on the basis of his or her sexual orientation has been forbidden. Moreover, many other laws were passed to protect the well-being of homosexuals serving in the army.[35] Today, at least officially, all the positions in the army, in combat units or other units, are open to gays and straights alike (some are not open to women and thus not to lesbians). This means that one's sexual orientation no longer affects one's security clearance and thereby which unit one can serve in. Moreover, the IDF allows soldiers to take part, as individuals, in gay parades, though without wearing the IDF uniform.[36] However, despite the Israel's army reputation as one of the most liberal in the world with respect to its official stance on integrating homosexuals and lesbians, it is not always so tolerant, either on the individual level or with respect to its social climate.[37]

The gap between the official IDF stance and the actual climate that gays and lesbians experience in the army can be attributed to the general social climate in Israel regarding homosexuality. Israeli society is socially conservative. Compared to other Western countries, Israeli society's attitudes toward gays and lesbians seem negative,[38] since the army's ground-level culture (if not its official policies) influences the society by establishing a machismo that denigrates homosexuality.[39] In this, Israelis are especially different from Jews in the United States, who tend to be strikingly liberal on issues of sexuality.

This general atmosphere explains why, according to research done in 2011 by IGI (organization of proud adolescence), most gay soldiers reported that the army environment was homophobic and full of verbal violence—saturated with derogatory phrases aimed at gay people. "Don't be a sissy" is just one common phrase, heard especially in combat units. The research demonstrated that 40 percent of homosexual soldiers said they were verbally abused because of their sexual orientation, 20 percent claimed they were sexually abused, 4 percent said they were physically abused and 44 percent claimed they experienced at least one kind of abuse related to their sexual orientation. These statistics were similar in all army units.

The research found a slight improvement in one area: an increase in the availability of information regarding gay and lesbian sexual orientation in different army units, although the informational scope is still narrow. Nevertheless, as a result of the homophobic atmosphere in the army, many soldiers become less open about their sexual orientation.[40] Many feel they must disguise their true identity—in contrast to their behavior in civil life, since most had already come out of the closet during their adolescence. Consequently, they live a split reality, with their civilian life separate from their army life. The resulting sense of living a false image takes them back to the years when they were hiding in the closet as adolescents, and it affects their well-being as soldiers.[41]

## Conclusion

The issue of gays in Israel is a window into the complexity of Israeli society, segments of which are characterized by conservatism, traditionalism, and machismo. Hence with respect to gay rights (as well as women's rights, for that matter), Israeli culture and society perform a delicate dance between tradition and modernity, liberalism and conservatism, openness and closedness. The dance reflects the complicated legal stance that Israel has created regarding gay rights. While the country has liberal, advanced laws on gay rights, the legal system makes it very difficult for gays and lesbians to create an Israeli Jewish home that includes children who have both an Israeli nationality and a Jewish identity. This complexity creates a gap between legal principle and social reality. While Israel has improved its legislation regarding gay rights, affecting both prescribed behavior for the army and civil life, research indicates that many gays and lesbians still feel unaccepted and discriminated against in daily life. For many gays and lesbians, Tel Aviv has become a sanctuary where they can live openly as gay couples and families. However, residents of that city are said to be living in a "bubble," since their political and social situation does not reflect the way people in general and gays and lesbians in particular feel in other parts of the country.

Israel is facing a serious, imminent challenge. It will need at some point to address the problem of hundreds of children categorized as Israelis with "no religion," a status that is an anomaly in Israeli society. Whether Israel will ignore this challenge or give it serious thought and consideration is yet to be seen. But the way Israel deals with this potentially explosive issue will either move the nation forward as a humanistic, democratic country or align it with its neighbors as a county influenced by the general Middle East environment, which seems increasingly to be characterized by reactionary attitudes toward gender unconventionality and sexual difference.

## NOTES

1. Amit Kama, *The Newspaper and the Closet* [Hebrew] (Tel Aviv: Kibbutz Hameuchad, 2003).
2. Ibid.
3. Yuval Yonai and Dori Spiback, "Between Silence and Condemnation: The Construction of Gay Identity in the Legislative Discourse in Israel, 1948–1988" [Hebrew], *Israeli Sociology: A Journal for the Study of Society in Israel* (1999): 2, 257–93.
4. Alon Harel, "The Rise and Fall of the Legislative Homosexual Revolution" [Hebrew], *HaMishpat: Law Review* (2004): 12, 10–29.
5. Michal Tamir, "'The Hebrew Language Did Not Invent a Title for Me': On the Dignity of Alternative Families in Israel" [Hebrew], *Kiryat H'amishpat* (2008): 8, 251–88.

6. Harel, "Rise and Fall of the Legislative Homosexual Revolution."
7. Dan Yakir and Yonatan Berman, "Marriage between Same-Sex Couples: Is It Necessary? Is It Wanted?" [Hebrew], *Ma'asey Mishpat: Tel Aviv University Journal of Law and Social Change* (2008): 1, 169–77.
8. Harel, "Rise and Fall of the Legislative Homosexual Revolution"; Yakir and Berman, "Marriage between Same-Sex Couples"; Yuval Marin, "Marriage between Same-Sex Couples and the Failure in the Alternatives Legal Regulations" [Hebrew], *HaMishpat: Law Review* (2001): 12, 20–33.
9. Yigal Mosku, "The Baby Boom of Gays and Lesbians," [Hebrew], *Uvda T.V. Series,* March 11, 2006, www.mako.co.il/tv-ilana_dayan/f66b3f491f97c110-b28d30564e97c110/Article-55086ce47951911004.htm.
10. Irit Rosenblum and Nurit Peleg, "Single-Gender Families (Same-Sex Families)" [Hebrew], *New Family* (n.d.), www.newfamily.org.il/blog/data-statistics/מיגדריות-חד-משפחות-אירי-עוד-מיניות-חד/.
11. Danna Harman, "The Trials and Treasures of Tel-Aviv's Gay-By Boom," *Haaretz*, February 18, 2013, www.haaretz.com/news/features/the-trials-and-treasures-of-tel-aviv-s-gay-by-boom.premium-1.504343.
12. Avraham Zlil, "Falling into the Bridge of Halachah" [Hebrew,] *Musaf 24 Hours, Yediot Achronot*, March 18, 2013, 4–5.
13. Harman, "Trials and Treasures of Tel-Aviv's Gay-By Boom."
14. Ibid.
15. Irit Koren, *Altering the Closet: Stories of Religious Homosexuals and Lesbians* [Hebrew] (Tel-Aviv: Yedhiot Achronot, 2003).
16. Tova Hartman and Irit Koren, "Between 'Being' and 'Doing': Conflict and Coherence in the Identity Formation," in *Identity and Story: Creating Self in Narrative* (Washington, DC: American Psychological Association, 2006), 37–62.
17. Koren, *Altering the Closet.*
18. "About HAVRUTA," http://havruta.org.il/English.
19. ANACHNU is a project under the auspice of Kamoha organization (Religious orthodox Gays), and can be found in their Website. See http://www.kamoha.org.il/?cat=3.
20. www.bat-kol.org.
21. This statement was originally published in the bulletin "Mayaney Hayeshua," later online at the website NRG Ma'ariv: www.nrg.co.il/online/11/ART/836/068.html, see also the site Moreshet: http://moreshet.co.il/parasha/print.asp?x=3844&co.deClient=64&pg=1.
22. Zeev Shvaidel, "(Br)others among Us: On the Place of Religious Gay-Lesbian in the Religious Society" [Hebrew], *Akdmot* 17 (2005): 85–114.
23. See, for example, "Rav Sherlow to Religious Gays: It Is Preferable to Come Out of the Closet" [Hebrew], *Yediot Aharonot,* December 21, 2008. www.ynet.co.il/articles/0,7340,L-3641851,00.html.
24. "A Gay Good Year: To Celebrate Rosh Hashanah Proudly" [Hebrew], www.mako.co.il/pride-news/local/Article-99459ff185ba231006.htm. This 2011 article refers religious gays to moder and gay-friendly synagogues in Jerusalem and Tel Aviv.
25. Orna Sasson-Levy, "Gendered Implications of the Transition to a Professional Military," *The Public Sphere* 5 (2011): 73–92.
26. Dafna Izraeli, "Gender in the Army Service," *Theory and Criticism* (1999): 14, 85–109; Orna Sasson-Levy, *Identities in Uniform: Masculinities and Femininities in the Israeli Military* [Hebrew] (Jerusalem: Eshkolot Series, Magnes Press, and Tel Aviv: Migdarim Series, Hakibutz Hameucahd Press, 2006).

27. Cynthia Enloe, *Maneuvers: The International Politics of Militarizing Women's Lives* (Berkeley: University of California Press, 2000).
28. Sasson-Levy, "Gendered Implications."
29. See Tamar Rappaport, Edna Lomski-Feder, Yechzek Dar and Haim Adler, "Youth and Adolescence in Israeli Society" [Hebrew], in *Adolescence in Israel* (Even Yehuda: Reches Publication, 1995), 17–40.
30. A. Ben-Ami, "'To Be a Proud Student': The School Experience of Gay Students" [Hebrew] (MA thesis, Tel-Aviv University, 2010).
31. Danny Kaplan, *David, Jonathan and Different life: On Identity and Sexuality in Combat Units in the IDF* [Hebrew] (Tel Aviv: Kibbutz Hameuchad, 1999).
32. Liora Sion, *Images of Manhood Among Combat Soldiers: Military Service in the Israeli Infantry as a Rite of Passage From Youth to Adulthood* [Hebrew] (Jerusalem: Shaine Center Hebrew University, 1997).
33. Kaplan, *David, Jonathan and Different Life.*
34. Eyal Gross, "Sexuality, Manhood, Army and Civil Life: The Service of Gays and Lesbians in the IDF in Comparative Glasses" [Hebrew], *Plilim* 9 (2000): 95–183.
35. Guy Shilo, Orna Pizmoni Levi, Amit Kamah, Sari Lavi, and Batya Pinchasi, "Proud in Uniform: The Situation of Gay, Lesbian and Bisexuals in the IDF" [Hebrew] (research report, Gay Youth Organization [IGI], Tel Aviv, 2006), www.igy.org.il/amuta/wp-content/uploads/2012/08/מחקר-דוח-במדים-גאים.pdf.
36. Idan Joseph, "New in the IDF: A Soldier Will Be Allowed to Parade in the Gay Parade" [Hebrew], *News1*, November, 19, 2006.
37. Shilo et al., "Proud in Uniform."
38. Daniel J. N. Weishut, "Attitudes toward Homosexuality: An Overview," *Israel Journal of Psychiatry and Related Science* 37, no. 4 (2000): 308–19.
39. Kaplan, *David, Jonathan and Different Life*; Shilo et al., "Proud in Uniform."
40. Shilo et al., "Proud in Uniform."
41. Gross, "Sexuality, Manhood, Army and Civil Life"; Sion, "Images of Manhood among Combat Soldiers"; Shilo et al., "Proud in Uniform."

# 2

# Family Transformations

# 5

## View from a Different Planet

### *Fertility Attitudes, Performances, and Policies among Jewish Israelis*

Sergio DellaPergola

FERTILITY LEVELS AND BIRTH RATES are among the great regulators of world population growth and composition, hence of societal scale and complexity.[1] In the more circumscribed realm of Jewish society, fertility constitutes both a mechanism of demographic change and—conditional upon the identification chosen for the children born—a fundamental precondition for cultural transmission and intergenerational continuity.[2] This article deals with fertility among Jews in Israel that, at first sight, ranges somewhere between puzzling and mysterious. Indeed, in 2012 Israel—a country ranked sixteenth out of 186 by the Index of Human Development—with 3.1 children currently born per family had the highest Total Fertility Rate (TFR) among the world's 94 more developed countries.[3] To find a country with higher fertility, one had to as far as Tonga, ranked 95th regarding development and with a TFR of 3.8. Combined with intensive immigration from a broad array of countries, Israel's sustained fertility generated persistently rapid population growth, alongside internal diversity and convergence.

Given these premises, fertility trends have significantly and unsurprisingly affected Israel's demographic balance, hence its regional and global strategic standing and relations in the context of the Israeli-Arab conflict. In turn, worldwide demographic trends across major Jewish communities—affecting their respective population growth, size, and composition—have constituted one of the cornerstones of Israel-Jewish Diaspora dialectics. Naturally then, fertility of Jews has long constituted a topic for policy debate.[4]

Routinely collected data and in-depth research help identify some of the most significant patterns and determinants in Israeli family formation. Research also brings us closer to appreciating the complex relationship that exists between popular perceptions and aspirations about having children, and public policies that may affect actual completed family size and composition.

In this article, we address four major themes: (1) main fertility trends in Israel in historical perspective; (2) main sociodemographic correlates of fertility levels; (3) differentials in contemporary preferences of intended and appropriate family size among Jewish married couples in Israel; and (4) perceptions of public policy options that might affect the future course of fertility. More specifically, we examine fertility patterns of Jews (79% of Israel's total population in 2013) and compare actual, intended, and appropriate family sizes in their variable demographic, socioeconomic, cultural, and policy contexts based on official documentation[5] and a special survey of family growth performances and attitudes undertaken in 2005.[6]

Earlier and later data on fertility in Israel point to a high level of continuity. The focus on Israel's Jews is especially interesting for comparative purposes, given both the general socioeconomic and technological similarities that exist with other developed countries and the documented low fertility of Jews in those countries. In comparison with other more developed societies, all featuring subreplacement fertility levels, the view from Israel looks much like that from another planet.

## Family Norms in Israel

As a general background, it is important to assess the nature of family norms that have long prevailed in Israeli society. Aiming to absorb Jewish immigration from disparate corners of the world, Israeli society incorporated many people from environments not yet modernized and Westernized. Wide demographic, social-structural, attitudinal, and behavioral gaps that prevailed before and during the early stages of immigrant absorption evolved into unique demographic patterns in the new country. At the same time, emerging family patterns were widespread, including relatively young marriage, greater marriage stability than in other developed countries, relatively large household size, and nearly universal endogamy. A modernizing social environment did affect the main demographic indicators, but change was comparatively conservative.

The median age at marriage among Jewish women and men has gradually increased, but the overall difference between the 1950s and 2010 was 4.5 years for women, from 21.6 to 25.9, and 2 years for men, from 26.1 to 28.2 (see figure 5.1).

More recent marriage postponement is illustrated by the percentages of never-married Jewish adults in 1994 and 2011. Israeli society did show change, but it was not nearly as striking as that in other Jewish communities. At ages 30–34 the never-married group increased from 10 percent for women and 20

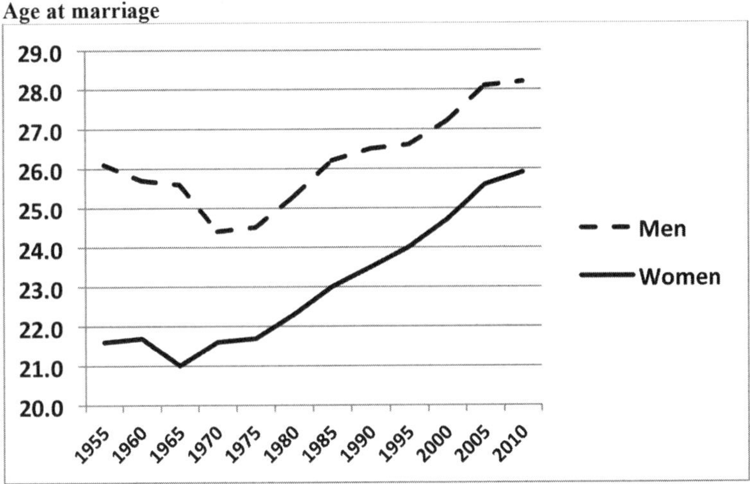


FIGURE 5.1. Median age at marriage among Jews, by gender—Israel, 1955–2010.
*Source*: Israel Central Bureau of Statistics.

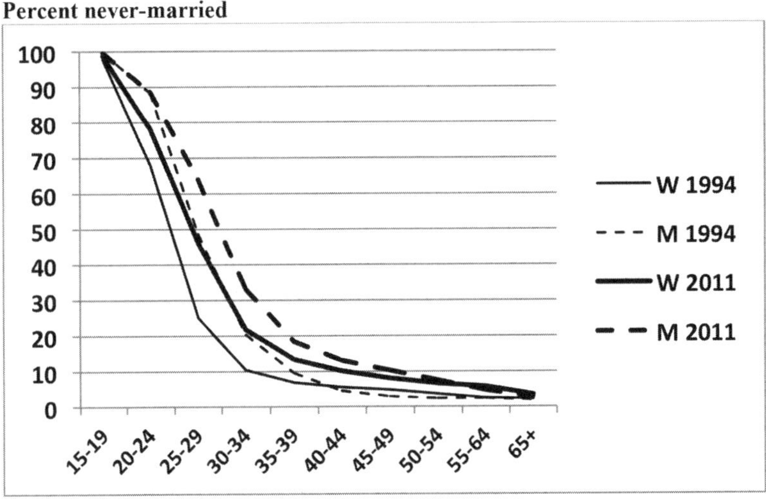


FIGURE 5.2. Percent Jews never married, by age and gender—Israel 1995 and 2011.
*Source*: Israel Central Bureau of Statistics.

percent for men in 1994 to 22 percent and 33 percent, respectively, in 2011. At ages 40–44, celibacy grew from 6 percent for women and 5 percent for men in 1994 to 10 percent and 13 percent, respectively, in 2011. But the overall propensity to marry remained high, as shown by the percentages of never married at 50–54, 7–8 percent in 2011 versus 3–4 percent in 1994 (see figure 5.2).

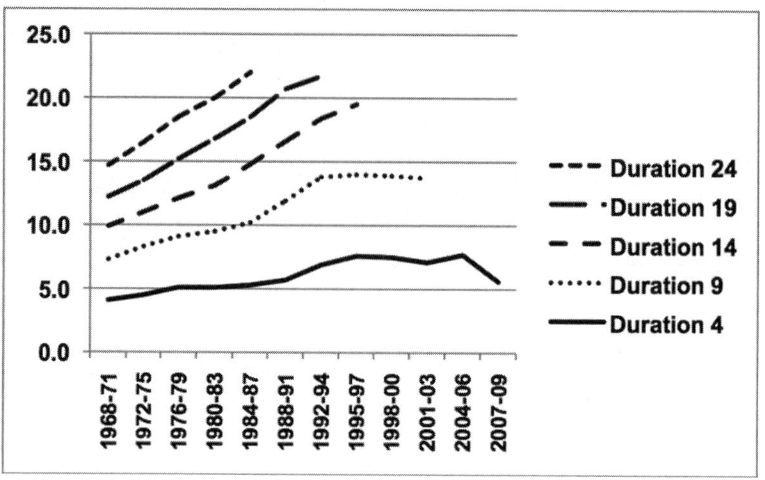


FIGURE 5.3. Percent ever divorced, by duration of marriage and year of marriage—couples married in Israel, 1968–2009. *Source*: Israel Central Bureau of Statistics.

Following a general trend, marriage stability decreased over time in Israel, yet without reaching the high divorce rate of some Western countries. Figure 5.3 shows the percent of Jewish marriages performed in Israel that were terminated at selected durations (four to twenty-four years of marriage). The longer the marriages' duration, the higher the divorces' cumulated incidence. A clearly rising trend emerged among marriages performed in Israel between the 1970s and the 1990s, approaching a cumulated break-down rate of about one in four. However the more recent marriage cohorts seemed prone to somewhat greater stability, or at least to a pattern that does not continue the increase in divorce frequencies.

Research on attitudes reflects conservative family norms in Israel and in several other societies throughout the 1990s and early 2000s.[7] Three—purposely conservative—propositions for evaluation by the public were as follows: (1) married people are usually happier than unmarried people; (2) it is better to have a bad marriage than not to marry; (3) people who wish to have children should marry. International comparisons of the attitudes expressed regarding these propositions cross-classified in about twenty countries are provided in figures 5.4 and 5.5, where the arrows connect the respective frequencies in 1994 and in 2002. High proportions of respondents in Israel viewed marriage as a nearly mandatory personal goal, a carrier of personal satisfaction, and the sole appropriate framework for procreation.

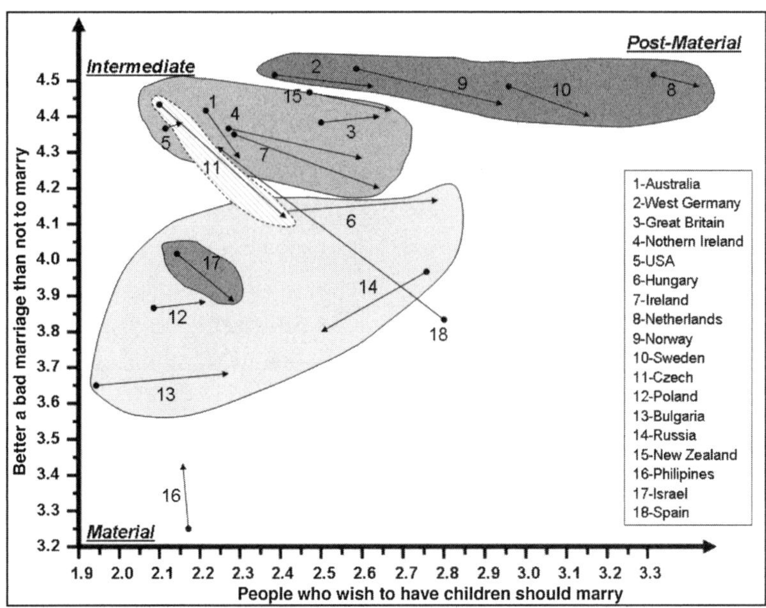


FIGURE 5.4. International comparison of family norms (1): country profiles and change—1994–2002. *Source*: Computed and processed from data of the International Social Survey Programme, coordinated by the Zentralarchiv für Empirische Sozialforschung at the University of Cologne, Germany (Kalushka, 2006).

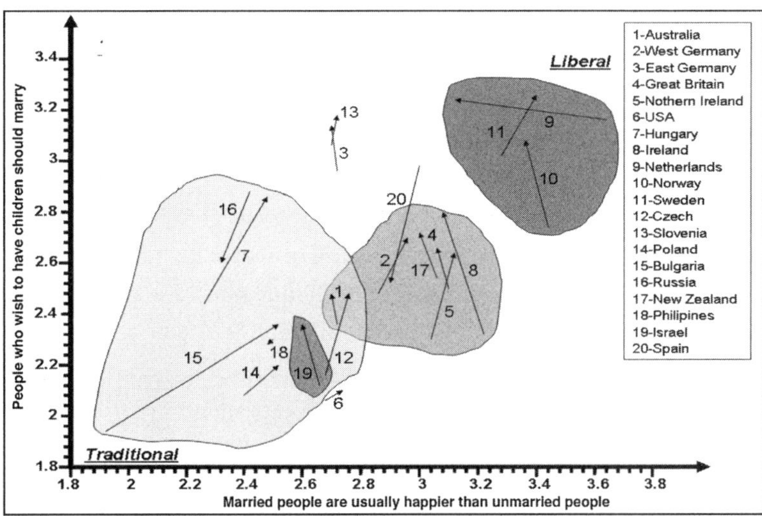


FIGURE 5.5. International comparison of family norms (2): country profiles and change—1994–2002. *Source*: Computed and processed from data of the International Social Survey Programme, coordinated by the Zentralarchiv für Empirische Sozialforschung at the University of Cologne, Germany (Kalushka, 2006).

Over time, Israelis expressed slightly declining support for the essentiality of marriage, together with growing propensity to associate having children with marriage (see notes 17 in figure 5.4 and 19 in figure 5.5). Family norms of the Israelis stood closer to the more conservative end of a country typology that ranges from traditional to liberal and from materialist to postmaterialist.[8] Yet Israeli society from the beginning developed a cultural blend that covered all possible shades of religious commitment, with a clear predominance of seculars or the moderately traditionalist over the strictly observing.[9] But in the process of cultural integration, elements of traditionalism—whether derived from long-standing Jewish religious norms or more broadly from the premigration environment—were preserved, informing the daily culture and life of the more modernized sectors.

## Fertility Patterns in Israel

Consistent with conservative perceptions of family in society, fertility in Israel has been characterized by stable, relatively high levels over time, through significant convergence across and within major religious and ethnic groups. This stability and convergence persisted in spite of tremendous cultural and socioeconomic transformations following repeated wars and other security challenges, the arrival of millions of new immigrants, speedy technological change, and rapidly rising standards of living. Modernization of immigrants from less developed countries resulted in shrinking family sizes, while immigrants from low-fertility countries raised their family sizes in Israel. The frequency of births outside marriage—less than 2 percent of Jewish births around 1990 and just over 4 percent in 2011–2012—remained among the lowest among developed countries.[10]

In 2012 Israel's TFR was 3.05, and different religious groups performed as follows: Muslims, 3.54; Jews, 3.04; Druze, 2.26; Christians, 2.17; and not classified by religion (mostly non-Jewish members of households immigrated from the Former Soviet Union FSU), 1.68. As noted, in 2012 Israel was ranked sixteenth globally by the Index of Human Development, trailing Iceland (TFR 2.1), Denmark (1.9), Canada (1.7), Korea (1.4), and Hong Kong (1.1), and preceding France (2.0), Finland (1.9), Belgium (1.8), Austria (1.3), and Singapore (1.3). Israel thus constituted the only societal context where the transition to below-replacement fertility—generational replacement being assessed at 2.1 children per woman—has not occurred, besides among relatively small minorities. Over the past fifty years, Israel-born Jewish women, who constitute the society's backbone, had a uniquely stable TFR at 2.5–3.1 children. If anything, the Jewish TFR steadily increased from 2.69 in 2005 to 3.04 in 2012. These unique patterns for a developed

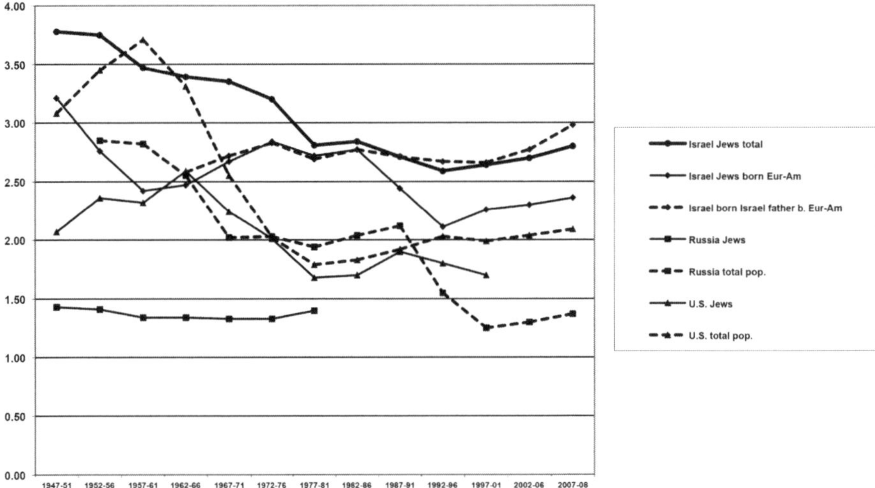


FIGURE 5.6. Total fertility rates among Jews in Israel, the US and Russia, 1947–2008. *Source*: Israel Central Bureau of Statistics, *Statistical Abstract of Israel*; *World Population Prospects, The 2008 Revision* (New York: United Nations Population Division, 2008); DellaPergola, "Actual, Intended, and Appropriate Family Size among Jews in Israel"; Tolts, "Post-Soviet Aliyah and Jewish Demographic Transformation."

country resulted from coalescence of more traditional and more modern family models into a stable new one. The result was intermediate between the larger families that prevailed among Jews in Asia and Africa longer than in Europe and America, and the smaller families of many developed countries.

Israel's total Jewish TFR can be compared with that of Jews in Israel born in Europe or America (including North and Latin America), Jews born in Israel from parents born in Europe or America, and Jews living in the Russian Republic and in the United States (see figure 5.6). The earlier histories, family ties, socioeconomic, and cultural backgrounds of these different Jewish populations—whether gone to Israel or remaining in the main countries of origin—were not substantially different. International migration usually involved a measure of self-selection among migrants,[11] and it may be assumed that there was a larger component of the more Jewishly committed among migrants, especially to Israel, than among stayers. But the more religious segment among immigrants from the Former Soviet Union (FSU) to Israel was extremely tiny, and in the case of the United States, the overall volume of migration to Israel was small.

The fertility contrast between Jews living in Israel and those in the United States and Russia is significant. Total fertility of US Jews at its highest point during the post–World War II baby boom years failed to reach even the lowest point ever recorded among the total Jewish population in Israel. It also was systematically lower than the fertility level of the total US population, although it followed similar temporal patterns.[12] In the Russian Republic, and overall in the FSU, Jewish fertility was very low and did not display any sign of a postwar baby boom.[13] The postwar TFR among Russia's total population was lower than that of Israel and the United States, and in the 1990s it rejoined the very low level anticipated by Jews. Among FSU immigrants to Israel, fertility grew among those who were Jewish but remained low among non-Jewish members of Jewish households.[14] In sum, the fertility of Jewish immigrants from Europe and America in Israel was significantly higher than among Jews in the countries of origin where Jews had a longstanding record of low or very low fertility, and it increased among the second generation of immigrants in Israel. This indicates a consistent tendency of intragenerational and intergenerational Jewish fertility increase in Israel.

As one of the paramount markers of the immigrants' cultural absorption in Israel, fertility levels became increasingly homogeneous. Initial diversity and significant convergence of fertility levels among different origin groups within the unified Israeli context can be seen in figure 5.7. During the 1950s Jewish women born in Asia and Africa (the Middle East and North Africa) had about three children more than their peers born in Europe and America, but by the mid-1980s convergence to a common pattern had nearly completed. With the arrival since the end of the 1980s of a massive immigration wave from the FSU, fertility of European-born women diminished and later gradually recovered, keeping above replacement. Opposite and symmetric effects can be observed among contemporary immigrants from Ethiopia. Thus, the intercontinental fertility gap temporarily rose, to diminish again in the most recent years.

The progressive disappearance of the so-called subethnic factor (*hagorem ha'adati* in Hebrew)—that is, the dependence of fertility on the geographic background of the Jewish population—is a critically important point. In the second generation of Israel-born women, classified by continent of birth of the respective fathers, the differential has been virtually zero since the 1960s. This conveys a very substantial sense of convergence in both family norms and behaviors. Convergence in demography could play a role, at least partially, as a moderating factor of other socioeconomic gaps tied to geographical origin and still visible in Israeli society.[15]

Another fundamental issue is the weak relationship of the mother's socioeconomic status—measured by level of education attained and labor force participation—to fertility. At the macro-social level, Israel's development, industrialization, infrastructure, and income—all supposedly related to fertility decline—rose rapidly, but in spite of this and of the recent absorption of 1 million Jewish immigrants from the very low fertility FSU, current fertility remained stable or moderately increased.

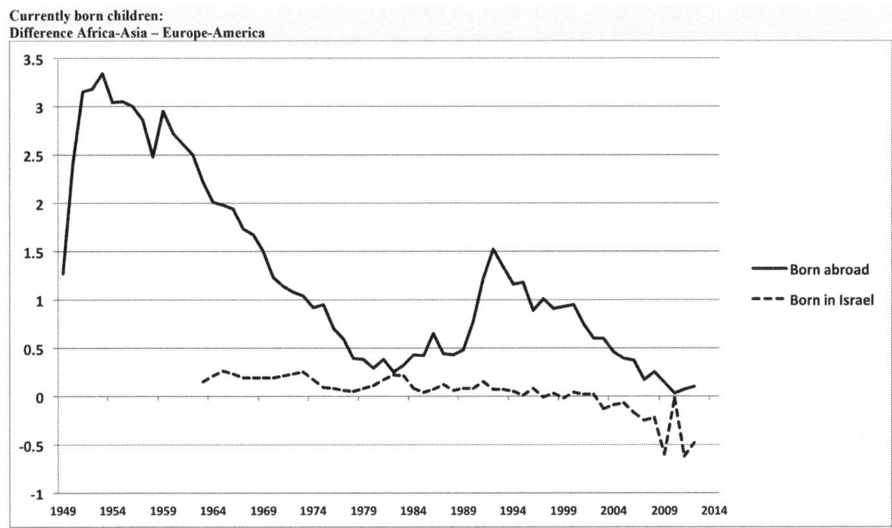


FIGURE 5.7. Jewish TFR gaps by mother's continents of origin and generation in israel—1949–2012. *Source*: Adjusted from Israel Central Bureau of Statistics, *Statistical Abstract of Israel*.

At the micro-social level, between the 1950s and the 2000s, a sharp surge occurred in the percent of women holding post-secondary education (thirteen or more years of schooling) especially among those aged 25–34. Women's labor force participation at reproductive ages rose overall from 30 percent to more than 70 percent. Labor diminished in the 14–17 age group consistently with an extension of compulsory schooling and significantly rose to more than 80 percent among those 18–34. Age-specific fertility rates markedly diminished among women below 20 and at 20–24, and also though less sharply at 25–29 and above 45. On the other hand, fertility rates increased significantly at 30–34, 35–39, and to some extent at 40–44. From the earlier peak of having children at 20–24 followed by 25–29, Jewish women shifted to a peak at age 25–29, closely followed by 30–34, postponing peaking at 30–34 in most recent years.

These shifts in the scheduling of childbearing reflect significant mutual accommodations between reproductive and socioeconomic patterns, though without affecting the TFR outcome. In particular, the extremely stable numbers of children born to native Jewish women over the last fifty years indicate a unique accommodation of reproduction levels and schedules facing a significant spread of higher education and employment among the more deeply Israel-acculturated.

While educational attainment and labor-force participation have lost much of their previous role as determinants of fertility levels and differentials, religiosity

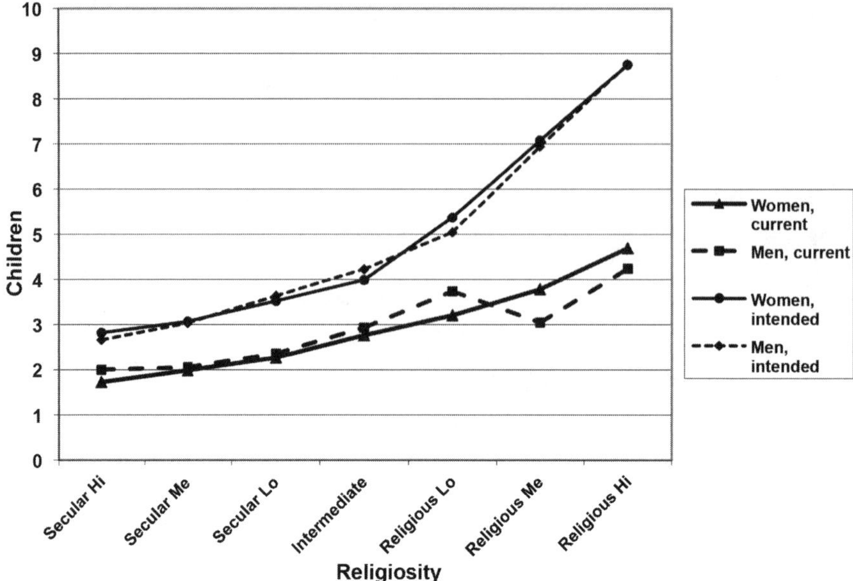


FIGURE 5.8. Current and intended number of children by self-assessed religiosity, currently married Jews, by gender—Israel, 2005. *Source*: *Survey of Attitudes and Behaviors Concerning Family Size among Israel's Jewish Population, 2005.*

continues to be the main correlate of Jewish fertility in Israel. Anticipating what will be illustrated later in greater detail, figure 5.8 reports on numbers of actual and intended children by Jewish married women and men by levels of religiosity, self-assessed on a scale with seven degrees of intensity.

Although intended and actual children do not necessarily coincide, religiosity continues to be prominently associated with fertility in Israel. The range of variation regarding the actual performance in 2005 among couples still in the middle of their reproductive lives shows that the most religious had already attained between four and five children per family, with the least religious approaching two. Regarding intended children, the preference was between close to nine children for the most religious and close to three for the most secular, with little variation between genders.

No less interesting than the very large ideal family size of the more religious—who constitute roughly 10 percent of the Jewish population—are the preferences of the large segment that defines itself most secular. A preference for three children appears extraordinarily high when compared to the prevailing norms in other developed countries. In fact, the predominant answer to an attitudinal question about what in Israel would constitute a family "too small," was 1.6 across the whole gamut of respondents, with virtually nobody saying none and 54 percent saying 1. The "too small" number averaged 2.6 children among those respondents intending to have larger families of more than five children, including the more religious. To the question of what would constitute a family "too large," the general average was 7, but among those planning the larger families it was 10.9. Other empirical data show that the fertility level actually attained by the more intensely religious sector—the *haredi* population—actually tends to be around 6–7, with fluctuations reflecting the economic opportunities available to families.[16]

## Fertility Attitudes and Intentions

The correspondence between fertility norms and ideals, their translation into practice, and the predictive value of declared fertility intentions constitute important questions for analysis in the overall assessment of family growth.[17] A national *Survey of Attitudes and Behaviors Concerning Family Size*, conducted in Israel in 2004–2005, covered a representative sample of 975 women aged 25 to 45 and 481 men aged 25 to 50, all Jewish, married or in stable unions, at a high response rate of 95 percent. The survey addressed personal demographic and socioeconomic variables, religiosity, norms about self-fulfillment and optimism, gender roles, and intended, most appropriate, and ideal family sizes. The survey also investigated the desirability and feasibility of public policies about family and reproduction in Israel.

In 2005 the average number of children attained by families with several years of further potential growth was about 2.5, exactly as in a previous 1988 survey (see table 5.1). Among those above age 40, married women had 3.7 children and men had 2.9. Expected, appropriate, and ideal fertility were similar in 1988 and in 2005, but showed some in increase in each area. Intended family size grew from 3.5 to 4.1, respectively. The most appropriate family size for a family of the respondents' same socioeconomic status increased from 3.4 to 4.0, and the ideal number of children for a generic Israeli family increased from 3.7 to 4.1. Excluding haredim, the average most-appropriate family size in 2005 still was 3.8 and, as noted, 3 among the most seculars. Hence, diffuse gaps existed between ideal perceptions (3–4 children) and actual performances (2–3 children).

Women wanted more children than did men. Among 63 percent of respondents, the numbers of *intended* and *appropriate* children matched. The most frequent preference for women was three children, followed by five or more. For men it was three followed by two or fewer. The latter group was largely dominated by parity two. A significant disjunction emerged between perceptions of family size eventually intended and most appropriate, based on the respondents'

Table 5.1. Number of intended[a] vs. appropriate[b] children among currently married[c] Jews, by gender—Israel, 2005

| | NUMBER OF INTENDED VS. APPROPRIATE CHILDREN | | | | | | | |
|---|---|---|---|---|---|---|---|---|
| | SAME | | | | DIFFERENT | | | |
| GENDER AND AGE | 0–2[d] | 3[d] | 4[d] | 5+[d] | I < A[e] | I > A[f] | TOTAL | N |
| Women, 25–40 | 12 | 25 | 11 | 16 | 8 | 28 | 100 | 975 |
| Men, 25–50 | 14 | 26 | 11 | 11 | 15 | 22 | 100 | 481 |
| Women % difference | −14 | −4 | = | +45 | −47 | +27 | = | |

a. Sum of total number of children born so far plus total additional children expected
b. Number of children most appropriate for family with standard of living same as respondent's
c. Including nonmarried persons in stable couple relations
d. Same number of children intended and appropriate
e. Number of children appropriate 3, 4, or 5, and fewer children intended
f. Number of children appropriate 2, 3, or 4, and more children intended

SOURCE: *Survey of Attitudes and Behaviors Concerning Family Size among Israel's Jewish Population, 2005.*

self-assessment of their own socioeconomic status. Indeed, 8 percent of women and 15 percent of men intended to have *fewer* children than they deemed appropriate, while 28 percent of women and 22 percent of men intended to have *more* children than appropriate. More women reported inconsistent parities than any consistently specified parity. Men more clearly preferred three children, while those intending to have more children than they deemed appropriate formed the second largest group.

Thus, while the first two children are nearly universally attained among Israeli couples, transitions from the second to the third and from the third to the fourth child have crucially shaped the current patterns and are likely to determine those of the future. In a policy-oriented context, fertility intentions, plans, attainments, and preferred policy options stand in an interactive determinant-consequence mode that needs to be explored in both directions (see figure 5.9).

When analyzing the relationships between social norms, individual background characteristics, perceptions of existing policy constraints and incentives, and fertility outcomes, alternative analytic paths may be considered. One option is to posit children intended and/or appropriate as the main dependent variable affected by personal and contextual background variables, as well as by the evaluation of available policy options and their anticipated effects on the final outcome. Alternatively, the perceived utility of policy options can be posited as the main dependent variable, with the number of children intended and/or appro-

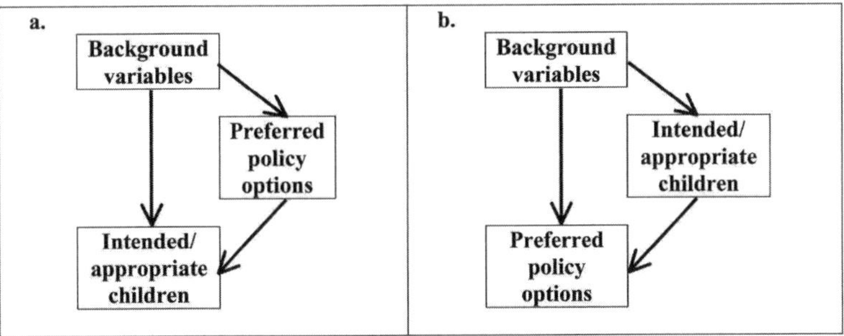


FIGURE 5.9. Alternative paths for intended/appropriate children and preferred policy options in Israel

priate as one of the explaining factors. An interpretative framework that incorporates background characteristics, social norms, and policy expectations should be able to catch the roots of the conservative dimensions that have led so far to stability or slow-motion change in the configuration of Jewish fertility in Israel. At the very least, such framework should help in revealing the beginnings of significant deviations from extant fertility patterns.

Fertility attitudes and actual performances among Jews in Israel were examined looking at the interplay of demographic factors (such as age and country of birth), socioeconomic factors (such as personal work status and family economic resources), religiosity, other ideational factors (such as norms about career and family), and policy attitudes (relative to a portfolio of possibilities). Based on an analysis of prospective parity progression ratios—that is, the likelihood of a person with a given attained parity to add one further child—we found that individuals and households who prefer different eventual parities constitute distinct subpopulations, each rooted in their preferences quite early in their adulthood and motivated by different causal paths. Rather than viewing parity preferences as a continuum, it seems eminently possible and analytically fruitful to study each final parity group as a separate subpopulation.

Multivariate analyses based on thirteen different possible determinants of fertility attitudes and performances, show that the strongest single predictor of fertility behaviors is by far religiosity, net of other factors. However, numerous other variables exert significant discriminatory power over fertility levels. Table 5.2 presents a synopsis of the relative strength of the various determinants when we contrast respondents, indicating each given parity or each type of inconsistency between intended and appropriate parity compared to the rest of the whole sample. The upper panel shows the explanatory power of each type of variable

Table 5.2. Synopsis of pseudo $r^2$ for binary logistic regressions[a]—currently married Jewish women and men, by preferred parity—Israel, 2005

| | NUMBER OF INTENDED VS. APPROPRIATE CHILDREN | | | | | |
|---|---|---|---|---|---|---|
| | SAME | | | | DIFFERENT | |
| EXPLANATORY VARIABLES | 0–2 | 3 | 4 | 5+ | I < A | I > A |
| N | 187 | 371 | 161 | 209 | 145 | 381 |
| EFFECT OF EACH GROUP OF VARIABLES ENTERED ALONE, $R^2$ | | | | | | |
| Demographic | .152 | .026 | .039 | .151 | **.104** | .043 |
| Socioeconomic | .014 | .023 | .025 | .033 | .051 | **.048** |
| Social norms | .011 | .035 | .015 | .096 | .010 | .010 |
| Religiosity | **.193** | **.122** | **.046** | **.578** | .023 | **.061** |
| Current children | **.260** | **.190** | **.087** | **.401** | **.062** | .021 |
| Preferred policy options | .032 | .016 | .010 | .077 | .023 | .040 |
| CUMULATED EFFECT OF ALL VARIABLES ENTERED TOGETHER, $R^2$ | | | | | | |
| | .456 | .279 | .189 | .679 | .216 | .169 |
| PERCENT INCREMENT IN $R^2$, GROUPS OF VARIABLES ENTERED STEP-WISE | | | | | | |
| + Socioeconomic | 5.3 | **69.2** | **53.8** | 23.2 | 35.6 | 86.0 |
| + Social norms | 2.5 | **52.3** | 18.3 | 41.4 | 5.7 | 18.8 |
| + Religiosity | **76.8** | **144.8** | **57.7** | **135.0** | 4.0 | **55.8** |
| + Current children | **50.7** | **65.2** | **62.5** | 8.7 | 3.3 | 4.7 |
| + Preferred policy options | 4.3 | 3.0 | 3.8 | 1.0 | 6.9 | 9.0 |

a. Conventionally known as amount of explained statistical variance. In the upper panel, the two groups of variables providing the higher explained variance in each column are outlined in bold. In the lower panel, groups of variables providing an increase of 50% or more over the variance explained by variables already entered in the model are outlined in bold.

SOURCE: *Survey of Attitudes and Behaviors Concerning Family Size among Israel's Jewish Population, 2005.*

separately. The bottom panel shows the additional explanatory power of each type of variable when entered on top of other variables already entered.

The amount of explained variance between choosers of a given parity group versus all other respondents, here indicated by pseudo R squares, varied as expected according to parity preferences. The overall explanatory effect of the thirteen variables considered in this study was stronger for lower parities (0–2 with 46% of explained variance) and higher parities (5+ with 68% of explained variance). These variations were highly influenced by religiosity, whether low or high, by current number of children, and to some extent by demographic and socioeconomic factors. On the other hand, respondents preferring intermediate parities (3 and 4), and those with intended different-than-appropriate parity were largely diffused across the population and therefore the explanatory variables exerted significant yet lower power of discrimination over other respondents (19–28% of explained variance).

In other words, preferring three or four children was less predictable based on respondent's characteristics and attitudes. Social norms about work and family, too, had a notable explanatory effect, especially among the largest group preferring parity 3. The additional effect of preferred policies in explaining a given parity choice was overall modest but not at all negligible. On top of all other explanations, preferred policy interventions added a further 1–9% to predicting a given parity choice, with the highest yield not surprisingly among those whose intended number of children was higher than what, in their view, would be the most appropriate.

More detailed data not shown here indicate a clear direct effect of age at low parities (0–2). While confirming the already noted lack of clear cohort effects in realizing parity intentions, the fertility expected by younger married women turned to be somewhat higher than that of older women. A definite reverse relationship prevailed between being born in the FSU and preferred parity. The turning of Israeli society from mostly foreign-born to mostly local-born residents was accompanied as already noted by fertility increase.

Overall, a positive relationship prevailed between years of education and preferred parity. The relationship with higher education (seventeen or more years of study) was negative at lower parities (0–2), and became positive at higher parities (5+). The high education of women who prefer higher parities testifies to the need to evaluate not only the amount of education received but also the cultural-ideological contents of that education, namely religious education. Labor force participation (ranging between "does not work" and "does not seek employment" to "currently employed") had a negative relationship to preferred parity. However, employment did not appear to have a systematic preventive effect on fertility, at least at intermediate parities. Perceptions of relative economic status at the household level were directly and positively related to preferred parity: there was clear evidence of a deterrent effect of poverty on fertility and of a positive relationship between household economic resources and parity. As noted above, the relationship of self-assessed religiosity to preferred parity was quite clearly positive. The visible effect of the more religious end of the distribution actually shows up only at parity 5 and above.

## Perceptional Inconsistencies

The presence of many actual and potential parents whose preferred intended family size differs from their own perceived most appropriate family size has significant policy implications. How do we interpret these inconsistencies? The intention to have a family smaller than is deemed socially appropriate may be related to age and health, as well as women's socioeconomic motives. When, as occurs more often, intentions are greater than one's perception of appropriateness, explanations are more complex and ambivalent. One explanation is that, first, people determine a family size more appropriate to their own social environment, and then the choice is made to outperform that norm. This implies investing more personal resources than others usually do to achieve the parity goal. An alternative explanation is that, first, people determine their expected performance, and then they evaluate that the same performance exceeds what would be appropriate given the available resources. Hence two completely different meanings may attach to similarly inconsistent parity answers.

In the case of *intended* parity being *lower* than appropriate, the stronger effects come from demographic background—especially from older ages and better-than-average economic success. We note additional gray areas of notable if statistically marginal effects, such as higher education, participation in the labor force, disagreeing with the placement of children at the center of one's own life, and lower current parity. Policy options are not really mentioned by this subgroup, but there is a hint—though statistically weak—of interest in fertility treatment to enhance one's own family size in the presence of health obstacles.

When *intended* parity is *higher* than appropriate, the data support the second explanation mentioned above, that is, a fear of outperforming appropriate family size norms grounded in insecurity about the availability of necessary resources. This climate of incertitude is disproportionately felt by women, younger adults, people not born in the FSU, and people who are at lower education levels, interested in working, but struggling with unemployment. The most powerful relationship concerns perceived poverty or lower-than-average economic status and economic pessimism, with no clear effects from career orientation. Religiosity is a significant factor, in reverse. Lack of self-confidence is related to a secular outlook, as the more religious would easily incorporate as natural some births that others would consider "excess" parity. Notable effects emerge from preferred policies. Nearly all possible options draw some attention, but housing and educational needs draw the most, with visible interest in direct monetary transfers and tax exemptions also. Only the mentioning of fertility treatment hints at the above-mentioned ideological explanation grounded on a wish to out-perform others.

In sum, assessing that one's own intended number of children will be higher than socially appropriate clearly conveys a sense of socioeconomic inadequacy. These families feel their own resources are not sufficient to the number of children that they nonetheless intend to have. This is the subgroup that more openly will be asking for economic support and these are the primary customers of possible sociodemographic policies. These may be people who already are in need of support asking for more support. The key question here is whether public resources should go to these needier families or to those who have a higher socioeconomic profile and greater resources but who for reasons related in part to age and work believe that they will not have enough children.

## Fertility Policy Preferences

Fertility policies have constituted a high profile and sensitive chapter in Israeli public discourse. The generally shared assumption is that Israel's government has steadily supported a higher birth rate, especially among the Jewish population.[18] The elaboration of population policies in Israel has long occupied public discourse, though rhetoric often exceeds the articulation of clear interventions. Economic policies and public discussion have focused mainly on family allowances, which have not been shown to effectively influence demographic trends. These money transfers have undergone repeated upward and downward changes reflecting short-term contingencies of economic policies. However, by international comparison, Israel performs about the same as or slightly above or below the average of other countries relative to most of the pertinent policy incentives to parenthood—providing not only direct money transfers, but also tax deductions, paid absences from work, flexible working hours, infrastructures for early childhood care, help with housing, subsidies of public services, and the like.[19]

Sensitivity to policy incentives cannot be understood separately from the public's general attitude toward children and fertility. It is not child-supporting policies that generate child-oriented attitudes, but rather the attitudes that generate the need for a policy. Therefore, the first question that should be asked concerns the reasons why one might intend or not to have another child (Table 5.3).

Interestingly, in attitudes and in reality, in terms of actual parenthood and of ideal family sizes, Jewish women in Israel appear to be more child-oriented than men. The male sample was somewhat older than the women's because men tend to be older than women at marriage, and remarriages tend to widen the gap, perhaps somewhat affecting outlook toward future children. The reasons for having or not having another child are also distributed somewhat differently by gender. Women tend to stress economic factors such as housing constraints,

Table 5.3. Main reasons for having or not having additional child—currently married Jews, by gender—Israel, 2005

| REASON | WOMEN | MEN | WOMEN % DIFFERENCE |
|---|---|---|---|
| N | 975 | 481 | |
| (IF INTENDING TO HAVE OTHER CHILD) | | | |
| Response % | 60 | 46 | +30 |
| MAIN FACTOR SUPPORTING ADDITIONAL CHILD | | | |
| Total | 100 | 100 | = |
| Child and family related | 72 | 66 | +9 |
| Ideological | 17 | 21 | −19 |
| Socially acceptable | 1 | 1 | = |
| Other | 10 | 13 | −23 |
| (IF NOT INTENDING TO HAVE OTHER CHILD) | | | |
| Response % | 46 | 54 | −15 |
| MAIN FACTOR PREVENTING ADDITIONAL CHILD | | | |
| Total | 100 | 100 | = |
| Economic, housing | 42 | 32 | +31 |
| Adult aspirations | 19 | 9 | +111 |
| Child and family related | 27 | 31 | −13 |
| Age, health | 12 | 28 | −57 |

SOURCE: *Survey of Attitudes and Behaviors Concerning Family Size among Israel's Jewish Population, 2005.*

but also their other aspirations, which significantly depend on their participation and achievements in the labor force and on conditions that would help to better facilitate the interplay between family and career.

Regarding reasons for having a child, a stereotypical perception is that people in Israel have children on behalf of the *medinah*—the state of Israel, for the Jewish people, for the army, as well as for God. These public, collective goals can be included under the general rubric of ideological reasons for childbearing. In reality, such ideological explanations obtain a rather modest return, about one respondent in five, more often among men than women. Strikingly stronger is the perception that an additional child is good for the already born children, for the household, for interpersonal woman-man relations within the couple, and for self. In other words, the fundamental explanation for willing another child tends to the intimate, micro-social, household framework rather than to the macro-social security or transcendental realm. In a country like Israel that constantly experiences security tensions, it is admittedly not easy to disentangle the micro from the macro. Personal preferences possibly reflect a broader perception and analysis of the externalities of Israeli society, including risks tied to ongoing conflicts. However, once the question is asked explicitly, the overwhelming majority of respondents offered a personal and intimate explanation of their rationale for more children.

Perceptions of incentives for, constraints to, and negotiations with family size provide the cognitive background to public attitudes toward policy options. Our survey data show that about 60 percent of the couples who responded do support public interventions designed to encourage larger families, while another 27 percent favor letting families to do what they wish, and only 4 percent favor smaller families. As noted, lack of socioeconomic security—real or perceived—generates some indetermination regarding intended and appropriate family size, while a clearly specified parity is a symptom of self-confidence.

A significant test of the potential effects of family policies in Israel is provided by a question about the main factor affecting adding one child more than the number finally intended—if the appropriate circumstances were in place. After having firmly ascertained what would be a family's preferred family size, one would expect a low propensity to consider adding further children. But in fact 78 percent of women and 67 percent of men did indicate one possible reason for having an additional child, showing that family size may remain negotiable until biologically sealed. Several main policy options were suggested as the background for possible family expansion by one, and the respective attitudes by gender are shown in table 5.4.

In Israel, education, including preschool childcare, is compulsory and nominally free but actually quite costly. Israel has a well-developed early-childhood network compared to the United States and most European countries. It is the cost more than the availability that constitutes a limiting factor in family-size preferences. In fact the expense of early-childhood education detracts huge shares from the income of working women and constitutes one of the main burdens on family life. Subsidy of early-childhood care is indeed the one policy option that women stressed the most, with a significant proportion mentioning later education, too. Men also primarily stressed the cost of education. Among women, the next two most advocated policy interventions were employment and housing. Women were significantly more sensitive than men regarding issues of equitable working conditions and rights, flexible careers and schedules, and remuneration. The importance of incentives to provide better housing was equally perceived by

Table 5.4. Policy options affecting having one additional child above number intended—currently married Jews, by gender—Israel, 2005

| REASON | WOMEN | MEN | WOMEN % DIFFERENCE |
|---|---|---|---|
| N | 975 | 481 | |
| Total | 100 | 100 | |
| None | 22 | 33 | −33 |
| Early childhood care | 28 | 19 | +47 |
| Child education cost | 10 | 16 | −38 |
| Woman employment | 18 | 10 | +80 |
| Housing | 14 | 14 | = |
| Money transfers | 5 | 9 | −44 |
| Tax exemptions | 5 | 9 | −44 |
| Fertility treatment | 3 | 4 | −25 |
| Good to children | 17 | 19 | −11 |

SOURCE: *Survey of Attitudes and Behaviors Concerning Family Size among Israel's Jewish Population, 2005.*

both genders. On the other hand, men stressed much more than women money transfers and tax exemptions, although altogether less than one-fifth mentioned these policy options. Such a gender gap is quite embarrassing if we wish to read it as if the men say, "Give us the money, and our women will provide the children," while the women say, "Give us the logistics, the conditions, and the infrastructure, and we will provide the children."

A small minority that asks for fertility treatment as the instrument for an additional child hints to infertility problems, probably in part related to age. Finally, an intriguing finding is that nearly one-fifth of the respondents—despite having identified their preferred final size—say that an additional child would be "good to children," expressing a general pronatal attitude, unrelated to specific policy incentives. Under generally improving economic conditions, a significant share of Israeli society may reconsider their family size targets. Perhaps one precondition is a general mood in the media and public discourse that is not hostile to larger families, that does not stigmatize them as anachronistic, and that sees them as fully compatible with personal human development and societal growth and modernity.

Attitudes to policy options that might incentivize Jewish women to have one more child, by intended and appropriate parity, are shown in table 5.5. The

Table 5.5. Policy options affecting decision to have one additional child above number intended, currently married Jewish women, by preferred parity—Israel, 2005

| | NUMBER OF INTENDED VS. APPROPRIATE CHILDREN | | | | | | |
|---|---|---|---|---|---|---|---|
| | SAME | | | | DIFFERENT | | |
| FACTORS | 0–2 | 3 | 4 | 5+ | I < A | I > A | TOTAL |
| Response rate % | 47 | 82 | 80 | 70 | 70 | 83 | 78 |
| Total | 100 | 100 | 100 | 100 | 100 | 100 | 100 |
| Early childhood care | **44** | **27** | **24** | 11 | **33** | **31** | **28** |
| Child education | 10 | 9 | 8 | 7 | 10 | 14 | 10 |
| Woman employment | **17** | **22** | 16 | 14 | 19 | 15 | **18** |
| Housing | 10 | 13 | 19 | 11 | 10 | **18** | 14 |
| Money transfers | 2 | 3 | 2 | **16** | 2 | 6 | 5 |
| Tax exemptions | 7 | 6 | 7 | 5 | 0 | 4 | 5 |
| Fertility treatment | 1 | 1 | 4 | 6 | 4 | 2 | 3 |
| Good for children | 8 | 19 | **20** | **30** | **23** | 10 | 17 |

NOTE: Top two priorities bold in each column.

SOURCE: *Survey of Attitudes and Behaviors Concerning Family Size among Israel's Jewish Population, 2005*

very response rates provide an interesting indication with the higher availability to consider the matter among people planning three or four children, and among those who feel their planning is higher than actually feasible. Early childhood provisions clearly dominate as the preferred provision at all parities except those preferring larger families of five or more children. That the latter more often allude to money transfers provides a sobering look at the shared socioeconomic rationale underlying the more ideological stance toward family growth. Concern with women's employment and housing cut across the different parity categories.

A more sophisticated statistical analysis is shown in table 5.6, where net effects of preferred parity on preferred policy option are examined for women and men together through odds ratios derived from logistical regressions that control for a host of other sociodemographic and attitudinal variables. The lowest, and especially the highest the desired parity, the more widespread appears to be the potential effect of preferred policy options. At the lowest parity (0–2), housing, fertility treatment, and "good for children" show up with significant weakening effects. This may be explained as a choice by the minority of respondents who opted for smaller families not contingent upon circumstances but rather unveiling

Table 5.6. Logistic regressions of policy options affecting decision to have one additional child above number intended, odds ratios[a], currently married Jewish women and men, by preferred parity—Israel, 2005

| EXPLANATORY VARIABLES | NUMBER OF INTENDED VS. APPROPRIATE CHILDREN | | | | | |
|---|---|---|---|---|---|---|
| | SAME | | | | DIFFERENT | |
| | 0–2 | 3 | 4 | 5+ | I < A | I > A |
| N | 187 | 371 | 161 | 209 | 145 | 381 |
| PREFERRED POLICY OPTIONS: FACTORS SUPPORTING HAVING ONE ADDITIONAL CHILD ABOVE CURRENTLY INTENDED. REF.: NONE | | | | | | |
| Early childhood care | .816 | .850 | 1.092 | .726 | 1.020 | 1.432* |
| Child education | .720 | .794 | 1.510 | 1.858 | .932 | 1.592* |
| Woman employment | .711 | 1.356 | 1.128 | 1.163 | .770 | 1.215 |
| Housing | .453** | .705 | 1.800* | 1.057 | .656 | 2.060*** |
| Money transfers | .663 | .878 | .810 | 1.246 | .612 | 1.558 |
| Tax exemptions | .656 | 1.263 | 1.195 | 1.226 | .281** | 1.687 |
| Fertility treatment | .084** | .545 | 1.886 | 4.557** | 1.602 | 2.319* |
| Good to children | .313*** | 1.156 | 1.430 | 1.595 | 1.414 | .985 |
| Constant | .235 | .570 | .125*** | .039*** | .013*** | .110*** |
| Pseudo $R^2$ | .456 | .279 | .189 | .679 | .216 | .169 |

*** $p < 0.01$ ** $p < 0.05$ * $p < 0.1$

a. Controlling for 12 other variables concerning personal characteristics and attitudes.

SOURCE: *Survey of Attitudes and Behaviors Concerning Family Size among Israel's Jewish Population, 2005.*

a rooted principle. The positive effect of housing is notable at parity 4, especially among those who think their intended fertility is higher than appropriate. The latter group also appears to be particularly sensitive to reductions in the burden of child-education costs. Sensitivity to women's employment conditions does not reach high statistical significance. Finally, the high sensitivity to fertility treatment among persons opting for higher parities confirms the presence of strongly felt pronatal attitudes in a sector that includes the most religious.

## Synthesis and Interpretation

Recent Jewish fertility trends in Israel reveal that economic resources affect birth performances and attitudes about final family size. Such resources include not only household income but also factors such as time allocated by grandmothers for babysitting and state policy incentives. A proxy used here is current wages per employee job in NIS among Israelis. Personal and household outlook founded on self-assuredness and *optimism* are also significant. This, under the prevailing conditions of a Jewish majority in Israel's society, in a sense, represents the symmetric and complementary of the *minority hypothesis* that has been suggested among the main explanations of low fertility across the Jewish Diaspora.[20]

A proxy used here is data on declared satisfaction from life obtained from Israel's annual Social Survey.[21] Figure 5.10, covering the period 2002–2011, demonstrates the relationships of both main explanatory variables with Jewish TFR, as well as the relationship between the two variables. During the period reviewed here, each of three variables—wages, satisfaction, and TFR—featured a short initial period of decline after the 2002 economic slump, followed by nearly constant increase. Interestingly, no visible negative consequences resulted in concomitance with the 2006 Lebanon war or with the 2008–2009 global financial crisis. The figures plotted are yearly data—each dot representing a single calendar year. In each of the three bivariate analyses, a nearly perfect linear relationship emerges, with coefficients of explained variance (R square) above 90 percent.

The emerging relationship between the two main explanatory factors (resources and optimism) and the dependent variable (children) is graphically illustrated in figure 5.11. This peculiar relationship can be visualized as a triangle in which each apex/variable affects the other two. Some of these relationships are quite expected and were just empirically demonstrated—resources explaining both optimism and children, and optimism explaining children. Optimism, in turn, appears to be highly and positively correlated with religiosity. But symmetric relationships can arguably operate, too, which if demonstrable would strongly reinforce the explanatory relevance of this parsimonious model. If it is true that optimism leads to more children, it is also true that children may lead to more optimism. If resources lead to more children, the argument about children leading to more resources, which in the past was surely true among rural societies in less developed countries,[22] today may perhaps transit through the macro influence of children stimulating greater consumption, in turn generating more employment and personal revenues. Finally, if resources lead to more optimism, optimism may generate more resources through risk-taking and entrepreneurship.

While such claims are largely speculative, the uniqueness of Israeli Jewish fertility patterns—high and stable or rising—cannot elude an explanation, and the mutually reinforcing triangular relationship is the main hypothesis submitted here. The acknowledged vulnerability of this interpretation is that it is

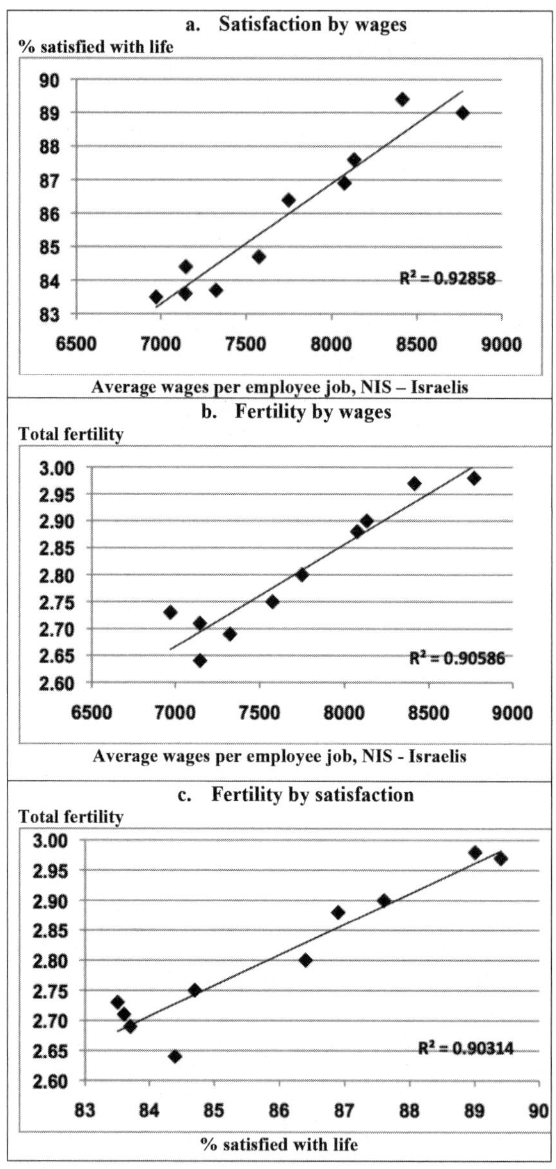


FIGURE 5.10. Relationships between wages, satisfaction with life, and total fertility in Israel—Jewish population, 2002–2011
Source: Adjusted from Israel Central Bureau of Statistics, *Statistical Abstract of Israel.*

contingent upon economic and motivational circumstances that are prone to change. Rather than turning to deterministic and preconstituted explanations, discourse and policies about family and fertility should consider if and how—among other goals—the fundamental pillars of demographic process might be preserved.

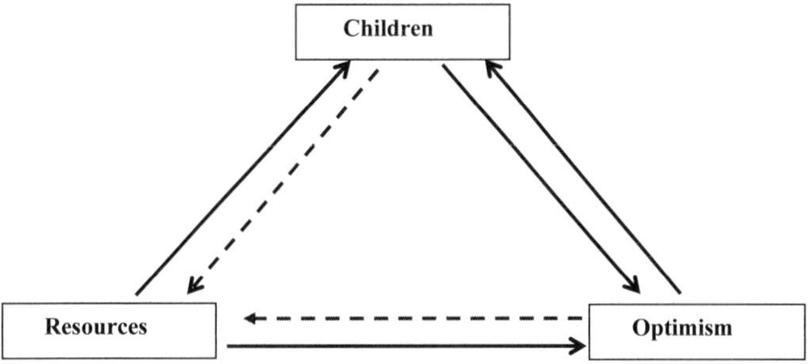


FIGURE 5.11. A parsimonious explanatory scheme of fertility levels in Israel

## Conclusion

This review of fertility performances and expectations, as well as attitudes toward possible family-oriented policies among Israel's Jewish population reveals intriguing facts significant to policy planners as well as to scholars of changing family formations. This study focused on the Jewish population and did not address the non-Jewish sector, which also represents an important part of Israel's overall population trends and policy concerns.[23]

Fertility trends in Israel have been uniquely stable over the past tens of years in spite of overwhelming demographic, social, cultural and economic change. As in the past, Israeli people and young adults, in particular, still do want children abundantly above mere replacement levels, and their explanations strongly point in the direction of the microsocial, household-level, affective sphere of family norms. Persistently, intensive family values appear not to be incompatible with personal aspirations, namely among working women—if the appropriate provisions for family formation and growth can be established. An emphasis on supporting the third and fourth child commands widespread public approval and has much greater societal impact than the support of very large families. Larger families characterize circumscribed sectors of society, namely the more religious and segregated, but have disproportionately been at the center of recent social policies concerning the family. Large proportions of Jewish households do not achieve the family size they intend and believe to be appropriate; their final outcome may be affected by emerging policy provisions.

Policy interventions are indeed highly welcome by most of the public and may significantly affect reproductive performance if they can relate to the crucial needs clearly expressed by the public. Concepts such as the encouragement of births [*yidud hayeludah*] are obsolete in the light of prevailing perceptions of intended and appropriate family sizes in Israel. The real policy issue is how to lower economic and logistic barriers that hinder the widespread desire for children among Israeli (Jewish) families, and how to facilitate families to have the children that they would like to have. Direct money transfers are not perceived as a significant tool in family-growth strategies. All in all, the clear indication is that the public asks for services and not for money transfers, unlike the noted prevailing emphasis in policy discourse and execution. Interestingly, this also was one of the main conclusions of the Israel government committee headed by Manuel Trajtenberg, set up to meet the emerging public needs after the massive street demonstrations in the summer of 2011.[24] The preferred emphasis goes to the infrastructure aimed at early childhood care, child education, housing, and women's empowerment. Policy discourse also passes through a deep process of reeducation of gender-related entrenched habits and inequalities. Bringing the male and the female side of the family equation on the same wavelength, in itself, is a main policy goal.

Our study unveils a paramount dilemma in public policy, namely the conflict of interests between universal and selective provisions. Indeed those more likely to respond to policy incentives and support are identifiable with lower socioeconomic strata—namely through their inconsistent stance on intended and appropriate family size. Additional births that might result from policy interventions would primarily reinforce population groups, which already are in quest for economic support. On the other hand, to try to particularly enhance the unexploited potential of wanted fertility among the socioeconomically stronger risks infringing basic rules of equal opportunity and social justice. The role of the state, obviously, cannot be one of imposing family planning targets but rather of facilitating what people actually desire. This may be a good starting point for a coherent approach to understanding and monitoring family trends in Israel in the conceivable future.

## ACKNOWLEDGMENTS

This essay reflects ongoing research at the Division of Jewish Demography and Statistics (DJDS) of the A. Harman Institute of Contemporary Jewry, The Hebrew University of Jerusalem. The *Survey of Attitudes and Behaviors Concerning Family Size* reported in this article was initiated in 2004–2005 as part of the Demographic Initiative of the Jewish Agency for Israel (JAFI) then chaired by Sallai Meridor. The survey was planned together with Rimona Wiesel, assisted by Moran Neuman, at JAFI and Ilana Ziegler at the Israel Family Planning Association. The Dahaf Institute directed by Mina Zemach undertook fieldwork. Research was directed by this author at the Jewish People Policy Institute (JPPI) in Jerusalem, then headed by Yehezkel Dror and Avinoam Bar Yosef. Israel Pupko ably assisted with data processing. Research continued during my stay in 2006 as senior fellow at the Steinhardt Social Research Institute (SSRI), the Cohen Center for Modern Jewish Studies, Brandeis University, Waltham, Massachusetts, headed by Leonard Saxe. Responsibility for the contents of this essay is solely the author's.

## NOTES

1. François Héran, "Fertility and Family-Support Policies: What Can We Learn From the European Experience?" (keynote speech presented at the 27th IUSSP International Population Conference, Busan, Korea, August 26, 2013).
2. Sergio DellaPergola, *Jewish Demographic Policies: Population Trends and Options in Israel and in the Diaspora* (Jerusalem: Jewish People Policy Institute, 2011), 324.
3. United Nations Development Programme, *Human Development Report 2013* (New York: United Nations, 2013).
4. Sergio DellaPergola and Lean Cohen, *World Jewish Population: Trends and Policies* (Jerusalem: Hebrew University, Jewish Population Studies, 1992); Shlomo Kupinsky, "Results of the Fertility Study Relevant to a Population Policy in Israel," in *World Jewish Population: Trends and Policies*, eds. Sergio DellaPergola and Leah Cohen (Jerusalem: Hebrew University, Jewish Population Studies, 1992), 301–18; DellaPergola, *Jewish Demographic Policies.*
5. Israel Central Bureau of Statistics, annual. *Statistical Abstract of Israel*, Jerusalem.
6. Sergio DellaPergola, "Actual, Intended, and Appropriate Family Size Among Jews in Israel," *Contemporary Jewry* 29, no. 2 (2009): 127–52; Sergio DellaPergola, "Fertility Prospects in Israel: Ever Below Replacement Level?" UN Department of Economic and Social Affairs, Population Division, expert paper no. 2011/9 (2011): 1–36.
7. Data taken from the International Social Survey coordinated by the Zentralarchiv für Empirische Sozialforschung at the University of Cologne and presented in Yulia Kalushka, "Change in Position toward the Marriage Institution, 1994–2002" [Hebrew] (unpublished paper, Hebrew University, Jerusalem, 2006). (in Hebrew)
8. Ronald Inglehart and Christian Welzel, *Modernization, Cultural Change, and Democracy: The Human Development Sequence* (New York: Cambridge University Press, 2005).
9. Shlomit Levy, Hanna Levinson, and Elihu Katz, *A Portrait of Israeli Jewry: Beliefs, Observances and Values among Israeli Jews 2000* (Jerusalem: Avi Chai and Israel Democracy Institute, 2002).
10. *Statistical Abstract of Israel.*
11. Sergio DellaPergola, "International Migration of Jews," in *Transnationalism: Diasporas and the Advent of a New (Dis)Order*, eds. Eliezer Ben-Rafael and Yitzhak Sternberg (Boston: Brill, 2009), 213–36.
12. Sergio DellaPergola, "Patterns of American Jewish Fertility," *Demography* 17, no. 3 (1980): 261–73; Sergio DellaPergola, "Contemporary Jewish Fertility: An Overview," in *Papers in Jewish Demography 1981*, eds. U. O. Schmelz et al. (Jerusalem: Hebrew University, 1983), 215–38; Laurence Kotler-Berkowitz et. al., *The National Jewish Population Survey 2000–01: Strength, Challenge and Diversity in the American Jewish Community* (New York: United Jewish Communities, 2003). The data series for US Jews combines for earlier years TFRs retrospectively estimated from NJPS surveys and for later years cross-sectional data on completed fertility assuming an average age at motherhood of 30.
13. Mark Tolts, "The Interrelationship between Emigration and the Socio-Demographic Profile of Russian Jewry," in *Russian Jews on Three Continents*, eds. Noah Lewin Epstein, Yaacov Ro'i, and Paul Ritterband (London: Frank Cass, 1997), 147–76.
14. Mark Tolts, "Post-Soviet Aliyah and Jewish Demographic Transformation" (paper presented at the 15th World Congress of Jewish Studies, Jerusalem, 2009), 1–36.
15. Momi Dahan, *Did the Melting Pot Succeed on the Economic Ground?* [Hebrew] (Jerusalem: Hebrew University, Feher Institute, 2013).

16. Ahmad Hleihel, "Fertility among Jewish and Muslim Women in Israel, by Level of Religiosity, 1979–2009" (working paper series no. 60, Israel Central Bureau of Statistics, Jerusalem, 2011); Jona Schellekens and Moshe Ophir, *Influence of Family Allowances and Marriage on Births* [Hebrew] (Jerusalem: Hebrew University, 2006).
17. Eric Peritz and Mario Baras, *Studies in the Fertility of Israel* (Jerusalem: Hebrew University, Jewish Population Studies series, vol. 24, 1992); Ilana Ziegler, "Family Growth in Israel and the 'Critical Child'" [Hebrew] (PhD diss., Hebrew University of Jerusalem, 1995).
18. Roberto Bachi, *The Population of Israel* (Jerusalem: Hebrew University, Jewish Population Studies, 1977); Dov Friedlander, "Israel," in *Population Policy in Developed Countries*, ed. Bernard Berelson (New York: McGraw-Hill, 1974), 42–97.
19. Massimo Livi Bacci, *The Narrow Path of Policies* (discussion paper no. 239, Hitotsubashi University, Institute of Economic Research, Tokyo, 2004).
20. Calvin Goldscheider, *Population, Modernization and Social Structure* (Boston: Little Brown, 1971).
21. *Statistical Abstract of Israel.*
22. John C. Caldwell, *Theory of Fertility Decline* (London: Academic Press, 1982).
23. DellaPergola, "Fertility Prospects in Israel."
24. Manuel Trajtenberg, *Creating a More Just Israeli Society* (Jerusalem: Israel Prime Minister's Office, 2012).

# 6

## Dreams and Realities

*American Jewish Young Adults' Decisions about Fertility*

Michelle Shain

THE COVER OF THE FOURTH ISSUE of the Jewish feminist magazine *Lilith*, released in fall 1977, featured an image of a pregnant woman and the provocative headline "The Population Panic: Why Jewish Leaders Want Jewish Women to be Fruitful and Multiply."[1] The lead article focused on how Jewish communal leaders viewed below-replacement fertility among American Jews as an acute threat to Jewish survival,[2] one that took on special significance in the wake of the murder of approximately 6 million Jews by the Nazi regime and its collaborators. Scholars studying the fertility of American Jews felt similarly, as evidenced by the poignant dedication in Ritterband's 1981 edited volume *Modern Jewish Fertility*: "For the Jewish Children, 1939–1945." Twenty-five years later, the Pew Research Center's 2013 Survey of U.S. Jews revealed that the fertility of American Jews remained below that of other Americans and below replacement level. The editorial board of *The Jewish Daily Forward* expressed its dismay, asking, "How will everything from support for Israel to campaigns for social justice be maintained if we become more of a minority than we are today?"[3]

Fertility is not a new concern within the American Jewish community, but today it is surrounded by a pronounced rhetoric of panic and crisis. Groups that are defined by a cultural trait such as language or religion survive by maintaining a balance between (1) births and deaths and (2) recruitment and defection.[4] The term "ethnomaintenance" is used to describe this basic process of group survival.[5] Studies repeatedly indicate that contemporary American Jews are not maintaining a balance of births and deaths.

To fully understand the implications of fertility trends for the future of American Jewry, it is necessary to understand how contemporary Jewish young adults make decisions about whether and when to have children. What are their primary concerns? What role does being Jewish play in fertility intentions and behavior? This paper begins by reviewing research relevant to understanding the fertility behaviors of contemporary American Jews and pointing to areas in need of further study. It goes on to explain the methodology of the present study, a series of in-depth interviews with young Jewish adults about their attitudes toward family formation. Key findings from the interviews are presented, including study participants' commitment to marriage as the context for childrearing, their struggle to balance career and family, and the limited role of Jewishness in their family-formation decisions. Finally, implications of these findings for future research and for Jewish communal policy are discussed.

## Review of Relevant Research

General fertility trends in the United States are well documented. The US total fertility rate in 2011 was 1.89 live births per woman, and the mean age at first birth was 25.6 years.[6] However, these aggregate figures mask substantial differences by race, ethnicity, and social class. A large body of research has documented that high levels of education and being white are associated with delayed childbearing and lower fertility, while lower socioeconomic status and being black or Hispanic are associated with higher fertility and an increasing prevalence of premarital births.[7] Because highly educated Americans are likely to postpone childbearing until after marriage, delayed marriage is a major driver of low fertility for this group.[8] Table 6.1 shows the clear educational gradients in age at marriage, age at first birth, and mean number of children born for American women of childbearing age. Women with a college education are more likely to marry by age 40, but they marry later, have children later, and give birth to fewer children overall.

Religiosity is also a powerful determinant of fertility in the United States. Among US women ages 15–39 in 2002, the total fertility rate was 2.3 among those who said that religion was "very" important to them, compared to 2.1 among those who said that religion was "somewhat" important and 1.8 among those who said that religion was not important.[10] The significant, positive relationship between religiosity and number of children ever born and intended persisted after controlling for sociodemographic covariates.[11] On the other hand, frequency of attendance at religious services was not significantly related to number of children ever born or intended;[12] neither were there significant differences between fundamentalist Protestants, other Protestants and Catholics on number of children ever born.[13]

Empirical evidence of recent fertility patterns among American Jews is limited. About 2 percent of all US adults identify as Jewish,[14] and national surveys often contain insufficient numbers of American Jews to allow for reliable infer-

Table 6.1. Marriage and fertility patterns by education (US women, ages 22–44)[9]

| | PROBABILITY OF 1ST MARRIAGE BY AGE | | | | | MEAN AGE AT 1ST BIRTH | MEAN CHILDREN EVER BORN |
|---|---|---|---|---|---|---|---|
| | 20 (%) | 25 (%) | 30 (%) | 35 (%) | 40 (%) | | |
| No high school diploma or GED | 27 | 50 | 66 | 72 | 77 | 19.9 | 2.5 |
| High school diploma or GED | 22 | 53 | 70 | 78 | 82 | 21.8 | 1.8 |
| Some college, no bachelor's degree | 14 | 47 | 68 | 77 | 82 | 22.9 | 1.5 |
| Bachelor's degree | 3 | 37 | 70 | 84 | 89 | 27.9[1] | 1.1[1] |
| Master's degree or higher | 2 | 29 | 63 | 78 | 88 | | |

1. Bachelor's degree or higher.

SOURCE: National Survey of Family Growth, 2006–2010.

ences. However, the number of Jewish respondents can be increased through pooled analysis of multiple national surveys. Pooling data from the 1991–2002 General Social Surveys revealed that the mean number of children born to Jewish respondents was 1.6, compared to 1.9 for Catholics, liberal Protestants, and moderate Protestants, and 2.1 for fundamentalist Protestants.[15] Lower fertility among Jews is unsurprising given that Jews display many of the key characteristics associated with lower fertility: they have high levels of educational attainment, occupational status, earnings, and wealth,[16] are considered white,[17] and are much more likely than other Americans to describe their religious outlook as essentially secular.[18]

Surveys of large, nationally representative samples of American Jews are another source of fertility data. Based on its 2013 Survey of U.S. Jews, the Pew Research Center reported that the mean number of children ever born to Jewish adults ages 40–59 was 1.9. However, this estimate reflects the fertility of younger baby boomers and older members of generation X, and a comparable estimate for Jews currently in their twenties and thirties was not provided.

Scholars have also used the 2000–01 National Jewish Population Study (NJPS) to examine the fertility of Jewish women. Comparing estimates from the 2000–01 NJPS to figures from the US Census Bureau, American Jewish women were older at marriage and first birth, had fewer children, and had a higher proportion of childlessness compared to all non-Hispanic white women.[19] Methodological problems with the 2000–01 NJPS cast doubt on the accuracy of point estimates derived from the study, but the data are useful for investigating the relationship between fertility and various sociodemographic and Jewish background characteristics.[20] A multivariate analysis isolated the relationships between number of children ever born and marital status, religion of spouse, education, age, distance from the immigrant generation, educational attainment, various measures of Jewish exposure, and Jewish denomination for female respondents ages 35–44.[21] Being married, regardless of religion of spouse, and having a college or post-college education were associated with lower fertility, while being Orthodox was associated with higher fertility.[22] Marriage, education, and Orthodox identification were also significant predictors of fertility for female respondents ages 45 and older.[23] The relationships of education and religiosity to fertility in these models reflect the patterns of the general US population.

The strong, negative relationship between socioeconomic status and fertility in the United States is well documented, as is the high socioeconomic status of American Jews. The limited quantitative evidence that directly examines the fertility patterns of American Jews suggests that their overall fertility is well below replacement level. However, valid, reliable estimates of the number, timing, and context of births in the American Jewish community are lacking. Furthermore, although one qualitative interview study suggested that some American Jewish women frame childbearing as part of their obligation to ensure the survival of the Jewish community,[24] there is very little research on how Jews of childbearing age think about family formation. Scholars have called for more research into American Jewish fertility, particularly the decision-making processes underlying fertility outcomes and differences within the American Jewish community.[25] The present study uses qualitative research methods to seek out the meanings behind American Jewish young adults' decisions about fertility. Methodological details of the study can be found in the next section, followed by findings from the research.

## Methods

Qualitative methods are ideally positioned to answer questions of meaning and capture the complexity of human motivations.[26] Although demography has traditionally been a qualitative discipline, mixed-methods approaches have become increasingly common as scholars have endeavored to understand the perceptions and attitudes that underlie quantifiable demographic behaviors.[27] The exploratory interview study described here was designed to examine ways in which a small group of American Jewish young adults think about fertility and family formation.[28]

Study participants were Jewish women and men ages 25–35, the middle decade of the childbearing age range (15–44). As a starting point, a purposeful sample of eight participants was selected from among respondents to the third wave of the Jewish Futures Project (JFP), an ongoing panel study of eligible applicants to the Taglit-Birthright Israel program between 2001 and 2006.[29] Since 2000, Taglit-Birthright Israel has provided free, ten-day trips to Israel for Jewish young adults, ages 18–26, who have never been on a peer trip to Israel. Taglit-Birthright Israel's eligibility criteria stipulate that applicants (1) identify as Jewish while not actively practicing another religion and (2) have at least one Jewish birth parent or have undergone formal conversion to Judaism. More than 300,000 young Jewish adults have applied.[30]

One advantage of recruiting participants from among JFP panelists was that a substantial amount of information was already known about them, including marital status, number of children, and Jewish background. Furthermore, although they are not perfectly representative of American Jewish young adults, JFP panelists reflect the diversity of the American Jewish community, including individuals with a broad range of Jewish backgrounds and commitments.[31] JFP panelists who were approached to participate in the present study had reported in a recent JFP survey that they were living in the Greater Boston or Greater Providence areas, the two largest metropolitan areas near the researcher's academic institution. The initial, purposeful sample of eight JFP panelists was composed of four unmarried and four married individuals, split evenly along gender lines. Two of the married individuals had Jewish spouses, while two had non-Jewish spouses. All four married individuals and the two unmarried women in the initial sample agreed to participate, but the two unmarried men declined. Two additional unmarried, male JFP panelists were approached, and one of these agreed to participate.

Married participants were asked to recruit their spouses into the study, and all spouses agreed to be interviewed. Interviewing spouses allowed for a more complete understanding of a couple's decision-making process regarding fertility and expanded the participant pool to include Jewish young adults who were either ineligible to apply to Taglit or uninterested in applying. All study participants were between the ages of 25 and 35. Two married couples had at least one child, and a third married couple were expecting their first child. Interviews with the eleven individuals who had been recruited were conducted between August and October 2012. Spouses were interviewed separately. Nine of the interviews were conducted face to face in coffee shops or participants' homes. One participant couple's location had been mis-specified in the JFP survey; they were living in the Greater New York area and were therefore interviewed by phone. Interviews followed a semistructured interview guide (see appendix) but were allowed to develop organically. Topics addressed included participants' earliest visions for their professional and family lives; how those visions evolved over time, particularly after marriage and the birth of a child; and the role of Judaism and Jewishness in participants' lives, both growing up and as adults. On average, interviews lasted just under an hour. Participants were given a fifty-dollar Amazon.com gift card to thank them for their time. All interviews were recorded and subsequently transcribed. Analysis of the interview transcripts followed the processes of coding, sorting, local integration, and inclusive integration.[32]

## Results

As participants described how they thought about family formation, they revealed a set of contradictions. They envisioned themselves in traditional families, but they had not made concrete plans to realize these visions. They wanted children, but they were fearful of the financial, emotional, and logistical strain that children bring. They believed that both men and women should have meaningful roles in both the professional and familial realm, but they had difficulties achieving this egalitarian balance. These contradictions are described in detail in the section below. The interviews revealed two other salient points. First, most participants did not consider their Jewishness as a factor in their family-formation decisions. Second, the Internet played a key role in all aspects of participants' lives, including family formation. Discussion of these two points bracket the discussion of the major contradictions described by participants.[33]

### JEWISH OBLIGATION

Only three participants cited their obligations as Jews as a reason to have children. One married couple believed that it was their "duty" to have children, both because their children would be the only Jewish children to carry on the male participant's family name and because, as the female participant put it, "We need more Jews in the world." In the wake of the Holocaust, she felt obliged to increase the Jewish population. Another participant said, "After I studied and learned a lot about Judaism and the heritage, I started feeling myself like part of the chain from Abraham to whatever. So I thought to myself that this chain shouldn't be stopped with me so I should I continue it, so I think the family is important." The rest of the participants did not explicitly connect their desire to have children to Jewish values or to the survival of the Jewish people.

### TRADITIONAL VISIONS AND VAGUE PLANS

All eleven participants expected to follow a traditional path to family formation. "This is how life progresses: you go to college, you get a job, you get married, you have kids," said one participant. "You get married and have children—that's what you do," said another. Across the board, participants stressed that they would have children only within the context of a marriage. "I can't have a family if I can't find a good wife," declared one male participant. "I have friends who want to have families on their own as single women, and that wasn't sort of my dream ever," said a female participant.

In explaining their commitments to the idea of marriage, participants reflected on their families of origin. Some were inspired by seeing successful marriages. One participant who grew up in "a very loving, supportive family" wanted to recreate that experience as an adult; another credits her sister's strong marriage as inspiring her to look for a healthy, serious relationship. Other participants described their family situation as a cautionary tale. A participant whose mother was widowed when she was young explained, "Watching my mom I thought—it was like, oh, if I'm going to have kids, I'm going to have kids with somebody else, and we'll be there together for each other and for the kids." A participant whose parents divorced when she was young expressed a similar sentiment.

Participants' visions for their own families also included at least two children. All but one participant grew up with siblings, and most participants described having close, loving sibling relationships. They did not want to deprive their children of that experience: "I can't imagine being without my sibling" was a common sentiment. Even the participant who grew up without siblings believed that children are better off growing up with a sibling. One participant went so far as to say that a second child would be "not even so much for ourselves, but for the kids to have a sibling and a friend." Sibling relationships also influenced one couple's desire to space their children close together, as their experiences with their respective siblings indicated that siblings who are closer in age have stronger bonds. Overall, reflecting on their own experiences growing up, participants expressed a strong desire for a family composed of two parents and at least two children.

Despite their commitment to a traditional family structure, participants thought about their future families only in very vague, general terms before getting married. Describing his image of his future family when he was in college, one participant said, "It was kind of very fuzzy, like at some point it might happen." Some participants harbored warm visions of a distant future: one dreamed of living on a cul-de-sac with her sisters and raising their children together; another dreamed of moving to Israel and spending Friday nights sitting around the Shabbat table with his wife and children, learning Torah; a third dreamed of having a vacation property where her extended family would gather. However, while they were unmarried, participants gave almost no thought to how they would actualize their dreams.

Even couples in serious relationships did not engage in detailed discussions about their plans for children. A participant who was engaged at the time of the interview reported discussing children with her fiancé in only a very "general" and half-joking way, and three of the married couples described their premarital conversations about children in the same vein: "abstract" and "vague." "It wasn't like one of us sat down and said we should talk about this," explained one participant. Only one married participant had insisted on discussing children with his then-girlfriend, explaining, "What's the point of getting engaged if you're not on the same page about having kids and other major things?" However, he said, "She freaked out a lot. The day I brought it up, it was really crazy to her." His wife recalled that the conversation "was a little scary," although she attributes the scariness more to her worries about being a successful parent than to the appropriateness of the subject.

Female participants' disinclination toward making concrete plans for childbearing existed alongside an expressed awareness of age-related fertility decline. All five female Jewish participants referred to a negative correlation between age and female fertility in their interviews. They worried about the possibility of having a baby in "that advanced maternal age range" or simply being "out of time." Nevertheless, in almost all cases, serious consideration of the number and timing of children was postponed well after a marriage took place.

## FINANCIAL, EMOTIONAL, AND LOGISTICAL STRAIN

Although all participants in this study wanted children, many expressed reservations about the financial, emotional, and logistical strain involved in childrearing. Having children was deemed "insanely expensive," and none of the married participants felt that they would be able to carry the financial burden without difficulty. One married graduate student who depended on his wife's salary was hesitant to bring a child into what he considers "a very perilous and serious" financial situation. Another married graduate student was grateful for a small inheritance that helped support her young family, noting, "I don't think that I would've been able to have two kids in grad school without living in a studio apartment and surviving on ramen noodles otherwise." The specific expenses mentioned by participants included basic necessities like food and clothing, early childhood education and care, a home with "more space" located "in a safe city with a good education," and savings for their child's college education and wedding.

Men were particularly worried about the financial burden of parenthood. Contemplating the angst he felt about this topic, one male participant said that a key piece of advice he plans to pass on to his child is, "Make a lot of money, kid."

He had started to regret not choosing a more lucrative career when his wife became pregnant for the first time. Another male participant changed professions when he started thinking about marriage to put himself in a position to better support a family. He reflected: "I think about all the things that are out to destroy us . . . that's probably what we're bred to do, born to do. You know, protect your family, and make sure everybody's safe and happy." Although female participants were also concerned about family income, they did not scrutinize their career decisions in this light, as the male participants did.

In addition to the general cost of raising children, the two married couples who wanted to send their children to Jewish day schools bemoaned the high cost of that type of education. One participant recounted, "Once I seriously started looking into it, I was like, 'Oh my God, this is impossible. We would never be able to afford this.'" Another participant said: "The cost of Jewish education, I think, is really, really scary. I don't know how people do it. The idea that you end up spending a quarter-million dollars to get your kid through high school is absolutely insane to me . . . I just can't imagine." All participants perceived finances as one of the biggest obstacles to having children, but the added dimension of day-school tuition was overwhelming for the participants who wanted to give their children an extensive Jewish education.

Participants were also wary of the intense demands that children make on their parents' time and energy. Words like "haggard" and "harried" were used to describe parents of young children, and parents as well as those contemplating having children spoke with dread about sleep deprivation. One childless participant observed that raising children "doesn't look like all that much fun." Among parents, one mother described her life as "a big juggling act" and herself as "a little overwhelmed," while a father noted that the birth of his first child increased conflict and decreased intimacy in his marriage. Childless participants were decidedly wary of the effect children would have on their lifestyles and intimate relationships. One participant without children said, "I try to look at people with kids when I'm out, like at the store or something. And more times than not, they're yelling at them to be quiet, or the kid is whining, or it's a negative situation. And it just makes me think, I don't know if I even want to do this at all." Another participant without children was slightly less circumspect, but nevertheless concluded that she wanted no more than two children, "one for each arm." The perceived burden of raising children went beyond the financial.

### MEETING EGALITARIAN EXPECTATIONS

When discussing how they would manage the demands of childrearing, participants overwhelmingly rejected a traditional, gendered division of labor. "I didn't want to be one of those guys who just kind of disappeared and came back for the kids' bedtime and wasn't so involved in parenting," said one male participant. Instead, men wanted to be active, involved fathers. Three couples discussed the possibility of the husband staying home with the children while the wife worked. Another couple jointly owns and operates a small business, which affords them both flexible hours and a family-friendly work environment: "I wanted to be able to have the time to be able to be with my family more than just being in a business," the male spouse explained. Fathers acknowledged that their wives did more of the work of childrearing, partly due to the demands of breastfeeding, but they were committed to finding an equitable way to share domestic responsibilities.

Among female participants, "I want it all" was the common sentiment. In their youth, women had imagined that combining career and family would be easy: "I had the vision that they would both just blossom as two neighboring flowers and bloom together over the years," said one participant. All female participants, as well as all but one of the male participants, had college or advanced degrees and professional aspirations. However, as participants grew into adulthood, they realized that achieving success in both their professional and personal lives would be challenging. Participants discovered that the workplace was not necessarily accommodating to parents. Finding good childcare and pumping breast milk at work posed challenges. One childless participant became discouraged when she realized that her colleagues with children "felt really torn" about working and "were not doing good at all" balancing their personal and professional responsibilities. Another participant was dismayed to learn that many people in her field believe that having more than two children is "excessive" and reflects a lack of professional commitment. In the personal realm, a professionally successful unmarried participant had been hurt by her grandmother's repeated query, "Don't you want a family like your friends?" Defensively, she said, "I didn't put my career first and avoid family. I was in relationships, but they ended. Like, it sucks." Both female and male participants expressed frustration at the difficulty of attaining both successful careers and rich family lives.

Thinking back to their childhoods, participants reported that they had imbibed egalitarian expectations without being exposed to successful models of egalitarian family life. Female participants remembered that most of the women they had known during childhood, often including their mothers, had not worked full-time. One participant recalled her mother being negative and "catty" about women who did work full-time. Male participants, for their part, had virtually no experience with infants and children during their youth. One male participant had never held a baby until his first child was born. Despite their desire to be active caregivers, men felt somewhat ill-prepared to take on that role.

Several participants said that they would have appreciated additional social support, both formal and informal, during the process of family formation. The topic of trying to conceive was considered "extremely taboo," particularly with professional colleagues, but with friends as well. "It's very taboo to talk about because, as my wife says, you're really talking about your sex life and no one wants to hear about it," joked one participant. Another participant wanted advice about how to time her pregnancies to minimize any negative consequences for her career, but she felt like such conversations were socially proscribed. This participant noted that the Jewish community provides a lot of resources to people with children, but no forum for discussing when to have children. A female participant who had experienced several years of fertility treatments and pregnancy loss made a similar observation: "I think the Jewish community does a good job of getting some resources out to people with children because it's like, the continuity piece is there. But if you don't have children or if you're trying to have children, it's like, where do you go? And I think I didn't quite know where I belonged and what resources, if any, I could access to get some support."

Furthermore, one male participant was irate that the hospital where his child was born offered a mothers' support group but no fathers' support group, and he complained that fathers receive no societal support for their role. A lack of childhood role models combined with a continuing lack of social support, particularly for childless couples and fathers, left many participants struggling with how to realize their dreams.

## THE INTERNET GENERATION

For this generation of Jewish young adults, the Internet fills some of their need for social connection, support, and information. One major use of the Internet is to help locate potential romantic partners. Several participants used dating sites like eHarmony.com, Match.com and OkCupid.com, and one single participant was a fan of the singles groups on Meetup.com. Among participants, an engaged participant met her fiancé through eHarmony.com, and another participant had met his ex-wife through an Internet forum. However, the role of the Internet in family formation goes beyond matchmaking. One participant used Metafilter, a blog to which anyone can contribute, to seek advice about the best time to have a baby for someone with her career aspirations. Another participant used the Internet to find resources about infertility and Judaism and said that she would have loved a virtual support group for Jews struggling with infertility, perhaps in the form of a message board. The importance of Jewish Internet resources extended beyond family formation, too: one participant used Facebook to stay connected to Israeli friends, read Israeli news online, and learn about Judaism from sites like Chabad.org. He recounted how, when his parents asked him for help placing a mezuzah on their door, "I just Googled it and I found out!" In all seriousness, he said, "I think maybe God helped us to invent the Internet."

## Discussion

Explicit discussions of Jewish identity and commitment were rare in participants' descriptions of their journeys toward family formation. Instead, the interviews revealed attitudes and behaviors typical of educated, middle-class young adults of their generation in general. Despite the dramatic increase in births to unmarried women over the past three decades, marriage and marital childbearing remains the dominant pattern among middle-class Americans,[34] and participants' commitment to the nuclear-family ideal reflects this reality. Similarly, participants' egalitarian attitudes toward the division of household labor are typical of their age cohort. As children of the late 1970s and early 1980s, they were raised in the era of the optimistic message of the popular children's album *Free to Be . . . You and Me*: "Mommies can be almost anything they want to be" and "Daddies are men, men with children/Busy with children."[35] In subsequent decades, the labor force participation rate for married women with young children increased dramatically,[36] and gendered differences in the allocation of time to paid and unpaid work reduced substantially.[37] These sweeping social changes are reflected in study participants' egalitarian expectations.

Participants described their difficulties of balancing the demands of the workplace with the extensive emotional and material commitments required for childrearing. Work overload and work-family conflict are common among well-paid professionals.[38] The demanding parenting ideology reflected in participants' descriptions of childrearing, referred to as "intensive mothering"[39] or "concerted cultivation,"[40] is also characteristic of middle-class parents. Like the persistence of the nuclear family ideal, the struggle to balance competing demands is indicative of the way social class shapes the lives of these young adults.

Interviews with a larger and more diverse sample should be conducted before drawing firm conclusions about how American Jewish young adults think about fertility. A complete understanding of American Jewish fertility also requires a reliable quantitative analysis based on recent data, which has not been conducted. Nevertheless, this study strongly suggests that Jewish young adults' attitudes toward family formation are shaped by the broad social forces that affect all Americans, not by particularistic concern for the Jewish community. For Jewish communal policymakers who wish to support Jewish young adults in the process of family formation, universal responses might therefore be more appropriate than parochial ones. Although the organized Jewish community's major efforts to influence US policy over the past fifty years have been in the field of foreign policy,[41] a few individuals have suggested making US family policy a communal priority as well.[42] Lobbying for public early childhood education and care services, paid parental leave and other family supports would be a reasonable response to young Jewish adults' desire for stronger social supports. In this way, the same steps that might ensure the wellbeing of American Jewish families would also contribute to the wellbeing of all American families.

## APPENDIX: INTERVIEW GUIDE

All participants:

- Thinking back, when do you first remember imagining what your life would be like someday, when you grew up? What did you imagine?
  - What were your first visions for your professional life?
  - What were your first visions for your family life? Did you expect to get married? Have children?
  - Was there anything else that you once imagined would be central to your life?
- Tell me a little bit about where you are in your life right now. Have any of those visions become reality, or have you moved in different directions?
  - Are you working or in school? Tell me about that.
  - Are you currently in a relationship?
  - Do you have children?

Married, no children:

- Tell me a little bit about your spouse and your "story" together.
- Before you got married, did you and your spouse discuss having children? Tell me about those conversations.
- Let's talk a little bit about the future. Have you [continued to discuss/discussed] having children since getting married? Tell me about those conversations.

Married, has children:

- Tell me a little bit about your spouse and your "story" together.
- Before you got married, did you and your spouse discuss having children? Tell me about those conversations.
- Tell me a little bit [more] about your child/ren. Name/s? Age/s? Biological children or adopted?
- [If biological:] What were you thinking about right before [oldest child's name] was conceived?
- [If adopted:] Tell me about when you made the decision to adopt [oldest child's name].
- Before [oldest child's name] was [born/adopted], what were you looking forward to the most? What were you most worried about?
- After [oldest child's name] was [born/adopted], what were your biggest joys and challenges?
- [If has multiple children:] Tell me about when your other child/ren was/were [born/adopted]. What were you thinking about then?

- Let's talk a little bit about the future. Do you and your spouse ever discuss having more children? Tell me about those conversations.

Unmarried, has children:

- Tell me a little bit [more] about your child/ren. Name/s? Age/s? Biological children or adopted?
- [If biological:] What were you thinking about right before [oldest child's name] was conceived?
- [If adopted:] Tell me about when you made the decision to adopt [oldest child's name].
- Before [oldest child's name] was [born/adopted], what were you looking forward to the most? What were you most worried about?
- After [oldest child's name] was [born/adopted], what were your biggest joys and challenges?
- [If has multiple children:] Tell me about when your other child/ren was/were [born/adopted]. What were you thinking about then?
- Let's talk a little bit about the future. Do you think you might get married [again] or have more children? What are the factors that will play into those decisions?

Unmarried, no partner, no children:

- How do you go about meeting people who you might want to date?
- When in the course of a relationship do you think it's a good idea to begin discussing marriage or children?
- Let's talk a little bit about the future. Where would you like to be five years from now?

Unmarried, with partner, no children:

- Tell me a little bit about your [fiancé/fiancée / partner / boyfriend / girlfriend] and your "story" together. What sort of future do you see with [him / her]?
- Have you discussed marriage or children?
    - [If yes:] Tell me about those conversations.
    - [If no:] When in the course of a relationship do you think it's a good idea to begin discussing marriage or children?

All participants:

- I'd like to talk a little bit [more] about how you grew up.
    - Were you raised Jewish or another religion? In your family growing up, what did it mean to be [X]?
    - Do you still identify as [X]? What role does being [X] play in your life today?
    - Are you happy with the role that being Jewish plays in your life now, or would you like it to play a different role? What are some of the challenges to creating the sort of [X] life that you want?
    - [If has children:] What sort of religious identity do you want your children to have? How are you trying to teach them about [X], e.g., did you have any type of religious ceremony or celebration when your child/ren was/were born?
- Is there anything else you haven't told me that would be important in order for me to understand how you think about creating a family?

## NOTES

1. Shirley Frank, "The Population Panic: Why Jewish Leaders Want Jewish Women to be Fruitful and Multiply," *Lilith* 1, no. 4 (January 1978): 12.
2. The word "fertility" denotes actual births, not the physiological capacity to reproduce (Sharon Estee, "Natality: Measures Based on Vital Statistics," in *The Methods and Materi-*

*als of Demography*, 2nd ed., eds. David A. Swanson and Jacob S. Siegel (Chippenham, England: Emerald Group, 2008), 371.

3. "Where Is the Good News in Pew Survey on #JewishAmerica?" *Jewish Daily Forward* editorial, October 17, 2013, http://forward.com/articles/185756/where-is-the-good-news-in-pew-survey-on-jewishame/.
4. Etienne van de Walle, "The View from the Past: Population Change and Group Survival," in *Zero Population Growth—For Whom? Differential Fertility and Minority Group Survival*, eds. Milton Himmelfarb and Victor Baras (Westport, CT: Greenwood Press, 1978), 6–25.
5. Sergio DellaPergola, "Demography," in *The Oxford Handbook of Jewish Studies*, ed. Martin Goodman (New York: Oxford University Press, 2002), 800.
6. Joyce Martin et al., "Births: Final Data for 2011," in *National Vital Statistics Reports*, vol. 62, no. 1 (Hyattsville, MD: National Center for Health Statistics, 2013).
7. Joyce C. Abma and Gladys M. Martinez, "Childlessness among Older Women in the United States: Trends and Profiles," *Journal of Marriage and Family* 68, no. 4 (2006): 1045–56; David T. Ellwood and Christopher Jencks, "The Spread of Single-Parent Families in the United States since 1960," in *The Future of the Family*, eds. David Patrick Moynihan, Tim Smeeding, and Lee Rainwater (New York: Russell Sage Foundation, 2004); Sarah R. Hayford, "The Evolution of Fertility Expectations over the Life Course," *Demography* 46, no. 4 (2009): 765–83; Sara McLanahan, "Diverging Destinies: How Children Are Faring under the Second Demographic Transition," *Demography* 41, no. 4 (2004): 607–27; Kelly Musick, "Planned and Unplanned Childbearing among Unmarried Women," *Journal of Marriage and Family* 64, no. 4 (2002): 915–29 and Kelly Musick, "Cohabitation, Nonmarital Childbearing, and the Marriage Process," *Demographic Research* 16 (2007): 249–58, 260–86; Kelly Musick et al., "Education Differences in Intended and Unintended Fertility," *Social Forces* 88, no. 2 (2009): 543–72; Lawrence L. Wu, "Cohort Estimates of Nonmarital Fertility for U.S. Women," *Demography* 45, no. 1 (2008): 193–207; Yang Yang and S. Philip Morgan, "How Big Are Educational and Racial Fertility Differentials in the U.S.? *Social Biology* 50, no. 3–4 (2003): 167–87.
8. Pamela J. Smock and Fiona R. Greenland, "Diversity in Pathways to Parenthood: Patterns, Implications, and Emerging Research Directions," *Journal of Marriage and Family* 72, no. 3 (2010): 576–93.
9. C. E. Copen, K. Daniels, J. Vespa, and W. D. Mosher, "First Marriages in the United States: Data from the 2006–2010 National Survey of Family Growth," *National Health Statistics Reports*, no. 49 (2012); G. M. Martinez, K. Daniels, and A. Chandra, "Fertility of Men and Women Aged 15–44 Years in the United States," *National Survey of Family Growth, 2006–2010, National Health Statistics Reports*, no. 51 (2012).
10. Sarah R. Hayford and S. Philip Morgan, "Religiosity and Fertility in the United States: The Role of Fertility Intentions," *Social Forces* 86, no. 3 (2008): 1163–88.
11. Li Zhang, "Religious Affiliation, Religiosity, and Male and Female Fertility," *Demographic Research* 18, no. 8 (2008) addresses the relationship between religiousity and children actually born. Hayford and Morgan, "Religiosity and Fertility" addresses the relationship between religiousity and intended family size.
12. Zhang, "Religious Affiliation," addresses church attendance and actual family size; Hayford and Morgan, "Religiosity and Fertility," addresses attendance and intended family size.
13. Zhang, "Religious Affiliation."
14. Pew Research Center, *A Portrait of Jewish Americans: Findings from a Pew Research Center Survey of U.S. Jews* (Washington, DC: Pew Research Center, 2013); Elizabeth Tighe et al.,

*American Jewish Population Estimates: 2012* (Waltham, MA: Steinhardt Social Research Institute, Brandeis University, 2013).

15. Tom W. Smith, *Jewish Distinctiveness in America: A Statistical Portrait* (New York: American Jewish Committee, 2005).
16. Paul Burstein, "Jewish Educational and Economic Success in the United States: A Search for Explanations" *Sociological Perspectives* 50, no. 2 (2007): 209–28; Barry R. Chiswick, "The Economic Progress of American Jewry: From 18th-Century Merchants to 21st-Century Professionals," in *Oxford Handbook of Judaism and Economics*, ed. Aaron Levine (New York: Oxford University Press, 2010): 625–45; Barry R. Chiswick and Carmel U. Chiswick, "The Economic Status of American Jews in the Twentieth Century," in *Encyclopedia of American Jewish History*, eds. Stephen. H. Norwood and Eunice G. Pollack (Santa Barbara, CA: ABC-CLIO, 2007): 62–65; Lisa A. Keister, "Religion and Wealth: The Role of Religious Affiliation and Participation in Early Adult Asset Accumulation," *Social Forces* 82, no. 1 (2003): 173–205.
17. Karen Brodkin, *How Jews Became White Folks and What That Says about Race in America* (New Brunswick, NJ: Rutgers University Press, 1998).
18. Barry A. Kosmin and Ariela Keysar, *Religion in a Free Market* (Ithaca, NY: Paramount Market Publishing, 2006); Pew Research Center, *A Portrait of Jewish Americans*.
19. Harriet Hartman and Moshe Hartman, *Gender and American Jews: Patterns in Work, Education and Family in Contemporary Life* (Hanover, NH: Brandeis University Press, 2009); Dawn S. Hurst and Frank L. Mott, *Jewish Fertility and Population Sustenance: Contemporary Issues and Evidence* (Columbus: Ohio State University, n.d.).
20. Charles Kadushin, Benjamin Phillips, and Leonard Saxe, "National Jewish Population Survey 2000–01: A Guide for the Perplexed," *Contemporary Jewry* 25 (2005): 1–31.
21. Hurst and Mott, *Jewish Fertility and Population Sustenance*.
22. Ibid.
23. Hartman and Hartman, *Gender and American Jews*.
24. Sylvia Barack Fishman, *A Breath of Life: Feminism in the American Jewish Community* (New York: Free Press, 1993).
25. Harriet Hartman, response to "Is the Prospect for the Future of American Jewry Positive or Negative?" (paper presented at the Association for Jewish Studies 42nd Annual Conference, Boston, MA, 2010); Linda J. Waite, "The American Jewish Family: What We Know, What We Need to Know," *Contemporary Jewry* 23 (2002): 35–63.
26. Norman K. Denzin and Yvonne S. Lincoln, Introduction, "The Discipline and Practice of Qualitative Research," in *The SAGE Handbook of Qualitative Research*, 4th ed., eds. Norman K. Denzin and Yvonne S. Lincoln (Thousand Oaks, CA: Sage, 2011).
27. Alaka M. Basu and Peter Aaby, eds., *The Methods and Uses of Anthropological Demography* (Oxford, England: Clarendon Press, 1998); David A. Kertzer and Tom Fricke, eds., *Anthropological Demography: Toward a New Synthesis* (Chicago: University of Chicago Press, 1997); Sara Randall and Todd Koppenhaver, "Qualitative Data in Demography: The Sound of Silence and Other Problems," *Demographic Research* 11 (2004): 57–94.
28. The protocols for both the present study and the Jewish Futures Project were approved by the Brandeis Committee for Protection of Human Subjects.
29. Leonard Saxe et al., *Generation Birthright Israel: The Impact of an Israel Experience on Jewish Identity and Choices* (Waltham, MA: Cohen Center for Modern Jewish Studies, Brandeis University, 2009); Leonard Saxe et al., *The Impact of Taglit-Birthright Israel: 2010 Update* (Waltham, MA: Cohen Center for Modern Jewish Studies, Brandeis University,

2011); Leonard Saxe et al., *The Impact of Taglit-Birthright Israel: 2012 Update* (Waltham, MA: Cohen Center for Modern Jewish Studies, Brandeis University, 2012).

30. Saxe et al., *Impact of Taglit-Birthright Israel*, 2011.
31. Saxe et al., *Impact of Taglit-Birthright Israel*, 2012.
32. Robert S. Weiss, *Learning from Strangers: The Art and Method of Qualitative Interview Studies* (New York: Free Press, 1995).
33. Direct quotes are indicated by double quotation marks or indented blocks of text. Minor grammatical errors in participants' speech have been corrected for ease of reading.
34. Smock and Greenland, "Diversity in Pathways to Parenthood."
35. Carol Hall, "Parents Are People," *Free to Be . . . You and Me* (New York: Bell Records, 1972).
36. Claudia Goldin, "The Quiet Revolution That Transformed Women's Employment, Education, and Family," *The American Economic Review* 96, no. 2 (2006): 1–21.
37. Suzanne M. Bianchi and Melissa A. Milkie, "Work and Family Research in the First Decade of the 21st Century," *Journal of Marriage & Family* 72, no. 3 (2010): 705–25, doi: 10.1111/j.1741-3737.2010.00726.x.
38. Ibid.
39. Sharon Hays, *The Cultural Contradictions of Motherhood* (New Haven, CT: Yale University Press, 1996).
40. Annette Lareau, *Unequal Childhoods: Class, Race, and Family Life*, 2nd ed. (Berkeley: University of California Press, 2011).
41. Henry L. Feingold, *Jewish Power in America: Myth and Reality* (New Brunswick, NJ: Transaction Publishers, 2008).
42. Charlotte Jacobson, "Increasing Public Awareness of Demographic Trends and Their Implications: A Jewish Leader's Perspective," *Jewish Population Studies* 23 (1992): 245–47; Letty C. Pogrebin, *Deborah, Golda and Me* (New York: Crown Publishers, 1991).

# 7

## Jewish Single Mothers by Choice

Tehilla Blumenthal

"When I was single, as I wandered through the streets in the night, I would always gaze into the lit windows and see families. Now I walk up to my home and have my own lit window." —Shira

### Introduction

SINCE THE ANCIENT NARRATIVES OF THE HEBREW BIBLE, motherhood has been perceived as an existential requisite for women in many traditional societies. The Israelite matriarch Rachel approached Jacob with a desperate cry because of her infertility: "Give me children, or else I die" (Genesis 30:1). Being married to Jacob was not enough for her, and she felt she was dead without children. This chapter discusses a similarly passionate yearning for motherhood in contemporary Jewish societies, especially in Israel, from the unique standpoint of women who separate motherhood from matrimony, that is, single women who decide to have children in a family that is, by definition, fatherless. Observers and many of these women often distinguish their situation from that of divorced women and from other types of unwed mothers' populations, such as poorly educated, impoverished teenagers, and they call themselves single mothers by choice. In recent decades, while single mothers by choice are not numerous, they have become part of the societal landscape in many Western societies, including Israel and America.

This chapter explores the phenomenon among US and Israeli Jewish single women, secular and religious, who chose to realize their motherhood without a husband. Previous studies have often focused upon the medical risks of single motherhood. This chapter, instead, examines these women's dedication to motherhood in light of society's reaction (the social risk attached to single motherhood) and examines the distinction between the desire for marriage and the longing for motherhood. Medical and biological realities have a profound impact on the phenomenon, as this chapter analyzes. Prior to medically assisted fertility strategies, modern birth control, easily accessible abortion, and diverse family-planning techniques, giving birth was possible only as a result of sexual intercourse, whether the pregnancy was desired or not. Nowadays, technology enables a certain amount of control of human birth processes, giving single women greater options to realize motherhood without a male partner. Moreover, advances in women's educational and occupational achievements have made single motherhood economically feasible: women are more likely than they were in the past to be able to support themselves and a child/children independently. The existence and acceptance of single motherhood also has important consequences for the relationship between the genders, raising essential questions about the need and place of the father in the family.

This chapter's primary research questions addresses the personal and social conflicts that accompany the creation of a family without a father among Jewish single mothers, with a special focus on Orthodox Jewish single mothers by choice who are examined in a case study. It examines the process of their decision, how these mothers see themselves, and how they think their communities and societies perceive them. In addition, this study examines whether or not Orthodox Jewish single mothers by choice demonstrate distinctive characteristics that derive from their beliefs and religion, compared to more secular women. The examination of the single-mother phenomenon in diverse Jewish societies may provide a window through which to clarify the relationships between the individuals, families of origin, and society. This study asks whether these women are perceived as belonging even though they have not followed an acceptable social order and what the social effects of this increasingly popular phenomenon are likely to be.

## Methodology of Original Research

After reviewing existing research in the United States and Israel, this chapter discusses this author's original study of unwed Orthodox Jewish mothers by choice.[1] This research used a qualitative, constructive paradigm with a phenomenological methodology to interpret the phenomenon from the point of view of the participants,[2] using semistructured, in-depth interviews.[3] The interviewer and others were the media for collecting information.[4] Subjects of the study were Jewish single women from Israel and the United States who opted to realize their motherhood without a partner. The goal was to learn about this phenomenon from the women who experienced it, and the study subjects were chosen to represent this population as realistically as possible.[5] The sampling was primarily achieved through the "snowball effect" and the mediation of mutual friends. The sample included thirty-four Jewish single women between the ages of 35 and 50, all mothers who gave birth without a partner to between one and three children using an anonymous sperm donation from a sperm bank. At the time of the study all children were under the age of 11. Nineteen of the women lived in Israel and fifteen lived in the United States; fourteen were secular and twenty religious (Modern Orthodox).[6]

Data collection was performed using semistructured, in-depth interviews.[7] Initially, contact was established to explain the research goals and present the central questions. Each woman was seen for an in-depth, in-person interview during which she was asked to tell her personal story about her decision to conceive and give birth without a partner. The interviews were audiotaped and transcribed. The information was analyzed by creating initial subject categories, assigning material to the different categories, interpreting the material, and, finally, identifying the main themes that emerged from the study.[8] Within this analysis, the interviewees' words were evaluated [perceived] as reflecting their feelings, thoughts, beliefs, and knowledge.[9]

## Earlier Research on Single Mothers by Choice

The modern family in the Western world was defined by Parsons as a nuclear family, consisting of a breadwinning father and a homemaker mother who are legally married and who live under one roof.[10] Together, they manage the household, and their biological or adopted children live with them.[11] Over the decades, women who gave birth to children but did not conform to this model often suffered from discrimination. For example, Chesler notes that in England during the 1920s, women were hospitalized against their will in a psychiatric hospital for as many as fifty years because they would not give up a child born out of wedlock.[12] Even recently, many policymakers cling to Parsons' model when developing societal family policy. As a result, social workers have labeled families who deviate from this model—such as those in which a spouse has died or there is a divorce—as a family "at risk" or a "broken family."[13] Some conservative social observers feel that reinforcement of the conventional model of the two-parent family is important to preventing societal chaos.[14] These assumptions and fears are also responsible for the establishment and continuation of negative stigmas attached to women who give birth to children out of wedlock; their children are often labeled with pejorative terms as well. Depending on the conservatism of the surrounding culture, children born out of wedlock may be considered "illegitimate," and the women who bore them are often assumed to be and are described as being young, poor, and under-educated because they became pregnant unintentionally. This language matters. Thompson and Gongla reasoned that the persistently ambivalent attitude toward single mothers by choice is attributable to the fact that the most relevant research was done in the 1950s and '60s and utilized the terminology "broken" or "damaged" for one-parent families.[15]

Working with a very different population of single mothers, somewhat older, educated, white-collar or middle-class women, Roberts determined that the language and the imagery assigned to poor teenage mothers was not appropriate.[16] Nevertheless, until very recently and today in some segments of society, attitudes toward women who bear children out of wedlock remains extremely negative. Some continue to describe single mothers as deviant and/or mentally unstable. While the latter years of the twentieth saw century less stigma attached to unwed mothers, they were often still characterized as selfish. Thus, for example, in some cases when women went for fertility treatment, unmarried women had to pass a mental-health evaluation that was not required of married women.[17] (Gay and lesbian applicants for medically assisted childbirth also sometimes encounter social or legal discrimination. For example, in Israel openly same sex couples are not allowed to use surrogacy to have a child, whereas heterosexual couples may do so.)

Analyzing the morally based objections of Western society toward women over age 30 who chose to become mothers out of wedlock, Linn distinguished between the deep and overpowering "moral imperative" that women felt about their bearing children, which was often seen to be in conflict with "the moral order" of society to allow childbearing only within the context of marriage.[18] She clarified states of conflict in which societal rules do not correlate with the internal, human need of the individual. This perceived moral conflict may be part of the reason that the phenomenon of single mothers by choice is not adequately represented in research, theory, or clinical findings,[19] despite the fact that the phenomenon is spreading in the Western world among bright, educated, upper-middle-class woman.[20] Linn notes that until her book was published in 2002, there only five published books had dealt directly with single, heterosexual motherhood.[21]

Recent demographic changes—later marriage and nonmarriage among substantial segments of the population—have helped to change the general climate and to create a more widespread understanding of the situation of single mothers and their decisions to give birth, stemming from biological realities of increasing age and the absence of partners.[22] In addition, because greater numbers of later-marrying women depend on medical interventions to help them conceive, there is growing understanding of single as well as married women's feelings of compulsion to experience motherhood before they are no longer fertile; society today better understands single women who also decide to control their fate and not remain alone in their old age.[23] These improved attitudes can be partially attributed to public lobbying focused on explaining the motives of the single mothers by choice in the writing of Jane Mattes and others.[24] In 1981 Mattes founded Single Mothers by Choice in New York, which has grown substantially and now includes women from fifty US states. In the chapter on the movement's philosophy and principles, Mattes stresses that the female members of the organization intrinsically believe that it is preferable that two parents raise a child. However, if a partner who can enable a healthy marital relationship is not found, responsible parenting for the child can be accomplished by a mother who is responsible, caring, and devoted.[25]

Despite studies on how the image of single mothers by choice has improved and how the world has generally grown more liberal, the topic of single motherhood seems to remain sensitive and to arouse ambivalence. Within the US general population, one still encounters conservative notions that counteract the acceptance of unwed mothers, and many people still warn against the phenomenon.[26] A 2011 American study, for example, found that 70 percent of those surveyed said that single motherhood is "bad for society."[27] American Jews, however, are less likely to hold such conservative beliefs, since they have a generally liberal attitudes on matters related to sexuality and reproduction.

## Extended Bachelorhood and the Desire for Children

As discussed in several other chapters in this book (see Parmer, Shain, and Bernstein and Fishman), many contemporary women in modern Western societies embrace principles of equality and aim to utilize their abilities to the fullest through study, self-development, and career development. In addition, women have greater longevity, and it appears to some that given their longer lifetimes they should be able to fulfill themselves by sequencing periods of focus—attending to studies and career early on, then seeking a life partner in a leisurely way. As a result of this and other social trends, the marriage age has been delayed in recent decades in the Western world in general and in Israel in particular, a phenomenon that is sometimes called extended bachelorhood.[28] Not only do many women look for life partners much later than they used to, they arguably look for different things. Women's expectations have shifted from a desire to achieve status and financial support through a partner to a desire for love.[29] At the same time, this extended schedule doesn't stop many women from having social and sexual relationships with men. The prevalence of bachelorhood has forced numerous scholars to conclude that it has become an important period of life and must therefore be prepared for appropriately. These scholars perceive bachelorhood as a status in itself rather than an interim phase before marriage.[30] In any case, there has been a documented, significant increase in the number of US families in which the head of the family is a single man or woman; some note that US society can no longer be defined as "a marrying society."[31] In Israel as well, the number of male bachelors aged 25–29 increased from 28 percent to 63 percent between 1970 and 2008, and female bachelors from 13 percent to 42 percent.[32]

Despite these profound changes, studies show that the personal urge for motherhood, as well as implicit and explicit social pressure for women to become mothers, operate among all strata of Western society, Jewish and non-Jewish alike.[33] A 2006 US study on infertile women reported that they expressed deep mourning and loss in the wake of discovering their inability to fulfill their longing for motherhood. In addition to feeling the loss of a physical experience, they expressed the psychological difficulty of damaged self-esteem as a result of feelings of failure and guilt and having to cope with social stigma. They felt that their personal identity was damaged, and their adulthood was not complete. McKaughan's 1994 survey of five thousand single women over age 30 found that about 60 percent felt threatened by the "biological clock," because they wanted to have a child.[34] Two-thirds of them stated that they had considered having a child without a husband because they felt "empty" without a child. Indeed, in 1998 Stern argued that when mothers were asked to identify what they were proudest of in their lives, the overwhelming majority—including successful career women in high positions—stated that of all their accomplishments they were proudest of all to be the mother of their children.[35]

To a surprising extent, societal changes and the granting of equal rights to women has not impinged upon women's yearning to give birth. On the contrary, women's ability to support themselves and run their own lives allows them to sustain and raise children without the support of a husband, making it easier to choose to be a single mother. Some observers have imagined that motherhood is such a basic aspect of essential femaleness that a woman cannot be a complete woman without it. Historically, because of the biological link between women and procreation, motherhood was usually perceived to be the most obvious and essential purpose of women's lives.[36] For example, in 1870, a physician explained the link between women and their biology by writing it was "as if the Almighty, in creating the female sex, had taken the uterus and built a woman around it."[37] Today, most psychologists, sociologists, and intellectuals are not so blatantly essentialist. Nevertheless, Louanne Brizendine, discussing the "female brain" in 2006 asserted that

> the deep-felt hunger to have a child, can hit a woman . . . suddenly, even the least child-focused females can start craving the tender, delicious feel and smell of babies . . . the real reason is that a brain change has occurred . . . and carries pheromones that stimulate the female brain to produce the potent love potion oxytocin—creating a chemical reaction that induces baby lust, and awakens the craving for a baby.[38]

Some sociologists have explored connections between the biological urge toward parenthood and sociology, stating that the yearning for motherhood is produced not only by factors within individual psychology, personality, and genetics, but also by society's influence. Individuals think they live their own lives and fulfill themselves; however, they actually register implicit directives from their society's ideology. The latter turns everyone into a "subject" of the social establishment of which one is part. Therefore, it is difficult for many women to distinguish between the personal longing to give birth and society's pressure to do so.[39] Even today, society expects women to give birth, and all the more so Jewish and Israeli society. In traditional Jewish sources especially, infertility is considered a curse, and fertility is an expression of God's blessing.[40] The mother is the one who bestows the Jewish identity.

Other observers, analyzing pronatalist pressure on women, challenge what the psychologist Nancy Russo calls "the motherhood mandate," where society forces women to define themselves through motherhood and its qualities.[41] This pronatalist pressure can make a woman who chooses not to give birth feel trapped, and she may often be considered deviant, selfish, and "socially sterile."[42]

Contemporary feminist social analysts sometimes emphasize that longing for motherhood does not consist only of giving birth, but also of raising children.[43] Gregory adds that nowadays, with all options available, there is apparently no need to "succumb" to societal pressures toward motherhood and claim that one was brainwashed.[44] Rather, today it is intrinsic longing that brings women to bear and nurture their children and to invest their passions in this creation. She found that even women who chose in advance to postpone motherhood because of their careers said, with satisfaction, that they did it to be freer, eventually to invest more in their children.

## Single Mothers by Choice in Israel

In Israel and in the United States, as in some other Western societies, the increase in later motherhood is accompanied by an increase in older unwed Jewish mothers.[45] Many of these women achieve motherhood through medically assisted conception. By 2010 the Israeli organization New Family was reporting increased numbers of single women in Israel applying for a sperm donation to realize their dreams of motherhood.[46] In addition, there has been an increase of 90 percent in the number of unwed Jewish mothers, from 8,400 in 2000 to 16,100 ten years later.[47] As elsewhere in the Western world, the historical attitude in Israel toward single mothers by choice was primarily negative. Bar, who compared self-image and the maternal role in married and single women, found that although there was no difference in their functioning as mothers, the single women suffered from a lower self-image.[48] According to her, this was the result of society's negative attitude toward unwed mothers.[49]

Yet increasing liberalization along with greater numbers of single mothers by choice has influenced societal status and brought about a change of attitude on the part of establishment policymakers in Israel. For example, in 1992 single mothers by choice were included in the group of those eligible for social security annuities according to the same criteria applied to single-parent families, and in 2000 the Israeli Supreme Court canceled the requirement of the Health Department for single women to undergo a psychiatric evaluation to obtain a sperm donation.[50] This latter change is mentioned in the research of Segal-Engelchin and Wozner from 2005, which compared married women, divorced women, and single mothers.[51] They concluded that regarding "quality of life," the highest level was found among single mothers by choice who felt that they had societal support and that their lives were full of gratification and interest.

Moreover, in Israel there are other social-psychological factors at play. In a paradoxical way, even though Israel is still a traditional society that emphasizes the sanctity of married life and family, when it comes to childbirth, the general population is very accepting and prepared to acknowledge children born by unwed mothers. Israel is a country that encourages procreation. Motherhood in Israel is much more than a role in the family—it is perceived as having a dimension of patriotism; it is a national role. Israeli society expects Jewish women to take on the demographic struggle (explicitly and implicitly) against the Arab population, to give birth to a nation after the annihilation of the Holocaust, and to provide soldiers for the people's army.[52] Therefore, there is no obstacle to "enlisting" a single woman to the task.

The actualization of the "Jewish mother" role, is the woman's "entrance ticket" to the Israeli collective and a well-regarded status within it. In a discussion at the first Israeli Knesset on passing the "Women's Equality Bill" (passed in 1951), then prime minister David Ben-Gurion said that "the simple and human reason" to grant women equality is their status as mothers. In his own words, "It is impossible to reconcile the fact that my mother, my sister who is also a mother, my daughter, who will be a mother, may be inferior to someone else."[53] Forty-five years later, in a study of free association, Friedman's representative sample of 512 Israeli subjects responded to the word "woman" with the association "mother" most frequently, while the association between "mother" and "wife" ranked only fifth.[54] These nationalistic and demographic facts are among the main reasons that Israel claims world leadership in the number of public clinics that deal with in vitro fertilization and was the first country that legally approved surrogate motherhood.[55] Israel allocates a substantial amount of money to encourage higher birth rates and finances up to eight fertility treatments for all women aged 18 to 45.[56]

## Single Mothers by Choice in the Jewish Orthodox Community

Jewish communities have historically incorporated features of surrounding societies. This is also true of segments of the Jewish community, which can "borrow" and adapt attitudes and behaviors even though while maintaining their own distinctive values and lifestyles. Today, Modern Orthodox Jewry clings religiously to tradition, all the while participating in the social and cultural life of surrounding secular groups. Since Modern Orthodoxy emerged in nineteenth-century Germany, observant Jews who embrace modern sciences and humanities as well as the Judaic heritage have taken as their motto a phrase from the ancient *Pirkei Avot*, the *Ethics of the Fathers*: "Torah learning is beautiful when combined with worldliness."[57] Modern Orthodox society is exposed to, and has to cope with, sociological and value changes in Western society, including changes in the status of women and the narrowing gap between the genders. Orthodox women can now participate in in-depth study of religious texts; they have broader options for education, career, and economic independence.[58]

As in secular society, postsecondary education has postponed the marriage age and having children in Modern Orthodox society and has created the phenomenon of Orthodox extended bachelorhood,[59] discussed in greater detail by Ari Engelberg in this volume (chapter 2). A survey prepared by sociologist Dafna Izraeli for the religious women's forum Kolech showed that only 50 percent of Modern Orthodox women marry before the age 25 and 30 percent remain single after age 30.[60] In this religious society, motherhood is seen not only as a means for self-actualization, but as part of the religious woman's role. The essence of her role as a "mother of Israel" is internalized in religious girls at an early age, when they are taught that their progeny is a sign of God's blessing, while being barren is a curse. Thus, the girl's preparation for her maternal role is part of the educational and cultural system to which she is exposed from a young age.[61] This author's research examining the phenomenon of single mothers by choice in religious single women has found that it is spreading into the Modern Orthodox community as well.[62] There is no clear, unequivocal assertion in *halakhah* (Jewish law) that allows single motherhood. However, there is clear preoccupation with it. Single motherhood can be found in the private legal responses and rulings (*p'sak halakhah*) of rabbis to single women, dealing with each case individually.[63] On the other hand, expressions of conservatism are certainly prevalent in Orthodox society, which is afraid of "loosening the harness," fearing that changes will have negative implications for the whole social system (see Yoel Finkelman and Lea Taragin-Zeller, chaps. 12 and 13 in this volume).[64]

## Interviews with Israeli Orthodox Single Mothers by Choice

Women interviewed in the current study, similar to the subjects of earlier studies, stated that they decided to pursue motherhood without spouses in a relatively late stage of their bachelorhood. Most of the interviewees did not rush to marry at the beginning of their twenties; they preferred to study and develop a career first and widen their cultural horizons. Of course, Israeli women have an additional delay because of required army or national service. Miriam said: "I really wanted to have fun and enjoy bachelorhood, study, travel the world, go to the theatre." Similarly, Shelly noted that during her bachelorhood she "earned a lot and took many amazing trips to various countries." Shlomit said, "It was a period of self-focus for me: personal development, movies, theatre, cafés." They did not feel unusual in their need to invest in themselves, and they felt they were behaving normally, as young people do in modern society. However, most of them, from age 25 (primarily the religious) into the 30s, hoped very much to eventually find a partner and get married.

At the time of their interviews, many said they now found their bachelorhood difficult: they felt hollow, lonely, different from family members and those around them, and essentially unfulfilled. For instance, Talya asked, "How many movies can one watch? And how many plays? It really stops being interesting, and one wants to advance towards a life of substance, family." Similarly, Engelberg found that among the religious Zionists, most bachelors regarded their status as temporary, a limbo that would be corrected by marriage. The majority longed to marry and reported they were miserable in their aloneness.[65] Women in the present study, both secular and religious, also described a feeling of emptiness: "One goes out on more and more 'dates,' acquires more and more acquaintances, and somehow it gradually grinds down one's personality." Frustration also derived from society's reactions to the single female, and particularly the religious society's. For example, Heftzi said that she dreaded "that feeling at friends' and family weddings where everyone is looking at me, the 'old maid,' telling me again, 'By you soon!' It was a terribly unpleasant experience."

Some women tried to cope with their bachelorhood by seeking a partner intensively. Shlomit said, "I dated of a lot; I think I was the first Israeli on JDate; it was certainly exhausting." And Rosie: "Men here in New York are not the marrying kind. Most of them are captives of 'the eternal search scene,' and it's interminable, an endless dating cycle." On the other hand, at some point, most women chose to accept their status as single and tried to make the most of that period. For example, Dafna said, "I decided I didn't wish to live in a constant state of anticipation. I convinced myself that bachelorhood was now my 'status' and I should at least try to enjoy every minute of it. I traveled and celebrated and did not apologize to anyone. But it's upsetting to live in anticipation; it was difficult."

The women interviewed were all independent and successful. Nevertheless, they said they felt unfulfilled. It was perfectly clear that at this point in their lives they felt their success in career and business was secondary to their wish to marry and have a family. Shir described it well:

> I think that anyone who hasn't had the experience of being an older single, who's looked for years and not found, cannot truly understand how hard it is. I was seemingly a very happy single woman, earning well. I went to India and had a lot of fun. I had always heard how married people envy me, and I had always resented that envy. What are you jealous of? The truth is that I lacked something so much that I compensated for it by doing things I loved, while what I actually wished for was something else entirely.

### MATRIMONY AND PARENTHOOD

The religious discourse clearly links matrimony with parenthood. Love is mentioned together with family and family together with children. Thus, for example, the 2005 "Single Woman's Prayer" written by Rabbi Joel Bin-Nun states: "Please Lord, hear the cry of single women who seek their partner and provide a match for them, so they will be blessed to build their house with happiness and purity and raise their children in health and with the Lord's blessing, Amen."[66] The discourse in the secular world is different, and under the umbrella of personal rights the longing for matrimony is regarded as distinct from the longing for parenthood.[67] The latter is expressed in terms of the right to get pregnant and to self-fulfillment through motherhood.[68] Under Israeli law as well, "The right to parenthood is a fundamental human right and derives from the right to self-fulfillment, freedom and honor."[69] Yet despite the difference between religious and secular discourses, the present study did not find significant differences between religious and secular women regarding the connection between marriage and giving birth. All the women said that, from the beginning, they planned to marry and wanted to give birth within the structure of marriage. This finding is in correlation with studies conducted on the general population of single mothers by choice in the United States.[70]

Importantly, being called a single mother by choice annoyed the women in the present study; they all stressed in one way or another that although they chose to get pregnant, they did not choose to be single mothers, and their initial hope had been to get the "package deal" that includes a husband with the children. According to them, they had made great efforts to find a partner, hoping to have a two-parent family and not become unwed mothers. Religious women made even further efforts. Four of them described agonizing, desperate attempts on their part to find a partner. Adina, for example, said: "I was willing to make pathetic decisions, compromise and date even men with a psychiatric background, just to have a child 'the right way.' "

With the goal of finding a father for their children, nine Israeli women (four religious and five secular) described attempts to find a partner through shared parenting, attempts which failed, mainly due to the man's reluctance to commit. For example, Abigail reported, "Can you imagine? He gave up so soon, after the third sperm donation that did not result in a pregnancy; so I decided to go solo and immediately made an appointment at the sperm bank." Nava expands from her own experience: "A man offered me coparenthood, and I counted on him. Then he withdrew from it very inconsiderately. It happened to my friends as well. They come, they promise, they delude us in a way, then withdraw when they don't feel like [going forward]."

In spite of a willingness to compromise, the interviewees certainly possessed principles and bright lines they were not prepared to cross for the sake of matrimony. For example, most religious women noted explicitly that they did not want to date secular men, and in the United States, nine women (representing both religious and secular lifestyles) said they would not marry a non-Jewish man. In addition, they did not agree to compromise when they encountered unsuitable characters and behaviors. Gali, an Israeli religious woman, clarifies: "I was not ready to compromise on men any more, just because I wanted children. There is a very serious problem in our circles with finding a partner. There are many religious girls and few religious guys, and they feel they are God's gift to the world." Dana, a secular US woman, adds: "I have just read a book about the way dynamics have changed in relationships between the genders and that nowadays, if a man wants a child, he should consider the woman's needs, so she would have a reason to have a child with him."

The women expressed considerable frustration at the difficulty of finding a suitable partner, but it was clear that their frustration did not decrease their longing to become mothers. Unlike in the past, when the longing to bear a child taught women they had to marry, scholars now believe women see motherhood and marriage as representing two distinct yearnings.[71] (Rosanna Hertz has examined the rift between the marriage institution and the role of motherhood, beginning in the early 1970s.[72]) When the women in the current study realized they would not find a suitable partner for life, they decided that their only choice was unwed motherhood. In their opinion, as Shirley said, "Matrimony is wonderful. Certainly, everyone would like both—wonderful matrimony and children, but I understood that if I can't find a partner, I should move on and give birth."

## LONGING FOR MOTHERHOOD

Once the interviewed women considered the option of giving birth, they described it as a compulsion that exploded from within, giving voice to a fierce sense of purpose also described in the literature. For example, as was expressed by the interviewee, Rosie: "Suddenly, at the age of thirty, I felt something really burning inside me. I knew I wanted to become a mother." Many of the women used the term "default" to refer to the decision to give birth. Lia said, "I felt I had absolutely no choice, because my default decision to be a mother was completely obvious to me."

In the present study, a deep longing for fulfillment through motherhood was expressed strongly by all the women. They spoke of primeval needs and social and ideological motivations. Nava put it this way: "Motherhood is a tendency that I feel is very natural to me, in the sense that I'm connected to it and crave it." Similarly, Rachel described a primeval urge: "There is something natural inside me that says, 'I want a child.' I think it began when I was 34." Among Jewish women in particular, there was a further catalyst founded in the need to perpetuate the Jewish nation and people: "You know," Shlomit said, "in the explanations of the book of Exodus, they say that women were the active ones who saved the Jewish nation. It seems so obvious to me that when one speaks of carrying on life, women are those who do what is required out of internal intuition." Several women spoke of their need to raise a family and define themselves within a family, as, for instance, Dafna noted: "I am not giving up on family. I need to have a family. I grew up in one, and I need it. It's important for society, for my Jewish identity, existence, my ego, continuity. I just need a family." Sima, a religious Israeli, tells a difficult story that clarifies the need and tremendous pressure to raise a family. She spoke of her roommate in national service who grew up in B'nei Brak (an Orthodox town). When she reached her thirties without finding a match, she committed suicide. At her grave, Sima decided to have a baby on her own. She said, "Which mother will eventually be happier, the one left with a daughter's name on a headstone, or the one whose daughter gives her grandchildren? Indeed, there is no husband, but there are grandchildren!"

Psychoanalytic theories link the need for motherhood to the narcissistic need for self-expansion and the illusion of being Godlike in creating life.[73] Erikson claimed that when a woman gives birth, she can find in herself the ability to continue her existence in the world.[74] According to Deutsch, motherhood provides opportunity of experiencing immortality.[75] A woman becomes a life-giving link in the constant struggle between life and death. One-third of the subjects expressed similar sentiments when giving reasons for their wish to give birth. In Bruriah's words: "I feel that my self-fulfillment is expressed by providing continuation to the next generation." They referred specifically to the need to preserve their genes. For example, Renana said: "I believe that if the body functions, it is important to give birth to your own child and not adopt; it is a privilege to pass on my genes to the next generation."

Because the study was conducted among women who define themselves as Jewish, nineteen of them from Israel and the United States, both religious and secular, expressed national Jewish arguments. For example, Rosie said: "I couldn't live with myself or forgive myself if I hadn't tried to have a baby. Especially after the Holocaust. . . . Our nation has a demographic problem after the Holocaust and because of assimilation." Or Gail: "It moves me so much that I'm one person who has brought two people into the world, two Jews, especially after the Holocaust." Similarly, Jane Bock's study on unwed mothers in the United States found that the Jewish subjects (who were not defined as Orthodox) expressed a motivation and the necessity to raise more generations for the Jewish nation after the Holocaust.[76] Six of the religious women added religious motivations and needs related to someone remembering them after their death. Gail: "I would like to have someone say *kaddish* for me after my death." Bruriah: "I want to have someone sit *shiva* for me (observe the Jewish week of mourning)."

### PLANNING THE MOTHERHOOD PROJECT

Most of the subjects reported that to fulfill their deep yearning to give birth during their bachelorhood involved much planning and organizing. Two-thirds of them participated in groups or Internet forums in preparation. All elaborated on how much thought and attention were devoted to advance planning for the economic, medical, and familial-social aspects of their decision. The religious also planned for the halakhic aspect. The women gave great thought to planning their financial affairs during the pregnancy and after the birth. As a result, half the women changed professions or jobs so they could take care of the baby properly, or took a job that required fixed hours or was closer to home so they could save commuting time. Annette said: "I was looking for a job suitable for a mother: convenient hours, not taking work home, not being expected to stay late. I know I won't make much. I earned almost twice as much previously, but now I can leave my job at 3:30 to collect the kids from daycare."

The women were well aware that their income would decrease and their lifestyle would change. However, this knowledge did not dissuade them from fulfilling their wishes. Rina, a religious woman from Israel, described this well: "I thought about the economic aspect. Mine would be a one-salary family, while usually the woman's income is the second in the family. I didn't know how I would manage, but I knew I was ready for it. I would try to prepare for it and I know how to economize. Of course, I also rely on God, for He retains the key to sustenance." Because the women interviewed were between 35 and 50 when they chose to receive sperm donations, their age and the need to have contact with the sperm bank forced them to contact doctors who were experts in in vitro fertilization. Six of them also needed an ovum donation. The women were aware of the complicated procedures they were expected to undergo and prepared accordingly.

It should be noted that women in the United States do not enjoy the reproductive-care options Israeli women receive, so their expenses are particularly high. As mentioned, Israel allocates a substantial amount of money to encourage higher birth rates and finances fertility treatments.[77] Nevertheless, even in Israel, women noted the expense, and many preferred American sperm banks to Israeli ones because the American provided more detailed donor information, while Israeli kept the donor's identity completely anonymous, apart from only very basic features and his nationality.

### PERSONAL AND FAMILIAL-SOCIETAL CONSIDERATIONS

The single women who decided to give birth alone in a somewhat conservative society (halachic for the religious ones) knew they were risking ostracism from the family community frameworks to which they were deeply connected and in whose norms they believed. Maya, referring to the conservatism of those around her, thought that if she "threatened" them with giving birth unwed, they would make more efforts to find her a "match." She said, "I decided that if I didn't get married until age 38, I'd make sure to have a child. I looked for a partner very openly and told everyone that I would have a child even unwed. It was as if I wanted to shock those close to me into understanding that they had to find me dates in a hurry."

In view of conservative influences in society and religious women's education (especially among the Orthodox), it is easy to understand these single mothers' fear of sharing their decision to become unwed mothers with their relatives, even though they were attempting not to design "a new family" but to preserve their traditional role as mothers. They were aware that and agreed with others that their behavior was not the norm, but they still longed to be accepted by their families, religious community, and the larger society. The single women deliberated long about the question of when to tell their family and friends about their wish to have children alone. Half of the subjects (mostly religious) chose not to tell their parents before getting pregnant. Six explained this delay as stemming from caring—the reluctance to disappoint their families in case the fertilization was not successful. The rest didn't want to generate conflicts with conservative relatives. Nava, for example, said, "I planned to tell them only when I got pregnant. I assumed they would accept it, but I did not share in advance, because they are a bit *alt-modish* ("old-fashioned" in Yiddish).

On the other hand, it is quite clear that all the subjects had at least one good female friend, with whom they deliberated and who helped later on. Shelly relates: "Michelle was always there for me. I discussed it all with her, and she accompanied me through all the inquiries and procedures." Two-thirds of the women participated in support groups for unwed mothers or in Internet forums. Many met other women there and became close friends. Elisheva met three other religious women, and they all decided to move close to each other, even before giving birth, to support and help one another with the procedure and babies. They also worked for acceptance by the community, although this clearly was not as much of an issue for the secular women as it was for the religious.

## HALAKHIC PREPARATION

From the halachic point of view, although there is still no explicit and unequivocal agreement to allow unwed motherhood, there is open discussion of the phenomenon, and permission is often granted in rabbis' private responses to single women. All the religious women considered it important to examine and clarify the halachic aspect of single motherhood and to receive permission for their plan. They gave much thought to the nationality of the sperm donor. They studied the halachic literature, on the Internet and directly with the community's rabbi. For example, Edna said: "I actually asked the rabbi, because the halakhah is very important to me." Rachel was very proud to receive sweeping permission from three rabbis.

Nevertheless, many of the women said that their yearning to have a child was so deep that they felt that they could not have handled a halachic prohibition, as was strongly articulated by Miriam: "I knew deep inside that it had to be 'kosher' to give birth alone without a spouse. I feel in my heart it has to be all right if a woman wants to bring a life into the world." They expressed no resentment of the halakhah, no desire to abandon their religious beliefs, but, rather, a feeling that, through childbirth, they were fulfilling their roles as Orthodox Jewish women. As Shlomit said: "I think that in matters of life and giving birth, women should decide. I'm not sure a man has that powerful inner feeling. Rabbis are men, after all. Even without their permission, I feel it is my role to bring life into the world." Despite that, all of the religious worked to get rabbinical permission, especially because of their concern for their children's future. They didn't want them to be halakhically banned from getting married.

Dafna explains: "I want my children to have no doubts. I don't want them to struggle, to have to prove themselves worthy of being married in the future." Naturally, the choice of sperm donor was a major issue for all the women. However, while the secular women focused mainly on such things as choosing a sperm bank, which genetic traits to stress, the price, quantities of the order, and so forth, the religious women without exception showed much more interest in whether the donor was Jewish or gentile, an issue that stems from the concern about the prospective child's halakhic status. Although most Jewish authorities agreed it was preferable according to halakhah to use a gentile's sperm to prevent unwitting incest among resulting children, others ruled against it and spoke of preserving the "Jewish spark." Two-thirds of the religious women said explicitly that they chose a gentile's sperm in order not to "get into trouble" with the rabbinate, but it was a very complicated issue for them. Maya in Israel expressed the paradox well: "Unfortunately, I used a gentile's sperm. It really wasn't easy for me, but I didn't want the child to suffer because of halakhah. I felt that for someone like me, who wouldn't marry a gentile, it would be preposterous to receive a gentile's sperm."

The other religious women insisted on using a Jew's sperm because of religious and national motivations. These women did so only after consulting with a rabbi, making sure they were not putting their future child in "halakhic risk." Batya said: "After much deliberation, I chose an Israeli Jewish donor. I felt I wanted someone from our nation. I wouldn't have felt comfortable if it had been a gentile's sperm. I immigrated to Israel and wanted to marry a Jew, so how could I have a baby from a gentile's sperm?" Shelly, an American, referred explicitly to the Jewish genome: "It was important to me to have a Jew's sperm because the Jewish genes are essential to me."

## THE PREGNANCY PHASE

The women arrived at the pregnancy phase after months and even years of deliberation. Due to their relatively older age, most of them had undergone difficult hormonal treatments. The pregnancies were usually considered "high risk" and required special medical care and attention. The women described that period as hard because of the mental and medical investments, but satisfying as well. Their visible pregnancy was a fait accompli and an explicit expression of their ultimate decision to become single mothers by choice. In fact, visible pregnancy was the first time they had to cope with other people's reactions to their decision.

The religious women in the United States were much more worried than the secular about the others' reactions. For example, Jenny said: "I know some people look at me oddly behind my back for not behaving normally and not getting married." The findings showed an additional, significant difference between religious women in the United States and in Israel. Some of the American religious women expressed concern that they might be suspected of getting pregnant in the context of unmarried sexual relationship and not by artificial insemination. For example, Susan said: "When people noticed my pregnancy, I felt a lot of embarrassment around me. I immediately clarified openly what I had done, and the reaction was usually very supportive, especially from women. Some said explicitly they were happy it was not an 'accident.'" Renana felt that her modest clothing could make a difference in how people would interpret her pregnancy: "I really make an effort to dress modestly, so people would understand that a girl like me would certainly do this according to halakhah." Interestingly, the religious women in Israel did not express such concern, probably because of the visibility of and easy accessibility to the sperm bank and in vitro fertilization in the country. The secular women did not even deal with the question of how or from whom they became pregnant, and they only referred to the functionality and efficiency of fertilization by a sperm donor during the process of becoming mothers.

During the pregnancy, the women continued to prepare and organize for their new family soberly and responsibly, by moving to a more convenient location or closer to their parents, changing job conditions, and building their social network. All twenty religious women noted that it was important to them to build a good connection with the religious establishment and the community's rabbi. It was essential for them to integrate into the religious framework and enable their children's participation in their religious community. These findings are similar to those of Hertz, who found that most unwed mothers in the United States made a conscious effort to do "social nesting" before becoming mothers, to be well-organized for the change in their roles, and to ensure that their needs as mothers were provided for.[78]

All the women interviewed, religious and secular, said they received mostly positive reactions from their surroundings, especially from women, and even stressed their amazement at the abundance of goodwill they received. Miriam, for example, commented, "I was a bit worried about the reactions, but was very surprised at how much everyone rooted for me," and Shirley said, "Everyone around me was very happy; I'd never received so much love and acceptance as I did during the pregnancy."

In spite of generally wide acceptance, one-quarter of the women, both secular and religious, experienced negative reactions and upsetting remarks from relatives, colleagues, or neighbors. Some reported relatives objecting because "the child would not have a father." Rachel referred to the "primitive, conformist neighbors" who objected and said she was "a 'strange one' to have a fatherless baby." And Shelly said, "At work, I felt that it disturbed some of the men because it seemed like sperm theft to them, although it's actually a purchase." Gali, an Israeli teacher at a secular school reported: "I had problems at work. They wanted to fire me during my fifth month of pregnancy. They claimed that I did not fit the proper school image."

The women in this study described the motherhood phase as the fulfillment of their awaited purpose. The many difficult years of yearning for a baby, deliberating, coping with social and physical difficulties were dwarfed by the powerful experience of holding the newborn baby in their arms and caring for it. Maya said, "My life is happy. It was not really happy before. Now there is joy in life. I feel I brought a gift to me and to the world. It's so good."

As Jews, the first expression of appreciation for having a child is the religious ceremony of naming girls and boys and ritual circumcision for boys (*brit milah*). It was important for the mothers in this study to perform ceremonies (brit milah for boys, and *zeved/simchat bat* for girls), although, for the secular women, the tradition is less a matter of faith than celebration of the birth. Regarding brit milah, most Orthodox women were busy finding a *mohel* (the man who performs the ritual of the circumcision) who would be willing to perform the ritual with special sensitivity to their needs. For them, the ceremony was also the first confirmation from the religious community that they were accepted as single mothers.

The ceremonies were mostly festive and grand. Some of the subjects said they invested in the event as a substitute for the wedding they did not have. Shira reported: "My mom said we would have a big celebration for our guests. Since I hadn't had a wedding, the money my parents saved for it would now be spent on the brit. Mom said, 'I want everyone to know that this is a wanted child. Our family accepts him and wants to celebrate him.'" And Maya, a mother of a girl, noted: "It was a very important event for me. Many close people in my life did not have the privilege of participating in my wedding, and this was the first opportunity for public celebration. This has been the most significant event in my life so far, and I explained to my guests that nothing was taken for granted." The names, traditional and modern, that the women gave their children expressed their emotions and included themes of gratitude, joy, and blessing. The names of deceased relatives and important people in their lives were also given to continue family dynasties.

Giving birth and experiencing motherhood may cause upsetting emotions as well, as a result of natural stress, such as chronic exhaustion. Moreover, the psychological literature is full of advice for mothers coping with the gap between their subjective needs and the necessity to respond to their children's needs.[79] The subjects certainly reported physical stress and difficulties in taking care of their children, but it was clear these feelings were dwarfed by their satisfaction with their roles as mothers. Perhaps the long journey following their choice to give birth made them appreciate even more the privilege of becoming mothers, especially as older women. Many studies show that giving birth at an older age allows for a deeper consolidation of the maternal consciousness and increases readiness and maturity.[80]

The difficulties the mothers did mention were mainly economic, such as having to support children on one salary, and emotional, such as coping with loneliness in stressful situations like a child's illness. For example, Bruriah recalled: "When my baby screamed in the middle of night because of an earache, I felt such loneliness. I don't think I would have felt it if I'd had a partner. The child woke the whole building, and I had nobody. It's impossible to describe how hard it is." However, most women noted that they had been aware in advance that they would have to cope alone. Therefore, despite the difficulties, they felt they had prepared well for their maternal role and did not feel bitter. Annette was very articulate on the subject of her struggles: "It's not as if I had expected something else and then I was suddenly alone and disappointed. I did not expect anything different. I knew I had to learn to deal with things on my own." Most of the mothers agreed with Gali: "Throughout the difficulty and sleeplessness I felt happy with my decision. I really didn't regret it for a second." The women distinguished between the experience of coping on their own and feelings of loneliness. Actually, since they became mothers, they had felt an improvement and did not experience the loneliness of their bachelorhood days. Gail said, "As a single woman you're alone a lot and there is much loneliness. Nowadays, I'm not alone: there is someone waiting for me at home."

Moreover, for both the secular and the religious, the change from a single woman to a mother significantly improved their status. The fulfillment of motherhood was accompanied for all the women by a central theme: the birth of the baby was also the birth of her own family, with her as head. The women mentioned how important it was for them to have the privilege of "establishing a family." They stress that they moved from the status of "being single" to the much more respectable one of "having a family." Becoming mothers strengthened their relationships with their relatives, improved their contacts with their surroundings and their status in society. Their parents call them much more to talk to the grandchildren and are more considerate about their needs when family decisions are made. The religious women were especially surprised by the sympathy they received from the religious society and friends, even when their rabbi opposed the idea of single motherhood. Heftsi tried to explain the sympathy she received from the religious society: "Our religious friends were so nice. I wouldn't say they encouraged it, since they want to preserve the traditional family unit. However, I felt that most of the families understood and blessed me, because the religious believe it is so important to bear children."

For the religious women, as mentioned, it was especially important to be in contact with the community's rabbi or synagogue. In communities where the rabbi supported the women, for example by inviting them for Sabbath dinners and offering assistance (mainly in the United States), they noted the positive connection with much warmth and satisfaction. Chana described excitedly how, on Friday nights, when the rabbi says Kiddush, children line up with their fathers to taste the wine: "I asked the rabbi if I can watch him from the men's section, and the rabbi answered, 'You can stand in line, beside him.'"

On the other hand, several women in Israel and the United States mentioned the negative attitude of a community's rabbi. For example, Susan and Heftsi's rabbi refused to give the special blessing for a woman giving birth. The religious women repeatedly stressed their frustration, hurt, and sense of insult in reaction to the attitude of the religious establishment. Gali said, "When establishment rabbis are interviewed on the subject, they never express the point of view of the world of halakhah, but rather their personal and social opinions." Dafna responded to the rabbis' claim that single mothers harm their children: "Before I had the baby, I reflected endlessly, 'How will I cope? Is it suitable for me? In which society will the child be raised? Where do I want to live? How much money do I have to support him?' How dare they say it is against the child's welfare! It's simply ridiculous."

All women paid a lot of attention to selecting the educational system suitable for their children. While the secular women stressed the choice of a high-quality education and a convenient location, the religious looked also for systems that were both religious and liberal enough to avoid stigma. The latter was a major concern because the people at the head of educational systems were often affiliated with the religious establishment and would bring any negative attitudes about single motherhood into direct contact with single mothers by choice and their children. Sima, a religious mother, explains, "As a single woman you are an addendum to society, as if you're somehow still in a state of waiting. Judaism is constructed around the family. Even when you're married you're in a state of anticipation until you have children." Interestingly, having children decreased some women's desire to engage socially with the religious community. The privilege of "raising a family" thrills them to the extent that, as one mother said: "Nowadays, I don't like to be invited to Sabbath dinners with the kids, as I used to when I was single. I want to cook for them and give them a home atmosphere, so they will have pride in our family."

Over time, one of the central assumptions about raising a family became quite obvious among the Israeli women, religious and secular alike—the need to have more than one child. It was quite apparent to them that a "real family" comprises many children. For their part, most of the American women emphasized economic concerns when considering family size. Chana said: "I live in a city where the annual school tuition fee for one child is $30,000. I have to take that into account when I consider having another child. And that doesn't include payment for the fertilization treatments. I have to think about what's best for the child. What would be preferable to him—having a sibling or good living conditions, good education, and my not having to be away from the house so much and always being concerned about earning a livelihood." The American women in this study saw no problem with having a family limited to one child. Shelly expressed the idea that a mother and child make a family: "I feel I have a real family. I've accepted that I have only one son. There are advantages to having more or fewer children, and the grass is always greener on the other side, but I'm very pleased with my family constellation."

Running parallel to the importance of having a family was the women's sense of the exceptionality of their families. All the women were aware of coping with the fact that their children did not have a father figure. They were helped by Internet forums, guidebooks, and professional support to acquire psychological and didactic tools to deal with that deficiency and the children's questions. However, some of the religious women stressed repeatedly their families' differentness and their anguish at not establishing a bi-parental family: "A true family has a father . . . I feel that we're a family, but I still think it's preferable for a child to have a father, too. I really believe a whole family should have a father, mother, and kids."

Occasionally, women expressed opinions similar to those of the rabbinical institutions regarding their exceptional status. Bruriah said that she didn't want to mention the names of the rabbis who gave her permission to have a baby out of concern that other women would improperly use it for themselves. She said she totally identified with the rabbis who worry that women will more readily choose to have a child without a husband. Despite being a single mother herself, she declared she still believed there was no substitute for a biological parent: "Mostly, children have two parents. Of course, one can live with only one, but if a child has only one, he certainly is at a great loss." In a religious family, the father's role is central, and his absence in social-religious events magnifies the feeling of differentness. Shira said: "At first, it really bothered me that the child wouldn't have a father. I thought about it for days and even cried . . . I wondered what will happen when the child grows up and has an *aliyah* to the Torah at the synagogue and won't have a father's name."

The religious single mothers were aware of the difference between themselves and the secular mothers regarding their conservatism and their belief in the ideal of a traditional family unit. Rosie: "I think that in secular Jewish society, 'liberalism' is the 'new religion' and because of that there are all kinds of family structures, and it is unacceptable to stigmatize any of them. I, however, am conservative and believe it's best to have two parents, and I don't mean of the same sex." Yet, it must be emphasized that among themselves, the religious women did not feel they were "sinners" because of their decision to have children out of wedlock. On the contrary, they described their motherhood as a sacred and spiritual experience and regarded their children as gifts from God and a manifestation of His blessing. From their standpoint, they had no choice but to utilize science, to make the most of several rabbis' openness to their plight, and to maximize their intellectual and financial skills to raise a family. They did not see their motivations as secular, but did everything within their power to preserve their traditional role.

All the subjects, both religious and secular, experienced motherhood as an existential good, one that made them feel complete. They did not regard their actions as a sociological attempt to create an alternative family model. Shlomit said: "I couldn't imagine my life without a child. I think that if I couldn't have given birth, I would have adopted. In order to feel fulfilled, I had to be a mother." Rachel stated, "Many people tell me I am brave; I don't consider myself brave—I think remaining alone and childless is much worse and braver." Miriam said: "When I began all this, I knew that I wouldn't regret it—you never regret having children. But I knew that if I didn't, I would regret it."

## Conclusion

During the 1960s, when the possibility of allowing in vitro fertilization in Israel was discussed, the British chief rabbi Emanuel Jakobovits objected forcefully out of his concern that "if artificial insemination were allowed for humans, it would mean severing the connection between marriage and giving birth . . . and would enable women to satisfy their hunger for children without a husband and a home."[81] Similarly, twenty years later, regarding single women who apply for artificial insemination, the Conservative rabbi David Golinkin, born in the United States and living in Israel for many years, said that adopting the artificial-insemination method for single women closes the book on the Jewish family.[82]

However, the words of the women in this study suggest that their yearning for marriage and companionship is as strong as ever. The independent and educated women want it very much, not for economic support or increased social status but to meet their psychological needs. All of them stressed that they hoped their children would marry in the conventional way. But their longing for motherhood is primary, and from their point of view, it is not connected to their desire for companionship and marriage. This study demonstrates that the possibility exists nowadays of distinguishing between the yearning for matrimony and the longing for children. This finding requires extensive examination of the changing relationship between the genders and its consequences, particularly regarding the role of the man in the family.

## NOTES

1. Tehilla Blumenthal, *Unwed Orthodox Jewish Mothers by Choice: The Decision Process and Its Consequences on Self-Image and Perceived Social Status* [Hebrew] (PhD diss., Hebrew University of Jerusalem, Israel, 2010).
2. Naama Sabar-Ben Yehoshua, *Qualitative Research in Teaching and Learning* [Hebrew] (Tel-Aviv: Modan, 1999).
3. Asher Shkedi, *Words of Meaning: Qualitative Research: Theory and Practice* [Hebrew] (Tel-Aviv: Ramot- Tel-Aviv University, n.d.).
4. Yvonna S. Lincoln and Egon G. Guba, *Naturalistic Inquiry* (Beverly Hills, CA: Sage Publications, 1985).
5. Jennifer Mason, *Qualitative Researching* (London: Sage Publications, 1996).
6. All names of subjects used for the purpose of this study have been changed to protect privacy, and all quotations in this chapter, unless otherwise cited, are drawn from this study.
7. Interview protocols followed Ben Yehoshua Shkedi and James P. Spradley, *The Ethnographic Interview* (New York: Holt, Rinehart and Winston, 1979).
8. J. W. Creswell, *Qualitative Inquiry and Research Design: Choosing among Five Traditions* (London: Sage Publications, 1998); S. Zalzberg, *The World of "Toldot Aharon" Chasidic Women: Their Status as Individuals and in a Group* [Hebrew] (PhD diss., Bar Ilan University, Israel, 2005).
9. Shkedi and Spradley, *Ethnographic Interview*.
10. Talcott Parsons, *The Social System* (Glencoe, IL: The Free Press, 1951); Talcott Parsons, "The American Family: Its Relation to Personality and Social Structure," in *Family,*

*Socialization and Interaction Process*, eds. Talcott Parsons and Robert F. Bales (London: Routledge, 1955).

11. Wilfried Dumon, "The Family and Its Status in Western Europe" [Hebrew], *Social Security* 44 (1995): 5–23; Judith Stacey, *Brave New Families* (New York: Basic Books, 1990); R. Bar-Josef, "Sociology of the Family in Light of Societal Changes and Bio-Technological Inventions" [Hebrew], *Megamot-Behavioral Sciences Quarterly* 38, no. 1 (1996): 5–29.
12. Phyllis Chesler, *Women and Madness* (New York: Avon Books, 1973).
13. Jetse Sprey, "The Study of Single Parenthood: Some Methodological Considerations," in *The One Parent Family: Perspectives and Annotated Bibliography*, 3rd. ed., ed. Benjamin Schlesinger (Toronto: University of Toronto Press, 1975), 48–60; Fred Deven, "A Review of Trends in the Research on One-Parent Families," in *One-Parent Families in Europe*, eds. Fred Deven and Robert L. Cliquet (Brussels: NIDI/CBGS, 1986), 13–27; Shirley M. H. Hanson and Michael J. Sporakowski, "One-Parent Families in Europe," *Family Relations* 35 (1986): 3–8; Anita Morawetz, "The Single-Parent Family: An Author's Reflection," *Family Process* 23 (1984): 571–76; William N. Stephens, "Judgment by Social Workers on Boys and Mothers in Fatherless Families," *The Journal of Genetic Psychology* 99 (1961): 59–64.
14. Jessie S. Bernard, *The Future of Marriage* (New York: Bantam Books, 1972); Hans J. Hoffman-Nowotny, "The Future of the Family," in *European Population Conference*, 1987, vol. 1, plenaries (Helsinki: IUSSP/EAPS/FINNCO, 1987), 113–98; Louise K. Howe, ed., *The Future of the Family* (New York: Simon and Schuster, 1972).
15. Edward H. Thompson and Patricia A. Gongla, "Single-Parent Families in the Mainstream of American Society," in *Contemporary Families and Alternative Lifestyles*, eds. Eleanor M. Macklin and Roger H. Rubin (Beverly Hills, CA: Sage Publications, 1983), 97–124.
16. Robert W. Roberts, Introduction and "A Theoretical Overview of the Unwed Mother," in *The Unwed Mother*, ed. Robert W. Roberts (New York: Harper and Row, 1966).
17. Ruth Linn, "'Thirty Nothing': What Do Counselors Know about Mature Single Women Who Wish for a Child and a Family," *International Journal of the Advancement of Counseling* 18 (1996): 69–84; Cheryl F. McCartney, "Decision by Single Women to Conceive by Artificial Donor Insemination," *Journal of Psychosomatic Obstetrics and Gynecology* 4, no. 4 (1985): 321–28; Denise Russel, *Women and Madness* (Cambridge, MA: Polity Press, 1995); V. Ravitzki, "'Children Mean Happiness': The Privilege of Parenting in an Age of Technological Reproduction" [Hebrew], *Deot* 8 (1999): 11–14.
18. Ruth Linn, *Mature Unwed Mothers: Narratives of Moral Resistance* (New York: Kluwer Academic/ Plenum Publishers, 2002).
19. K. G. Lewis, "A Life Style Model Should Include Single Women: Clinical Implications for Addressing Ambivalence," *Journal of Feminist Family Therapy*, 10, no. 2 (1998):1–22; Edward H. Thompson and Patricia A. Gongla, "Single-Parent Families in the Mainstream of American Society," in *Contemporary Families and Alternative Life Styles*, eds. Eleanor M. Macklin and Roger H. Rubin (Beverly Hills, CA: Sage Publications, 1983), 97–124.
20. M. Kornfein, T. S. Weisner, and J. C. Martin, "Women into Mothers," in *Women into Wives: The Legal and Economic Impact of Marriage*, vol. 2, eds. Jane R. Chapman and Margaret Gates (Beverly Hills, CA: Sage Publications, 1977), 259–91; Esther Watenberg, "The Fate of Baby Boomers and Their Children," *Social Work* 31, no. 1(1986): 20–28.
21. Melissa Ludtke, *On Our Own: Unmarried Motherhood in America* (Berkeley, CA: University of California Press, 1997); Jane Mattes, *Single Mothers by Choice: A Guidebook for Single Women Who Are Considering or Have Chosen Motherhood* (New York: Times Books, 1994); Sharyne Merrit and Linda Steiner, *And Baby Makes Two: Motherhood without*

*Marriage* (New York: Franklin Watts, 1984); Jean Renovize, *Going Solo: Single Mothers by Choice* (London: Routledge, 1985); Molly McKaughan, *The Biological Clock: Balancing Marriage, Motherhood and Career* (New York: Penguin, 1987).

22. Regarding age, R. Bar Tzuri and M. Tal's *Information Book* (Jerusalem: Ministry of Health and Welfare, 2002), which addresses the employment of single mothers by choice, found that in Israel 40% of single mothers by choice were aged 40 and above. Jane K. Bock addresses women who do not find partners in "Doing the Right Thing? Single Mothers by Choice and the Struggle for Legitimacy," *Gender and Society* 14, no. 1 (2000): 62–86.
23. A. Sabbatlo, "Birth Patterns Outside of Marriage in Israel" [Hebrew], *Society and Welfare* A, no. 1:31–44; Linn, *Mature Unwed Mothers*; Betty Friedan, *The Second Stage* (New York: Summit Books, 1986); Renovize, *Going Sol*; G. Gera, "SMCs: Ego and Moral Development and Sexual Identity" [Hebrew] (master's thesis, Hebrew University of Jerusalem, Israel, 1991).
24. Mattes, *Single Mothers by Choice.*
25. Ibid., principles 4 and 6.
26. See, for example, David Popenoe, *Life without Father: Compelling New Evidence That Fatherhood and Marriage Are Indispensable for the Good of Children and Society* (New York: Free Press, 1996).
27. Rich Morin, "The Public Renders a Split Verdict on Changes in Family Structure," in *Social and Demographic Trends* (Center: Pew Research Center, February 2011).
28. Lori Gottlieb, *Marry Him: The Case for Settling for Mr. Good Enough* (New York: Dutton, 2010); Marlene Wasserman, "Is Marriage the Best Form of Relationship Recognition?" *Sexual and Relationship Therapy* 22, no. 2 (2007): 57–158; Laurie A. Hughes, "The Effects of Relationship States on Empathy, Narcissism, and Resilience in Women," *Dissertation Abstracts International* 64, no. 1-B (2003): 464; David Yount, *Celebrating the Single Life: Keys to Successful Living on Your Own* (Santa Barbara, CA: Praeger/ABC-CLIO, 2009).
29. Elizabeth Gregory, *Ready: Why Women Are Embracing the New Later Motherhood* (New York: Basic Books, 2007); Sylvie Fogel-Bijaoui, "Families in Israel: Between Familialism and Postmodernism" [Hebrew], in *Sex, Gender and Politics*, eds. Dafna N. Izraeli et al. (Tel Aviv: Hakibbutz Hameuchad, 1999), 107–66.
30. Gottlieb, *Marry Him*; Wasserman, "Is Marriage the Best Form"; Hughes, "Effects of Relationship States."
31. Yount, *Celebrating the Single Life*; Bella DePaulo, *Single Out: How Singles Are Stereotyped, Stigmatized, Ignored and Still Live Happily Ever After* (New York: St. Martin's Press, 2006).
32. Israel Central Bureau of Statistics, July 21, 2010.
33. Rosanna Hertz, *Single by Chance, Mothers by Choice: How Women are Choosing Parenthood Without Marriage and Creating the New American Family* (New York: Oxford University Press, 2006).
34. McKaughan, *Biological Clock.*
35. Daniel N. Stern, Nadia Bruschweiler-Stern, and Alison Freeland, *The Birth of a Mother: How the Motherhood Experience Changes You Forever* (New York: Basic Books, 1998).
36. Simone De Beauvoir, *The Second Sex: Woman's Life Today*, vol. 2, ed. and trans. H. M. Parshley (London: Lowe and Brydone, 1956).
37. Cited in Carroll Smith-Rosenberg and Charles Rosenberg, "The Female Animal: Medical and Biological Views of Woman and Her Role in Ninteenth-Century America," *The Journal of American History* 60, no. 2 (September 1973): 332–56, esp. 335.
38. Louann Brizendine, *The Female Brain* (New York: Broadway Books, 2006), 97.

39. For example, Louis Althusser, "Ideology and Ideological State Apparatuses," in *The Anthropology of the State: A Reader*, eds. Aradhana Sharma and Akhil Gupta (Malden, MA: Blackwell Publishing, 2006 [1969]), 86–111; Emile Durkheim, *Suicide: A Study in Sociology*, trans. and eds. John A. Spaulding and George Simpson (London: International Library of Sociology and Social Reconstruction, Routledge, 1952 [1897]).
40. Deuteronomy 7:13–14.
41. Nancy F. Russo, "The Mothering Mandate," *Journal of Social Issues* 32 (1976): 143–53.
42. Grace Baruch, Rosalind Barnett, and Caryl Rivers, *Lifeprints: New Patterns of Love and Work for Today's Women* (New York: New American Library, 1983); Linn, "'Thirty Nothing'"; Robyn Rowland, *Woman Herself: A Transdisciplinary Perspective on Women's Identity* (Melbourne: Oxford University Press, 1989).
43. Daphne DeMarneffe, *Maternal Desire* (New York: Little, Brown and Company, 2004).
44. Elizabeth Gregory, *Ready: Why Women Are Embracing the New Later Motherhood* (New York: Basic Books, 2007).
45. E. Fuchs, "The Number of Singles Who Gave Birth Has Doubled in the Last Decade," *MAKO Home & Family*, February 21, 2012, www.mako.co.il/home-family-relationship/family/Article-f84a8a67a40a531006.htm.
46. M. Della Torre, "Puah Institution Regarding the Halachic Status of Artificial Insemination," *Srugim*, May 10, 2010, www.srugim.co.il.
47. Fuchs, "Number of Singles."
48. A. Bar, "SMCs: Self-Image, Attitudes Toward Motherhood and Perception of the Child. Comparison with Married Mothers" [Hebrew] (PhD diss., Bar Ilan University, Israel, 1989).
49. S. Albeck. S. and A. Bar, "Single Mothers by Choice," *Health and Welfare* 14, no. 1 (1993): 67–79.
50. Ravitzki, "'Children Mean Happiness.'"
51. Dorit Segal-Engelchin and Yochanan Wozner, "Quality of Life of Single Mothers by Choice in Israel: A Comparison to Divorced Mothers and Married Mothers," *Marriage and Family Review* 37, no. 4 (2005): 7–28.
52. Dafna Izraeli, "Culture, Politics, and Women in Israeli Families with Two Breadwinners," in *Family and Science: A Current View on the Family*, eds. R. Weller and R. Cohen [Hebrew] (Jerusalem: Ministry of Education, 1997), 80–107; Dafna N. Izraeli, *Sex, Gender, and Politics* [Hebrew] (Tel Aviv: Hakibbutz Hameuchad, 1999); Linn, 2002.
53. Knesset Minutes 2132, July 2, 1951.
54. Ariela Friedman, *Coming from Love: Intimacy and Power in the Female Identity* [Hebrew] (Tel Aviv: United Kibbutz, 1996).
55. Susan Martha Kahn, *Reproducing Jews: A Cultural Account of Assisted Conception in Israel* (Durham, NC: Duke University Press, 2000); Ruth Landau, "Policies about Fertility Treatments in Israel," in *Spotlight on Social Policy* [Hebrew] (Jerusalem: School of Social Work and Social Welfare, Hebrew University, 2004/5); V. Levi Barzilai, "Have Six, Have Seven, Have Eight Children" [Hebrew], in *Haaretz*, January 28, 2005.
56. According to new 2014 regulations www.health.gov.il/Subjects/fertility/Pages/IVF.aspx. M. Sarig, "Spilling the Baby" [Hebrew], *Haaretz*, August 17, 2003, 33–38; para. 6(d), 2nd ed., Israel Social Security Law, 1994.
57. Mishna, *Ethics of the Fathers*, 2:2.
58. Tamar El-Or, *Next Pesach: Literacy and Identity of Young Religious Women* [Hebrew] (Tel Aviv: Am Oved, 1998); Y. Bowmel, "Thank G d, I'm Religious?" [Hebrew], *Haaretz*, September 10, 2003.

59. H. Shtol, "Singles Aren't Waiting Anymore" [Hebrew], *Deot* 11 (2001):16–20; H. Bartov, "The Challenge of Bachelorhood" [Hebrew], *Deot* 17 (2003/4): 28–30.
60. Y. Griver, "Between Him and Her: Halachah and Reality" [Hebrew], *Deot* 20 (2005):8–10, esp. 9.
61. Menachem Friedman, *The Charedi Woman* [Hebrew] (Jerusalem: Jerusalem Institute for Israeli Research, 1988); Yehudit Rotem, *Distant Sisters: The Women I Left Behind* (Philadelphia: Jewish Publication Society, 1997).
62. Blumenthal, "Unwed."
63. Dvora Ross, "Artificial Insemination for Single Women," in *Jewish Legal Writings by Women*, eds. Micah Halpern and Chana Safray (Jerusalem: Urim Publications, 1998), 45–72.
64. Tamar Ross, *Expanding the Palace of Torah* [Hebrew] (Tel Aviv: Am Oved Publishers, 2007); Tova Hartman, "Between Tradition and Revolution: The Confrontation between Women's Voices and Rabbinical Authority" [Hebrew], *Ravgoni* 3 (2000): 44–49.
65. Ari Engelberg, "Love Conquers All? The National-Religious 'Singles Problem'" [Hebrew], *Theory and Criticism* 35 (2009): 280–91.
66. Aliza Lavie, *Jewish Women's Prayers Throughout the Ages* [Hebrew] (Tel-Aviv: Miskal-Yedioth Ahronoth Books and Chemed Books, 2005), 56.
67. R. Gombo and S. Schwartz, "A Comparative Perspective of Young Charedi Women's Values," *Megamot* 32, no. 3 (1989): 332–60.
68. Stephanie Coontz, *The Way We Never Were: American Families and the Nostalgia Gap* (New York: Basic Books, 1992); Arlene Skolnick, *Embattled Paradise: The American Family in an Age of Uncertainty* (New York: Basic Books, 1991).
69. *Nahmani v. Nahmani* CFH 2401/95, Israel Law Reports (1995–1996).
70. N. L. Cole, The *Experience of Never-Married Women in Their 30's Who Desire Marriage and Children*, in *Dissertation Abstracts International*, sec. A, *Humanities and Social Sciences* 60, no. 9-A (2000): 3526 and others.
71. Lewis, "Life Style Model"; McKaughan, *Biological Clock*; Ann Oakley, *Woman's Work* (New York: Pantheon, 1974).
72. Hertz, *Single by Chance*.
73. Malkah Notman and Elizabeth Lester, "Pregnancy: Theoretical Considerations," *Psychoanalytic Inquiry* 8 (1988): 139–59.
74. Erik Erikson, *Childhood and Society* (New York: W. W. Norton, 1950).
75. Helene Deutsch, "The Psychology of Women in Relation to the Functions of Reproduction," in *The Psychoanalytic Reader: An Anthology of Essential Papers with Critical Introduction*, ed. Robert Fliess (New York: International University Press, 1969 [1925]), 165–79.
76. Bock, "Doing the Right Thing?"
77. Sarig, "Spilling the Baby."
78. Hertz, *Single by Chance*.
79. Anat Palgi-Hecker, *Mother in Psychoanalysis: A Feminist View* [Hebrew] (Tel Aviv: Am Oved publishers, 2006).
80. Pauline M. Shershefsky and Leon J. Yarrow, *Psychological Aspects of First Pregnancy and Early Post-Natal Adaptation* (New York: Raven Press, 1973).
81. Immanuel Jakobovits, *Medicine and Judaism* [Hebrew] (Jerusalem: Mossad Harav Kook, 1966) Chapter 15.
82. David Golinkin, "A Halachic Response ('*Teshuva*') Regarding Artificial Insemination," *"Vaad Hahalacha" Responses of Israel Rabbinical Committee*, vol. 3 (Jerusalem: Schecter Institute, 1988).

# 8

## Judaism as the "Third Shift"

### *Jewish Families Negotiating Work, Family, and Religious Lives*

Rachel S. Bernstein and Sylvia Barack Fishman

"WE JOKE SOMETIMES ABOUT DECISIONS that would earn B grades instead A grades, because sometimes it's not worth the mental effort of an A-level decision," muses Lisa, a Jewish convert in her late thirties, about family decision-making. Like Lisa and her husband, the majority of contemporary American-Jewish men and women pursue higher education in above-average numbers and create dual-earner families at rates typical of Americans in their socioeconomic cohort. But these families must confront many decisions specific to Judaism beyond those they share with their non-Jewish neighbors. They comment that they can make "B-grade" decisions about what to cook for dinner, but intersecting decisions about personal investments in paid and unpaid work, religious life, family ritual practices, worship, and education require careful thought. These negotiations often weigh heavily on Jewish parents, who say they strive for a "grade of an A" when it comes to their decisions for their Jewish homes and children.

This chapter studies American Jewish families balancing their work, home, and Jewish responsibilities. Few prior studies have examined the role of Judaism in family-life interactions and how Jewish families manage their religion, parenting, careers, and household.[1] This chapter draws on two phases of original research: first, a pilot phase analyzed the responses of fifty-nine Jewish women and men with children participating in an online survey investigating how married and partnered Jewish parents decide upon and accomplish childcare, household labor, and other related tasks.[2] Second, interviews with fifteen married Jewish individuals interrogated how Jewish families envision and configure the role of Judaism in their lives and their family decisions and interactions, and the ways in which Judaism affects the balancing of their work and home lives.[3]

Our study shows that Judaism for these families is work, constituting another set of responsibilities demanding time, money, and emotional energy. Men and women today enter Jewish marriages and life partnerships expecting to negotiate roles and tasks. Many fall back on aspects of established gender roles in some areas of life but forge new patterns in other areas. Respondents describe their investments of time and energy into religion as another "shift" that has to be worked into full family schedules. Judaism as a "third shift" necessitates negotiations: who assumes responsibility and devotes time, energy, and financial resources into Jewish connections in light of other responsibilities. Despite the additional burdens that religion imposes, our study demonstrates that many are eager to do this "work," for Judaism serves as the "framing frame of [their] family life."

## Dual-Earning and "Postmodern" Changing Families

After the social revolutions of the 1960s and 1970s, American families began to move past bourgeois conventions of the breadwinner father and homemaker mother. Kathleen Gerson notes, "By 2000, 60 percent of all married couples had two earners, while only 26 percent depended solely on a husband's income, down from 51 percent in 1970."[4] Increasing female labor-force participants changed workplaces and created profound structural changes in American families. Now dual-earner families negotiate working hours, housework, and childcare in strategies that sometimes depart from and sometimes default to conventional gender norms. These new family constructions were publicized and deplored by the "new familists," professors and policy analysts who warned that shifting trends in American marital status are precipitating social and moral decline, and contemporary preoccupations with individual rights and material success undermine more productive emphasis on social groupings and their interwoven responsibilities.[5] But opposing scholarship argued that the 1950s-style nuclear family, with its isolated suburban mothers and economically driven fathers was a relatively recent—and gravely flawed—social construction.[6] Examining the children of the watershed generation—the 1970s—Gerson found female children were positively affected by the energy and focus dual-earner mothers put into paid labor. The children overwhelmingly supported their dual-earner parents; females hoped to remain independent as wage earners themselves and produce dual-earning families, whereas young men still envisioned themselves as primary breadwinners if a more egalitarian family form failed.[7] Reflecting on these patterns, Stacey defined contemporary families as "postmodern" because "contemporary family arrangements are diverse, fluid, and unresolved" and there is "no longer a single culturally dominant family pattern to which the majority of Americans conform."[8]

These American trends in labor-force participation are especially salient to Jewish families. Over two decades ago sociologist Calvin Goldscheider wrote,

"American Jews are located in social statuses and geographic locations that are most responsive to changes in marriage and the family."[9] Riv-Ellen Prell noted, "The Jewish family economy has changed since the 1970s,"[10] as Jewish women have entered the workforce in increasing numbers, especially affecting married women with children. Jewish women's life choices have continued to reflect patterns of American society: 66% of American Jewish men and 54% of American Jewish women work in the paid labor force, according Harriet Hartman and Moshe Hartman's analysis of the National Jewish Population Survey 2000–01. Married women with children tend to work part-time more than nonmarried women, but in patterns similar to those in the broader population. As Hartman and Hartman relate, "45 percent of Jewish couples in 2000-01 (down from 54.8% in the 1990 NJPS)" were dual-earners, less than the national average of "57.0% in 2000, 59.3% in 2001."[11] Extended years in higher education and retirement within aging populations could account for this lower percentage of dual-earners—among those aged 25–64, "around 74% were dual earners," which was "more comparable to the national average." Significantly, among those with children under 18 at home, "72.3% [were] dual-earners,"[12] which is above the average of the broader population. As Fishman argued elsewhere, "Today, dual-career Jewish households have become the new normative Jewish family."[13] Financial resources, free time, and time for childcare and housework, as well as the gender strategies for handling all of these responsibilities, have changed for the Jewish family, as they have for families generally since the 1970s.

## The American Second Shift

Women have assumed more paid work since the 1970s, but they continue to bear responsibility for more unpaid work inside their homes, according to Arlie Hochschild and Anne Machung, who emphasized that unpaid work is still work by calling it the "second shift" and by discussing the unequal distribution of this work.[14] Women feel most of the responsibility for and complete far more cooking, cleaning, and childcare. While unpaid work varies by gender ideology, and despite real changes in gender norms, women continue to contribute about a month more domestic work per year than men do.[15] Contemporary dual-earner families find themselves in a "time bind," for they experience their home lives as work just as much as paid labor is considered work.[16]

Hochschild's calculations launched her own further research and that of other scholars analyzing the unpaid household work of men and women. Milkie, Raley, and Bianchi, for example, calculated time spent in housework, childcare, and paid labor in the work force for married men and women with preschool-aged children, finding, "the gap in total workloads—the combination of hours in paid and unpaid work—is around five hours per week . . . not 15 hours per week," as in Hochschild's calculation. Mothers in paid work do slightly less paid work and more unpaid work, and husbands do more paid work and less unpaid work. The total time spent in unpaid and paid work is closer to equal among parents with young children—"with mothers averaging 65 hours per week compared with fathers' total load of 68 hours."[17] Emotionally, however, women overwhelmingly felt responsible for almost all of the household work and childcare, in addition to their paid labor. While housework hours have decreased since 1965 due in part to the outsourcing of many family services, women still assume core household tasks. Notably, "women's and men's hours have become more similar, but women still do much more of this [unpaid] work."[18] Perhaps the most striking conclusion in the research by Bianchi et al. was that children and marriage increased housework much more for women than for men.

The advances of feminism and the entry of women into the paid labor force have not completely transformed gender relationships within families but instead have created a "stalled revolution" or an "unfinished revolution."[19] The continuing gendered division of labor, including expectations and emotions involved in leaving the workplace, only to return home to another shift of work around the house, takes its toll on contemporary families.

## The Division of Labor in Jewish Homes

Households buzz with the activities of daily life—cooking, cleaning, going to work, going to school, mowing the lawn—quotidian necessities demanding a division of labor between partners. The Jewish respondents in our studies often expressed exasperation or unhappiness with the realities of these many tasks. Some described traditional arrangements—what Hochschild would define as a transitional gender ideology—with heterosexual female partners doing less paid work and taking care of cooking, carpooling, and caregiving more than their male partners, especially when men worked long hours with little flexibility. However, even when men had more flexibility or women worked longer hours, the *impression* of the spouses was that childcare or cooking was more the role of one than the other, just as Hochschild found.[20] Most of our research participants described the duties of the male as the one who cleans up after dinner, perhaps doing some laundry, and often taking charge of financial matters and household repairs. Rebecca, an Orthodox participant currently in Israel, said childcare activities and decisions are her "ultimate responsibility." Jessica underscored she is in charge of the "day to day" even if she and her husband make decisions about their children's activities together.

Families sometimes approach household and childcare activities with less structured gender roles but still default to traditionalist assignments, although with less rigidity, as Gerson has noted.[21] Our respondents described their division of labor as having "evolved," frequently without negotiations or deliberate discussions to decide who would do what. The functioning of the family in terms of household and childcare is reported as developing a kind of "rhythm." Often partners rely on what Hochschild calls "family myths" to describe their personal tasks as based on personality and ability,[22] when in fact the roles they assume seem ultimately embedded in culture-wide traditional understandings of male and female personalities, rather than family. For example, a Reform man in his early forties in a dual-career marriage, responded to the survey that he and his wife organically "decide who does what on a day by day basis":

> Whoever is best available physically and emotionally. My wife gets off work earlier than I. When I get home, I work on [the children's] homework if there is still some left to do. My wife usually goes to the gym after I get home. My wife usually cooks dinner and cleans up the dishes, while I deal with finishing homework, getting the girls bathed and to bed. This arrangement evolved organically: my wife prefers to do the dishes to getting the girls ready for bed, and this gives me extra time with them.

Especially noteworthy, both husband and wife recognize that she "prefers to do the dishes to getting the girls ready for bed," and they create their own arrangements that take this into account, and her need to work out at the gym is taken for granted.

Often families are in a position to outsource household care such as cleaning and lawn care, an approach which may be present in family negotiations from the outset. Ruth, a secular humanist in her early seventies, says, "We reached an agreement when we got married that we would always have house-cleaning help, somebody to clean the house, and we would always have somebody to mow the lawn." In addition, childcare is frequently outsourced to nannies, babysitters, and daycare centers. This alleviates some pressure on the partners who might otherwise have had to complete these tasks, but it also costs money—and sometimes generates family tension related to finances.[23] Several respondents bemoaned the move away from a beloved babysitter or anxiety over feeling uncomfortable with the daycare center their children attend. Michelle, in her mid-forties with two children, even describes how a "stressful" daycare experience affected decisions about having another baby: "I mean, I really didn't want a third child, but I was really discouraged from having a third child by having to deal with childcare again."

In many, perhaps most, younger Jewish families with children where both parents are employed outside the home, our online survey suggests that active negotiation is considered a given.

When husbands and wives assume they will fall back on conventional family roles, not everyone may be satisfied with their roles but the roles tend to be clear. However, when roles are negotiated—and judging from our respondents who renegotiated repeatedly—success depends not only on negotiating skill but also on the responsiveness and flexibility of both parties and their willingness to follow through on agreements. Sometimes, the expectation that responsibilities will be divided exactly equally creates its own stress for the spouse who feels the other spouse is not living up to agreements. Some participants detailed what they presented as rather successful negotiations of egalitarian, nonconventional role divisions, such as one Conservative woman in her early thirties who works four days a week and is married to a man, also in his early thirties, who works full-time:

> We both handle all aspects of childcare . . . much of it has to do with which parent is with the kids at the time. For example: on evenings when my partner is working, I am responsible for meal preparation, clean up, hygiene, and bedtime. When I am working the same is true in reverse. When we are both home, we "divide and conquer," and who does what mostly depends on a spur-of-the-moment decision (though there are some things that we consistently divide up—for example, when we are both home, he generally does baths and I generally do more of the kitchen clean-up).

This virtuous circle of (1) flexibility, (2) responsiveness, and (3) follow-through did not happen by accident. This woman describes the process of negotiation in which the she and her husband worked out how to accommodate two sets of rather inflexible professional responsibilities with the needs of their family. Similarly, a 1989 study of successful married mothers by Vannoy-Hiller and Philliber found that these attitudinal issues were crucial to the overall sense of marital satisfaction. A husband's assuming responsibility often meant more than merely doing the laundry. Husbands in the Vannoy-Hiller and Philliber study who were perceived as sharing familial responsibilities generally were part of exceptionally satisfying relationships.[24]

Spousal negotiations to plan in advance and set responsibilities are part of the quotidian lives of Orthodox, Conservative, Reform, post-denominational, and secular Jewish families. One Conservative father, in his forties with a doctoral degree, suggests that how the family spends Sundays has a powerful impact on how he feels they are doing as a family. A successful Sunday mapped out in advance provides needed recreation for all:

> Sundays are always a challenge because both of us have professional responsibilities that require weekend work time, we both want to get out and get some exercise and even have some fun, and we also have responsibilities to our children, who are ages 9, 15 and 18. We successfully deal with Sundays when we sit down and map out the day (who needs to go where at what time and who needs personal work and exercise time more urgently).

An unsuccessful Sunday, by contrast, leaves them feeling out of control, frazzled, and unsatisfied: "Sundays when we don't plan . . . we end up careening from one event or errand to another in what feels like a haphazard situation."

## Judaism as the Third Shift

In *The Time Bind*, Hochschild defined a "third shift" for working parents in her study of employees at a major American corporation. Employees working a full shift of paid labor returned home not only to complicated childcare arrangements and plentiful housework but also to the intricacies of family relationships demanding "noticing, understanding, and coping with the emotional consequences of the compressed second shift."[25] Families also need time to manage the demands and stresses of the combination of their work, family, and religious lives—the third shift. Sociologist Kathleen Jenkins addressed specifically the notion of religion as a third shift within conservative Christian communities in her work on the International Churches of Christ.[26] She argues that disciples in the ICOC were often stressed by their responsibilities to paid labor, their households and families, and the expectations of the church to disciple other members of the church, perfect themselves and their homes, and proselytize both through the church and their homes.[27] Especially considering the demands of Judaism, which—depending on levels of observance—may include daily prayers and synagogue attendance, weekly Shabbat preparations, consistent planning around the preparation of kosher food, and concerns about imparting Jewish knowledge to one's children or negotiating the family's level of religious practice, Judaism can have wide-ranging (and often unrecognized) impacts on the family.

In addition, just as the "second shift" of unpaid childcare and housework imposes differing degrees of weight on men and women and often conforms to traditional gender ideology, so too does the "third shift" of religion. Jewish law and tradition assign different tasks to each gender—often expecting more of fathers religiously; however, American mores put women in charge of religious observance in the home.[28] Jewish fathers and mothers now negotiate how they will divide and complete Jewish tasks in their household. While sometimes the emotional investment and input of time into Jewish matters is not clearly divided by gender, often, as previous research has shown, one spouse more than the other must shoulder most of the responsibility for defining religious rituals for the family, encouraging synagogue attendance, implementing kosher food preparation, and planning family celebrations for holidays and life-cycle events. For families in which Judaism is more episodic, the "third shift" may be less obtrusive—taking time off from work to celebrate the High Holidays, postponing leisure time to carpool children to Sunday school. For families who observe Shabbat and the laws of *kashrut* (Jewish dietary laws), the "third shift" emerges as a constant condition, creating pressure, pulling time from the workplace, childcare, and housework. Framing Judaism as a "third shift" underscores the substantial nature of religion in the family, a feature to be managed and negotiated.

## The Division of Labor and Religion

Paid labor, unpaid labor, and religious involvement all have an influence on each other, and religious involvement is highly correlated with marriage and childbearing.[29] In her mixed-methods study of Christian families in upstate New York, Penny Edgell documented the often differing levels of involvement in paid labor, household labor, childcare, and religious involvement between spouses. She showed church attendance affected men and women differently in relation to their responsibilities at work and in the home. On one hand, married men with children spent less time on household tasks if they were regular church attenders, and were less likely to feel a tension between their work, home, and religious lives. On the other hand, Edgell found that married women with children saw themselves in a "time bind" without adequate time to spend with their families and participate in religion due to the demands of their work and home lives. As Edgell argues, "women who try to balance work and family and still be involved in a local church are more likely [than men] to report that both their work and their family lives are draining; fitting together all three activities may not be as easy for women as for men, perhaps because of the longer hours that women put into housework of all kinds."[30] Women feel drained due to their involvement in work, family, and religion, but still find each sphere meaningful.

Similar to Edgell's findings,[31] Hartman and Hartman noted that a "stronger Jewish identity is associated with fewer hours of paid employment for the wife."[32]

They also found that dual-earning was related to religious investments individuals make, perhaps due to the nature of spending more time in paid labor and the resulting exposure to broader American norms: Jewish dual-earners were "more likely to see being Jewish as being part of a universal moral community and heritage,"[33] and less likely to place emphasis on ritual behaviors such as kashrut and Sabbath observance.

## Gender and Religious Involvement

Women are disproportionately responsible for both unpaid labor in the household and their family's religious expression. Research on gender and religion in the United States shows that women are more religious than men, mainly in terms of their frequency of religious service attendance and often too in their personal beliefs and practices.[34] Scholars propose several theories to explain gendered differences in religiosity, including risk-related behaviors, gender-role socialization, and life-course effects.[35] One branch of this research defines the source of the differences as structural, claiming that women's greater roles in childrearing and fewer hours in the paid labor force encourage them to be more religious.[36]

Hartman and Hartman dismiss the so-called structural location theory as an explanation within the Jewish community because Jewish women's connections to family-based rituals and roles might be stronger in relation to their labor force participation even when their Jewish identity is negatively correlated with paid labor.[37] They showed that "women express stronger Jewish identity than do men on all but two of the factors" of Jewish identity, excluding Orthodox practice, which neutralizes this difference, and personal attachment to Israel, which is stronger for men.[38] Jewish women exhibited stronger Jewish identities especially in regard to beliefs, public ritual practices, activity in the community, and attachment to the Jewish people. Other studies confirm that American Jewish women often direct their family's practices and the Jewish education of their children, as well as are more personally involved in synagogues and Jewish volunteer opportunities.[39]

## Judaism as the Family's "Lens on Life"

Judaism and the family overlap to such an extent in our surveys and our interviews that it can be hard to separate the two spheres. Judaism informed family life in its moral underpinning, day-to-day interactions and scheduling, and as a key factor in personal identity, and the requisite preparations for and enactment of Judaism constituted a necessary "third shift" in busy family lives. Joel,[40] who identifies as Conservative, framed the idea of Judaism and the family as something beyond the synthesis of two spheres: "For me, Judaism and family—there is no intersection; they're one and the same." Mark, who connected with the philosophic and cultural dimensions of Judaism rather than its ritual practices, framed Judaism as a source that "answers a lot of the question [of] what kind of person am I or what kind of a person do I aspire to be." Judaism thus provides Mark with a reference point in both his family life and work life.

Much as Maureen Semans and Linda Fish found that Jews "dissect life with a Jewish scalpel," [41] with Judaism providing a way to understand the world and family life, our respondents, who practice Judaism in diverse ways, described their lives as "pretty enmeshed" in Judaism, for it served as their "lens on life" or "the prism through which we do everything else." Especially in terms of decision-making and the structure of their family life, they rely on Judaism to provide the "organizing frame of our family life" that informs "every single decision we make," including those about education, scheduling, morality, family time, and monetary investments. Families turn to Judaism to "ground" their lives and provide an "anchor in [their] life," which reiterates the importance of religion in these families' lives, however diversely they express it, and positions Judaism as an integral part of the family in relation to their other responsibilities.

Judaism also provides a religious and moral system for the family, affecting family-life interactions. Erica, who identifies as Orthodox in her mid-forties, discusses her family's "completely integrated Jewish lives" where discussions of allowance "also involves talking about *tzedakah*," or Jewish practices of charity. "Even the stuff that doesn't look Jewish," Erica claims, "for us always brings in Jewish elements, and Jewish grounding in our thinking." Robert, a convert to Judaism in a same-sex marriage,[42] describes Judaism as part of the "experience in every single decision [he and his husband] make." Robert especially valued Judaism's promotion of social justice and the importance of modeling the value of helping others for his daughter. By using Judaism as one's lens on life and having it inform most personal and familial decisions and practices, Judaism makes a major impression on family life, necessitating personal commitment, knowledge, time, and money.

Many respondents discussed how Judaism shapes their yearly family calendar. The rhythm of Judaism builds in "dedicated family time" according to Jonathan, an Orthodox Jew in his mid-thirties, who treasures the "totally sacred time" of Shabbat as one without technology and distractions for him and his family. Taking time to go to synagogue, take Jewish education classes, and celebrate the holidays is an important part of family life for several of our respondents. The schedule of Jewish day schools, with activities around Jewish observance, also affects family lives and underscores Judaism as "a constant presence" in the participants' lives. Joel details how weekly commitments to Hebrew school influence decisions about his children's other extracurricular activities, making it difficult to commit to some. Beyond quotidian schedules of Jewish observance, several respondents emphasized Judaism as "a guidepost" that "[gives] you a direction" during major life events and a system for interpreting and practicing events related to childbirth, the bar or bat mitzvah, and death. Some felt that the structure Jewish tradition provides makes life less complicated.

Spouses and families work through their Jewish commitments to make decisions about family activities, ritual practices, and religious education. Our respondents spoke about Judaism as a factor similar to gender that affects how they approach their family structure and the balancing of their family, work, and religious lives—it is so integral, almost imperceptibly so sometimes, that it informs everything else that they do.

## Negotiating Jewish Observance

Respondents described their family negotiations and Jewish practices as draining on time and emotions, although also personally meaningful and a fulfilling part of their lives. Time may be spent on committees, shepherding children to Jewish activities, and preparing for large meals around holidays. While women are not always more religiously involved or invested than men, women are often in charge of religious practice in the family, adding pressure and scheduling challenges along with emotional stress, as women balance their own and their families' religious observance with other responsibilities. Many mentioned the tension of balancing wives' investments in Judaism against their husband's or family's lack of interest. Monica, a Conservative Jew in her late thirties, admits, "I am very involved in Judaism, and my husband isn't at all," which creates an imbalance in desire and energy to pursue Jewish activities. She says, "I would like to get out into a synagogue and maybe have my kids being active there as well as my husband. So I think my husband prevents me from doing a lot of things that I would like to do." Susan concurs: "I love to go to synagogue. I find it very comforting for me, and often I don't get my family to come with me as much as I would like." Often having less free time than men,[43] when women choose to invest their free time in religious activities that are not supported by the rest of their families, they experience additional time-management anxiety amid all of their responsibilities.

At the same time, women's general control of religious activities allows them to increase or decrease religious observance or activities to their taste. Joel discusses his desire for more religious observance in his family, including more frequent synagogue attendance and higher standards of kashrut, but adds, laughing, "I wish we could go to *shul* more often. But that's just me. That's why we don't." Michelle, Joel's wife, also mentions the imbalance of religious sentiment, ultimately realizing that the final religious decision-making falls to her. While she expresses respect for her husband's religious feelings and involvement, she says Jewish practice is not as spiritually meaningful for her. When she had to deal with children resisting synagogue, she says, "it just started to have a different feeling for me," and she became "a little resentful." She ultimately decided to decrease the level of kashrut, which created waves in the family as her daughter followed suit. She explains, "I feel like we had more of [kashrut] and now we have less of it, and I think a lot of that is my doing and I feel somewhat guilty about that because I know it's not ideal for Joel, but I also know he would never challenge me on it." Tellingly, the power that women in many families hold over religious observance and connections can be accompanied by tension and guilt.

Time is usually a scarce resource in families and Judaism can take up a lot of it, so Judaism necessitates negotiations in families to balance all their responsibilities. Jonathan described his family's decision-making and scheduling around work, synagogue board meetings, and childcare, for he says, "There are some Sundays when I work, so I'll probably be needing to arrange for a babysitter, so my wife can fulfill our duty to go to the board meetings or go to whatever the meetings need to happen." Jewish responsibilities take time, and can take time "away" from other things. Jonathan also mentions his practice of regularly reading Torah on Shabbat, which requires preparation the week before, which he notes, "usually will take away from either some family time or some just time for myself [or] for my wife and I to just spend together." While Jonathan feels all of these activities—Torah reading, family time, and alone time—are important, their overlapping nature initiates a balancing act of Judaism, home, and work that can sometimes require sacrifices of time and investment in one or all of the activities.

## The Impact of Kashrut

Any cooking consumes time and effort and constitutes a major part of the second shift, but for Jewish families where kashrut is a factor in their Jewish observance, the availability of kosher food, personal stringency, and the time it takes to ensure they have kosher options in diverse secular settings increase demands on parents' time, work, and thus stress. The management of individual family members' practices around kashrut, and the change over time in their level of observance, often creates moments of tension and a retooling of Jewish practice, affecting the practical, emotional, and spiritual interests of the family as a whole. Time must be set aside to prepare kosher food and make it available in secular settings. Rebecca frames the work it takes to keep kosher as "part of the rules" and "part of the context of my life," and Jonathan underscores that kashrut is "one of the things we find most meaningful and we care to impart in a positive way for our kids." Yet Jonathan confirms that kashrut is a factor that must be managed in relation to his family's non-Jewish workplaces and his children's day-care. One example Jonathan discusses: "Tomorrow our son is having a party at school, which means that tonight we're going to make pizza for dinner so that we can send some of the kosher alternative for tomorrow." In addition, he packs and brings his own lunch every day to the office and also frequently takes time to explain to colleagues why he does not eat at group lunches at work. Rebecca comments that kosher food is a consideration "when I go on vacation, or plan a trip, or whatever; decide where my kid is going to go to school," which complicates things and requires time for research, planning, and preparation.

Negotiating family practices around kashrut requires time, money, and also emotional input from members of the family. Several respondents discussed how kashrut became a topic of negotiation soon after marriage as couples first worked out their system of religious observance. Not only did this first encounter with kashrut create a sticking point around which they had to decide family practice, but the issue appeared again as children were added and family members changed opinions about keeping kosher. Susan, who grew up keeping kosher, describes deciding with her husband, who grew up in a non-kosher home, how they would incorporate kashrut into their family. In the beginning, she says, "I think he kind of sabotaged things—the wrong fork, the wrong spoon," but "that stopped eventually." Some defined similar debates as emotionally taxing, as well as time-consuming. Erica details negotiations around kashrut as "kind of navigating the gray," for the ways and means to observe kashrut are varied. Navigating the gray involved considering "when we eat out; eating cheese, not eating cheese, drinking wine, not drinking wine. Like, what's our practice? Kashrut outside of the home, with the kids, without the kids? We're trying to figure that out, or come to a place of agreement on that. Right now we have slightly different practices. . . . We each have our areas where we're a little stricter than the other." Monica ultimately drew the line for her family, making kashrut a firm household practice because she wanted to be sure that kashrut was a meaningful system for them even though her husband was not willing to invest the same amount of time or punctiliousness in the project: "My husband doesn't keep kosher when he is not at home, but I told him that in front of our kids he needs to keep kosher so my kids don't know that he does not eat kosher."

Such expenditures of time and energy, and the emotional jockeying, take their toll, and when practices change over time, they often send a shockwave through the family. Michelle "grew up eating everything" but was "willing to give that up when [her husband] wanted to keep kosher." Later Michelle found herself questioning the kosher practices of the family, finding them too costly, time-consuming, and not spiritually meaningful: "Decisions that I initiated because I was doing the shopping and the cooking and the Weight Watchers or whatever it was that made it harder and more expensive to keep strictly kosher. And I started resenting it." As Michelle began to eat non-kosher food outside the home and rearranged the family food system to make things easier in the home, her children started to follow. While the family still separates milk and meat in the home, their kosher observance is not as strict as it was. Michelle says of her and her husband, "I'm a bit conflicted about it, [and] he's a bit conflicted about it. And we check-in every once in a while . . . but that's what we've decided to do." Not only the physical management of kosher food, but also the negotiations between family members over expectations, desires, and abilities around kashrut exact expenditures of time and energy in many Jewish families.

## The Impact of Children on Jewish Negotiations

Jewish education and the activities of children are viewed by American Jewish parents as significant Jewish responsibilities and an expression of their own Jewishness. Balancing the demands of secular and religious activities such as synagogue attendance, Hebrew school, and youth group, and juggling complicated schedules with soccer matches and birthday parties create stress for Jewish families, and also all these activities take time and money. While teaching children to swim is a *mitzvah*, commanded of Jewish parents by the Talmud, Jessica confesses controversy in her family over conflicts between synagogue attendance and swim lessons for her children, who are growing up in a major coastal city. To avoid heavy traffic, and finding time limited because of full work weeks, Jessica finally decided her family would have to compromise by attending synagogue every other week and attending swim lessons in the interim weeks because "given the amount of water around . . . we recognize what the priorities are, and we have to balance it that way."

Geography, schedule conflicts, and changing personal priorities—which can differ among family members—have profound effects on familial Judaic practice. Many people who live in geographical regions outside of major metropolitan areas with dense Jewish populations must compromise when scheduling activities that do not take Jewish practice into account. Michelle recounts conflicts over her family's participation in synagogue and local soccer teams that play on Saturdays. When the whole family is involved in both synagogue and soccer, sometimes secular, extracurricular activities take precedence over religion: "So . . . we're a little bit concerned, and then we're also kind of philosophical, like we chose this kind of ambiguous route where we played soccer on Saturdays. And now it's hard to get to temple on Saturdays." Changing investments of individual family members in Jewish practice—especially during the teen years—create conflict within the family. Susan found it "very upsetting" when her daughter who moved from a Jewish day school to a public high school but was still active in supplementary schools and trips to Israel announced that she did not "feel as Jewish anymore." Michelle describes a "crisis for our family" because "we're on different pages" about Jewish attachment and observance. After her bat mitzvah, Michelle's oldest daughter gave up participation at their synagogue, and the rest of the family was left dealing with the "reverberations because she won't go to temple anymore, and we won't make her." Parents sometimes unwittingly find their children acting out their own (sometimes unacknowledged) ambivalences toward Judaism.

## Managing Judaism and the Workforce

The balancing of Judaism and paid labor outside the home is influenced by the typical workplace schedule and its frequent conflict with Jewish holidays. How onerous these conflicts are ranges broadly. Several respondents set their work schedules for the year by taking vacation or personal days to observe Jewish holidays. Taking this time off was often the only overlap they report between their work lives and Jewish lives. More contentious arrangements occur with careers that make it difficult to observe Jewish holidays, especially if work interferes with Shabbat observance. Even for respondents who do not observe all of the laws of Shabbat, getting home in time to prepare the weekly Friday-night family dinner in honor of Shabbat is often complicated by work schedules that leave little time before sundown. Michelle must work late into the afternoon on Fridays, and she says she feels "pressured to put a Shabbat dinner on the table." Jonathan, who is *shomer Shabbat* (observes the laws of the Jewish Sabbath), feels particularly harried on "Friday afternoons, especially in the wintertime when Shabbat starts very early":

> I have to somehow sneak out of work very early, long before, say, our colleagues might . . . to pick up the groceries for my wife . . . there aren't a lot of things I have to get done on Friday afternoon that would cut [to] the wire in terms of Sabbath starting, but for my wife, who has a normal work-

> day [until] at least 5 p.m. . . . that's actually challenging. And so sometimes on Friday, I will take the full responsibility of just getting everything ready at home, so my wife can kind of walk in, take a bath, and be ready for Shabbat when it starts, and yet our house will still be ready.

Several respondents similarly describe challenges they face when they have to figure out some way to get it all done and fulfill their personal responsibilities to their Jewish lives. They describe decisions that are made on the basis of both logistics and ideology. Debby, who identifies as Orthodox, recalls when she and her husband had to book a hotel within walking distance to the location where her husband was interviewing for a job on Shabbat, affecting their travel plans as well as their religious views. Like working a separate second shift, both men and women strive to balance their career responsibilities and their Jewish lives, splitting responsibilities when it comes to preparing for Jewish holidays on top of their paid workdays. Jewish families face these issues by negotiating their priorities to work, Judaism, and family, and arrange their lives to accommodate all of these responsibilities.

## The Costs of Jewish Living

As others have noted, a major change for Jewish families in the United States in the twentieth century was the outsourcing Jewish education.[44] Families are no longer solely responsible for teaching their children about Jewish texts, traditions, and ethics. This relieves some of the burden of Jewish education from parents, but comes at an emotional—and certainly a financial—cost. Several respondents discussed their desire for their children to "have a strong Jewish education" and "a strong Jewish background," choosing to send their children to day school or combining public school with several kinds of supplementary and informal forms of Jewish education. While such schools and programs took on some of the responsibility for educating Jewish children, they also necessitated family discussions and decision-making between spouses and children.[45] Monica described the eventual end of her child's day school after the fifth grade and how she and her husband disagree about continuing with day school or using a combination of public school and supplementary school: "We are not fighting yet, but there is going to be a fight!" Without regard to her husband's opinion, Monica would like to have her children attend a day school closer to her home that is not Orthodox "because that's not what we practice here at home." Decisions about which schools or programs to choose required research, emotional processing, and negotiations between family members.

Similar to the ways in which outsourcing housecleaning and daycare can ease demands on a family's time and energy but come with a price tag, so too does the outsourcing of Jewish education. Erica lamented the toll on her family when "we have to pay a day school tuition bill that's thousands upon thousands of dollars, or when we can't afford a tuition bill, because we, who worked in the Jewish community our whole lives, don't get paid enough to pay for the tuition." Even those who identify as upper-middle-class professionals found themselves taking the cost of Jewish education into account when family planning. Jonathan, who works in a medical profession and is married to a lawyer, underscored the necessity of constructing a dual-earning family for the very reason that Jewish education is expensive. He described their negotiations over family planning and Judaism as follows:

> Both of us come from families of four, so that was kind of the family size we had envisioned, though recognizing that at current rates, that would be $100,000 a year in day school tuition. That gives us pause, because . . . we recognize we have to make some sacrifices, not going to Israel as often or not having vacations, but it's one thing to sacrifice certain luxuries; it's another thing to realize that you're barely going to make ends meet with that kind of obligation to carry.

Even if they did not personally have the need or did not choose to send their children to a Jewish day school, many respondents mentioned its expense, as well as the cost of other elements of Jewish life such as synagogue membership and kosher food, as major stressors. The expression of their concern ranged from detached remarks about the cost to fellow community members to descriptions of full-blown family planning and sacrifice due to the cost of education. For several respondents with careers in the Jewish community, the irony of struggling to pay for tuition and afford kosher food was not lost. Erica described a time when she and her husband, both of whom work in the Jewish community, realized they were paying almost a thousand dollars for Passover food, and she exclaimed, "This is a crazy religion; what the hell are we doing here?"

Additionally, the cost of synagogue membership is a source of frustration for some Jewish families. Erica exclaimed, "[There are] times where we're like, 'This is ridiculous, we can't afford our lives, and it's all because we're Jewish, and we're committed to living a practicing Jewish life.'" Sometimes financial limits forced families to choose alternatives to synagogue membership and Jewish involvement. For those families who seek to practice, balancing income, the general cost of living, and the cost of living a Jewish life can be a significant source of tension. While the burden of balancing work, family, and the financial and emotional costs of religion may not be unique to Judaism, it certainly weighs on Jewish families. Even for families who do not factor in kashrut or other costs, the cost of summer camp, synagogue membership, and the annual Jewish holidays necessitating special or extra foods, complicate Jewish families' schedules and negotiations, and greatly increase their personal and budget stress.

## Conclusion

In our survey data and in our interviews with Jewish spouses and parents, it became clear that Judaism is work. Contemporary families struggle to balance their roles in paid labor with their responsibilities in raising children and maintaining a home; their devotion to Judaism adds obligations that further complicate that balance, such as the need to earn enough to pay for kosher or holiday foods, set aside time for Shabbat preparations, run Hebrew-school carpools that do not conform to the 9-to-5 workday, and other religious duties. Understanding the profound practical and ideological connection of the Jewish religion to home and family, and using the contemporary framing of Judaism in the home as *work* also helps us better understand the emotional, temporal, and financial pressures on contemporary families.

Jewish families in particular, as members of a minority religion that adapts to—and resists—many of the broader societal changes in gender and family practice, provide an interesting case for examining the work that goes into religion in the family. The clash between the Jewish calendar and the typical rhythm of broader American society provides insight into and a symbol of the added "shift" that Judaism demands. Some issues are easily resolved between family members, but at other times the Jewish "third shift" generates extended discussions and emotionally laden compromises. In addition, budgeting for day school, kosher and holiday foods, and synagogue memberships and activities places strain on Jewish families. Even though Jewish families are overwhelmingly in socioeconomic statuses conducive to family life, the cost of Jewish living is still a factor these families must consider, calculate, and collaborate on together.

This research opens up many questions for further research, especially considering the unique place of American Judaism. How do other religious groups experience religion as work that must be negotiated in their families in relation to their roles in the labor force and the division of labor in their homes? In religious groups with strong cultural components and with family-focused religious rituals and practices—such as Italian or Irish Catholics, Hindus, or Muslims—is religion another "shift" in their already busy days? Future research should consider the role of religion in family life more broadly and comparatively.

Our central questions about the role of Judaism in family life and its impact on the division of labor and how families balance work and home life highlight not only the many ways in which Judaism is important to Jewish families but also the many stressors it places on their time, emotions, and budgets. In a society with increasing prominence (and necessity) of dual-earner families, and with a persistent at least partially gendered division of labor in the home, families who seek to incorporate religion into their family life also face challenges in dividing their responsibilities to religion, paid labor, and home environment. Just as the traditional division of household labor continues to influence individuals as they strive for more egalitarian arrangements, so too do traditional divisions of religious work factor in as background, as we have seen with Jewish families who negotiate between partners' desires for religious expression in the home. As the broader society continues to change in relation to gendered labor, with American Jews overwhelmingly adopting those changes, how might the third shift of Judaism continue to change as Jewish families negotiate who does what in their Jewish homes? In addition, just as corporations have worked to create better work-family policies, family-leave practices, and childcare options, how might the Jewish community work to better support families who struggle to balance their work, home, and religious lives and all of the resulting issues with schedules, budgets, and personal commitments?

The confluence of Judaism and the family is a theme highlighted in traditional Jewish ritual expressions and in our online survey and interview data. Our study takes a step toward disaggregating the influences, benefits, and stressors that accompany that melding of religion and family life. As Judaism takes up time, energy, and money, Jewish families face choices and negotiations to organize their lives around all of their responsibilities. Judaism may be for many a "lens on life," but it is also work.

## NOTES

1. Maureen P. Semans and Linda Stone Fish, "Dissecting Life with a Jewish Scalpel: A Qualitative Analysis of Jewish-Centered Family Life," *Family Process* 39, no. 1 (2000): 121–39; Riv-Ellen Prell, "Family Formation, Educational Choice, and American Jewish Identity," in *Family Matters: Jewish Education in an Age of Choice*, ed. Jack Wertheimer (Waltham, MA: Brandeis University Press, 2007); Shelly Tenenbaum, "Good or Bad for the Jews? Moving Beyond the Continuity Debate," *Contemporary Jewry* 21, no. 1 (2000): 91–97.
2. The Negotiations in the Jewish Home survey was created and facilitated by the Internet-based survey tool SurveyMonkey. The researchers chose SurveyMonkey because it provides easy-to-use and accessible surveys online, with membership options allowing for advanced internet security (SSL) and statistical analysis both on the website and through

SPSS. To collect narratives and understand the breadth of responses to the survey questions, the researchers conducted a pilot study through nonrepresentative convenience sampling. Information about the study and a link to the survey were sent to several communities available to the researchers: the ASSJ and Wexner listservs, local synagogues, and friends and colleagues (with the request to further distribute). Each respondent received the same link, but the web survey allowed participants to access their individual survey and reenter the survey based on their IP address. No geographic or personally identifying data was collected from participants such as name or address. By December 2011, 173 individuals had accessed the survey and 82 had completed it.

To understand the ways in which Jewish families juggle and negotiate their work, homes, and religion, Rachel Bernstein conducted interviews with 15 Jewish individuals who were married or partnered and had children of any age in 2012–2013.

3. In total, 9 respondents were interviewed in the Greater Boston area, 4 respondents were from other major cities along the East Coast, 1 respondent lived in the Midwest, and 1 respondent lived with her family in Israel, but grew up in the Boston area and met her husband there before moving to Israel. The average age of the respondents was 48.7, with a median age of 46. The gender distribution of interview respondents was 10 female respondents and 5 male respondents. One male and one female respondent were married to one another. The average number of children was 2.2, with two mixed families with children from previous marriages. Two respondents had converted to Judaism before their marriages, and most respondents identified as Orthodox (4), Conservative (6), and Reform (3), but respondents also identified as culturally Jewish (1) and secular humanist (1).
4. Kathleen Gerson, *The Unfinished Revolution: Coming of Age in a New Era of Gender, Work, and Family* (New York: Oxford University Press, 2010), 4.
5. Mary Jo Bane, *Here to Stay: American Families in the Twentieth Century* (New York: Basic Books, 1976); Sylvia Ann Hewlett, *A Lesser Life: The Myth of Women's Liberation in America* (New York: Warner Books, 1986); Christopher Lasch, *Haven in a Heartless World: The Family Besieged* (New York: Basic Books, 1977); May Ann Glendon, *Abortion and Divorce and Western Law* (Cambridge, MA: Harvard University Press, 1987); David Blankenhorn, Steven Bayme, and Jean Bethke Elshtain, eds., *Rebuilding the Nest: A New Commitment to the American Family* (Milwaukee, WI: Family Service America, 1990).
6. A few of the many important works on the creation of American domestic life include the following: Stephanie Coontz, *The Social Origins of Private Life: A History of American Families* (London: Verso, 1998); Marcia Millman, *Warm Hearts, Cold Cash: The Intimate Dynamics of Families and Money* (New York: Free Press, 1991); Elaine Tyler May, *Homeward Bound: American Families in the Cold War Era* (New York: Basic Books, 1988); Steven Mintz and Susan Kellogg, *Domestic Revolutions: A Social History of American Family Life* (New York: Free Press, 1988); Barbara Ehrenreich, *The Hearts of Men: American Dreams and the Flight from Commitment* (Garden City, NY: Anchor Press, 1983); Gerson, *Unfinished Revolution;* Judith Stacey, *Brave New Families: Stories of Domestic Upheaval in Late-Twentieth Century America* (Los Angeles: University of California Press, 1998).
7. Gerson, *Unfinished Revolution.*
8. Stacey, *Brave New Families*, 17.
9. Calvin Goldscheider, *Jewish Continuity and Change: Emerging Patterns in America* (Bloomington: Indiana University Press, 1986); Jay Y. Brodbar-Nemzer, "The Contemporary American Jewish Family," in *The Religion and Family Connection: Social Science Perspectives*, ed. Darwin L. Thomas (Provo, UT: Brigham Young University Press, 1988), 2.

10. Prell, "Family Formation," 6.
11. Harriet Hartman and Moshe Hartman, *Gender and American Jews: Patterns in Work, Education and Family in Contemporary Life* (Waltham, MA: Brandeis University Press, 2009), 93.
12. Ibid., 101.
13. Sylvia Barack Fishman, "Choosing Lives: Evolving Gender Roles in American Jewish families," in *The Cambridge Companion to American Judaism*, ed. Dana E. Kaplan (New York: Cambridge University Press, 2005), 248.
14. Arlie Hochschild and Anne Machung, *The Second Shift: Working Families and the Revolution at Home* (New York: Penguin Books, 2012 [1989]).
15. Ibid. Hochschild and Machung define these three gender ideologies as traditional—wife identifies with the home and husband identifies with paid work; egalitarian—both wife and husband identify equally with household labor and paid labor; and transitional—wife identifies with household labor and paid work and husband identifies mostly with paid labor (15).
16. Arlie Russell Hochschild, *The Time Bind: When Work Becomes Home and Home Becomes Work* (New York: Metropolitan Books, 1997).
17. Melissa A. Milkie, Sara B. Raley, and Suzanne M. Bianchi, "Taking on the Second Shift: Time Allocations and Time Pressures of US Parents with Preschoolers," *Social Forces* 88, no. 2 (2009): 498.
18. Suzanne M. Bianchi et al., "Is Anyone Doing the Housework? Trends in the Gender Division of Household Labor," *Social Forces* 79 (2000): 207.
19. Hochschild and Machung, *Second Shift*; Gerson, *Unfinished Revolution*.
20. Hochschild, *Time Bind*.
21. Gerson, *Unfinished Revolution*.
22. Hochschild and Machung, *Second Shift*.
23. Ibid.
24. Dana Vannoy-Hiller and William W. Philliber, *Equal Partners: Successful Women in Marriage* (Newbury Park: Sage Publications, 1989), 120–22.
25. Hochschild, *Time Bind*, 215.
26. Kathleen E. Jenkins, *Awesome Families: The Promise of Healing Family in the International Churches of Christ* (Piscataway, NJ: Rutgers University Press, 2005); Kathleen E. Jenkins and Gerardo Marti, "Warrior Chicks: Youthful Aging in a Postfeminist Prosperity Discourse," *Journal for the Scientific Study of Religion* 51, no. 2 (2012): 241–56.
27. Jenkins, *Awesome Families*, 223.
28. Fishman, "Choosing Lives"; Jack Wertheimer, "What Is a Jewish Family? The Radicalization of Rabbinic Discourse," in *American Religions and the Family*, eds. Don S. Browning and David A. Clairmont (New York: Columbia University Press); Prell, "Family Formation."
29. Penny Edgell, *Religion and Family in a Changing Society* (Princeton, NJ: Princeton University Press, 2006); Hartman and Hartman, *Gender and American Jews*; Robert Wuthnow, *After the Baby Boomers: How Twenty- and Thirty-Somethings Are Shaping the Future of American Religion* (Princeton, NJ: Princeton University Press, 2010).
30. Edgell, *Religion and Family*, 64–65.
31. Edgell found that women in part-time work tended to have higher levels of church attendance, while working full-time in paid labor often decreased the amount of time they spent attending religious services in order to compensate for their longer hours in the paid labor

force. In addition, in an earlier study, Hofmeister and Edgell (2003) found that the husband's number of working hours and their commuting time does not impact their religious attendance to the extent that it does women's.

32. Hartman and Hartman, *Gender and American Jews*, 216–17.
33. Ibid., 219.
34. Alan S. Miller and John Hoffmann, "Risk and Religion: An Explanation of Gender Differences in Religiosity," *Journal for the Scientific Study of Religion* 34, no. 1 (1995): 63–75; Alan Miller and Rodney Stark, "Gender and Religiousness: Can Socialization Explanations Be Saved?" *The American Journal of Sociology* 107, no. 6 (2002): 1399–1423.
35. Miller and Hoffmann, "Risk and Religion"; Rodney Stark, "Physiology and Faith: Addressing the 'Universal' Gender Difference in Religious Commitment," *Journal for the Scientific Study of Religion* 41, no. 3 (2002): 495–507; Jessica L. Collett and Omar Lizardo," A Power-Control Theory of Gender and Religiosity," *Journal for the Scientific Study of Religion* 48, no. 2 (2009): 213–31; Louise Marie Roth and Jeffrey C. Kroll, "Risky Business: Assessing Risk Preference Explanations for Gender Differences in Religiosity," *American Sociological Review* 72, no. 2 (2007): 205–20.
36. Edgell, *Religion and Family*; David DeVaus and Ian Mcallister, "Gender Differences in Religion: A Test of the Structural Location Theory," *American Sociological Review* 52, no. 4 (1987): 472–81.
37. Hartman and Hartman, *Gender and American Jews.*
38. Ibid., 142.
39. Sylvia Barack Fishman and Daniel Parmer, "Matrilineal Ascent/Patrilineal Descent: The Gender Imbalance in American Jewish Life" (Waltham, MA: Maurice and Marilyn Cohen Center for Modern Jewish Studies and Hadassah-Brandeis Institute, 2008); Prell, "Family Formation."
40. All names are pseudonyms and any identifying characteristics have been omitted.
41. Semans and Fish, "Dissecting Life with a Jewish Scalpel."
42. Only one respondent in our study was in a same-sex marriage. While scholars argue that gay and lesbian families may have unique experiences, this study does not have sufficient data and makes no claims about the similarities and differences between same-sex marriages and opposite-sex marriages. See Judith Stacey and Timothy Biblarz, "(How) Does the Sexual Orientation of Parents Matter?" *American Sociological Review*, 66, no. 2 (2001): 159–83.
43. Hochschild and Machung, *Second Shift*; Milkie, "Taking on the Second Shift."
44. Prell, "Family Formation"; Jack Wertheimer, "Jewish Education in the United States: Recent Trends and Issues" in *American Jewish Year Book*, vol. 99, ed. David Singer (New York: American Jewish Committee, 1999); Jonathan B. Krasner, *The Benderly Boys and American Jewish Education* (Waltham, MA: Brandeis University Press, 2011).
45. See also Prell, "Family Formation."

# 3

# Marriage and the Law

# 9

## Behold You Are [Fill in the Blank] to Me

*Contemporary Legal and Ritual Approaches to* Qiddushin

Gail Labovitz

### Introduction: The Traditional Jewish Marriage

THE TERM *QIDDUSHIN* (BETROTHAL) has designated both the central act that legally binds a couple in marriage and the state of being so bound since at least the time of the composition and redaction of the Mishnah, the foundational text of rabbinic Judaism, sometime around the beginning of the third century CE. The legal mechanism that creates qiddushin is under scrutiny today because it is not one in which the man and woman play equal roles—indeed, in the most traditional ceremonies the woman hardly plays a role at all beyond a form of passive acquiescence to the proceedings. As the Mishnah relates, at the very opening of the tractate on this topic, mQiddushin 1:1: a woman is acquired (*niqnet*) in three ways: by money, by document, or by sexual intercourse.[1] The Tosefta, a roughly contemporaneous, roughly parallel document to the Mishnah, elaborates:

> By money how (*is the acquisition effected*)? He gave her money [or the equivalent of money], (*and*) he said to her "Behold, you are betrothed (*m'quddeshet*) to me," "Behold, you are betrothed (*m'oresset*) to me," "Behold, you are a woman/wife[2] to me," she is betrothed . . . (tQiddushin 1:1)
>
> And by document? . . . Even if he wrote (*one of the formulae*) on a potsherd and gave it to her, (*or*) on blemished parchment and gave it to her, she is betrothed. (t. Qiddushin 1:2)
>
> And by sexual intercourse? Any act of sexual intercourse that is for the sake of *kiddushin*, she is betrothed . . . (tQiddushin 1:3)

To this day, when a Jewish man gives a Jewish woman a ring as part of a Jewish wedding ceremony in the presence of two valid witnesses and says to her, "You are betrothed to me by this ring, according to the laws of Moses and Israel," he is fulfilling the requirement of betrothal by money or the equivalent thereof (i.e., the ring, as an item of monetary value).[3]

The Jewish wedding in fact entails a two-step process—qiddushin should be followed by *nissuin* (which is enacted through the recitation of the *sheva b'rakhot*, the seven blessings) before the couple consummate the relationship and begin to cohabitate—and at certain times in Jewish history the two could be separated in time by as much as a year or more. Nonetheless, it is qiddushin that is the legally constitutive act, and once it occurs, even if nissuin does not follow, significant legal consequences apply: notably, the laws of adultery come into force, and the couple must be divorced to sever their connection to each other. Similarly, the signing of a *ketubah* (marriage contract) is also not, in and of itself, constitutive of a legally binding marriage; as the flip side of the same coin, qiddushin will take effect even in the absence of a ketubah.

Examining contemporary responses to the traditional Jewish process of marriage, several points are worthy of note. First, qiddushin is understood as a form of acquisition or purchase in these passages.[4] Although the word that opens the Mishnah is niqnet (acquired), the Toseftan text makes clear that when the acquisition is properly performed, the result is that the woman is "betrothed"—*nitqadeshet*. The man does not have to use the language of qiddushin specifically to create the bond; other terms and phrases that indicate his intent to acquire her are sufficient to be legally binding. Second, the man is the active party in this transaction, and the woman the object of his acquisition. He is the active party linguistically: he betroths, he declares, he acquires. In contrast, the bride is designated by passive language: she is acquired, she is betrothed. The woman is not assigned any act she must perform or statement she must make. As both the Tosefta and later texts further make clear (see particularly the part of tQiddushin 1:1 elided above and bQiddushin 5b), the statements that the man can use to effect the qiddushin all designate that he is doing something to change her status. His status does not change (whether through something she says, or even through something he himself says about himself), nor can she be the agent to change either his or her own status.[5]

Most significantly in the modern context, the legal nature of Jewish marriage through qiddushin is directly tied to the legal nature of divorce. Because marriage is understood as a form of acquisition, it is the acquirer, that is, the husband, who must relinquish his acquisition. Divorce too, then, is a unilateral act in which the husband presents his (soon to be ex-)wife with a divorce document known as a *get*. In the text of the get, the husband reverses and releases the claim on the woman, which was enacted at her qiddushin: "Behold you are permitted to any man." Again, this act (and formula) has its origins in the earliest of rabbinic texts (see mGittin 9:3[6]) and despite much legal development in the interim, has not significantly changed its underlying basis. The divorce must happen at the husband's free will and with his full consent (mYevamot 14:1, tBava Batra 11:5), a criterion that has, if anything, been strengthened over time such that any suspicion of coercive pressure brought to bear may be considered by some arbiters to invalidate the get. The result, particularly in modern times, is what a colleague in this project felicitously named "the exit problem": the get can be and all too frequently is withheld by the (ex-)husband as a matter of spite or extortion. In addition, if a man becomes unable to give a get (if his whereabouts are unknown, if his death cannot be confirmed, or if he is not mentally competent), the wife has little if any recourse to free herself from the marriage. Women in these situations are known as *agunot*; those whose husbands are withholding divorce are sometimes distinguished by the term *m'suravot get*. In either case, the wife is prevented from remarrying or even having another relationship under Jewish law. Any relationship she does enter will be deemed adulterous (with the additional result that she may be prohibited from marrying the second man if and when a divorce is forthcoming), and any children she bears are considered *mamzerim*, whose future marital choices are severely limited by their "impaired" status.[7]

## Giving Brides a Voice

As we have seen, in the most traditional form of marriage, the bride need only accept the ring given to her as the token of qiddushin, and she does not speak. For some, a first, minimal step toward acknowledging this imbalance in Jewish marriage rites has been to seek a way in which the marriage ceremony can be reconfigured to give the woman an active role. Several proposals are now in use and more widely under discussion that suggest responses the bride can make to actively indicate her willing acceptance of the qiddushin. Some permit her to present the groom with a ring as a reciprocal gesture, though without the intent of thereby "acquiring" him.[8] In other suggested ceremonial changes, depending often on denominational context, the solution has been to "mutualize" qiddushin, such that each of the two parties declares the other "set aside." Some authorities (mostly, but not exclusively Orthodox) do not allow such an exchange (even without "mutualized" qiddushin), precisely because its nature as an exchange thereby throws into question or entirely vitiates the nature of the transaction as an acquisition:

> When a woman gives a man a ring in return, they are simply exchanging articles of value . . . The legal transaction implied by the groom giving

> the bride a ring has now been matched one for one, and thereby cancelled. Her status remains unchanged. It is as if the bride has not received anything at all, or as if she has given back the gift.[9]

Others allow the exchange, but only after the person solemnizing the ceremony (usually a rabbi) uses rhetoric making it clear that this liturgical activity is not part of the wedding ceremony but instead is a kind of ceremonial epilogue.

Yet even when allowed—and though such statements may reflect actual expectations by both spouses for a union of sexual and emotional exclusivity on both sides—it is frequently the case that one or both of the spouses will *not* thereby have control over the legal meaning given to the mutual qiddushin, whether at the time of a divorce or possibly even from the outset according to the rabbi who oversees the wedding ceremony. Consider, for example, the view expressed by Rabbi Isaac Klein, considered one of the outstanding legal authorities of the Conservative movement, in *A Guide to Jewish Religious Practice* (1976): "Some authorities object to this practice . . . especially if the formula used by the bride is the same as the one used by the groom. Legally, however, there can be no objection. Once the traditional formula has been recited the betrothal is binding, and whatever is added *is of no legal significance*."[10] Today, it is still the case within the Conservative movement, and all the more among the Orthodox, that when a marriage ends, the formal requirement for severing the bond is for the man to give the woman a get regardless of whether "mutual" qiddushin took place; in no case is she ever required or able to give him a get instead or in return.[11] "Mutualized" qiddushin gives the appearance of egalitarianism, but at the end of the day in no way addresses the underlying inequities of qiddushin, nor does it avert the "exit problem."[12]

More comprehensive responses to these inequities of Jewish marital law and the Jewish marriage ceremony, or at least to the detrimental outcomes those inequities may facilitate, have taken several forms within those segments of the Jewish community that consider Jewish law (though interpreted and understood in different ways in different sub-groups) to be compelling (again, in the multiple possible meanings of that word) in their religious lives. In what follows, I explore proposals that attempt to address the negative outcomes of qiddushin by altering or adapting the rites and legal acts that create a marriage from the outset;[13] these fall into two broad trends, roughly corresponding to two broad approaches to the nature and authority of Jewish law. In the first, traditional, or "formalist," methods and categories of legal interpretation are brought to bear. These approaches tend to work to eliminate or ameliorate most particularly the likelihood and ability of the husband to withhold a religious divorce from the wife, but they do not fundamentally alter the role of unilateral qiddushin as the constitutive act of creating marriage (or, therefore, of a get as the preferred means of severing it). Such proposals can be found in both Orthodox and Conservative contexts, and often have histories that extend back through the twentieth century or even a bit beyond.

More recently—in approximately the last twenty-five years or so—a more "radical" approach has started to develop. The question now beginning to be considered by those who wish to proceed in more egalitarian or fair directions (not only between men and women, but in some cases also between different-sex and same-sex couples) while also working within or taking into consideration the Jewish legal framework of marriage is this: Can there be Jewish marriage (or at least sanctioned monogamous partnerships) without unilateral qiddushin—that is, either through a reconfiguration of qiddushin to make it genuinely mutual or to introduce a level of legally significant female agency, or through a method other than qiddushin altogether?

## "Formalist" Approaches

Within this category is a further subdivision into two key approaches that are most commonly in current use, though they do not by any means exhaust all possible approaches that have been suggested or tried: *qiddushin al t'nai* (conditional marriage) and prenuptial agreements. These also track with what Mark Washofsky has identified as "solutions" and "inducements" among the means by which halakhic authorities have typically addressed the global problem (as opposed to individual cases) of women held hostage to failed marriages through the recalcitrance of husbands to grant *gittin*:

> "Solutions," as the name implies, seek to *solve* the *agunah* problem; they do so by suggesting means of terminating a marriage that do not require that the husband issue a divorce in response to his wife's suit in rabbinic court . . . other authorities have suggested "inducements": enactments designed to bring pressure to bear upon the recalcitrant husband so as to "induce" him to submit to the decision of the rabbinic court.[14]

As will be shown below, qiddushin al t'nai is intended to invalidate the marriage in the case of the inability or unwillingness of the husband to grant a divorce, while the variety of prenuptial agreements in use aim in various ways to create penalties for a partner who refuses to participate in the divorce process in good faith. It may also be noted from the outset that even these two options are met with varying forms of acceptability and implementation between groups—that is, both between the Orthodox and Conservative movements, and within Orthodox subcommunities.

The legal issues involved in conditional betrothal/marriage are quite complex, and as they have been explored in great depth in several other locations, it is not my intent to delve into them in detail here.[15] Presented in brief and somewhat reductively, the essence of such proposals is that at the time of the qiddushin (and again at the nissuin; see just below) the husband makes his actions contingent on certain conditions; if these conditions are not subsequently met, the qiddushin is null and void ab initio, that is, it never existed legally. Conditions may be set that limit the husband's ability to withhold a religious divorce: for example, if the marriage is ended by civil divorce and no get is given (or accepted) within a set period afterward, then the marriage is retroactively annulled (but if a get is given, the validity of the marriage remains intact and the couple are legally divorced). Alternately or in addition, the condition(s) may extend to prevent the wife from becoming an agunah in other circumstances as well: if the man disappears and makes no contact with the wife for a set period, or suffers a condition that makes him legally incompetent to give a get for a set period, then the marriage becomes void. A religious court might be designated as the arbiter to verify that the conditions have or have not been met, but once such a determination is made, the marriage automatically and retroactively ceases to have existed, and no get would be necessary to allow either partner to enter a subsequent (re)marriage.

While the possibility of conditional qiddushin is debated even in rabbinic texts, and there are examples of the technique being used in various circumstances elsewhere in halakhic history,[16] proposals for the use of conditional marriage to counter the modern-day problems of (civil) divorce, agunot, and mamzerim go back at least as far as the late nineteenth century. In fact, the first proposal that opened modern debate came from French rabbis responding to the introduction of civil marriage and divorce in their country in 1884, and sought to forestall the problems resulting from women who had been civilly divorced and subsequently remarried (or who had entered other relationships) under civil law without having received a religious divorce. This both created a precedent for later proposals and elicited numerous concerns and challenges. Among the most crucial (and interrelated) concerns and objections raised (then and now) by this tactic are the following:

a) Can a condition made at the time of qiddushin remain valid once the marriage (nissuin) is completed, and more importantly, consummated? Does the fact of the couple subsequently living and presenting themselves as married override the condition and indicate at least a doubtful desire to be married through "proper" qiddushin, which may then have been enacted through their sexual intercourse?

b) Were the marriage to be retroactively annulled, what then is the status of the sexual relations between the couple—do they retroactively become classified as licentious, non-marital sex, which most consider to be prohibited, or at least to be strongly discouraged?[17]

c) Should the functioning of secular/civil law (i.e., the granting of a civil divorce) be able to affect the legal status of a halakhic Jewish marriage?

The gravity of these concerns explains why proposals for conditional qiddushin have met significant resistance in much of the Orthodox world.[18] In the Conservative movement, however, a proposal of this type was presented to the Committee on Jewish Law and Standards and adopted in 1968, thereby making it a legitimate option for Conservative rabbis, many of whom use it regularly to this day.[19]

The use of a prenuptial agreement, formulated as an addition to the traditional marriage document, the ketubah, was first adopted in the Conservative movement in 1953,[20] and prenuptial agreements continue to be used—with some adaptations in language—by some Conservative rabbis. A ketubah containing such a provision, known as the "Lieberman clause" after the author of the original version, Rabbi Saul Lieberman, is meant to be enforceable in a civil court as a civil contract between the parties; in this formulation, the bride and groom each agree that

> should our marriage be dissolved in the civil courts, each of us is bound to appear before the Joint Bet Din [Jewish court] of the Conservative Movement, or such Bet Din as shall be designated by the Joint Bet Din, if so requested by the other, and to abide by its instruction and decision with respect to the dissolution of our marriage under Jewish law. Each of us intends that the undertaking to appear before and to be bound by the directions of the Bet Din may be enforced by civil court of law.[21]

The Conservative ketubah clause is less clear, however, that the joint bet din must come to a ruling regarding issuance of a get, what additional penalties the Joint Bet Din might be able to impose in the face of refusal to grant or accept a get,[22] or whether either the Joint Bet Din or a civil court can enforce not just the summons to appear but also compliance with the Joint Bet Din's subsequent rulings (see further discussion below). One further significant challenge that has been raised (particularly by Orthodox authorities) to this formulation[23] is that the parties are not fully aware at the time of the agreement of the possible penalties that might be subsequently imposed, and therefore cannot be said to have consented to them in full knowledge.[24]

Prenuptial agreement proposals coming from Orthodox sources thus take a somewhat different tack and also tend to function as separate and distinct prenuptial agreements rather than as addenda to the ketubah.[25] Typically in such agreements a specific set of financial consequences is delineated—the recalcitrant party is required to make regular payments to the other, for example—to take effect under specific circumstances such as when the marriage has been civilly dissolved (outside of Israel) or when a religious court determines that reconciliation is not possible and a divorce is in order. To avoid the question of whether the husband is being fined for his noncompliance (thereby raising the concern that perhaps he gives the get under compulsion and not by his own free will), the language of the agreement may be worded as a promise to pay his wife's maintenance, an obligation that Jewish husbands have under halakhah already (even if it is typically superseded by secular law or private arrangements between the couple during the course of marriage).

There are several remaining practical, as well as halakhic difficulties, with this solution (in all its forms). Beyond the fact that it addresses only situations of recalcitrance to grant (or receive) a get and does not provide help for a woman whose husband has disappeared or is not competent is the thorny issue of effectiveness and enforceability. The agreement (particularly in the Orthodox formulations) may actually present the parties with a choice, and one party might opt to pay the penalties despite the expense rather than divorce; alternately, the party against whom a claim is made might lack (or hide) resources to avoid payment. There must also be a mechanism in place to enforce payment or compliance when recalcitrance occurs (as, for example, civil courts outside of Israel, or religious courts so empowered in Israel). Above and beyond the issue of having to invoke external legal mechanisms to resolve an internal halakhic problem (already discussed in relation to conditional qiddushin), it is unclear if such enforcement would actually prove effective;[26] moreover, even if or when it might be effective, the need to invoke such authority and have claims adjudicated would likely further delay the process, to the detriment of the party seeking the get.

## Foundational Changes beyond Formalism

What both of the approaches above—and all the various proposals that fall within their parameters—share is that they avoid altering the underlying unilateral nature of qiddushin, focusing instead on the inequity of its effects rather than its basic structure. Given that this has been the basic legal form of Jewish marriage for an extended part of Jewish history, a question that follows is, Can there be a legal basis for Jewish marriage (or monogamous partnerships) that addresses both the problematic functional and the problematic structural aspects of qiddushin? A small but potentially innovative subset of Jewish thinkers and writers has begun in recent years to develop a body of literature on new ways of thinking about and conducting Jewish marriage in dialogue with Jewish law. The remainder of this chapter explores several such proposals and approaches that are currently being pursued or that are available in the public record, while noting that the examples are still limited. I have loosely grouped them in relation to each other—or perhaps they can be seen as points along a continuum—and wish to be clear that the categories are likely to change and/or develop and/or grow over time.

### MAKE QIDDUSHIN A PROCESS IN WHICH BOTH PARTIES EXERCISE LEGAL AGENCY, AND/OR ONE THAT IS LEGALLY MUTUALLY BINDING.

Under this heading are two items; intriguingly, both were developed by the authors for personal use and were implemented at their own wedding ceremonies. These are (1) a qiddushin formula composed by Jill Jacobs and Guy Izhak Austrian,[27] and (2) the wedding ceremony devised and discussed in a series of five posts by Ben Dreyfus on the blog "Mah Rabu," to be used by the author and his wife (as well as two other friends also in the process of marrying).[28] Both sets of authors discuss the value they find in preserving a form of qiddushin if possible, balanced with their desire to find a way to open up its legal meanings and effects—as well as their understanding of the legitimacy of such endeavors:

> We remained committed to reconstruct *ḳiddushin* if at all possible, and thereby to affirm our position both as legitimate inheritors of Jewish tradition and as shapers of the continually evolving legal system . . . We therefore sought to develop a new form of *ḳiddushin* that would enable us to make clear our intentions to enter into an equal partnership that would take effect only with both of our participation.[29]
>
> The bottom-line essence of *ḳiddushin* as marital exclusivity is uncontroversial to us and to most people. In fact, we thought it was so important that it should be multiplied by two, so that *both* partners are subject to *ḳiddushin* . . . our place is to continue the movement that the rabbis began, moving our understanding of *ḳiddushin* even further away from unilateral acquisition.[30]

To this end, both make recourse to the legal mechanisms of qiddushin al t'nai, already discussed above, but based on more immediate and ongoing considerations rather than conditions that may not arise for some time, if ever. Each embeds conditions into the qiddushin declarations that are meant to make the statements of the two parties provisional upon each other.

In Jacobs and Austrian's ceremony, each party made the qiddushin contingent on the other's willingness to be obligated by the terms of the egalitarian ketubah that they had drafted;[31] additionally, each also invited the other to "be my life partner" (*shutaf/at hayyim*) rather than using traditional language of qiddushin. Whether this is a mutual qiddushin or a form of qiddushin that makes explicit the need for female consent is not entirely clear, nor is it clear that a new protocol would be necessary for dissolving this qiddushin or whether the woman could dissolve the qiddushin herself by subsequent removal of her consent to the conditions.[32] The Mah Rabu proposal, on the other hand, explicitly means to create mutual qiddushin, with conditions built into the statements each party makes to the other such that one qiddushin should not go into effect, or stay in effect, unless the other does also, and vice versa. In regards to the possibility of divorce, the intent is that if one of the parties chooses to terminate his or her act of qiddushin, then the condition on which the other person's act of qiddushin rests is no longer valid, and the second qiddushin is automatically ended as well (see especially part 5 of the series). It may be noted, though, that a discussion ensued in the comments section of part 5 about the nature of the abrogation of the second qiddushin; that is, was it negated as of the time of the giving of the get by the other party, or might it be considered retroactively annulled altogether in the absence of the condition that was set at the outset being met? Also, although not a prominent point in the blog itself, this format would appear to be applicable to a marriage of same-sex partners, since it presumes that a woman may betroth someone else, and a man may be betrothed.

### USE A FORMULA THAT SHOULD NOT CREATE QIDDUSHIN LEGALLY, BUT THAT PRESERVES SOMETHING OF THE LANGUAGE AND/OR APPEARANCE OF QIDDUSHIN—SUCH AS AN EXCHANGE OF RINGS AND STATEMENTS OF INTENT.

Here, I bring together two proposals from very different ideological perspectives and with very different intent, which nonetheless come to very similar conclusions about method. The key in these proposals is the use of attempted betrothal declarations found in rabbinic sources but specifically designated there as invalid or of doubtful legal status toward creating legally binding qiddushin. Meir Simha Feldblum writes from an Orthodox (and Israeli) perspective, and with the intent to address the social problems of agunot/m'suravot get and mamzerim.[33] He further notes that many modern, nonreligious women would reject the premises of qiddushin were such premises fully understood (a point that calls into question whether most women are in fact consenting to qiddushin, as legally required, meaning that the validity of the qiddushin in such cases should be doubtful). Thus, while he continues to privilege qiddushin as the optimal form of marriage within Jewish law and tradition, he also describes what he believes to be an acceptable alternative hinted at in writings of medieval halakhists and Talmudic commentators: *derekh kiddushin*, "in the manner of qiddushin." Discussing a case in which the two parties were not able to legally create a marriage,[34] he notes that

> Most of the decisors, earlier and later, emphasize that "the manner of *qiddushin* and *nissuin*" is not considered licentiousness . . . That is to say, despite the fact that there is no [legally binding] Toraitic *qiddushin* here, nor even rabbinical[ly recognized] *qiddushin*, the essence of the case is that they are defined as exclusive to each other . . . and in a connection of this sort the woman does not require a get [to sever the relationship].[35]

He thus argues that this alternative kind of exclusivity can serve as the model by which a non-qiddushin form of marriage may be allowed and recognized within the legal system as a form of valid connection between a man and a woman that is not to be deemed prohibited licentiousness—but that is not legally binding qiddushin and hence not requiring a get to be severed. In the ceremony Feldblum proposes, the groom uses the words *harei at m'yuhedet li* (behold, you are singled out for me), a formula that is mentioned in bQiddushin 6a and later codes as only doubtfully creating qiddushin.[36] Although the couple therefore foregoes the acquisitional nature of qiddushin and the unilateral divorce process if the marriage does not last, and doing so is materially beneficial to women, it is worth noting that the ceremony, as Feldblum imagines it, is still hardly an egalitarian one and hews almost exactly in its ritual structure to a "traditional" Jewish wedding.

David Greenstein argues for a more thoroughgoing rejection of qiddushin in its traditional form, given that it relies on a "theory of marriage" that is built on exclusive sexual access for the man to the woman that is nonreciprocal (she does not, legally, have exclusive sexual access to him) and hence, in conjunction, assumes heteronormativity.[37] Nonetheless, his rejection of mutualizing traditional qiddushin rests as much on legalistic grounds (in keeping with the view of the Conservative movement's Klein, cited above, who allows an outside authority to accept the husband's act of qiddushin as binding while treating the wife's reciprocal statement as legally meaningless) as on those of ideology.[38] He does, however, embrace the concept of sexual exclusivity that qiddushin and the metaphor of ownership represent on a symbolic as well as a legal level (similar to the position taken in the Mah Rabu blog), writing, "The sense of exclusive 'ownership' that is inherent in feeling love for another should be preserved and acknowledged—as a feeling and claim that each is entitled to have regarding the other."[39] Following

Feldman's lead, he also turns to a form of marital declaration that is mentioned but explicitly rejected as nonbinding in rabbinic and later halakhic writings. Taking such a statement from Maimonides' Mishneh Torah (*Hilkhot Ishut* 3:1–2 and 6), Greenstein proposes a ceremony in which each partner (of any gender combination) does not attempt to "acquire" the other, but rather makes a statement of his or her own sense of giving him or herself to a spouse: "Behold, I am betrothed/set aside for you" and "The gift of the ring is declared by this formula to exemplify a gift of self . . . each is creating a change of status to themselves and dedicating that changed status to the other."[40]

While both of these proposals explicitly aim to avoid creating a legally binding state of qiddushin, it is somewhat less clear by what alternative means marriages enacted through these methods might be considered legally binding on the participants. Feldblum asserts that the relationship created by derekh qiddushin is a valid form of marriage in its own right and is not to be considered *pilagshut*, "concubinage," a category of relationship with a long and intricate halakhic history and considered by most at this time to be forbidden at least ab initio.[41] Indeed, one of the factors that should distinguish the two, he argues, is that "according to our proposal . . . a procedure would be introduced for counseling and divorce, which is not the case regarding the concubine."[42] But while it may be argued that the need to *legally* undo an act is itself a marker that the initial act had legally binding force, neither article delineates how such relationships are undone with the same degree of specificity given to their creation; Greenstein refers his readers in a single end note to the work of Rachel Adler (see below), while Feldblum appears to assign the task of creating a procedure to the (Israeli) rabbinic court system that would also oversee the original marriages.[43]

## Replacing Qiddushin

Those proposing the most foundational changes claim that qiddushin and the metaphor of ownership cannot or should not be redeemed, mutually or otherwise. The best known and most fully developed example of this type at the moment is Rachel Adler's ceremony of "*B'rit Ahuvim*"/Lovers' Covenant (though models that invoke the laws of vows—*nedarim*—would also fit here).[44] While Adler embraces the position that two "reciprocal" acts of qiddushin ought to legally cancel each other out (see above), nonetheless, "the problem with marital *kinyan* is not simply that it is a unilateral act, but that it commodifies human beings. The groom's commodification and acquisition of the bride is not rectified by the bride's retaliation in kind."[45] Rather, a new ceremony with a new legal basis is needed. Seeking a different metaphor and legal model of marriage, Adler turned to rabbinic discussions on forming business partnerships. This process, known as "placing [money] in a pouch" (*she-hitilu la-kis*), appears in rabbinic and later halakhic sources (see tKetubot 10:4; Mishneh Torah, *Hilkhot Shluhin v'Shutafin* 4:1 and 3); it is enacted by the symbolic—but also legally binding—act of the two (or more) partners each placing their contributions to the common fund into a pouch and lifting it together, thereby acquiring rights in and duties toward the partnership. Adler's proposed ceremony thus centers around the ritual moment at which the two partners (the ceremony accommodates partners of any gender combination) each place an item of value—be it a ring or something else chosen for its significance to the participant—into a bag and lift the bag together, thereby forming a legally binding partnership and each committing themselves to all the reciprocal obligations and responsibilities the partnership entails (such as sexual fidelity, mutual support, joint responsibility for children from the marriage, etc.). These are further outlined in a *b'rit* document, which is also an essential part of the marriage.[46] An advantage of this method, Adler suggests, is that the laws of partnership allow either (or any) party to the partnership to withdraw from and dissolve it should they feel dissolution is necessary. Adler devotes much less of her chapter to this aspect of b'rit ahuvim, but states that "this procedure should be conducted by a court of three learned Jews";[47] the termination of the marriage and arrangements agreed to by the couple for division of assets or continuing obligations between them should also be documented by the court in Hebrew and the vernacular, and signed by witnesses.

As regards all of these newer innovations, the concerns that remain to be considered and investigated are several. I conclude by highlighting two, which are interrelated. Both hinge on the impulse among "traditionalist" decisors of Jewish law (and other legal systems) to assimilate new cases and unfamiliar acts into already established categories. In the realm of marriage law, this means that exclusive and binding relationships between heterosexual partners, however initiated, may be brought under the rubric of qiddushin, such that they must be severed by the (unilateral) get process. The closer an alternative ceremony looks to traditional qiddushin, the more likely it may be that it will be assimilated into the dominant regime. Four of the five works outlined here address this concern directly, providing arguments and reasons why their alternate marriage forms ought not to be understood even by outside observers as qiddushin.[48] The author of the Mah Rabu blog, however, also raises the question of whether one ought to be overly concerned about legal meanings that might be imposed from outside, at the expense of creating one's own egalitarian legal meanings. Hence, even if such arguments are successful, further questions follows: If not deemed qiddushin, are such connections still at risk of being "absorbed" into the traditional system under other definitions, such as licentiousness, or even concubinage? If no get is demanded, is this sufficient? Are negative, undesirable definitions imposed from outside relevant? To what extent do the authors of these proposals, and others that might follow in their wake, hope to create new legal meanings, and for whom?

## Conclusion

Both integration of Jews and Jewish communities into the larger civil society, and the changed circumstances of women's status (and also the increasing societal acceptance of homosexuality and same-sex partnerships), particularly in modern, "Western" societies, have put the longstanding legal structures of Jewish marriage and divorce in a new spotlight. The still increasing number of women who have been extorted for or entirely prevented from receiving a get due to a husband's recalcitrance has become a significant social crisis, notably in Israel and some Orthodox communities, and has alerted Jewish women (and men) across the Jewish spectrum to the real and material damage the legalities of qiddushin can inflict. And while there are those who may have proposed, advocated for, or personally employed measures to forestall problematic potential outcomes, it is hard to overlook the underlying and systemic gender imbalance embedded in qiddushin that originally set the stage for such abuses. Intriguingly, even some who might be expected to be among the strongest defenders of traditional forms—(male) rabbis and scholars of Jewish legal sources—have on occasion demonstrated some understanding of the problematic underlying assumptions and legal results of creating marriage through qiddushin. David Novak, for example, tellingly, if somewhat backhandedly, remarks on the "risk" of other marital options being available: "If the Jewish public, especially the female Jewish public found out about [those options], Jewish marriage with its greater contemporary liabilities and fewer contemporary assets, would become an option fit only for fools."[49] Going forward, it will be for each of us who continue to seek—individually and communally—Jewish forms to solemnize our marriages to determine whether there is continued value in preserving traditional forms and whether strategies of "solutions" and "inducements" (presuming they are successful in relieving the most obvious abuses in Jewish divorce procedures) are sufficient to "redeem" qiddushin. If not, the questions before us will be, How shall we marry? How shall we create ceremonies and legal forms to enact binding commitments to each other that we can also understand as "authentically" Jewish?[50] The possibilities discussed here are, it is to be hoped, only a beginning in a rich and vital conversation.

## NOTES

1. All translations of primary and secondary sources are my own.
2. The Hebrew *isha* can carry either meaning (this is true in biblical, rabbinic, and modern Hebrew).
3. "Valid" being traditionally defined as "religiously observant Jewish adult male."
4. Elsewhere I have argued at length that this ownership should be understood as a cognitive metaphor and the primary model by which rabbinic texts across the rabbinic period construct their understanding and legal reasoning regarding marriage and resultant gender roles. See Gail Labovitz, *Marriage and Metaphor: Constructions of Gender in Rabbinic Literature* (Lantham, MD: Lexington Books, 2009).
5. For a more extended discussion of qiddushin relative to the question of same-sex marriage, see Gail Labovitz, "By Any Other Name? Kiddushin, Same-Sex Relationships, and Halakhic Discourse in the Liberal Movements," *Jewish Law Association Studies* 23 (2012): 120–37.
6. Note that this Mishnah also juxtaposes divorcing a wife with manumitting a slave. This pairing recurs regularly in rabbinic texts (as in tBava Batra mentioned just below); see the discussion in Labovitz, *Marriage and Metaphor*, 160–67, and Daniela Piatelli, "*Get* and *Get Shihrur*," *Jewish Law Association Studies* 1 (1985): 93–99.
7. It is true that since the "Decree of Rabbenu Gershom" at the end of the tenth or beginning of the eleventh century, a woman, at least in Ashkenazi communities, must also accept the get of her own free will. Some remedies, however, exist for a man whose wife refuses to accept a get, while the opposite is less, if at all, the case; similarly, the severity of the penalties that result from a relationship he conducts despite the absence of a divorce, either for him or for the status of any children he might father, in no way begin to approach those that result for an undivorced woman.
8. For a discussion of recent implementation of this and similar innovations in an (Israeli) Orthodox context, see, for example, some of the recent work of Irit Koren: "The Bride's Voice: Religious Women Challenge the Wedding Ritual," *Nashim* 10 (2005): 29–52; "Behold, I Agree to Be Betrothed to You as We Stipulated According to the Torah: An Orthodox Wedding Not by Way of the Rabbanut" [Hebrew], *De'ot* 32 (2007): 21–26; *You Are Hereby Renewed Unto Me: Gender, Religion and Power Relations In the Jewish Wedding Ritual* [Hebrew] (Jerusalem: Magnes Press, the Hebrew University, 2011).
9. Resnik, Yosef, "Is a 'Double Ring' Wedding Okay?" http://www.chabad.org/library/article_cdo/aid/477319/jewish/Is-a-Double-Ring-wedding-ceremony-okay.htm.
10. Isaac Klein, *A Guide to Jewish Religious Practice* (New York: Jewish Theological Seminary of America, 1979), 396; emphasis added.
11. In the Reform movement, which does not consider itself bound by Jewish law, a civil divorce is deemed sufficient to sever the marriage, and the couple may participate in a mutualized religious ceremony of divorce or none at all.
12. See also Rachel Adler's critique of even the symbolism of mutual qiddushin, cited in note 44 and discussed below.
13. There is also an extensive literature on means by which authorities might resolve situations of women unable to obtain a divorce from a marriage that was already established through traditional qiddushin, but these materials are quite complex in their own right and deserve a separate treatment. The interested reader may see the latter half of Monique Susskind

Goldberg and Diana Villa, *Za'akat Dolot: Halakhic Solutions for the* Agunot *of Our Time* [Hebrew] (Jerusalem: Schechter Institute of Jewish Studies, 2006).

14. Mark Washofsky, "The Recalcitrant Husband: The Problem of Definition," *The Jewish Law Annual* 4 (1981): 146.
15. Some particularly accessible overviews in English and Hebrew can be found in Susskind Goldberg and Villa, *Za'akat Dolot*, 119–49; Melanie Landau, *Tradition and Equality in Jewish Marriage: Beyond the Sanctification of Subordination* (New York: Continuum, 2012), 95–125; Yehudah Abel, "The Plight of the Agunah and Conditional Marriage," www.mucjs.org/MELILAH/2005/1.pdf.
16. A noted example is attributed to Rabbi Israel of Bruna (Germany), known as the Mahari Brin, in the fifteenth century. The proposal in this case is meant to address the situation in which a man seeking to be married has a brother who is an apostate; were the man to die childless, his widow might be trapped by the laws of levirate marriage and the brother's unwillingness to participate in the ceremony that would release her to remarry. This ruling does not appear in Rabbi Israel's known writings, but is cited by Rabbi Moses Isserles in the *Shulhan Arukh, Even haEzer* 157:4: "And one who betroths a woman, but he has an apostate brother—he may betroth and make a condition . . . that if she were to fall before the apostate for levirate marriage that she would not have been betrothed [in the first place]." Similar discussions appear in other roughly contemporaneous sources.
17. It may be noted, however, that Orthodox legal thinkers seem to have dedicated much thought and concern to the possible, retroactive sin of "licentiousness" due to a man engaging in sex that was determined after the fact—although this was not understood at the time it was happening—to have taken place outside the legal framework of marriage. In contrast, they have dedicated relatively little thought to and concern for confronting the ethics of using religious law to in essence hold a woman and her marital future—and any potential Jewish progeny—for ransom.
18. Although some prominent Orthodox thinkers have provided arguments in favor of conditional qiddushin. Most well known is Eliezer Berkovits's *Tenai Be-Nissu'in uv-Get* [Hebrew] (Jerusalem: Mossad HaRav Kook, 1966). See also Michael J. Broyde, "A Proposed Tripartite Agreement to Solve Some of the *Agunah* Problems: A Solution without Any Innovation," *Jewish Law Association Studies* 20 (2010): 1–15, esp. 5–6 and 12–14. Irit Koren, in "Behold, I Agree to Be Betrothed to You," describes using conditional marriage for her own wedding, with the assistance of Noam Zohar, a professor at Bar Ilan University and Modern Orthodox rabbi.
19. Eli Bohnen et al., "T'nai B'Kiddushin," *Proceedings of the Rabbinical Assembly*, 1968, 229–41; also reprinted in David Golinkin, ed., *Proceedings of the Committee on Jewish Law and Standards of the Conservative Movement, 1927–1970*, vol. 2, *The Agunah Problem* (Jerusalem: Rabbinical Assembly and Institute of Applied Halakhah, 1997), 914–26. Note that the authors rely on many of Berkovits's arguments. See also Perry Raphael Rank and Gordon M. Freedman, eds., *Moreh Derekh: The Rabbinical Assembly Rabbi's Manual* (New York: Rabbinical Assembly, 1998), C-35–39, which specifies the recommended procedures within the Conservative movement for enacting conditional qiddushin.
20. *Proceedings of the Rabbinical Assembly* 1954, 64–68; also reprinted in David Golinkin, ed., *Proceedings of the Committee on Jewish Law and Standards of the Conservative Movement, 1927–1970*, vol. 2, 818–22.
21. *Moreh Derekh*, C-33.
22. Lieberman's original version included the provision "We authorize the Beth Din to impose such terms of compensation as it may see fit for failure to respond to its summons or to carry

out its decision." *Proceedings of the Rabbinical Assembly* 1954, 67–68; Golinkin, *Proceedings*, 821–22.

23. Even in its original form as drafted by Lieberman; see note 22.
24. This challenge was raised even in the proposal's original form as drafted by Lieberman; see note 22. For further discussion of the Lieberman clause and some of the challenges to it, see Susskind Goldberg and Villa, *Za'akat Dolot*, 104–11.
25. For an overview of the history of some proposals within the Orthodox world beginning in the mid-twentieth century, see Rachel Levmore, "Rabbinic Responses in Favor of Prenuptial Agreements," *Tradition* 42:1 (2009): 29–49. See also the discussion in Susskind Goldberg and Villa, *Za'akat Dolot*, 3–100. Two prenuptial agreements that are currently in common use can be found on-line at www.theprenup.org/ (Beth Din of American) and www.youngisraelrabbis.org.il/prenup.htm (Council of Young Israel Rabbis in Israel). See also www.agunot-campaign.org.uk/pre_nuptial_agreement.htm (Court of the Chief Rabbi, Great Britain).
26. Among the concerns that arise at least in the American context is that of separation of church and state, and whether a civil court may enforce a private contract if it entails compelling a person to perform a religious act. The Conservative Lieberman clause has been tested only once (to the best of my knowledge) in American civil courts, in *Avitzur v. Avitzur*. The husband was ordered to fulfill his commitment to appear before the Jewish court, as the ketubbah clause was ruled an enforceable contract under civil law, but was still under no obligation thereby to grant a get. See *Avitzur v. Avitzur* 86 A.D.2d 133 (1982) (NY: Appellate Div, 3rd Dept.), http://scholar.google.com/scholar_case?case=14399906263480799747&q=avitzur+v+avitzur&hl=en&as_sdt=4,33; and *Avitzur v. Avitzur* 58 N.Y.2d 108 (1983) (NY: Court of Appeals), http://scholar.google.com/scholar_case?case=7857121138287506037&q=avitzur+v+avitzur&hl=en&as_sdt=4,33. Warshofsky also notes that civil jurisdiction might be thwarted by the recalcitrant party fleeing beyond its sphere of influence ("Recalcitrant Husband," 156).
27. Jill Jacobs and Guy Izhak Austrian, "The Choices of Marriage: One Couple's Attempt to Create an Egalitarian Jewish Wedding Ceremony within the Traditional Framework of *Kiddushin*," *Conservative Judaism* 63, no. 3 (2012): 32–41.
28. Beginning at mahrabu.blogspot.com/2010/06/wedding-industrial-complex-and-kant-as.html. See also Ben Dreyfus et al., "Marriage by Document," *Sh'ma*, June 2010, 18.
29. Jacobs and Austrian, "Choices of Marriage," 37.
30. Dreyfus et al., "Marriage by Document"; emphasis in the original.
31. Based on a version by Rabbi Gordon Tucker (which can be viewed at www.ritualwell.org/ritual/egalitarian-ketubah), together with their own additions delineating mutual commitments and responsibilities.
32. The authors also note that "our ceremony seeks to solve problems of patriarchy and sexism in *ḳiddushin* between a man and a woman, and therefore does not necessarily address the particular needs of same sex couples" (Jacobs and Austrian, "Choices of Marriage," 40).
33. Meir Simha Feldblum, "Ba'ayot Agunot uMamzerim: Hatza'at Pitron Maqifah u'Kolelet" [Hebrew], *Dine Yisra'el* 19, no. 5757–5758: 203–16.
34. In short, the case is one in which the father of a minor girl has gone abroad and failed to maintain contact with his family. Due to the girl's age, only her father should be able to contract a marriage for her; she cannot do so herself, and no other family member has rights over her in this regard. Some authorities, however, permit her mother and/or brothers to arrange a marriage (this was considered, by these authors, to be to her benefit) and further rule that because marital relations between the young woman and her "husband" take place

"in the way of *qiddushin*" and with the intent to be a married couple, they are not to be considered licentious or forbidden.

35. Feldblum, "Ba'ayot Agunot uMamzerim," 109.
36. That it may create doubtful qiddushin—which would then demand a *get m'safek*, a divorce out of doubt (or "just in case")—is, however, a source of critique to Feldblum's proposal. See Suskind, Goldberg, and Villa, *Za'akat Dalot*, 247, esp. n517; "Agunah: The Manchester Analysis" (draft final report of the Agunah Research Unit University of Manchester), 207, point 7.47, www.mucjs.org/ARUDraftFinalv.2.pdf. Note that the alternate formula suggested in the latter as preferable is similar to that of David Greenstein, discussed just below.
37. David Greenstein, "Equality and Sanctity: Rethinking Jewish Marriage in Theory and in Ceremony," *G'vanim* 5 (2009): 1–35.
38. See also the discussion of Rachel Adler's work, below.
39. Greenstein, "Equality and Sanctity," 26.
40. Ibid., 27. Greenstein also writes that an additional advantage of this method is that it can be used for a same-sex pairing: "The trivial truism that traditional *qiddushin* has never applied to gay couples contributes nothing toward determining the essential nature of *qiddushin* as we value it . . . this approach recognizes that gender roles are not determinative in defining a sacred relationship" (27).
41. Feldblum, "Ba'ayot Agunot uMamzerim," 113–14. But see also J. David Bleich, "Can There Be Marriage without Marriage?" *Tradition* 33, no. 2 (1999): 39–49, esp. 42. On pilagshut more generally, and as a possible (but rejected) alternative to marriage by qiddushin, see Elyakim G. Ellinson, *Non-Halachic Marriage: A Study of the Rabbinic Sources* [Hebrew] (Tel Aviv: Dvir Co. Ltd., 1975); and Susskind Goldberg and Villa, *Za'akat Dolot*.
42. Feldblum, "Ba'ayot Agunot uMamzerim," 114.
43. Greenstein, "Equality and Sanctity," 27, 33, n77; Feldblum, "Ba'ayot Agunot uMamzerim," 110. In the course of articulating possible objections to his proposal, Feldblum also admits the possibility that "in practice, civil marriages are within the sense of 'the way of *qiddushin*'—in that they [the couple] are exclusive to one another—even without a religious ceremony and without rabbinic involvement. . . . " He argues in response, however, that his method is preferable in that it retains a religious element to the ceremony ("Ba'ayot Agunot uMamzerim," 114–15).

This possibility of foregoing qiddushin or another other religious ceremony in favor of civil marriage has become a topic of discourse particularly in Israel, where Jewish citizens currently have no option for marriage within the country except through the state-sanctioned (ultra-)Orthodox rabbinate. The suggestion that civil marriage might serve as the basis for an ab initio solution for the problems and inequities occasioned by qiddushin, however, while common from a secular perspective (especially in Israel), is far less likely to come from within a halakhic argument. I would thus like to make note of one other item, a recent article by Ariel Picard, "'According to the Law of Moses and Israel': The Essence of Marriage According to the Halakhic Decisors of the Twentieth Century, Civil Marriage as a Test Case," *Democratic Culture* 12 (2011): 141–95. After reviewing the reasoning of several prominent Orthodox authorities of the twentieth century on the status of civil marriage vis-à-vis Jewish marriage, and the current stance of the Israeli religious court system, Picard suggests an opening for "the halakhic recognition of civil marriage as a Noahide marriage . . . a solution also for religious couples who find themselves in internal conflict regarding marriage [through qiddushin]" (192). Two key points underlie his argument: (a) Jewish tradition has long recognized that most human cultures (which, since they descend from the children of the biblical Noah, are known as "Noahide") have forms of marriage guided by their own social and legal norms, and that these "marriages" have legitimacy and (hence) certain binding effects (most notably a prohibition on adultery, especially female adultery) so long as they last; and (b) Jews too are descendants of Noah and hence "Noahides." From these flow an argument (adopted by the Israeli Rabbinate) "which treated civil marriage as a situation valid 'in retrospect,'" and which can "open the option of seeing civil marriage and divorce as an act that carries religious significance also before the act . . . "; 194. Such non-qiddushin marriages could therefore be conducted even under the auspices of the rabbinate.

Picard does not then propose a ceremony of his own, but rather refers his readers to Feldblum's work. It thus seems to me he suggests an alternate understanding (albeit indirectly) for grounding the halakhic force of derekh qiddushin as a Noahide marriage.

44. Rachel Adler, *Engendering Judaism: An Inclusive Theology and Ethics* (Philadelphia, PA: Jewish Publication Society, 1998), esp. chap. 5, "*B'rit Ahuvim:* A Marriage between Subjects," 169–207.
45. Ibid., 191. Jacobs and Austrian also briefly mention a similar idea in "Choices of Marriage," 36–7; note also the testimony of "Tehila," one of Irit Koren's interview subjects in *You Are Hereby Renewed Unto Me*, 38–39.
46. Indeed, a couple may negotiate stipulations particular to their own circumstances (arrangements regarding children in blended families, for example) and bind themselves to them through inclusion in the document.
47. Adler, *Engendering Judaism*, 199.
48. The exception is Jacobs and Austrian, "Choices of Marriage," who briefly and somewhat obliquely hint that a marriage enacted by the ceremony they devised would require get, by noting that *other* options (such as Adler's ceremony) that they did *not* choose might not activate the get process (37, 40).
49. David Novak, "The Marital Status of Jews Married Under Non-Jewish Auspices," *Jewish Law Association Studies* 1 (1985): 76.
50. Along these lines, Adler takes guidance from the sociologist Barbara Myerhoff, who "observes that although ritual actually changes all the time, convincing rituals make us feel as if they have always been done this way." Adler, *Engendering Judaism*, 84; see also page 197, where Adler (re)invokes this insight in regards to her own liturgical innovations for marriage.

# 10

# Negotiating Divorce at the Intersection of Jewish and Civil Law in North America

Lisa Fishbayn Joffe

## Introduction: Legal Pluralism

OVER THE COURSE OF THE TWENTIETH CENTURY, the rights and responsibilities granted to spouses under family law in Western Europe and North America have changed dramatically. Divorce has gone from being a remedy available exclusively based upon the demonstrable, legally defined fault of one of the parties to an option that can be based on the spouses' subjective perception of their own incompatibility. Divorce may now be initiated by either spouse and be finalized over the opposition of the other spouse. Property is no longer divided based upon the name that appears upon a deed of title but is divided equally between the spouses based on the notion that building a family is a joint enterprise where contributions of care count as much as those of cash. Women do not lose their legal personality upon marriage under the doctrine of *couverture*, nor do they surrender their right to reject unwanted sexual encounters with their spouse. Maintenance after divorce has shifted from a lifelong obligation from husband to ex-wife to a transitional short-term support to enable the spouses to make a clean break of their financial ties. Conversely, child custody upon divorce is now based on the assumption that a clean break of parenting responsibilities is undesirable and that ex-spouses should rise above their differences to collaborate as coparents through some form of shared custody.

Jewish family law, however, has not developed along the same path as these civil family laws on questions of finance, property, or custody. The most glaring difference between Western family law and Jewish law can be seen in the context of divorce. Although the consent of both parties is required to divorce in Jewish law, husbands enjoy disproportionate power to initiate or thwart the divorce process. While effective remedies exist to assist a husband whose wife refuses to receive a divorce, women whose husbands refuse to grant one may face a choice between remaining chained to a dead marriage or acceding to bribery demands to secure their freedom.

Outside Israel, Jewish citizens may choose to govern their affairs with reference only to state codes of family law and to ignore provisions of Jewish family law. Some might choose to solemnize their marriages using the rituals of Jewish law, but turn to the civil courts to dissolve their marriage should it come to an end. Jewish spouses may thus be subject to multiple regimes of family law, as a matter of law in the state of Israel and as a matter of voluntary choice in nations outside it.

This state of affairs in which multiple, overlapping, and possibly conflicting regimes of legal regulation exist within a single state is described as legal pluralism.[1] The overlapping nature of these legal arrangements can impede attempts to secure gender equality under civil family law, but this overlap may itself be a resource for bringing religious norms into line with civil ones. Lawyers and legal theorists who seek to reconcile the dual commitments to the preservation of collective religious practices and to the individual human rights of female members of religious communities have focused on the role institutional form can play in shaping the nature of these conflicts. Institutional arrangements that distribute the power to regulate areas of social life and to review actions of courts and government can be designed to enable, encourage, or impede a dialogue between state institutions and religious groups over how discriminatory practices can be brought in line with relevant human rights norms.[2]

In this chapter, I examine the notion that offering civil law remedies to women subject to *get* (Jewish divorce) refusal can both be an occasion for dialogue about the reconciliation of Jewish and civil law norms in divorce disputes and the catalyst for a broader dialogue within the Jewish community about finding solutions to these problems. In previous work, I have described how the processes of drafting get laws and negotiating *halakhically* (in accordance with Jewish law) permissible forms of enforcement have spread awareness of the *agunah* (literally, a woman chained to a dead marriage) problem in the Canadian Jewish community. I explore the extent to which the operation of get laws has provided the basis for a fruitful dialogue between legal authorities in the rabbinical and civil law courts on issues of doctrine. A central notion of this project to use civil law to spur changes in religious law is that there can be some kind of genuine dialogue across legal traditions that allows adherents of religious norms to affirm egalitarian change from within their legal tradition. I study the extent to which these traditions are able to speak to each other comprehensibly in the context of disputes over Jewish divorce. I conclude that the potential for this dialogue is limited.

While philosophers might envision a thorough reconciliation of conflicting values or a better understanding of the points of intractable disagreement, the form this dialogue takes in actual disputes is largely a strategic engagement in which litigants deploy elements from both regimes in an ad hoc fashion to achieve their desired ends.

I begin by evaluating the doctrinal differences between Anglo-American and Jewish law on the grounds for divorce, the role of personal choice in exit from marriage, and the role of negotiation to resolve disputes over marital assets. In particular, I draw out how the two legal regimes model how preferences may be legitimately shaped by background legal entitlements and bargaining between spouses. I describe the sorts of pressure and incentives that are viewed as unavoidable aspects of divorce proceedings and those that constitute an inappropriate intrusion into what should be a protected sphere of free choice. I conclude this section by pointing to the sometimes paradoxical relationship between validity under Jewish law and validity under civil law. What appears to be essential bargaining under Jewish law to remove the possibility that a get will be held to be invalid may look to civil courts like coercive extortion. Conversely, what looks like legitimate intervention to redress an underlying gendered inequality of bargaining power between spouses to civil lawyers may be perceived as impermissible coercion by Jewish courts.

Recent decades have seen a trend toward the use of civil law to redress women's inequality under Jewish laws relating to divorce. Canada, Britain, South Africa, and New York State have all passed "get laws" that allow civil courts to attach financial or legal consequences to men's failure to remove barriers to their spouse's religious remarriage. These laws allow courts to withhold a civil divorce until a religious divorce has been granted, impose financial penalties for delay or refusal to grant a divorce, or refuse to hear arguments from spouses who refuse to cooperate in delivering a religious divorce. Civil courts in the United States have sought to enforce promises to appear before a *beit din* (rabbinical court) or to give a get that was included in prenuptial contracts, *ketubot* (marriage contracts), or divorce agreements. Courts in France, Israel, Canada, and the Netherlands have awarded civil damages for breach of such contracts or for negligent infliction of emotional harm against men for refusal to deliver a get. These new laws and legal remedies have all been founded on the notion that women have a right to exercise autonomy in determining the course of their marital lives, a right that is being thwarted by their husband's refusal to grant them a divorce. The analysis by civil courts envisions these remedies as a means to equalize the capacity of men and women to exercise such autonomy. While Jewish law also contains a commitment to personal freedom in choosing to end a marriage, it is a gendered one that reserves this right to men while denying it to women.

## Doctrinal Differences

### GROUNDS FOR DIVORCE

In civil law regimes, the most prevalent contemporary ground for divorce is irretrievable marriage breakdown proven by the spouses having lived separately for some statutorily set period (generally between six months to five years). Regimes usually also offer alternate grounds based on the fault of one party, such as adultery, cruel and inhuman treatment, unreasonable behavior, imprisonment, or abandonment. While adultery, for example, was initially only a ground for divorce when committed by the wife, all grounds are now equally available to both spouses. Where grounds exist, the divorce will proceed over the objections of an unwilling spouse, regardless of gender.

In Jewish law, the picture is a bit different. The *Tanakh* (Hebrew Bible) states in *Devarim* (Deuteronomy 24:1) that a husband may divorce his wife if "she fails to please him because he finds something obnoxious about her." A husband once had an almost absolute right to divorce his wife at will for virtually no reason, and her consent was not required.[3] This freedom to divorce at will was later narrowed. In the eleventh century, Rabbenu Gershom imposed a rabbinical enactment requiring the consent of the wife in the absence of specific grounds, including infertility, her refusal of sexual cohabitation, or abandonment.[4] Grounds might be cited affecting her rights to property and maintenance or might form the basis for an order *heter mea rabbanim* (permission of one hundred rabbis) dispensing with the need for her consent if she refused to receive the divorce.[5]

In current Jewish law, a wife cannot issue a divorce, but she can initiate legal proceedings requesting that a beit din determine whether the husband is morally or legally obligated to divorce her. She must cite grounds cognizable under *halakhah* for the issuance of such an order. These include the husband's affliction with a loathsome disease, impotence, sterility, failure to support, refusal to cohabit, physical or verbal abuse, forcing the wife to violate Jewish law, engagement in an occupation that makes him smell bad, becoming an apostate, and habitual infidelity.[6] The beit din may find that the husband is morally obliged to give a divorce or that that the demonstrated grounds are so egregious that the court orders that he be forced to give the get. The beit din cannot, however, dispense with his consent and issue the get itself.

Divorce may thus be available to the husband who simply believes that the marriage is irretrievably broken down, as the need for the wife's consent may be subject to waiver. Divorce is available to a wife who can allege grounds, but only to the extent that her husband obeys an order to deliver a get. It is not available at all to the wife who does not allege a specified ground but who feels simply that the marriage is over.[7]

Certain lines of authority in Jewish law would permit no-fault divorce to be initiated by women. Gaonic authorities permitted a rebellious wife to seek divorce by abandoning her husband for a period of twelve months. While she might walk away without her ketubah money, she was entitled to walk away. Other authorities permitted a wife's unilateral right to demand divorce to be written into the ketubah itself.[8] Several key decisions have held that where the parties have been unable to reconcile for an extended period, the husband should be ordered to grant a divorce. However, some rabbinical court judges in contemporary Israel decline to follow these authorities, arguing that this model of irretrievable marriage breakdown is an alien concept imported from civil law.[9]

## JEWISH DIVORCE NEGOTIATIONS

While civil divorce can be sought by either spouse without the other's consent, Jewish divorce can only occur with the husband's consent. A man's consent to divorce must be freely given, a product of the unfettered exercise of his will.[10] A get may be rendered *meusah* (invalid) if executed under improper duress or compulsion.[11] Such compulsion can only be imposed by a rabbinical court or consequent upon a ruling by such a court, under the circumstances set out below.

Where the wife has initiated proceedings and has demonstrated that the husband is afflicted by or has committed a cognizable marital fault, rabbinical courts may order an obligatory get. While they cannot themselves issue the divorce, they can use all powers at their disposal to pressure the husband to divorce. Paradoxically, a divorce coerced under these conditions is still considered to be an exercise of the husband's free will. Breitowitz explains:

> It is assumed that every Jew truly wishes to comply with the dictates of religious law and any refusal to do so is merely the result of an "evil disposition" which temporarily overpowers or vanquishes his "free will." Duress is therefore applied not to overcome the husband's exercise of will but to remove the impediment that prevents that "free will" from emerging.[12]

The husband may thus be coerced until he declares his willingness to comply. Any coercion is permissible under these circumstances and does not invalidate the get. Indeed, once an obligation to give the get is found to exist, this coercion authorized by halakhic authorities is expressly permitted to be imposed by non-Jewish authorities.[13] The victim is also free to invoke self-help remedies to enforce compliance with a beit din order, including "posting his picture all over town or, in extreme cases, even hiring a band of thugs to "teach the husband a lesson."[14] However, in most cases that make it to the civil courts outside Israel, the parties have not received, or even sought, any sort of order from a beit din.

Some American Jewish law authorities hold that where the husband actually wishes to end the marriage (evinced perhaps, by his having already gone through civil divorce) but withholds consent only to achieve economic benefits, coercion applied to win his consent without satisfying his financial demands does not render the get invalid.[15] However, the dominant view is that this coercion must be coupled with some payment of money by the wife to the husband to "cure" the possibility of the get being perceived as invalid. As Broyde explains it, this practice "is certainly accepted by many great *poskim* (decisors) as normative halakhah, and validates any get given in the process of a settlement where the wife gives anything of value to the husband to which he is not entitled."[16] Broyde argues that given that most civil regimes treat property acquired during the marriage as jointly owned, any concession in property negotiations by the wife should satisfy this criteria and such give and take likely exists in every divorce transaction.[17] Others suggest that giving the husband property to which he is already notionally entitled under marital property laws is not sufficient—she must give him something out of her excluded property or a payment from her family to him,[18] such as waiving rights to maintenance and child support owed to her under the civil law.[19]

In difficult cases of get refusal, Jewish law not only permits the surrender of payments or rights the wife enjoys under civil law to secure her husband's consent to divorce, it may encourage such surrender as a solution to the important doctrinal problem of avoidance of coercion. Additional payments beyond what the husband may be entitled to under civil law can be cited as a financial motive for granting the get that refutes any later claim a husband may make that his consent to granting the divorce was impermissibly coerced.

Unfortunately, these arrangements may appear very different in the eyes of a civil court. While civil law doctrine expects divorcing parties to engage in hard bargaining about terms of separation, it also requires that such bargaining occur against a backdrop of fundamental policies of gender equality, fairness, and the primacy of the best interests of the children. Where it appears to the courts that agreement has been achieved through improper coercion, such agreements can be set aside.

Negotiations in which the husband seeks to use his power to withhold the get to secure economic or custodial advantages come to the attention of civil courts both as aspects of ongoing divorce negotiations and post-divorce, when women may sue in civil court to recover what they consider to be extortionate payments given to secure the divorce. Below are some illustrative examples.

*(1) The husband refuses to give the get in violation of his undertaking to do so.* In the absence of a get law or some sort of contractual undertaking to grant a get or appear before a beit din, civil courts have no pretext for getting involved in Jewish divorce disputes. US courts have gone both ways on the enforceability of contracts in relation to the get. Some American courts have been willing to order specific performance of an undertaking *in a ketubah* to appear before a beit din for purposes of giving a get.[20] Some have gone further, ordering a husband to actually deliver a get to free his wife.[21] Some US courts have held the husband in contempt for failure to comply with his undertaking *to the civil court* that he would attend at the beit din to give a get and have fined or imprisoned him.[22] Conversely, the New Jersey case of *Aflalo v. Aflalo* found use of coercion to force the get was invalid under both civil and Jewish law.[23]

*(2) The husband wants to give the get only when he is beyond the reach of the get law.* Canada's get law includes an exemption for those who allege that they have a religious objection to removing the barriers to their spouse's remarriage, that is, delivering or receiving the get. For the most part, the civil courts in Canada assume that the husband is being manipulative when he seeks to refuse to give the get for religious reasons. The religious objection was most directly raised in a Quebec case in 2000. The husband appeared before the beit din after receiving notice under the get law, claiming that he had been willing to give the get but was appearing there on that day because he felt coerced to do so by the get law. Not surprisingly, the beit din refused to supervise the get under these circumstances. The wife then asked the civil court to throw out his pleadings in the civil divorce by virtue of his failure to remove the barriers to her religious remarriage. He argued that he fell into the religious reasons exemption because, in his words: "I have every reason to believe that the coercive nature of the request and the conditions under which I am being forced to make such a request would result in the refusal of the *ghet* [French transliteration of *get*] by any valid Rabbinical Authority or in the alternative, if granted by coercion, would be invalid in any event."[24] The judge noted that in spite of having told his rabbi months before that he was willing to give the get, he had not shown up to do so. If he was willing to give it in any event, there was no reason for him to mention his views on the coercive nature of the act to the beit din, other than to deploy the ghet as "weapon in negotiations" against the wife.[25]

In another leading Quebec case, the husband stated he was willing to give the get, but only after the civil proceedings were concluded. In widely cited reasons, the judge held that "[the husband's] willingness to grant the 'Ghet' only after the civil divorce is completed leads me to conclude that is his intention to use this power over his wife in settlement negotiations. His offer to consent to the 'Ghet' after the civil divorce is meaningless since he would, in no way, be bound to do so."[26] The judge concluded that the husband was attempting to game the system by delaying to the point where he was beyond the reach of the get law. His pleadings were, accordingly, struck out.

*(3) The husband secures agreement to his property demands with a promise to deliver the get but then exercises his free choice not to give it.* In 2007, the Supreme Court of Canada rendered its decision in *Bruker v. Markowitz*. The couple had divorced civilly in 1980, with the husband agreeing in the divorce agreement to immediately attend before the beit din of Montreal to deliver the get. He did not show up—for fifteen years. After the get law was passed in 1990, the wife sued him under it, and he delivered the get within days. She did not let the matter rest there. She sued him for breach of his contractual commitment to give the get and sought damages for the pain and suffering of being an agunah from the age of 31 to 46. The Supreme Court of Canada pointed out that the get law received "overwhelming support from the Jewish community, including its more religious elements, reflecting a consensus that the refusal to provide a get was an unwarranted indignity imposed on Jewish women and, to the extent possible, one that should not be countenanced by Canada's legal system."[27] Justice Abella outlined the differences between Jewish and Canadian understandings of marriage:

> We also accept the right of Canadians to decide for themselves whether their marriage has irretrievably broken down and we attempt to facilitate, rather than impede, their ability to continue their lives, including with new families. Moreover, under Canadian law, marriage and divorce are available equally to men and women. A *get*, on the other hand, can only be given under Jewish law by a husband. For those Jewish women whose religious principles prevent them from considering remarriage unless they are able to do so in accordance with Jewish law, the denial of a *get* is the denial of the right to remarry. . . . The refusal of a husband to provide a *get*, therefore, arbitrarily denies the wife access to a remedy she independently has under Canadian law and denies her the ability to remarry and get on with her life in accordance with her religious beliefs.[28]

She concluded by stressing that the decision of the court should not be understood to alter the husband's prerogatives under Jewish law. He retains those intact. It does, however, reshape the structure of incentives created by the interaction between Jewish and civil law. While his refusal to grant the get was costless under Jewish law—he went merrily on his way for fifteen years—the civil courts redirected the burden of his decision back on to him, concluding, "It is his right to refuse to give a get if he is so inclined, but not without accepting responsibility for the consequences to Ms. Bruker of his decision to resile from this civil obligation."[29]

The Supreme Court of Canada upheld the lower court's order that the husband pay damages for pain and suffering in the amount of $47,500.

*(4) The husband seeks to impose conditions upon which he will grant the divorce.* Radzyner,[30] and Weiss and Gross-Horowitz,[31] have reported on the disturbing trend in Israeli rabbinical courts to impose conditions post-divorce. Men have granted divorces on condition, for example, that the wife agree never to seek maintenance for herself or child support for children of the marriage. When the wife later sought child support, a right that incidentally cannot be bargained away under civil law because it is an inalienable right of the child to be supported by the parent, the husband returned to the rabbinical court asking that the get be revoked. This remedy has been ordered in several cases. One judge even opined that the husband could impose conditions related to the wife's dress, food, and lifestyle after divorce in a get agreement.[32]

Conversely, this is how a Quebec civil court responded to a husband's demand to continue to exert control over his wife's lifestyle after divorce. He stated that he would not give the get because he feared that his wife would remarry while the five young daughters of the marriage remained in the home. He argued that it would violate what he understood to be Jewish norms of modesty to have his daughters live in the house with a man who was not a blood relative. The court responded that his argument was

> just another way for Monsieur to impose on Madame his beliefs, his way of being, his way of life, his way of doing things despite the dissolution of the civil marriage." . . . Monsieur has the right to his beliefs. However, he does not have the right to impose them on others, . . . Madame has the right to obtain the *get* and Monsieur cannot refuse her by hiding behind the rights of the children.[33]

*(5) The wife agrees to give up rights to obtain consent to divorce—and then tries to get them back.* As noted above, Jewish law encourages a woman to give her

husband property to which he is not otherwise entitled to persuade him to grant the get of his own free will. In several American cases, wives sued successfully to get back money and property they had given their husbands to receive the get. For example, in *Perl v. Perl*, the wife agreed to sign over her rights to investments, house, car, and jewelry and to make cash payments to her husband in exchange for being granted the get. Once the get was received, Mrs. Perl stopped payment. Mr. Perl sued for the money he had been promised. The wife argued that she had agreed to pay under duress and should not have to honor the commitment. The New York Supreme Court Appellate Division found that the agreement amounted to "nothing less than a total surrender of her rights" as a quid pro quo for granting the divorce. The agreement was set aside as unenforceable under the civil law for duress.[34]

*Perl* was followed in *Golding v. Golding*, in which the wife was told by her husband to sign increasingly extreme written sets of demands or he would not give her a get. Rabbis involved advised her to sign whatever he presented her with to be free. She also sought to set aside the civil divorce agreement once the get had been issued. The trial court agreed, finding that "by exploiting the power differential between the parties, so as to completely dominate a process which should have entailed honest negotiating, the defendant engaged in 'inequitable conduct' which 'vitiates the execution of the agreement.'"[35]

The husband appealed, arguing in part that both parties' claims had already been heard and arbitrated by the beit din. The New York Appeals Division actually found that no matter what the beit din thought it was doing, it was not arbitrating, because all the rabbinical court had done was translate the husband's demands into Hebrew and tell her to sign. The court failed to entertain the possibility that enabling the husband to enforce his arbitrary will upon the wife might actually reflect the beit din's interpretation of its role under Jewish law.[36]

## Conclusion: Barriers to Genuine Dialogue between Legal Authorities in Jewish and Civil Law

In this chapter, I've sought to contrast the ways Jewish law and civil law conceive consent to divorce and appropriate forms of bargaining couples may employ to reach consensus on whether to divorce and on what terms. I have cited examples in which Jewish law and civil law promote different ideals about what constitute acceptable tactics in divorce negotiations. However, most of the civil cases treat unacceptable negotiating tactics as instances of individual misconduct by the husband, rather than as the manifestation of doctrinal differences between the religious and civil legal regimes. In this final section, I will describe some of the factors that contribute to this picture.

## AGENCY OF PARTIES

Civil courts may be getting an inaccurate picture of Jewish legal norms from the parties who appear before them. Fournier argues that to understand the relationship between civil and religious law under conditions of liberal legal pluralism, one needs to take into account the perspective of the Holmesian "bad man." In his classic work, *The Path of Law*, American Justice Oliver Wendell Holmes argued: "If you want to know the law and nothing else, you must look at it as bad man, who cares only for the material consequences which such knowledge enables him to predict, not as a good one, who finds his reasons for conduct whether inside the law or outside of it, in the vaguer sanctions of conscience."[37]

Fournier points out that religious law is rarely invoked by plaintiffs because they truly want to parse the meaning of religious precepts in the context of a civil dispute. Rather, it is invoked as a strategic tactic to secure that party's best advantage in the contest. Accordingly, litigants do not aim to paint the most accurate picture of religious law. They aim, rather, to describe an account of religious law, including Jewish law, that best supports their position. Therefore, a wife may give an account of Jewish law that highlights practices that seek to avoid get refusal, while a husband may present schools of thought within Jewish law that support and enable get refusal and get-based extortion.

This approach is enabled by the conception of religion used by civil courts. In the context of freedom-of-religion cases, it is well-established law that plaintiffs are entitled to demand accommodation of the religious conception they genuinely hold, however idiosyncratic or doctrinally unsound it may be.[38] The court will consider whether an alleged belief is consistent with the way the individual lives his life, taking into account the possibility that people change over time, as do their beliefs.[39] A religious authority may be called as an expert witness, but such evidence is not necessary.[40] The segment of cases that come before civil courts may thus over-represent those who understand Jewish law instrumentally and are using Jewish law strategically. On the facts presented, parties generally have often not appeared before a beit din, because one party refuses to accept its jurisdiction. Indeed, in the *Bruker* case before the Supreme Court of Canada, the husband refused to appear, and there is no evidence that Ms. Bruker sought or received any sort of order compelling a divorce from a beit din. The civil courts treated her as an agunah because she said she was one, not because any beit din had declared her to be one.

The small number of divorce cases that go to trial on any matter also involve couples where there is some degree of belligerence. It may be that those get refusal cases that are reported involve genuinely more hostile bargaining tactics and vengeful motives than are present in the general population seeking a Jewish divorce. Indeed, most cases proceed on the assumption that the Jewish and civil marriages will be dissolved at the same time. Judges in Canada and the United States routinely ask Jewish parties how the husband plans to deliver the get and will coordinate their activities to ensure it is done before the civil divorce is finalized.[41]

## AGENCY OF RABBINICAL AUTHORITIES

The relative power of rabbinical courts in Israel and North America shapes both their doctrine and practice. Westreich suggests that halakhic commentators in Israel take a more stringent line on showing sympathy and lenience toward women in family law disputes because they are concerned to defend their authority. They resist lenient positions taken by academic and modern Orthodox interlocutors to protect their internal dominance in the Jewish law world and to protect the field of Jewish law from encroachment by civil law authorities.[42]

In a fascinating recent study, Hacker compared the practice of Israeli rabbinical courts that address marriage breakdown (where they have exclusive jurisdiction) to those that address inheritance issues (where they must compete with civil courts for jurisdiction). She found that rabbinical courts are much less sympathetic to women's claims for relief from gender discriminatory norms in the family courts as compared to inheritance courts. She concludes that the greater the competition from the civil courts, the more willing the religious tribunal will be to accommodate liberal values and practices.[43] Her suspicions are borne out when we consider the practice and discourse of mainstream rabbinical courts outside Israel. Because they must compete for customers, they may tend to be much more accommodating.

What is sometimes invisible in these reported cases before the civil courts are the ways in which Modern Orthodox rabbinical court judges in North America use get laws strategically to free women but remain within the bounds of halakhic validity. While in theory ringing sentiments like those enunciated in the Canadian case law might be taken up as incentives to reform the actual doctrines of Jewish law, the legal devices approved in these get law cases are instead taken up by North American rabbinical court judges to be used in ways consonant with their conceptions of Jewish law.

The *Va'ad Ha Rabbonim* (rabbinical council) of Toronto, home to the largest Jewish community in Canada, initially welcomed the role of the get law in getting recalcitrant husbands through the door of the beit din. Once the court made contact, it could theoretically enter into a relationship with the husband that might eventually result in the issuance of a valid get. This process includes, however, the wife formally waiving rights under the get law and testifying that the law has not played a role in husbands' decision to divorce to ensure the validity of the get.[44] Broyde describes the interweaving of civil and religious norms among the large Modern Orthodox community that appear before the Beit Din of America in New York State, where he sat as a judge, as "an extremely complex and largely invisible dance."[45] Civil and rabbinical court judges work closely on contested cases to coordinate the granting of civil and religious divorces in ways which are valid under both regimes.

In North America, unlike in some cases in Israel, the practice of Jewish law on these issues is open textured and expansive enough that it may prove possible for modern Orthodox *batei din* and civil courts to work with couples to resolve many agunah disputes. This difference in responsiveness to women's claims to gender equality in exit from marriage may flow, in part, from doctrinal differences as the customary norms of the Jewish community in North America have now adapted to incorporate many of the commitments and expectations to the of civil marriage.[46] It is also shaped by the relative strength of rabbinical courts as legal and communal institutions. Their lack of significant enforcement powers and location in competition with other non-Jewish courts for the business of marriage dissolution and dispute resolution may make them more willing to adapt their role to remain relevant. North American rabbinical courts judges who serve Modern Orthodox and Conservative populations rely on the voluntary submission of individuals to their jurisdiction. They can thus defend what turf they have by being uncontroversial, flexible, and, to the extent possible, helpful.

The underlying promise of dialogic remedies is that with enough good-faith open dialogue, common ground can be found between diverse interlocutors on values that are shared by both religious and civil law. However, the dialogue I have discovered at the intersection of civil and religious law is not the one envisioned by political philosophers where public reason measures and reshapes values in an open debate that is then reflected in legislative debates and judicial decisions. Rather, it is a strategic dialogue in which individual agents and institutional actors use rhetorical moves to achieve their objectives and best advantage. In the North American context, this strategic dialogue has sometimes worked to the advantage of Jewish women seeking assistance in persuading their recalcitrant husbands to grant them a divorce. The implication of this ongoing dialogue in Israel remains to be seen.

## NOTES

1. Under conditions of legal pluralism, a situation that pertains in some form in every complex modern state: "law and legal institutions are not all subsumable within one 'system' but have their sources in the self-regulatory activities of all the multifarious social fields present, activities which may support, complement, ignore or frustrate one another, so that the 'law' which is actually effective on the 'ground floor' of society is the result of enormously complex and usually in practice unpredictable patterns of competition, interaction, negotiation, isolationism and the like." John Griffiths, "What Is Legal Pluralism?" *Journal of Legal Pluralism* 18, no. 4 (1986): 1, 39.
2. See, for example, Ayelet Shachar, *Multicultural Jurisdictions: Cultural Differences and Women's Rights* (Cambridge, MA: Cambridge University Press, 2001); Monique Deveaux, *Gender and Justice in Multicultural Liberal State* (Oxford: Oxford University Press, 2006).
3. There were a few exceptions. The husband could not divorce his wife, where, for example, he had been forced to marry his rape victim or where he had falsely accused his betrothed of adultery, both presumably because his actions had rendered her unmarriageable in the eyes of others. Irving A. Breitowitz, *Between Civil and Religious Law: The Plight of the Agunah in American Society* (Westport, CT: Greenwood Press, 1993), 9–10.
4. Ibid., 13.
5. Ibid., 42.
6. Ibid.
7. However, Michael Broyde and Jonathan Reiss stress that there is no divorce without mutual consent now and that intervention by the state to compel a man to give a divorce would be an alteration of this essential equality. They argue that the fact that a wife must go to court to ask the court to compel divorce while the husband can grant it directly is a difference in form without significance in terms of their capacity to initiate divorce. "The Ketubah in America; Its Value in Dollars, Its Significance in *Halacha* and Its Enforceability in Secular Law," *Journal of Halacha and Contemporary Society* (2004): 101–24, n42 and accompanying text.
8. Avishalom Westreich, "Divorce on Demand: The History, Dogmatics and Hermeneutics of the Wife's Right to Divorce in Jewish Law," *Journal of Jewish Studies* 62, no. 2 (2011): 340–63, esp. 341.
9. Avishalom Westreich, "The Right to Divorce in Jewish Law: Between Politics and Ideology," *International Journal of the Jurisprudence of the Family* 1 (2011), 19–22.
10. Breitowitz notes that halakhah generally validates other conveyances in spite of duress unless they are gratuitous. He suggests that the different treatment accorded to divorce underscores the crucial importance of consent (for men) in this context. He states that this doctrine is the main stumbling block in dealing the recalcitrant spouse, and how to circumvent it is central to finding a resolution. Breitowitz, *Between Civil and Religious Law*, 20n61.
11. Ibid, 20.
12. Ibid, 35.
13. Ibid.
14. Ibid, 36–7.
15. Michael J. Broyde, *Marriage, Divorce and the Abandoned Wife in Jewish Law* (Hoboken: Ktav, 2001), 105–6.
16. Ibid, 108.

17. Ibid.
18. Ibid.
19. R. Feinstein validated a get granted by a husband who had been imprisoned for nonpayment of maintenance. The wife agreed to waive her maintenance arrears claim in exchange for the get. Breitowitz, *Between Civil and Religious Law*, 135.
20. *Avitzur v. Avitzur*, 459 N.Y.S.2d 572 (1983) (New York). See also *Waxstein v. Waxstein*, 395 N.Y.S.2d 877 (Sup. Ct. 1976) (aff'd 394 N.Y.S.2d 253) (App. Div. 1977).
21. In *Minkin v. Minkin*, the husband had alleged adultery on the part of the wife in the civil divorce. The court found that Jewish law required him to divorce his wife if he believed her to be adulterous and ordered him to do so. *Minkin v. Minkin* 434 A.2d 665 (1981) (N.J. Super. Ct. Ch. Div.). See also *In Re Scholl* 621 A.2d 808; (1992) (Del. Fam. Ct. LEXIS 106); *Goldman v. Goldman* 196 Ill. App. 3d 785; 554 N.E.2d 1016; (1990) (Ill. App. LEXIS 448); 143 Ill. Dec. 944 (Illinois). Conversely, in *Mayer-Kolker v. Mayer-Kolker*, the court found that it did not have enough evidence about what Jewish law required to decide that the ketubah required the husband to do anything. 819 A. 2d 17 (N.J. Appellate Div. 2003).
22. In *Margulies v. Marguilies*, 42 A.D.2d 517; 344 N.Y.S.2d 482 (1973) (N.Y. App. Div. LEXIS 3798), the US Supreme Court declined to hear an appeal from the New York appellate court decision allowing an order of incarceration of a husband for failure to give his wife a get. In *Shragai v. Shragai*, cert denied, 89 U.S. 1073; 109 S. Ct. 1360; 103 L. Ed. 2d 827 (1989) (U.S. LEXIS 1341), an appellate court struck down a further order for incarceration for contempt because such coercion might render any get given invalid. They upheld the contempt finding and related fines because the husband's later behavior was clearly contumacious. He never intended to grant the get despite having since remarried and was clearly using the civil court to serve his own motives in freeing himself. Other cases have founded a contempt citation on undertakings to give a get made as part of a civil divorce settlement. In *Kaplinsky v. Kaplinsky*, 198 A.D.2d 212; 603 N.Y.S.2d 574; (1993) (N.Y. App. Div. LEXIS 10208), the Supreme Court of New York, Appellate Division, upheld an order of contempt and ordered an uneven distribution of the couple's assets under s. 253 of New York's Domestic Relations Law (the get law) giving the wife 75% of the family assets.
23. In *Aflalo*, the court determined that the Establishment Clause did *not* permit the court to compel the husband to submit to a beit din to initiate get proceedings. Moreover, the court found that coercing the husband to provide the get would not have the effect sought because it would invalidate the get. They determined that it is the role of Jewish legal authorities to resolve cases of get refusal: "If the *get* is something which can be coerced then it should be the Beth Din which does the coercing. In coercing the husband, the civil court is, in essence, overruling or superseding any judgment which the Beth Din can or will enter, contrary to accepted First Amendment principles." Any unfairness that the wife suffers thereby is a result of her free choice to have subjected herself to Jewish law by entering into a Jewish marriage (para. 19). A New York court took a similar position in a case in which the wife had waived her rights to go to civil court for child support in favor of accepting the judgment of a beit din under threat that she would be made subject to a *seruv* (contempt citation). The court rejected her attempt to bring her claim in civil court, finding that "the wife freely submitted herself to the jurisdiction of the Bais Din and that this was a manifestation of her having voluntarily undertaken obedience to the religious law which such tribunals interpret and enforce." *Greenberg v. Greenberg*, 238 A.D.2d 420; 656 N.Y.S.2d 369; (1997) (N.Y. App. Div. LEXIS 3788).
24. *K.N.H. v. J.S.* [2000] R.D.F. 268 Quebec Superior Crt.
25. Ibid., para. 17.

26. *E.S. v. O.S.* Droit de la Famille, 2296 [1995] R.D.F 729.
27. *Bruker v. Marcovitz* [2007] 3S.C.R. 607 (Supreme court of Canada), para. 81.
28. Ibid., para. 82.
29. Ibid., para. 96.
30. Amihai Radzyner, "Problematic Halakhic 'Creativity' in Israeli Rabbinical Court Rulings," *Jewish Law Annual* 20 (London: Routledge, 2013), 103–78.
31. Susan Weiss and Netty Gross-Horowitz, *Marriage and Divorce in the Jewish State: Israel's Civil War* (Waltham, MA: Brandeis University Press, 2012).
32. P.D.R. (Israeli Rabbinical Courts Judgments, 2 (2005), 176, 182 (as excerpted in Radzyner, "Problematic Halachic 'Creativity.'"
33. *D.A. v. J.H.* [2008] R.D.F. 273. para. 66, 72, 86.
34. *Perl v. Perl* 126 A.D. 2d 91, 512 N.Y.S. 2d 372. (1987).
35. *Golding v. Golding* 581 N.Y.S. 2d 4 (1992) (N.Y. App. Div), 22.
36. Some Jewish law commentators object that using the civil courts to rescind coerced agreements means a woman can make property promises in order to get a get and later renege on her promises. Breitowitz cautions that a revocable waiver is of no legal effect and does not remove the coercive pressure on the husband to give the get or lose property, so we are not moved forward at all. Breitowitz, *Between Civil and Religious Law*, 117n643.
37. Quoted in Pascale Fournier, "Flirting with God in Western Secular Courts: Mahr in the West," in *Gender, Religion and Family Law: Theorizing Conflicts between Women's Rights and Cultural Traditions*, eds. Lisa Fishbayn Joffe and Sylvia Neil (Waltham, MA: Brandeis University Press, 2012).
38. In Canadian jurisprudence, the belief must be sincerely held and good faith. The court will determine only that the belief is not "fictitious or capricious, and that it is not an artifice." *Syndicat Northcrest v. Amselem* [2004] 2 S.C.R. 551, para. 52–54. This is similar to the US approach. See *Thomas v. Review Bd.*, 450 U.S. 707 (1981), holding that the "guarantee of free exercise is not limited to beliefs which are shared by all of the members of a religious sect." Christopher L. Eisgruber and Lawrence G. Sager, "Symposium: The Supreme Court's Hands-off Approach to Religious Doctrine: Does it Matter What Religion Is?" *Notre Dame Law Review* 84 (2009): 807, 824.
39. *Syndicat Northcrest v. Anselem*, 53.
40. Ibid., 54.
41. Lisa Fishbayn, "Gender, Multiculturalism and Dialogue: The Case of Jewish Divorce," 21 Can. J. L. & Jurisprudence 71 (2008); Michael Broyde, "New York's Regulation of Jewish Marriage: Covenant, Contract, or Statute?" in *Marriage and Divorce in a Multicultural Context*, ed. Joel A. Nichols (Cambridge, MA: Cambridge University Press, 2013).
42. Avishalom Westreich, "'The Gatekeepers' of Jewish Family Law: Marriage Annulment as a Test Case," *Journal of Law and Religion* 27 (2011–2012): 125–28.
43. Daphna Hacker, "Religious Tribunals in Democratic States: Lessons from the Israeli Rabbinical Courts," *Journal of Law and Religion* (2012): 59–81, 78–79.
44. Fishbayn, "Gender, Multiculturalism and Dialogue," 93. More recent work suggests that this court has become less willing to use the get law and less responsive to claims from agunot. See Yael Machtinger, "Socio-Legal Gendered Remedies to Get Refusal: Top Down, Bottom Up," in *Women's Rights and Religious Law*, eds. Fareda Banda and Lisa Fishbayn Joffe (London: Routledge, forthcoming).
45. Broyde, "New York's Regulation of Jewish Marriage," 145.
46. Ibid., 142.

# 11

## Women, Divorce, and *Mamzer* Status in the State of Israel

Susan Weiss

> "If someone wants to understand and feel how horrible is the fate of the *mamzer* in the eyes of our sages and how his suffering is unbearable, it is enough to consider the *halakha* as it is set forth in the Shulkhan Aruch (Yoreh Deah, Siman 265, Seif 4). There it is written that, in contradistinction to the newborn male child for whom it is our custom to beseech [the Lord] to have mercy on him and to pray for his survival and long life, we do not say this prayer for the *mamzer*!" —Judge Zvi Weitzman, Kfar Sava Family Court, 2012 (rejecting a woman's petition for paternity and child support).[1]

SOMETIME IN 1999, a client informed me that she was pregnant. Though the fetus was perfectly healthy and the client very much wanted the baby, news of the pregnancy was the source of great distress. For the past seven years she had been trying unsuccessfully to obtain a Jewish bill of divorce, a *get*, from her husband. The husband was not the baby's father. This meant that the fetus would be a *mamzer* according to Jewish law—which is also the law of the land in Israel with respect to marriage and divorce.[2] A mamzer is a child conceived of a relationship between a married woman and a man who is not her husband, regardless of whether the husband is a convict, missing, held hostage, unconscious, or refuses to divorce his wife unless he receives a king's ransom. If the father of the fetus is not the mother's lawful husband, the state, through its rabbinic courts and the institution known as the "Chief Rabbinate," will ostracize the child and his progeny for all generations, prohibiting them from marrying a fellow Jew unless that Jew is also a mamzer or a convert.

In Israel, rabbinic courts and the Council of the Chief Rabbinate (henceforth "Rabbinate") are part of the state's legal apparatus. Both are financed by the state and governed by laws passed by the state legislature (the Knesset). By law, the state cedes authority to rabbinic courts to decide matters of "personal status"—marriage and divorce—in accordance with *din torah* (the law of the Torah).[3] By law, the state acknowledges the authority of the Rabbinate to engage in "activities aimed at bringing the public closer to the values of Torah."[4] Applying Torah laws and Torah values incorporated into Israeli statutory laws, rabbinic judges can declare a Jewish child a mamzer, and the Rabbinate, in coordination with the rabbinic judges, can keep track of those *mamzerim* (pl. of mamzer), as well as other persons deemed ineligible to marry, creating a blacklist of untouchables and making the very ancient taboo of mamzer a real fact of the modern life in the State of Israel. Worried that her child might be placed on the state-backed blacklist, my client wondered—should she abort the baby? Two out of three rabbis with whom she consulted said "yes."

This chapter explores the way Israel has responded to the mamzer taboo. It shows that the state has promulgated laws, published regulations, set up blacklists, and established special tribunals that have reified the troubling prohibition, legitimating it and keeping it very much alive. This chapter demystifies the social construction of mamzer, explaining how it is a man-made idea that has changed over time. I describe the place of the mamzer taboo under contemporary Israeli law and expose how Israel's elaborate system of addressing mamzer enables the taboo and its accompanying rules to seed disorder, to delay stigmatization rather than avoid it, to sustain a discriminatory divorce regime, and to symbolize the dangers that the rabbis imagine threaten the Jewish People. I suggest that the presumptions adopted by the state through legislation to ameliorate the problem of the mamzer are "weak" fictions that do not do justice for innocent children. And I conclude by calling for the state to repeal all regulations, legislations, courts, and blacklists that perpetuate the notion of mamzer.

## Mamzer, a Social Construction

The State of Israel takes the legal concept of mamzer seriously—supporting a blacklists of mamzerim (section IIA), establishing special rabbinic tribunals that adjudicate if a person is a mamzer (section IIB); passing laws meant to limit the number of mamzerim (section IIC); and issuing circulars and regulations—all of which are meant to make sure that mamzerim do not marry non-mamzerim. For Israel citizens, mamzer is not an irrational, antediluvian taboo. It is a normative, taken-for-granted, commonsensical institution grounded in revered texts and traditions, as well as in state laws and regulations. It just is, covered by a sacred, legal, symbolic, and complex canopy of legitimation, and it appears immutable: "[A]s if [it] were something else other than a human product—such as . . . [the] result of cosmic laws, or manifestations of divine will."[5]

## CONSTRUCTION OF MAMZER STATUS IN THE BIBLE AND RABBINICAL LITERATURE

However, the stigma of mamzer is *not*, in fact, written in stone. Rather, it is an idea that has changed over time, a man-made social construction that is, theoretically at least, in the hands of Israeli society to want or to will away. The parameters of mamzer have adjusted over the millennia—as reflected in the Bible, the Mishnah, and the codices.

In the Bible it is written that "No mamzer shall be admitted into the Congregation of the LORD."[6] Rabbinic authorities have historically referred to this passage as proof text in support of the idea that a "mamzer" is the child of a forbidden union who is not permitted to marry a fellow Jew. But Biblical scholars have questioned this definition in the Biblical context. For example, Jeffrey Tigay, the author of the JPS commentary to Deuteronomy, argues that there is "no evidence that the term [mamzer] refers to a bastard." He writes:

> The meaning of Hebrew *mamzer* is not certain. Derivation from a root m-z-r, "rot," has been suggested. There is no evidence that the term refers to a bastard, a child born out of wedlock. Talmudic exegesis holds that it refers to the offspring of incestuous or adulterous intercourse. The Septuagint and Targum Jonathan understand the terms as referring to the offspring of a prostitute, while others take it as a term for foreigners or the name of a particular foreign nation.[7]

Tigay also claims that the term "Congregation (*ḳahal*) of the Lord" refers to the national governing assembly of Israelites, not to the rite of matrimony. He explains that "assembly" is a more suitable translation for the Hebrew word kahal than the JPS's term "congregation." Hence the Biblical rule barring certain people from entering the Assembly of the Lord is about who is entitled to *citizenship*, not who is entitled to *marry*. He states:

> [The term *ḳahal*] refers to the national governing assembly of the Israelites, that is, the entire people, of all the adult males, meeting in a plenary session, and perhaps sometime to their representatives acting as an executive committee. This Assembly convenes to conduct public business such as war, crowning a king, adjudicating legal cases, distribution of land, and worship. . . . This Assembly seems to have been of a type similar to popu-

> lar assemblies in the ancient world. . . . Eligibility for membership in the Assembly seems to have been tantamount to eligibility for full citizenship.[8]

Thus, the plain reading of the biblical text in Deuteronomy suggests that the rule barring mamzer from the Assembly of the Lord refers to a type of person or ethnic group ineligible for citizenship in the Israelite polity. It's about preventing foreigners or persons of other liminal status from owning land, conducting businesses, or having a say in how the polity operates. In a similar vein, the next sentence in the Bible states that "no Ammonite or Moabite or any of their descendants may enter the Assembly of the LORD."

In other words, in the Bible, the mamzer rule would appear to be the attempt to guard against dangerous foreign elements infiltrating the *external* cohesive boundaries of the Israeli body politic. It is not about ordering the *internal* boundaries that distinguish different sects of Jews or that define sexual conduct and mores of Jewish men, punishing dangerous infractions to those boundaries. Indeed, sexual conduct is monitored under other passages in the Bible where infringements are punished directly by death or excommunication, not indirectly by imposing taboos on innocent children.[9] As it is written, with regard to adultery: "If a man is found lying with another man's wife, both of them—the man and the woman with whom he lay—shall die. Thus you will sweep away evil from Israel."[10]

By late antiquity, rabbinic literature uses the term mamzer not to refer to undesirable foreigners who wanted to join the Israelite polity, but to a taboo imposed on children who are the product of "forbidden unions." Scholars note that different Jewish[11] sects from the Second Temple period may have had different opinions about what type of forbidden sexual unions would result in the mamzer stigma.[12] It is possible to discern a glimpse of these different opinions in the dialectics set forth in Mishnah Yevamot, chapters 4–7. One opinion related in Mishnah Yev. 4:13 is that of R. Akiva. For him, mamzer is the child of a union with a relative with whom cohabitation is forbidden by a biblical commandment that begins with the words: "thou shalt not lie." This reading would confine the mamzer stigma to children born of sexual relations with a "consanguine," or blood relative, such as a mother or sister. Adulterous relations or sexual relations with a person who is not related by blood but only by "affinity"—an in-law, for example—would not be included in Akiva's category.[13]

A second opinion in the same Mishnah is that of R. Shimon HaTimni. He maintains that mamzer is a child born of a union that carries the punishment of *ḳaret* in the Bible—excommunication or death at the hands of God.[14] This has been interpreted as meaning children born of *all* sexual unions forbidden in the

Bible—whether of adulterous relations or incestuous ones, be they consanguine or affinal. A third opinion in the same Mishnah is accredited to R. Yehoshua. According to him, mamzer is a child born of unions that carry the *punishment of death*. This would limit the mamzer stigma to children born of relations with another man's wife,[15] in particular the wife of one's father,[16] or one's son;[17] or to a child born to a man who has had licentious relations with a mother and daughter at the same time.[18] Still another opinion stated in Mishnah Yev. 7:5 suggests that some Jews may have considered a child born to an Israelite woman and a gentile to be a mamzer.[19] Yet another ruling, reflected in Mishnah Yev. 4:12, states that a child is also a mamzer if born to a man and his prohibited ex-wife, or to a man and his ex-sister-in-law who he manumitted in a levirate ceremony.

Just as different sects in late antiquity disagreed on definitions of mamzer,[20] so too did they disagree about punishment. Bar Ilan describes the Qumran sect as barring mamzerim from entering the Sanctuary and perhaps from the sect itself.[21] Some Jews compared mamzerim with lepers and forbade them from entering Jerusalem, learning Torah, or inheriting;[22] others marked mamzerim in ways that made them readily recognizable—by painting their graves and houses with white plaster,[23] or by shaving their heads in a circle so that their hair could not grow back.[24]

However construed and however punished, the notion of mamzer in late antiquity appears to have been fluid—a matter of debate, change, and social construction. In addition, mamzer may indeed have been a way that different sects of Jews distinguished among themselves. While biblical mamzer rules created boundaries that set apart foreigners from members of the Israelite polity, Mishnaic mamzer rules created boundaries that set apart one group of Jews from the other.

In the middle ages, codifiers of Jewish law resolved the Mishnaic debate regarding mamzer. Rabbi Moses Ben Maimon (1135–1204) and Rabbi Yoseph Karo (1488–1575) agreed that the mamzer stigma applied to children born of *all* unions that were forbidden in the Bible, whether adulterous or incestuous, including children born of relations entered into under duress or rape, that is, without specific intent to commit adultery or incest, but not to children born of relations with menstruating women.[25] What's more, the codifiers gave broad discretion to husbands to impose the mamzer taboo or to ignore it. On one hand, they held that a husband could deem his child a mamzer simply by declaring that the child was not his (*din yaḳir*).[26] On the other hand, they ruled that a husband could discredit any claim made by his wife,[27] or anyone else, regarding the child's paternity, relying on the marital paternity presumption that most of a wife's sexual activity must, statistically, have been with her husband.[28]

In his "Guide for the Perplexed," Maimonides rationalized the mamzer taboo. With regard to forbidden relations with relatives, including in-laws, Maimonides explained that such relatives were very accessible and thus a source of temptation. Clear lines had to be drawn to govern proper sexual activity and to inculcate a sense of "chastity."[29]

Regarding adultery, Maimonides explained that the taboo guarded against this "horrible act" that is "universally condemned," as well as ensured the purity of the "seed" of the Jewish people:

> In order to create a horror of illicit marriages, a bastard was not allowed to marry an Israelite woman . . . the adulterer and the adulteress were thus taught that by their act they bring upon their seed irreparable injury. In every language and in every nation the issue of licentious conduct has a bad name; the Law therefore raises the name of the Israelites by keeping them free from the admixture of bastards.[30]

Rabbi Karo called on the mamzer taboo to buttress the mandate of religious authorities to oversee marriage and divorce, warning that secular officials—increasingly involved in the conduct of marriages and divorces[31]—could not be expected to handle Jewish marriages and divorces in ways that would protect against the taboo: "Anyone who is not an expert in matters of divorce and betrothal should not deal with such issues, since it easy to err and thus to allow for abominations which may lead to mamzerim."[32]

Thus, in the Middle Ages, the mamzer taboo regulated the sexual activity of Jews, keeping the patriarchal unit intact with Jewish men in control and Jewish women under their thumb, making sure that the *internal* borders between Jews were clear. Few married women probably had the courage or economic independence to leave a failed marriage, let alone enter into adulterous relations that might result in a stigmatized child. If a wife were unfaithful, or simply out of favor with her husband, he could wield the taboo to discredit her and her children. With the mamzer taboo codified, Jewish men were given a powerful tool with which to control the sexual lives of their wives. And just as the taboo consolidated the power of men over their wives, so too did it consolidate the power of rabbinic authorities over marriage and divorce.

## MAMZER, AS CONSTRUCTED IN THE CONTEMPORARY JEWISH STATE

The modern state of Israel could have discarded mamzer as an ancient, religious taboo that was not worthy of inclusion in its legal repertoire. Instead, the state embraced the taboo when it adopted the "millet" (religious community) system of the Ottoman Empire as the law of the land.[33] Under the millet system the governing body rejects the notion of one "territorially" bound law for all persons under its jurisdiction. Instead, the state delegates authority to religious communities and their clerics to determine marriage, divorce, and personal status according to their respective religious rules. From the establishment of the state between 1948 and 1971, Israel formally rendered such power onto fourteen religious millets and their clerics.[34] All the clerics of those recognized millets are male, and they impose religious rules on the men and women who appear before them without regard to the religious sensibilities of those persons. Israel does not recognize marriages conducted within its territory between persons of different millets (intermarriages), nor will it recognize marriages officiated by clerics of unrecognized millets.[35]

With regard to Israeli Jews, the state has promulgated laws that specifically authorize rabbinic judges to apply *din torah* religious rules[36] (also referred to often as *halakhah* or Jewish law). According to din torah, a Jewish woman remains married until her Jewish husband agrees to deliver a *get* to her of his own free will.[37] A forced divorce is invalid.[38] If a husband is missing, incapacitated, or simply refuses to deliver a get, his wife remains anchored to her failed marriage indefinitely, an *agunah*. If an agunah has a relationship with a man who is not her husband while waiting for a get, any child born of that union is a mamzer. So are children born of any "forbidden relations" set forth in the Bible, whether conceived intentionally or as a result of rape (except a child conceived during the forbidden menstruating period). Thus, in the state of Israel today, a mamzer and a mamzer's progeny forever cannot marry a fellow Jew unless the intended partner is another mamzer or a convert.[39] In contrast, a child born to a married man who had an adulterous relationship with a single Jewish woman is not similarly assigned the status of mamzer and is not condemned by din torah or by Israeli law.

In addition to deferring to rabbinic courts in the matter of mamzer, the state sustains the construction of the taboo in a variety of ways through its civil courts, laws, and public offices. The state Attorney General's Office has acknowledged the right—indeed the obligation—of rabbinic judges to determine if a person is a mamzer.[40] Submitting to the general provisions of the Chief Rabbinate Law, the state has allowed the Rabbinate to issue regulations that permit marriage registrars to ferret out mamzerim from among persons requesting marriage licenses. Both the Attorney General's Office and the Chief Rabbinate have joined forces to set up special tribunals that conduct trials to establish if a child is a mamzer. The Knesset has passed a variety of civil laws meant to mitigate the harsh results of the taboo, but instead entrench it. Most disturbingly, the Rabbinate maintains a "blacklist" that includes the names of persons who the rabbis declare are, or may be, mamzerim. Referred to euphemistically as a "list of those prevented from marrying," the list can, at any given time, contain the names of gentiles, converts, adulteresses, married persons masquerading as singles, as well as mamzerim.[41]

Before 1951, there was no official, state-sponsored blacklist. Information regarding persons "unfit to marry" was gleaned informally, often from persons bearing ill tidings in response to marriage announcements placed by the state in local newspapers. In 1951, the Ministry of Religious Affairs directed marriage registrars to keep "special notebooks" that would include the names of persons suspected of being unfit to marry, from whatever source derived.[42] In 1954, the ministry took responsibility for the administration of those notebooks. By 1976, 2,218 persons were on the blacklist.

In 1976, State Attorney General Aharon Barak (later president of the Supreme Court) decided to review the legality of the list. Did rabbinic courts have authority to keep such lists? And if so, were the lists being managed in a manner consistent with due process? In an internal memo referred to as Directive 6.4501,[43] Barak proclaimed that since rabbis had jurisdiction to determine who is able to marry in accordance with din torah, they also had, ipso facto, the authority to prevent persons from circumventing din torah and hence were entitled to keep the blacklist. With respect to due process, he adjured the marriage registrars to refrain from putting a person on the blacklist if that person had not requested a marriage license. The rabbis and their emissaries, Barak explained, must not act as if they were the police: "Moreover, the authority of the Marriage Registrar arises only when a person requests to register a [future] marriage. If there is no such request, there is no authority. The status of the Marriage Registers is not the same as the status of the Police who collects information about potential criminals."[44]

By 1989, 8,379 persons were on the list. Despite Barak's adjurations, it contained third parties who had never appeared before a marriage registrar or rabbinic court for any purpose, including children. The ombudsman called for reform. In 1994, 5,200 persons were on the list. Determined to lower that number, MK Shimon Shitrit and Chief Rabbi Bakshi-Doron pared the list down to 200, eliminating children and third parties. At the same time, they recommended that no persons be placed on the blacklist without a full hearing or without a final determination as to their status. Their recommendations were not adopted.[45]

In 2003, the Ministry of Religious Affairs issued a circular outlining how marriage registrars should go about collecting and evaluating information regarding persons applying for a marriage license. The circular gave broad authority to registrars: to question applicants;[46] to examine witnesses;[47] to engage in independent inquiry regarding written evidence;[48] to withhold the right of a person to marry if the applicant was already on the blacklist,[49] or should be on the blacklist.[50] In 2009, the blacklist had burgeoned to 4,334 persons. This included 93 mamzerim.[51] In 2013, the state controller reported that the blacklist had included 4,865 persons as of March 2011, and 5,397 persons as of August of 2012.[52]

In 2003, at the same time the Ministry of Religious Affairs published the circular defining the scope of the power of marriage registrars, the High Rabbinic Court asked to convene a special committee with the Justice Department to establish directives on how to deal with mamzer children. Could a marriage registrar who established that a person is a mamzer also place that person's child on the blacklist? If a rabbinic judge suspected that a pregnant litigant had committed adultery, could he put her unborn child on the list? In both cases the minor had not asked to marry or divorce and, as such, the matter was not directly within the jurisdiction of the rabbinic courts. If it were permissible to blacklist a child, what were the procedures for doing so? On December 23, 2003, a special committee made up of nine men[53] issued two and a half pages of directives titled "Procedural Guidelines for the Ineligible for Marriage."[54] Despite the exhortations of Barak to limit the blacklist to persons who requested a marriage license, the guidelines took for granted that rabbinic courts had authority to conduct trials regarding children. Asserting laconically in a way that echoed Barak's general acceptance of the blacklist in his 1976 directives, the committee announced that such authority arose from the rabbis' power to decide who can marry.[55] Though lamenting the awful plight of the mamzer, the committee proclaimed that sometimes a rabbinic court had "no choice" but to decide such matters.[56]

The 2003 guidelines outlined the procedures for determining whether a child is a mamzer. They required that a separate file be opened; a special tribunal be convened; an attorney from the Social Welfare Office be present at all hearings to protect the "best interests" of the child; a determination of legitimacy be final and not subject to appeal, whereas a determination of mamzer could be appealed and, if affirmed, reopened when the minor reached majority.[57] In the guidelines, the committee also clarified that if the state waited till a child reached majority to conduct a trial, important evidence might be lost,[58] and authorized the social welfare officers to collect such evidence. All this, it proclaimed, to protect the best interests of the child while at the same time protecting the "interests of the public" from unwittingly marrying a mamzer.[59]

In addition to blacklists, regulations, and tribunals that allow rabbinic civil servants to hunt out mamzerim of all ages, the Knesset has passed civil legislation that further ensconces the taboo even as it attempts to limit the number of persons declared mamzer. These laws incorporate the spirit of the din torah marital paternity presumption. According to section 22 of the Population Registration Law of 1964, a child born within 300 days (ten months) of his mother's divorce must be registered as the child of his mother's ex-husband. Paternity cannot be attributed to anyone else except by court order. According to section 28 (E) of the Genetics Testing Law of 2008, a court cannot order a paternity test without first receiving the expert opinion of the chief rabbis that such test would not raise the specter of mamzer. If mamzer is suspected, testing is not permitted except in matters of "life and death, or serious, irreversible disability."

## Mamzer in Israel, a System at War with Itself

In the modern state of Israel, the mamzer taboo operates within a social arena that Mary Douglas might refer to as "a social system at war with itself,"[60] or that Berger and Luckmann would refer to as a "universe" that is looking "strange and uninhabitable."[61] Drawing on twenty-eight cases brought, hesitatingly and surreptitiously, to the attention of the Center for Women's Justice (CWJ) by mamzerim or their mothers, as well as published decisions, I posit that the embrace of the mamzer taboo by the state has seeded moral disorder and abdication of familial responsibilities; has punished innocent children for fabricated sins, delaying their stigmatization but not preventing it; has buttressed what has become the keystone of the state's gendered and discriminatory marriage and divorce regime; and has exacerbated the great symbolic weight still given to the taboo as somehow protecting the threatened boundaries of the Jewish people from dangerous infiltrators.

### DISORDER: LEGAL INCONSISTENCIES IN ISRAELI POLICIES

In Israel today, the mamzer taboo is not instrumental in guiding Israelis toward "proper" sexual mores or familial responsibilities. Disorder prevails. The taboo does not prevent women from having extramarital sex. Nor does it prevent "incestuous" sexual relations between relatives. Rather, the taboo confounds the proper order of things, sometimes allowing men to escape their responsibilities to support their children and, at other times, preventing them from having any contact with their biological children.

If a Jewish woman in Israel has had an extramarital relationship, and if she and her husband agree to stay married, her marriage will remain intact and the taboo will not be imposed on her children. Her children—and by implication her own sexual activities—will be "legitimated" by the marital paternity presumption. This assumes, of course, that her lover, the child's biological father, makes no claims to paternity or connection with the child. In such cases, the taboo and paternity presumption will not have prevented extramarital sex but instead will have exonerated it. Similarly, if an unhappy Jewish wife wants a divorce from her Israeli husband, she is free to physically leave him and engage in extramarital sex while waiting for a get if her religious conscience permits her to do so. So long as she has no children, the state will not punish her activities. In this situation too, the taboo will not prevent extramarital sex, though it could very well encourage the use of birth control. It may also provide, as described above, an incentive for an abortion—entered into with the blessing of rabbis.

The taboo is ineffectual in preventing incestuous relations, whether the consanguine type or affinal type. It would appear obvious that the taboo will not prevent malevolent fathers or brothers from forcing incestuous sexual relations on their vulnerable daughters or sisters. Nor will it prevent relations with distant relatives or in-laws. Most people are unaware that the taboo applies at all in such cases. Today, most states outside of Israel allow marriages between distant blood relatives and in-laws.[62] Aunts may marry nephews, just as uncles may marry nieces. Men may marry the widows or ex-wives of their brothers. They may also marry the sisters of their ex-wives.

In contrast to the modern latitude and freedoms with respect to relations with distant relatives, din torah law is not only out-dated, it is also not rational to the modern mind. Under din torah rules, a man *must* marry his brother's widow if his brother died without children.[63] But he is *prohibited* from marrying her if his brother died with children.[64] He is also prohibited from marrying his ex-wife's sister, but only if his ex-wife is still alive.[65] Thus, in Israel today, children born to a man who has had sexual relations with his brother's widow or with his ex-sister-law under prohibited din torah circumstances will be blacklisted and ostracized by the state's Chief Rabbinate, rabbinic courts, and marriage registrars. In one case brought to the attention of CWJ, an Israeli rabbi actually married a man and his ex-sister-in-law. When the rabbi asked them if they were related, they (correctly) said, no. Only many years later did the rabbi discover his error. By that time the couple had numerous children, all mamzerim. Though CWJ could not corroborate whether the children had actually made the blacklist, it has confirmed that the rabbi who performed the wedding informed the parents of his mistake and of the resulting, devastating consequences.

Moreover, and perhaps most importantly, the taboo confounds the proper ordering of responsibilities between family members. Because of the taboo, children are denied child support and are kept from knowing who their fathers are,[66] and men are denied contact with their children. From my experience, if a woman is divorced or estranged from her husband, she will not sue him to support someone else's biological child. It does not matter that the state has registered the child as his under the Population Registration Law of 1965. First, because registration is not proof of paternity,[67] and second, because such estranged husbands or ex-husbands can defend against a support claim simply by denying paternity and thus raising the specter of the mamzer taboo. This would cause the mother to immediately withdraw her claim. Mothers will similarly hesitate to sue biological fathers for support. Like an estranged husband or ex-husband, the biological father can avoid responsibility by denying paternity and wielding the threat of the taboo. Moreover, he can invoke the Genetics Testing Law of 2008 to prevent any definitive proof that he is indeed the father.

A case brought by a mother before the Kfar Sava Family Court illustrates the support conundrum well. A judge dismissed a mother's petition for child support brought against a child's alleged biological father and *not* against her ex-husband. The judge held that the best interest of the child was to deny presentation of any evidence that might link the child to the defendant. Quoting the din torah opinion of Chief Rabbi Amar that the judge himself had solicited, the court ruled that a civil court support obligation would be dispositive proof of the defendant's paternity and would result in the stigmatization of the child. Thus, despite acknowledging the clear adverse economic consequences to the single mother of two, the judge rejected the petition for support. He wanted to avoid the mamzer stigma, literally at all costs. In defense of this position, the judge cited the wisdom of the Shulkan Aruch quoted in the epigraph to this chapter that suggests that a mamzer is better off dead. The judge rationalized that the child was doing well enough:

> The bottom line in the case at hand . . . is that the child before us is being nurtured, well taken care of, and is socially adept. And so it appears, on the face of things, that despite his mother's economic difficulties, she is able through her resourcefulness, conduct, and by girding her loins, and perhaps also with the good help of friends and family, to raise a child who is the source of pride and joy, without anything substantial lacking from his everyday needs.[68]

In another difficult case, a Jerusalem family court judge rejected a man's petition for visitation rights with a child over whom he claimed paternity. Fearing the mamzer stigma, the judge refused to allow the father to introduce any evidence that might prove paternity. Referring to the Genetic Testing Law, the judge held that, the "legislature has taken away any discretion of the court and placed the halakhic status of the minor as its single priority."[69]

A Tel Aviv family court similarly refused to accept a man's paternity claim in the case of a child who was calling two men "*abba*."[70] Intent on avoiding the mamzer taboo but unable to ignore the fact that the child had been conceived when the petitioner had been living with the mother and was being raised by him, the judge declared the petitioner to be the "psychological parent" of the child but not the child's biological father. The father appealed. In August 2012, the Tel Aviv District Court accepted the appeal. Not only did the district court award paternity to the petitioner, it also ordered the Population Registrar to register him as the child's biological father. Taking express issue with the state's way of handling mamzer cases and noting the implicit human rights violations, the judge held that the family courts must separate civil law from din torah rule. He ruled that if a family court determines by a preponderance of the evidence that a man is the biological parent, this does not mean that a rabbinic court must similarly rule. Arguably, the standard of proof under din torah to construct a mamzer is different and much greater than the standard necessary to prove paternity. And most interestingly, the court underscored the disorder and chaos that reigned in the life of a child who called two men "abba." Quoting the expert psychologists who had implored the court to "establish certainty" and to "make order," the court wrote: "The most important thing to do here is to 'make order' in the minor child's life and to base that order on realistic data."[71]

### DELAY: COMPLICATIONS RESULTING FROM DELAYED CONFRONTATION

In addition to seeding disorder, state involvement in the mamzer taboo fails to protect innocent children from stigmatization. At best, state involvement delays stigmatization. At worst, it can exacerbate it.

It is the prevalent assumption that section 22 of the Population Registration Law of 1964 prevents stigmatization of a child. It is supposed that registering a child as the offspring of his mother's ex-husband is a modern adaptation of the din torah marital paternity presumption, and that such registration and presumption are absolute and not subject to rebuttal. Such assumptions are wrong. By law, registration is not legal proof of paternity, just as registration is not irrefutable proof of any other fact alleged, such as religion, nationality, or even sex.[72] Registration is always open to rebuttal by evidence brought before a court of law. According to din torah, the presumption is also rebuttable. In the Kfar Sava case described above, the chief rabbi held that any evidence brought in support of a child-maintenance claim would be enough to refute the presumption.

Thus registration of a child under the name of the mother's ex-husband provides little protection. Such registration is a lie. And it is a fragile lie held in place by an even more fragile, and in many ways deceptive, din torah "fiction." The forced paternal registration is a fragile lie because "everybody" knows when the child does not belong to the reputed father, including the child's mother, biological father, reputed father, and extended (and not-so-extended) family and friendship circles. Those who know the truth may also include teachers, doctors, health-care professionals, population registrars, rabbinic court officials, immigration officers, and often the child himself or herself. The registered father may not even know that the state has registered the child as his in the Population Registry. Most often the child's family will ignore registration and refer to the child by the biological father's surname for most purposes, requiring awkward maneuvering when official purposes reveal the child's "true/false" identity. Other times, a (hidden) mamzer will participate all his life in the lie, waiting anxiously for it to be revealed.

Rivkah Lubitch, a rabbinic *toenet* (advocate or pleader) who conducted many conversations with mamzerim and their family members, describes the feelings of grief and anxiety that this lie engenders in the people forced to take part in it. They live on edge, waiting for the lie to be uncovered and for the stigma, which they know to be "true," to erupt.[73] Unveiling of the lie and eruption of the stigma can occur when a rabbinic court has "no choice" but to examine the facts. This can happen, for example, when a woman is pregnant during the course of a divorce and her husband claims that the child is not his. On such occasion, state rabbinic courts have authority by virtue of the 2003 Procedural Guidelines to summon the mother, the husband, and the suspected father, as well as any other relevant witness, to appear before the "special rabbinic tribunal" and subject all of them to intense cross-examination, mostly about the mother's sexual habits. An attorney from the state will then appear on behalf of the child and try to perpetrate more lies or raise more legal fictions and loopholes to exonerate the suspected mamzer. For example, there have been cases where the state attorney has suggested that the mother had sex with the Arab gardener because if the biological father of the child is a non-Jew, the child is not a mamzer.

Unveiling of the lie and eruption of the stigma may also occur at the moment of birth. If a mother objects to the automatic (false) registration of her child as her ex-husband's, she is precluded by law from listing any other man as the child's father. (Many women are unaware of why they cannot accurately report who the child's father is and will adamantly refuse to attribute paternity to their ex-spouse!) The registration will be left open, literally marking this child as special and announcing to all with access to the registry that there is a question regarding the child's paternity. If the mother then asks for a marriage license while the child is still a minor, the marriage registrar who has easy access to the Population Registry will refer her and the child to the special tribunal to determine who the father is. The special tribunal will then initiate the inquisitorial fact-finding and cross-examination mandated by the Procedural Guidelines.

Unveiling of the lie and eruption of the stigma are very likely at the moment a (still hidden) mamzer appears before the marriage registrar asking for permission to marry. At that point the marriage registrar can ask questions, examine papers, inspect the Population Registry, and make enough inquiries to reveal the lie and raise the specter of mamzer from its long, but temporary, rest. For example, the registrar could summon the person's registered "father" as witness to the person's genealogy. The "father" will be hard-pressed to continue perpetrating the lie and will in all likelihood refuse to appear. The (still hidden) mamzer would be best to avoid marrying in Israel altogether, even though it is, among other things, to ensure this very right to marry that he has been hiding all his life. Alternatively, the mamzer can continue to participate in the lie before the marriage registrar, making excuses for why the registered "father" cannot appear and waiting for the lie to be revealed at still another time, perhaps when the mamzer's child wants to marry—or perhaps when the registered father writes a will disinheriting his "child," asks a court for a declaratory judgment that he is not the child's father, or refuses to take part in the "adoption" of "his child" by the person who is the child's biological father, the method preferred by the Social Welfare Office to "correct" the situation. Even if exonerated by the special rabbinic tribunal at some juncture, the child is still not safe. Attorney Eddie Weiss, legal advisor for the state Social Welfare Office who has represented many mamzerim, informs me that determinations of the special tribunal are never final, regulations notwithstanding. The stigma can erupt again, and the lie, now hidden by another lie, can be unveiled if new facts are "discovered" by a rabbinic court. The tribunal is even authorized to solicit such evidence, including medical records, for example.

Sometimes registration will create a mamzer where one does not exist in fact. If a child is conceived *after* a divorce but is born within three hundred days (ten months) of divorce, the child will still be registered on the name of his mother's ex-husband. This requires parents to take legal steps to rebut the false registration and to prove that the child was premature or conceived immediately subsequent to the get.

Moreover, the marital paternity presumption is of no help at all if a mother is not married at the time of conception. A child of a man who has had sexual relations with his daughter, his ex-wife's sister, or with his brother's widow when he is helping take care of his nieces and nephews will not be helped by the presumption. And there is no dissimulating registration. The taboo is forever.

In short, the state mandates a lie at the point of birth and registration, apparently to try to prevent stigmatization of innocent children for the "sins" of their parent.[74] And then it authorizes rabbinic bureaucrats to "reveal" that lie at various junctures of the child's life or to engage in further lies and fictions to try to bury the truth once again, until those bureaucrats decide that they have no choice but to confront the lie at yet another juncture.

Registration of a child on the name of the ex-husband does not remove the stigma of mamzer. It, at best, *delays* it, and only in cases where the mother is married.

### DISCRIMINATION: AGAINST WOMEN

In addition to seeding disorder and delaying stigmatization, state rabbinic court involvement with the mamzer taboo disciplines and punishes women, keeping them, if you will, in their proper "subordinate" place. The taboo punishes unfaithful wives for their marital transgression but does not similarly punish unfaithful husbands, and it inhibits women from making valid legal claims against both ex-husbands and recalcitrant husbands. Mamzer is the ultimate "trump card" that men hold against their wives in cases of divorce.

Historically, rabbis have applied the mamzer taboo only to the offspring of unfaithful wives, not to the offspring of unfaithful husbands if those husbands restrict their extramarital relations to single women. If a husband has extramarital relations with a single woman, such sexual activity is not unlawful fornication prohibited under the Bible, and, hence, under din torah. It is only unlawful if the Jewish man has relations with a Jewish *married* women, thus infringing on what is effectively the property rights of another Jewish man.[75] As such, a child born of a Jewish man's adulterous relationship with a single woman is not stigmatized by the state (nor, for that matter, is it necessarily grounds for divorce[76]).

In a recent spate of cases, rabbis called on the taboo not only to punish wayward, adulterous, wives but also to prevent divorced women from breaching their divorce agreements or from suing to set them aside. The rabbis declared that husbands would not have agreed to the get if they had known that their wives would contest or breach their divorce agreements. The rabbis announced that *gittin* delivered under such "fraudulent" or "mistaken circumstances"[77] were void, effectively making mamzerim of the children born to these women after they received the "mistaken" get. One such holding was rebuked and overturned by Rabbi Dichovsky who wondered: "Will we go to such extremes as to establish *mamzerut* [status of religious illegitimacy preventing marriage to Jews under Jewish law] even after a woman has had children with another man? . . . It seems to me that we have to separate completely between the arrangement of the *get* and all other matters, as did authorities in the past who were responsible for arranging the *get*."[78] Notwithstanding Rabbi Dichovsky's objections and express reproach regarding the misuse of mamzer by disgruntled ex-husbands, many such decisions have stood unchallenged and the threat of repealed gittin remains.[79] A similar threat does not hover over men who breach or challenge divorce agreements. They are not only free to breach and challenge, but to even set the terms for divorce.[80]

In similar spirit, the High Rabbinic Court has called on the mamzer card to prevent women from suing their husbands for damages for get refusal in family courts. The High Rabbinic Court has held that no rabbinic court should arrange a get so long as a damage claim is outstanding. Rabbi Hashai warned that if a man was forced to give a get under such conditions, "such get is not a get and the children are mamzerim."[81] In an analogous case in 2011, Rabbi Amos of the Netanya Court explained: "This is the place to express dissatisfaction with regard to legal proceedings in the form of 'damages claims,' whose purpose is to force husbands to divorce against the laws of the Torah, indirectly and 'through the back door,' actions that lead to invalid forced divorces and the surge of mamzerim." Dov Frimer, a law professor and prominent Israeli divorce attorney, agrees. In an academic article written in support of the position that women who file damage claims are exerting "unlawful compulsion" and putting both their get and children at risk, he argues:

> It must be stressed that the legal and halakhic ramifications of "unlawful compulsion" are extremely severe: the *get* is void, i.e., the couple is still considered *halakhically* married, even retroactively, and the woman's subsequent children from another man would be considered offspring of an incestuous or adulterous union (*mamzerim*). These are not consequences that any responsible rabbinical authority can take lightly.[82] (Frimer 2012, 45–46)

In general, rabbis draw on the taboo to prevent women from putting any type of pressure on their recalcitrant husbands to deliver a get—lest the get be invalid, a woman remarry, and the resulting child a mamzer. Rav Elayashiv (1910–2012), a modern decisor who set the tone for Israeli rabbinic courts, warned rabbinic judges that using even the slightest force against recalcitrant husbands would result in mamzerim: "All of the ahronim [early rabbinic religious authorities] hesitated to use force even when the law would allow for it . . . thus it is appropriate to follow their opinion and to refrain from applying force since it is likely to lead to an [invalid] forced divorce and mamzerim" PD"R 4: 164 (1950).

The taboo is often called into play to deny proposed systemic solutions to the agunah problem in Israel and abroad. Take, for example, Michael Broyde's threatening use of mamzer to support his sweeping dismissal of Aviad HaCohen's proposal to allow rabbinic courts to declare marriages void if entered into on the basis of mistake: "Courage implies taking risks with one's own status. But Hacohen's courage entails inflicting the possible status of mamzerut on the children of women who rely on these unorthodox approaches. Advising women to take that risk for their children is not courageous but irresponsible."[83]

Rabbinic pleader Rivkah Lubitch calls mamzer the "trump card" that a man holds over his wife in matters of divorce.[84] If not for the threat of mamzer, women could dismiss the need for a get and continue on with their normal lives. The mamzer taboo is a great inhibiter on women's autonomy. Women will not put their children at risk, even for the sake of their freedom.

### DANGER: TO THE PURITY OF THE JEWISH PEOPLE

Mamzer is the conceptual keystone of a rabbinic meaningful order—a *nomos*—that is structured in such a way to keep women subordinate to men.[85] This gendered order may be disintegrating, fragmenting, unstable, "a system at war with itself," more symbolic than diabolic.[86] It may be the product of good men trapped in conceptual apparatuses who are trying to keep their nomos whole and coherent,[87] and not the invention of misogynists who want to dominate and oppress women. But this gendered order does, nonetheless, result in the subordination of women to men and the discrimination against women in favor of men.[88] Any threat to this order of things is said to be "dangerous." Mamzer and the dangers it represents are the taboo that anthropologist Mary Douglas might suggest function to keep the gendered order in place.[89]

In the spirit of Douglas, I further posit that for the rabbis—and for many Jewish citizens of the State of Israel—the body of a married Jewish woman is a symbol for the whole of the Jewish people. The mamzer, a child born to a Jewish woman as a result of a foreign man invading her body, stands for the "polluting" dangers that can invade the Jewish people (the "admixture of bastards" in the words of Maimonides[90]) and threaten their physical and spiritual integrity, or "holiness"—that is, damage the "vineyards" of Israel.

That the rabbis see their job as protecting the integrity of the Jewish people—their holiness—and keeping them separate, apart, and pure is articulated in astonishing clarity in what was, until recently, the introduction to the website of the rabbinic courts. Chief Rabbi Amar wrote:

> By the grace of God, we have been blessed with a legal system that operates according to the laws of our *holy* Torah, and this is the rabbinic court system in the Holy Land, which was founded by our brilliant sages to serve

> the *holy* people of this land, a system which is incredibly organized and well managed, and which respects our People and our Land, which was passed down from our forefathers. All of the *People of Israel in this Land and in the Diaspora* can be proud of this court system. It directs the paths and ways of the rabbinic courts and rabbis of Jews wherever they are found. It is a system that protects the fundamentals of Torah and the *purity of the lineage of our People* and its *holiness*.[91]

In 2006, a Tel Aviv rabbinic court made the direct connection between the mamzer taboo and the holiness of the Jewish family and purity of the Jewish people in response to learning that a woman had sued for damages for get refusal in family court. Claiming that they could not arrange a get so long as the wife had sued her husband for damages, the Tel Aviv District Court noted that the very sanctity of the Jewish family was at stake. The court asserted that

> [o]ne must leave all matters ancillary to the obligation of a get and its execution or enforcement to a rabbinic court. It alone knows how to operate in accordance with the halakha and it alone knows how to take into consideration the sanctity of the Jewish family and to make sure that the release of a wife into the public sphere will be done without blemish [alluding to that which makes the carcass of an animal unkosher and to the mamzer].[92]

In 2011, a Netanya rabbinic court echoed similar sentiments, again in response to a woman who had filed for damages for get refusal in family court:

> This court will do everything in its power not to injure the "vineyard of Israel" as a result of the delivery of a forced divorce that is void, and whose consequences lead to mamzerut and the destruction of the family unit which, by itself, causes damage to the vineyard of Israel.[93]

Another member of the Netanya tribunal expressed his worry about the "proliferation" of the (polluting) damage claims "without restraint":

> [W]e are talking about issues that among the most substantive and serious ones in our personal status laws—the validity of the get, and the possibility of mamzer. Should this difficult phenomenon expand and proliferate without restraint—who can imagine what all this will lead to?[94]

So powerful were the words written by the Netanya court that they were quoted in full by Rabbi Shimon Yaakobi, the legal advisor to the rabbinic courts in a "response" filed with the Israeli Supreme Court.[95] The Netanya court also expressed clearly the "danger" that rabbinic courts register at the possibility of the proliferation of mamzerim. Rabbi Yanai wrote:

> [T]o my regret, with the proliferation of the phenomenon of damages claims with regard to personal status we are reverting to the "Dark Ages" of jurisdictional struggles and wars. . . . Only this time, the war has taken on a more severe shape. . . . Unfortunately, this is not just any battle, but, on the contrary, it is a "World War."[96]

## Mamzer, a Religious Concept That Should Have No Israeli Legal Status

The "gospel truth" is that mamzer and presumptions that sustain it should be rejected by the State of Israel. A democratic state government dedicated to civil liberties should not be punishing innocent children for the "sins" of their parents, conducting mamzer trials, maintaining mamzer blacklists, or passing legislation to that end. It should, instead, be protecting the right of children to support and to know who their parents are, as well as the rights of biological fathers to have contact with their children. In fact, Israel expressed its commitment to those universal human rights when it signed the UN Convention on the Rights of the Child. At the very least, the secular arm of the state, including its courts, should be conducting business without attempting to take into consideration the din torah, halakhic determinations of its religious arm, the rabbinic courts. This is what the Tel Aviv District Court did when it overturned the family court decision that deferred to the taboo to reject a father's petition for paternity. This is what Judge Weitzman of the Kfar Sava court, the author of the epigraph to this chapter, did *not* do when he denied a woman child support and quoted the Shulhan Aruch to back up his decision. The value system and priorities of the two courts are not, and should not necessarily be, in sync.

### FALSE: *DIN TORAH* PRESUMPTION THAT "MOST FORNICATION OCCURS WITH THE OWNER/HUSBAND" PROTECTS THE MAMZER

Arguably, the state should also protect children from the harmful stigma of mamzer imposed by religious traditions and its resulting infringements on human rights. But neither the secular nor the religious arm of the state does this by incorporating the din torah marital paternity presumption that is rebuttable and tantamount to a "fiction" that the rabbis themselves do not believe. The din torah presumption that "most fornication occurs with the owner/husband (*ba'al*)"—what I have often referred to more delicately as the "marital paternity presumption" but which I will refer to here as the "fornication presumption"—is a legal fiction that, paraphrasing Jeremy Bentham (1748–1832), is of no use in the doing of justice. It is a false statement made with only "partial consciousness" of its falsity and with only the most vague understanding of what use and purpose it is meant to serve. It does not protect children from stigmatization.

The presumption that "most fornication occurs with the owner/husband" is false because even if it were absolutely statistically true that "most fornication occurs with the owner/husband," that truth would not necessarily and conclusively lead to the determination that a particular child is the offspring of a particular owner/husband. To the extent that the presumption is conclusive, or not subject to rebuttal, it is still a false presumption. It is simply false to say that because of X (most fornications) then Y (the child is the husband's). A simple blood test would accurately test paternity.

The rabbis are what Fuller would refer to as only "partially conscious" of the fact that the fornication presumption is false since they appear to be equivocal about whether, and to what extent, the presumption is rebuttable.[97] If the rabbis were fully conscious that the presumption is false but useful, they would deem it irrefutable. It would not matter that "because X then Y" is false, since Y—the child is the husband's—is the outcome desired, and that outcome cannot be rebutted whether by genetic testing, registration, or circumstantial evidence. But since the rabbis are only partially conscious that the presumption is false, they equivocally allow for rebuttal while at the same time claiming to "protect the presumption."

Civil legislation passed by the Israeli legislature is an example of such equivocation. Section 22 of the Population Registration Law of 1965 protects the presumption by requiring children born within ten months of a divorce to be registered in the names of their mother's ex-husbands, but at the same time the rabbis and courts do not recognize that registration as conclusive. Such registration can be rebutted by substantiated petitions to family court for support or paternity, by genetic testing, and by "information" from whatever source derived and brought before the attention of a rabbinic court—even after that court has made a determination that a child is kosher. Similarly, the Genetic Testing Law of 2008 is meant to protect the presumption, but it at the same time can be refuted by violation of the law itself—undergoing genetic testing. Thus the very passing of the Genetic Testing Law underscores the fact that the presumption is rebuttable.

To the extent that the fornication presumption is rebuttable, the presumption is of no use in protecting a suspected mamzer from stigmatization. Support of legislation that buttresses such "weak" legal fictions would appear to be supporting just that—the fictions and the institutions that propagate those fictions—and nothing else. A weak legal fiction is like no fiction at all.

There are those who argue that the fornication presumption is not rebuttable and hence advocate a "strong" fiction—unabashedly false—that could protect a child from din torah stigmatization by attributing paternity to the husband. This is the position taken by Judge Shneller of the Tel Aviv District Court, who claimed that even if a family court were to decide that a third party was the child's father, this would not rebut the presumption nor in any way compromise a rabbinic court finding that, for din torah purposes, the husband was the child's father. Shneller would "split the status" of the child and suggests that the din torah fornication presumption is only rebuttable by conclusive 100 percent proof—that is, beyond any doubt at all, a factual impossibility but a strong legal fiction.[98] This would appear to be also the position taken by Rabbi Aviner, who suggests that, according to din torah, microscopes and telescopes cannot prove a person to be a mamzer, though Rabbi Mordechai disagrees with him.[99]

Indeed it would appear that most rabbis disagree with Shneller's and R. Aviner's strong conceptualization of the fornication presumption. They treat the presumption as "weak" and rebuttable, certainly by genetic testing. It would also appear that the rabbis would rebut the fornication presumption if the mother herself admitted that the child was not her husband's or ex-husband's and such admission was corroborated by his unequivocal denial of having had sexual relations with her at the time of conception.[100] And here, perhaps, lies the rub. The historical origins of the din torah fornication presumption would seem to be with the aim of protecting a husband's patriarchal rights to decide whether or not to recognize a child as his, and not to protect the child from stigmatization—hence the *fornication* presumption and not *a marital paternity* presumption. This reading would explain several things—why the presumption is weak; why, even in the most complicated cases that are resolved, the rabbis will deem a child the husband's and not the lover's; and, why, as described above, the taboo is serving a gendered and rabbinic hegemonic order of things rather than justice for an innocent child.

## TRUE: WE ARE ALL MAMZERIM

To protect innocent children from unfair stigmatization, to make sure children know who their fathers are and that those fathers support them, to respect the paternity rights of fathers, and to hold the privacy of women in highest regard, rabbis should reject the notion of mamzer completely. This is essentially what Rabbi Spitz of the Conservative movement has done by advocating to "render *mamzerut* inoperative" and refusing to consider any evidence of mamzerut. He declares: "We will give permission to any Jew to marry and will perform the marriage of a Jew regardless of the possible sins of his or her parent."[101]

Other policies might emerge from rabbinic leaders. Rabbis could also redefine the notion of mamzer, eliminating it almost completely, by adopting "strong" fictions that were irrefutable and whose "falseness" the rabbis are fully conscious of. Rivkah Lubitch has suggested a series of such fictions.[102] For example, rabbis could adopt the presumption that all contemporary Jews fall into the status of mamzerim—a presumption that is in all likelihood a statistical truth.[103] Or they could presume that we were all conceived though in vitro fertilization and *not* through sexual intercourse, a prerequisite to mamzerut under din torah.[104] Lubitch has also suggested that rabbis could allow Jews to marry "conditionally" in a way that would allow the rabbis to void the marriage retroactively if a mamzer were suspected. But, as Lubitch notes, this last suggestion would solve the problem for children of adulterous relations but not incestuous ones.

Whether by rejection or redefinition, there appear to be ways for the rabbinic establishment to eliminate the stigma of mamzer in a manner that would allow for the recognition of the paternity of biological fathers if that were indeed their din torah will.

The goal of this chapter has been to demystify the stigma of mamzer, uncover its constructed and gendered roots, and to urge the State of Israel to reject all legislation, regulations, and courts that support this unfortunate notion and the witch hunt that it has, perhaps inadvertently, engendered. In this chapter, I have described the social construction of mamzer and the errors of its embrace by the State of Israel. I hope that in so doing I have convinced the reader that the state must cut itself loose of the idea and let mamzer languish in the dustbin of cultural wrongs—along with female genital mutilation and foot binding, for example.

The state cannot justify the taboo. It serves no reasonable end. Worse, embracing the taboo, the state infringes on the human rights of Israeli citizens, men and women, old and young. It compromises the rights of Jewish women to privacy, property and divorce; it denies Jewish men access to their biological children; it refuses Jewish children's requests for support and to know who their fathers are; and it punishes innocent children for the "sins" of their parents. To improve the condition of Israeli society as well as the lives of those affected directly, rabbis would do well to look for ways to redefine mamzer in manners that render it inoperative—perhaps by adopting the empirical fact that, statistically, we are all mamzerim and therefore can marry each other. But until the rabbis figure out what to do about mamzer, the state must take no part in it at all.

## NOTES

1. FamCt. 32690/09, *Plonit, et. al. v. Ploni et.al.* (Kfar Saba), July 16, 2012 [Hebrew].
2. Rabbinic Court Jurisdiction (Marriage and Divorce) Law, 1952 [Hebrew].
3. Yüksel Sezgin, "The Israeli Millet System: Examining Legal Pluralism Through Lenses of Nation-Building and Human Rights," *Israel Law Review* 43 (2010): 631–54 (describing at length the confessional system referred to as the "millet system").
4. "Chief Rabbinate of Israel Law, 5740–1980," www.israellawresourcecenter.org/israellaws /fulltext/chiefrabbinateisrael.htm.
5. Peter L. Berger and Thomas Luckmann, *The Social Construction of Reality* (New York: Anchor Books Doubleday, 1966), 89.
6. Deut. 23:3 (JPS trans.).
7. Jeffrey H. Tigay, "Adultery," in *Encyclopedia Judaica Jerusalem* (Jerusalem: Keter Publishing, 1972), 313. For further discussion, see Simcha Fishbane, "The Case of the Modified Mamzer in Early Rabbinic Texts," in *Deviancy in Early Rabbinic Literature: A Collection of Socio-Anthopological Essays* (Leiden: Brill, 2007), 4–15 (supporting the idea that the term mamzer referred first to reviled ethnic groups and only later to children of forbidden relations).
8. Jeffrey H. Tigay, *The JPS Torah Commentary, Deuteronomy* (Philadelphia, PA: Jewish Publication Society, 1996), 210.
9. Rules regarding prohibited adulterous and incestuous sexual behavior are set forth in three places in the Bible—twice in Leviticus (18:8–18; 20:11–21) and briefly in Deuteronomy (22:22, 23:1, 27:20–23). Forbidden incestuous relations include both "consanguine" (blood) relations, as well as "affinal" (in-law) relations. For further discussion, see Baruch A. Levine, "Excurses 5," in *The JPS Torah Commentary, Leviticus* (Philadelphia, PA: Jewish Publication Society, 1989), 253–55 (claiming that biblical incest rules underwent "considerable development" and "can be understood as an attempt to prevent too much inbreeding within families that were otherwise bound together as social units"). For a completely different understanding of biblical incest rules, compare with Calum M. Carmichael, *Law, Legend and Incest in the Bible: Leviticus* 18–20 (Ithaca, NY: Cornell University Press, 1997) (claiming that conduct of biblical ancestors inspired the "idiosyncratic" incest rules in Leviticus); L. William Countryman, *Dirt, Greed, and Sex: Sexual Ethics in the New Testament and Their Implications for Today* (Minneapolis, MN: Fortress Press, 1988) (maintaining that rules of forbidden relations can be understood only in the context of the purity and property rules of the priestly sect).
10. Deut. 22:22 (JPS trans.); see also Lev. 20:10.
11. Compare the term "Jewish" with the term "Judahist," Donald H. Akenson, *Surpassing Wonder: The Invention of the Bible and the Talmuds* (New York: Harcourt Brace, 1998), 28 (preferring the term "Judahist" to "Jewish" when referring to the spectrum of religious expression that thrived in ancient Israel prior to the destruction of the Second Temple in 70 CE, and which he argues must be used to distinguish between what later became known as Rabbinic Judaism).
12. See Meir Bar Ilan, "The Attitude Toward Mamzerim in Jewish Society in Late Antiquity," *Jewish History* 14 (2000): 125–70.
13. Expanding on this point, see Simcha Fishbane, "The Case of the Modified Mamzer in Early Rabbinic Texts," in *Deviancy in Early Rabbinic Literature: A Collection of Socio-Anthropological Essays*, Simcha Fishbane (Leiden: Brill, 2007), 4–15.

14. Levine, "Excurses 5," 41–42 (defining *karet*).
15. Lev. 20:10.
16. Lev. 20:11.
17. Lev. 20:12.
18. Lev. 20:14.
19. For the opposite opinion, compare with *tosefta* Yev. 6:9 (Lieberman ed., 21), cited in Bar Ilan, "Attitude Toward Mamzerim," 131. The Babylonian Talmud concludes that a child born to a Jewish woman and gentile man is not a mamzer (Yev. 23a, 45a). For a historical survey of the attitude toward intermarriage, see Christine E. Hayes, *Gentile Impurities and Jewish Identities: Intermarriage and Conversion from the Bible to the Talmud* (New York: Oxford University Press, 2002), 184 (describing the consistent, chronological trend toward legitimation of a child born to a male Israelite and female Gentile).
20. Jacob Neusner, *The Evidence of the Mishnah* (Chicago: University of Chicago Press, 1981) (stating that the Mishnah is a compendium of different sectarian opinions).
21. Bar Ilan, "Attitude Toward Mamzerim," 132–34.
22. Ibid., 134–35.
23. Ibid., 136–39.
24. Ibid., 139–41 (noting that the ways of punishing mamzer were eventually limited to the marriage prohibition, perhaps as a result of exposure to Graeco-Roman democratic values).
25. Rambam, Mishnah Torah, Laws of Forbidden Unions 15:1,16, 19; Caro, Shulkhan Aruch, Even Ha'Ezer, Peria Ve'Rivia, siman 4, seif 13.
26. There are those who claim that the power given to husbands to declare a child a mamzer was circumscribed; see Stephen M. Passamamneck, "Some Medieval Problems in Mamzeruth," *HUCA* 37 (1966): 121–45 (showing how medieval authorities tried to limit the power of married men to deem their children mamzerim).
27. Maimonides, Mishnah Torah, "Laws of Forbidden Unions" 15:19.
28. Caro, Shulkhan Aruch, Even Ha'Ezer, Peria Ve'Rivia, siman 4, seif 15.
29. Maimonides, "Guide for the Perplexed," chap. 49, 376, trans. Friedländer (1904), www.sacred-texts.com/jud/gfp/gfp185.htm.
30. Ibid.
31. See Mary Ann Glendon, *The Transformation of Family Law: State, Law and Family in the United States and Western Europe* (Chicago: University of Chicago Press, 1989), 30–34 (describing the gradual secularization of family law beginning from the sixteenth century).
32. Caro, Shulkhan Aruch, Even Ha'Ezer, Ishut siman 49, seif 3.
33. Ron Harris, "Absent-Minded Misses and Historical Opportunities: Jewish Law, Israeli Law and the Establishment of the State of Israel" [Hebrew], in *On Both Sides of the Bridge: Religion and State in the Early Years of Israel,* eds. Mordechai Bar-On and Zvi Zameret (Jerusalem: Yad Ben Zvi, 2002) (describing the "absent-minded" ways that the millet system was embraced by the new state).
34. Before the establishment of the state, the following eleven communities were recognized millets under the Palestine Order in Council: Sunni Muslim, Eastern Orthodox, Latin Catholic, Gregorian Armenian, Armenian Catholic, Syrian Catholic, Chaldean Uniate, Jewish, Greek Catholic Melkite, the Maronite, and the Syrian Orthodox. After the establishment of the state, three more communities were officially recognized: the Druze, the Evangelical Episcopal Church, and the Baha'i. See Sezgin, "The Israeli Millet System," 632nn2 and 4.
35. But all marriages conducted outside of Israel will be registered by the minister of interior, HCJ 143/62 *Funk-Schlesinger v. Minister of Interior,* IsrSC 17(1) 225, 1963. But this does not

mean that couples who marry abroad will avoid religious courts upon divorce; see Zvi H. Triger, "Freedom from Religion in Israel: Civil Marriages and Cohabitation of Jews Enter the Rabbinical Courts," *Israel Studies Review* 27, no. 2 (2012): 1–17.

36. Rabbinic Court Jurisdiction (Marriage and Divorce) Law, 1953 [Hebrew].
37. Yev. 112b.
38. Git. 88b.
39. Sulkhan Aruch, Even Ha'Ezer 4, seif 20, 24. A male or female mamzer can marry a convert, but the child will still be a mamzer (seif 20), but if a male mamzer marries a *shifcha*, a servant woman, the children obtains the status of a servant and not a mamzer. Upon manumission, the child of a mamzer and servant woman can then marry an "untainted" Israelite (seif 24). There have been Israeli men who have taken advantage of this loophole to end the stigma attributable to them. Israeli women have no similar loophole.
40. Israeli Department of Justice, Directive no. 6.4501 of Attorney General (List of Those Prevented from Marrying) [Hebrew], 1976, updated 2003, http://index.justice.gov.il/Units/YoezMespati/HanchayotNew/Seven/64501.pdf. Special thanks to Akiva Miller who, on behalf of CWJ, did much research on the history of the blacklist and how it operates.
41. Ibid. (outlining the history of the blacklist).
42. Ibid., section18: "All [marriage] registrars must conduct a special notebook in which they list, in alphabetical order, the names of persons who they ascertain, through the newspaper or other sources, are prohibited from marrying in the Jewish manner; and they must consult that notebook with regard to all persons wanting to marry in order to make sure they are not on that list."
43. Ibid.
44. Ibid., section16.
45. Shimon Shitrit, *The Good Country: Between Power and Religion* [Hebrew] (Tel Aviv: Yedi'ot Aharonot, 1998), 265–74.
46. Ministry of Religious Affairs, circular of CEO 2003, rule 12 [Hebrew], www.dat.gov.il/NR/rdonlyres/D6621BEC-0680-4F3F-8B32-4BEC1D90564D/0/022003.pdf.
47. Ibid.
48. Ibid., rules 11, 14, 17.
49. Ibid., rule 37.
50. Ibid., rule 35.
51. Zalman Quitner, Rabbinic Court's Administration Office, "Those Prevented from Marrying" (internal letter to Center for Women's Justice) [Hebrew], March 5, 2009.
52. Micha Lindenstraus, State Comptroller's Office and Omnubudsman, Report 63c 2012 [Hebrew], 248, www.mevaker.gov.il/he/Reports/Report_114/f1e98fb8-ad35-4ef4-8cc2-ffbd51567b58/7923.pdf.
53. All nine members of the committee were observant Jews and all were important civil servants. The committee included Chief Rabbi Shlomo Amar; Rabbis Shlomo Dichovsky, Avraham Sherman, and Chaim Izerer, rabbinic judges; Elyakim Rubenstein, Attorney General and later Supreme Court Justice; and Yaakov Shapira, advisor to Rubinstein; Rabbi Shimon Yaakobi, the legal advisor to the Office of the Rabbinic Courts; Eli Ben Dahan, secretary to Office of the Rabbinic Courts; and Eddie Weiss, the deputy legal advisor to the State Welfare Office.
54. Shlomo M. Amar and Elyakim Rubenstein, "Procedural Guidelines for those Ineligible for Marriage" [Hebrew] (Jerusalem: Justice Department, 2003), www.justice.gov.il/NR/rdonlyres/EC880D06-9620-44AC-9CC2-3A1ED52643F8/0/lineage.pdf.

55. Ibid., para. 1.
56. Ibid., paras. 2, 3.
57. Ibid., para. 9.
58. Ibid., para. 10.
59. Ibid., paras. 3–10, 14, 15.
60. Mary Douglas, *Purity and Danger: An Analysis of the Concept of Pollution and Taboo* (Routledge: 1966), 141–59.
61. Berger and Luckmann, *Social Construction*. In the following sections, I also draw upon cases published by the Israeli family and rabbinic courts.
62. See Glendon, *Transformation of Family Law*, 55–58 (distinguishing between prohibitions regarding marriage and taboos pertaining to mating, and describing how legal systems in the United States and Western Europe have gradually reduced marriage prohibition between distant relatives).
63. Deut. 25:5–10.
64. Lev. 18:18.
65. Lev. 18:16; compare with decision of J. Levine in FamCt 10779–02–10, *Doe v. Doe* (Beer Sheva, March 21, 2012) (rejecting motion to dismiss action against brother in law for paternity despite the mamzer threat).
66. See UN Convention on the Rights of the Child, article 3 (regarding best interest of child) and article 7 (stating that child has right to know who father is).
67. HCJ 143/62 *Funk-Schlesinger v. Minister of Interior.*
68. FamCt. 32690/09, *Plonit, et. al. v. Ploni et.al.*, 30–31.
69. FamCt File No. 13632/08, *Ploni v. Almonit* (Jerusalem), December 6, 2009.
70. File No. 24955–03–11, *M. v. H.* (Court of Appeals, Tel Aviv), August 28, 2012.
71. Ibid., 6.
72. HCJ 143/62, *Funk-Schlesinger v. Minister of Interior.*
73. Rivkah Lubitch, "Mamzeruth in Israel: Hardship and Solutions" (forthcoming).
74. 406 U.S. 164, 175, *Weber v. Aetna Cas. & Sur. Co.*, 1972 (striking down a Louisiana workman's compensation law that denied benefits to unacknowledged illegitimate children ("bastards"), stating: "[I]mposing disabilities on the illegitimate child is contrary to the basic concept of our system that legal burdens should bear some relationship to individual responsibility or wrongdoing. Obviously, no child is responsible for his birth, and penalizing the illegitimate child is an ineffectual—as well as an unjust—way of deterring the parent."
75. Countryman, *Dirt, Greed and Sex* (explaining that the Bible seems more intent on preventing one man from infringing on the property of another man—his wife—than on securing the fidelity and sanctity of marriage, and declaring that adultery in the Bible is about "dirt and greed"—i.e., purity and property—not about trust and fidelity.) Moreover, rabbinic courts are more vigilant in scrutinizing the extramarital sexual behavior of women, in general, than of men. This is because *din torah* prohibits an unfaithful wife from remarrying her ex-husband and lover, even if she has not had children with the lover. Israeli rabbinic courts feel compelled to indicate such prohibition in the act of court (מעשה בית דין) issued with the *get*. Such act of court applies to the status of the wife who is being set free and not the husband who is doing the freeing.
76. Ruth Halperin, "Adultery on the Part of the Husband as Grounds for Compelling Him to Divorce His Wife" [Hebrew], *Mehkarei Mishpat* 7 (1989): 297.
77. See also, RabCt. 041987009–24–1 C v. C, Law and its Decisor 9 (2005), no.6 (Haifa, November 25, 2003); RabCt. 037537164–21–1, Law and its Decisor 12 (2006), no. 4 (Tel

Aviv, November 21, 2005); RabCt. 9997–23–1 Ploni v. Plonit, Law and its Decisor 14 (2007), no. 7 (Tel Aviv, July 10, 2006); HRabCt. 8894–21–1 Plonit v. Ploni, *Da'at (Herzog Academy, Gush Ezion)*, www.daat.ac.il/daat/psk/psk.asp?id=258, Plonit v. Ploni PD 13 5(08) 2008 (Isr.) (Jerusalem, January 27, 2008).

78. HRabCt. 032675951–21–1, "*Ploni v. Plonit*," Law and Its Decisor 17, no. 8 (Jerusalem, January 15, 2008).
79. Atara Konigsberg, "in re: Declaring a Get Void after Delivery of Same" [Hebrew] (seminar paper, October 2004).
80. Susan Weiss, "The Three Methods of Jewish Divorce Resolutions: Fundamentalism, Extortion and Violence" [Hebrew], *Eretz Aheret* 13 (2002): 42.
81. HRabCt. 7041–21–1, *Plonit v. Ploni*, 16 (Jerusalem, March 11, 2008), *Da'at (Herzog Academy, Gush Ezion)*, www.daat.ac.il/daat/psk/psk.asp?id=252.
82. Dov Frimer, "Refusal to Give a Get: Tort Damages and the Recalcitrant Spouse in Contemporary Jewish Law," *Jewish Law Annual* 12 (2012): 39–52.
83. Michael R. Broyde, "An Unsuccessful Defense of the Beit Din of Rabbi Emanuel Rackman: The Tears of the Oppressed by Aviad Hacohen," *Edah* 4, no. 2 (2004): 2–28, esp. 4.
84. Lubitch, "Mamzeruth in Israel."
85. See argument that keeping women in their place is symbolic of the theological order God:man as man:woman; see Susan Weiss, "Not Just Words: The Tort of Get Refusal" (PhD diss., Tel Aviv University, December 2012), esp. chap. 7, 170–85.
86. Gerda Lerner, *The Creation of Patriarchy* (New York: Oxford University Press, 1986) (distinguishing between subordination and domination and describing the power of symbols to sustain subordination).
87. Lon L. Fuller, "Legal Fictions," *Illinois Law Review* 25, no. 4 (1930–1931): 363–99, 513–46, 877–910 (explaining how persons who adopt legal fictions may be caught in an "existing conceptual apparatus" [513–46], adhering to rules that make their world seem "coherent" and "simple" [877–910]).
88. It must also be noted that the taboo hurts female mamzerim more than it hurts male mamzerim. A male mamzer can put an end to the stigma attached to his progeny by marrying a gentile woman (or "maidservant") and then converting her and their gentile children; see Kid, 69, a.; Mishnah Torah, Prohibited Unions 15:3, 4. This legal loophole is used to this very day. A similar loophole is not available to women. Gentiles do not bear the stigma of mamz*er* even when they are the offspring of incestuous or adulterous relationships.
89. Douglas, *Purity and Danger*.
90. Maimonides, "Guide for the Perplexed," chap. 44, 377.
91. Rabbi Shlomo Amar (n.d.), "Greetings from the President," (Hebrew), [Israel] Rabbinic Courts [of Israel], accessed June 13, 2012, www.rbc.gov.il/president/index.asp (link has since expired); emphasis mine.
92. RabCt 027862614–21–1, *K. v. K.* (Tel Aviv), December 6, 2006 (unpublished, on record with author).
93. RabCt. 272088/6, *Ploni v. Plonit*, Law and its Decisor 27 (2011), no. 5 (Netanya, January 23, 2011), also available at. *Da'at (Herzog Academy, Gush Ezion)*, www.daat.ac.il/daat/psk/psk.asp?id=521.
94. Ibid. The language of the rabbinic court is especially curious since, in the case at hand there was no chance of mamzerut at all. The wife had three adult children and was past childbearing age when the rabbis ruled.

95. FamApp. 2374/11, *N. v. N.* (Israel Supreme Court), July 12, 2011, *Rulings, Interim Orders, And Protocols of State of Israel,* www.ruling.co.il/%D7%91%D7%A2%22%D7%9E-2374-11-%D7%A4%D7%9C%D7%95%D7%A0%D7%99-%D7%A0.-%D7%A4%D7%9C%D7%95%D7%A0%D7%99_d253521c-78cc-6a3f-25cf-391db091df9e.
96. RabCt. 272088/6, *Ploni v. Plonit.*
97. Fuller, "Legal Fictions."
98. File No. 24955–03–11, *M. v. H.*
99. Rabbi Shlomo Aviner and Rabbi Mordechai Halperon. "Tissue Testing to Determine Paternity" [Hebrew], *Da'at* (Herzog Academy, Gush Ezion), www.daat.ac.il/daat/psk/psk.asp?id=388, www.daat.ac.il/daat/kitveyet/assia/kviat-4.htm.
100. See Yev. 47a; Maimonides, above section 2; Rabbi Elie Kaplan Spitz, "Mamzerut," *Responsa of the CLJS 1999–2000,* 559 (March 15, 2000): 572–73 (published by the Rabbinical Assembly), http://www.rabbinicalassembly.org/sites/default/files/public/halakhah/teshuvot/19912000/spitz_mamzerut.pdf; Michael Wigoda, "Investigating Suspicions Regarding the Purity of Geneology in Rabbinic Courts" [Hebrew], *State of Israel, Justice Department, Mishpat Ivri* (2000), www.daat.ac.il/mishpat-ivri/havat/45-2.htm (urging rabbinic courts to limit investigation into the concept of mamzer but noting that it is sometimes unavoidable—for example, upon declaration of husband that child is not his). Compare this with position taken by Passamaneck, "Medieval Problems," 135–45) (arguing that medieval decisors try to limit ability of father to declare his child a mamzer); RabCt. 4981–31–1, *Plonit v. Ploni* (Haifa), April 19, 2009 (unpublished, available from author) (denying admission of mother that child was not her husband's and corroboration of husband, but only after allowing woman to rescind her testimony and after husband admitted that he had had sexual relations with mother a few weeks before the get); RabCt. 9830–63–1, *Plonit* (Netanya), May 21, 2007, *Da'at* (Herzog Academy, Gush Ezion), www.daat.ac.il/daat/psk/psk.asp?id=388 (denying admission of mother and corroboration of husband, but only after hearing testimony that would suggest that husband might have been the father and that child might have been conceived from relations with a non-Jew).
101. Spitz, "Mamzerut," 586.
102. Lubitch, "Mamzeruth."
103. Avi Rosenthal, "We are All Mamzerim" [Hebrew], *VeTashar Devora*, May 12, 2013, http://vatashardevoraivrit.blogspot.co.il/2013/05/blog-post_12.html.
104. Lubitch, "Mamzeruth," 11n20.

# 4

# Backlash and Reaction

# 12

## The Secret of Jewish Masculinity

### *Contemporary Haredi Gender Ideology*

Yoel Finkelman

TRADITIONAL JUDAISM, like most ancient religious cultures, has typically been patriarchal to a greater or lesser degree. While much of contemporary Judaism has pushed against that tradition by expanding women's roles, Haredi Orthodoxy remains profoundly committed to patriarchy and reinforces supposedly traditional gender roles. Recently, as part of a complicated interaction with and critique of feminism,[1] Haredi spokespeople, both men and women, have articulated the notion of "separate but equal" to help explain and defend the patriarchy. Women are responsible for the domestic sphere, while men deal with public life. According to this representation of Haredi gender roles, neither sphere is more important than the other, because a Torah community requires both. In fact, in some ways the domestic sphere is more important than the public because it is a place of purity and sanctity. This distinction between roles is not misogynistic, the claim goes, but rather places members of each gender in roles that are appropriate to their God-given and immutable essences. The male active and rational essence belongs in public, while the female connectedness and emotionality belong in the interpersonal domestic sphere.

Yet an examination of the socioeconomic structure of Haredi culture as well as the rhetoric about male and female gender roles suggest a more complicated situation. Economic necessity requires women to exit the domestic sphere and enter the workplace, while the complexities of raising large child-centered families encourage men to take on tasks in the domestic sphere. The boundaries between gendered domains are actually far more blurry than the official separate-but-equal doctrine would suggest. An asymmetry appears in Haredi communal perceptions of this crossing over of one gender into the putative sphere of the other. Female exposure to the public sphere, even when necessary, such as when entering the workplace, is perceived as being fraught with danger. In contrast, male entrance into the female sphere of domestic work is celebrated as an ideal—reflecting to a startling extent the values of contemporary Western cultures.

In this chapter, I interrogate the gap between the dominant separate-but-equal doctrine and competing Haredi images of gender roles. I offer explanations for the asymmetry that discourages women from entering the masculine realm but encourages men to enter the feminine realm. In fact, Haredi gender ideology reveals a community pushed in several directions simultaneously. Robert Merton refers to this kind of dual pull within a culture as "sociological ambivalence,"[2] and I argue that this sort of ambivalence is central to understanding the Haredi community in general and its gender images in particular.

## Gender Roles in Jewish Tradition and History

Countless Jewish texts emphasize the value of feminine modesty and women's secondary status within the gender hierarchy. Women in the Jewish tradition are expected to do housework and to care for the food, child care, and household work (e.g., Mishnah Ketubot 5:5)—though historically these task often did not come at the exclusion of income-earning work inside or outside the home.[3] Women were generally excluded from both Torah study and formal communal authority. Gender practices took on different forms in varying historical environments. So women in Ashkenazic culture were seldom confined to the home and were active in the marketplace and in business. In contrast, within Jewish communities in medieval Muslim lands, women were generally much more confined.[4]

Traditional Jewish sources offer various explanations for differences between women, men, and other gender categories.[5] The Talmud (Bava Metziah 59a) for example, conceptualizes masculinity and femininity in two related but different ways. One opinion suggests that a man should rely on his wife regarding matters of the home but not regarding matters of the world, while the other opinion suggests he should rely on her in worldly matters but not spiritual ones.[6] Medieval rationalistic Jewish philosophers famously associated masculinity with form and femininity with matter.[7] In Kabbalistic literature, flesh-and-blood men and women became linked to conceptions of masculine and feminine aspects of the Godhead and the Sephirot.[8]

But in the modern period, the key term for making sense of gender distinctions became "domesticity." Historians show that the industrial revolution and concurrent urbanization transformed the relationship between home and the public space, with far-reaching gender consequences. If, in premodern cultures, production, distribution, and consumption could move seamlessly between the home and outside the home, the industrial revolution moved production into factories, distribution into stores, and consumption into homes. The mixing and merging of the public and private that characterized preindustrial culture gave way to sharpening separation between the public and private. Public realms became associated with depersonalized, alienating, and morally problematic work, while the home became linked to the personal, emotional, and morally pure. Marriage slowly transformed from a primarily functional, biological, and financial arrangement to one with increased emphasis on emotional and sentimental factors.[9]

This change profoundly affected how home, housework, women, and children were conceptualized. The lines between the public-workplace and the private-home became clearer and more delineated. Home and its associated housework became a feminine realm, and the wife-mother became responsible for creating a "haven in a heartless world" for herself, her children, and her husband,[10] who were to be bound together in bonds of affection, warmth, innocence, and love. The home was viewed a wholesome private zone protected from the dangers of the outside world, in which women and children could be kept safe; it was women's religious and social responsibility to ensure the purity, safety, and sanctity of the domestic space. Men, who spent their days in the contaminated public spaces, could retreat into the safety of the home for religious edification, privacy, comfort, and personal refueling. Thus masculinity came to be associated with strength, physicality, and worldliness, while femininity became linked to notions of weakness, purity, and domesticity.[11]

## Haredi Retrenchment

Orthodox Jews in Western Europe in the nineteenth century, and in the United States, England, and Israel in the twentieth century, incorporated these modern Western European notion of domesticity to frame and conceptualize "traditional" Jewish gender ideals. R. Samson Raphael Hirsch, with his German middle-class notions of *bildung* (character building) and respectability, became a leading advocate of Orthodox feminine domesticity.[12] In Eastern Europe, Jewish culture was less urban and industrialized, and modernistic gender notions took longer to arrive. Still, both Mitnagdic (non-Hassidic) and Hassidic communities underwent a transformation beginning at the end of the nineteenth century. In place of Hasidic courts and yeshivas containing essentially only men, these modernizing Orthodox movements shifted to include families, whether as part of Hassidic communities or in yeshiva-centered neighborhoods.[13] Hence, these religious groups needed a new conceptualization of the roles of women; emerging notions of idyllic domesticity were central to this project. By the twentieth century—and certainly after the Holocaust—formulations of female domesticity separate from a male public life became central in Orthodox discourse throughout the world.

Picking up on these themes, contemporary Haredi Jews have "doubled down" on the notion of domesticity. Haredi spokespeople not only reiterate the link between women and domesticity, but they form it into a clearly articulated doctrine, expanding its importance in Jewish ideas, elevating it to the level of a near dogma, and using the doctrine to combat various attempts to expand women's roles. Borrowing from the traditional view that has always seen women as the "other" Jews, as second to the more dominant and authoritative men, as responsible for housework and childcare, contemporary Haredi Jews have adopted the modern notions of domesticity to explain their own tradition and make conceptual sense out of it. As Rabbis Shlomo Wolbe and Yoel Schwartz have written, "The woman is not involved in Torah study and deals quite a bit with the daily needs of life, because without that it is impossible [for a man] to acquire Torah. . . . A woman's goal is her place—her home. Even if she does not have prominent roles, when she builds her home, she can achieve perfection. She builds the tabernacle of God—the Jewish home."[14]

In the eighteenth and nineteenth centuries, feminine domesticity was a new and even progressive ideology. Indeed, many *maskilim* (thinkers of the Jewish Enlightenment) espoused this ideology in their attempts to save women from the trials and tribulations of the marketplace. Today, however, Western societies and their ideologies have moved past domesticity, with advancements in feminism pushing toward (though not achieving) gender equality and sexual liberation. Haredi Judaism, like many religious traditions, sees feminism as a threat. Haredi reinforcement of the link between women and the domestic represents a conservative response to feminism, using the rhetoric of feminine domesticity to reinforce the patriarchy and protect it from the gathering forces of gender equality, second- and third-wave feminism, and the sexual revolution. The idea that the female from her very essence and by nature chooses to focus on the home can appear as a traditional notion of femininity to combat contemporary feminism, and that ideology is likely to appeal to women who do find the domestic sphere comfortable and desirable. Haredi domesticity, according to this ideology, plays to a woman's advantage: "A Torah lifestyle would enhance her ability to express her femininity, whereas the values that modern society held out as the idea for women ignored this aspect of her personality."[15]

One of the first English-language works to explain Haredi theology to non-Haredi Jews links femininity to childrearing and to creating a safe domestic space for the husband:

> Her prime responsibility is creation in the physical realm, and in this area she feels the greatest satisfaction. The woman's desire to bear children despite all the difficulties and pain reflects her need to create in the way that she can best do so. . . . The Torah woman creates a home, an atmosphere, an environment where not only do her children receive their foundations of life but also her husband receives the haven and support without which he could not create in his primary area of activity.[16]

This leads to a neat division of labor between men, who are responsible for communal public life by virtue of their rational natures, and women, whose emotional natures make them responsible for interpersonal relations and the domestic tasks of the home: "Just as God divided men and women physically, he gave each one separate roles to play, which combined to produce spiritual completion for the couple. Man's sphere is the external world, while woman is the instiller and protector of the vital, internal values of the Jew."[17] These sharply delineated gender roles emerge as a variation on the Victorian ideal. In Victorian culture the male sphere involved the workplace and communal political leadership, while in contemporary Haredi culture the male public space includes those things as well as the long-term Torah study that qualifies men for communal leadership.

Within contemporary Haredi popular literature, the cultural prescription is that women are to find spiritual success and meaning in domestic tasks. Examine a poem, published in the Agudath Israel monthly *Jewish Observer*, titled "Washing Dishes": "But one day the sun hits a frying pan in soapy water/and she's holding a rainbow/ The thought flashes through her like lightning:/G-d's creating light! And she sees/all this/the light, the water, her hands, herself,/are miracles."[18] But the home is valuable to the entire community, not only to the woman. The home, in its modern sense of domesticity, becomes central to the cultural imagination of Haredi Jews, representing security and shelter, the best environment for a warm holiness, unsullied by the secular outside world: "The woman represents the home . . . And home means a safe and protected place."[19] This connects the notion of privacy and domesticity with the Haredi emphasis on segregation from a dangerous secular culture. One author waxes nostalgic for "a time, not so long ago" when homes were genuinely protected. "When one physically crossed the threshold of one's home, it was understood that they were stepping into another domain, a *reshus hayachid* [private domain], the domain of the family. What was outside had to remain there, unless invited to cross the threshold with you. . . . A *bayis* contains, encompasses, surrounds, at the same time that it stands as a physical symbol excluding that which must remain outside its walls."[20]

This perception of the Haredi home as a bulwark against secularization makes the feminine/domestic role particularly important, since nothing matters more to the Haredi worldview than keeping Judaism safe from negative outside influences:

> The crucial role of the family must never be underestimated nor permitted to be undermined. This is especially vital in today's world, where values contrary to Torah have gained so much currency, insinuating themselves into the finest of homes; at the same time, now more than ever, the family as a viable unit is suffering and the woman's traditional role as homemakers is under attack from so many quarters. It is thus more imperative than ever that the Jewish woman appreciate her function as *akeres habayis* [homemaker].[21]

Rejecting feminist and other theories that identify gender as a potentially fluid social construct, Haredi rhetoric argues, within a larger context of Haredi commitment to philosophical essentialism,[22] that women's domesticity is rooted in core Jewish ideas: "The man was given the public role in Judaism, while the inner role, the private sector, was assigned to the woman."[23] Indeed, trying to make gender roles more interchangeable is seen as an attack on the Creator's plan for creation itself, as explained in biblical narratives and explicated by the rabbis:

> The advocates of exchanging roles have, perhaps, not studied well the early history of the Jewish People. When Pharaoh and the Egyptians were looking for ways to oppress their Jewish slaves, they . . . switched the roles of men and women: the men worked in the house; the women, in the fields.[24] In revealing this incident, the Torah is not discussing role-conditioning or even the physical and emotional limitations of the different sexes. . . . The Creator obviously created everything for a purpose and that purpose was set from the beginning. The Torah explains and defines the purpose and function of everyone and everything. When one goes against this system, he is trying to undo the creation, bringing havoc and misery to all concerned.[25]

A recent book builds on this essentialism to undermine the very notion of women's history, or at least Jewish women's history. Men's lives may change over history, this thinking goes, but if we would examine great Jewish women over the generations we would not be able to distinguish them from one another: "Among women, nothing has changed. The lifestyle of the wife of a Torah student, a Haredi woman—is the same lifestyle of a woman from one hundred or one thousand years ago."[26] That is because the Jewish home "has kept its form, unchanging . . . from Sarah, Rebecca, Miriam the prophetess, until this very day."[27] This author goes so far as to suggest that the central Haredi doctrine of *yeridat hadorot* (the decline of the generations[28]) applies only to men, as "the spirit of the time has no influence on" the Jewish woman.[29] Other writers do not go quite this far. Today women "have fought for equal rights" and a woman has "taken on professional roles that were closed to her in the past." Yet, there is no need for this to have any profound effect on the structure of family life because "the nature of women remains the same in our day."[30]

Some Haredi ideologues speak of this conceptualization of gender roles explicitly as "different but equal."[31] Prolific Israeli Haredi author Yoel Schwartz argues that feminism developed among gentiles because they needed it. Gentile culture has always viewed women as second-class citizens. But Judaism never required a feminist movement because Jewish women have always been viewed as equal to men. "Israel is unique due to its near equality between fathers and mothers," he writes, "which is unlike gentile nations, where the attitude toward women is more harsh than the attitude toward men. . . . Their [children's relationship to the mother] relationship is a physical one, unlike a Jewish relationship to parents, which is also spiritual."[32] Or as another writer puts it, "The Torah woman understands that her role is the necessary compliment of her husband's; that each part is equal, separate and dependent on the other."[33] In other versions, female separateness and protection stem from women's supposedly greater level of holiness, her "natural, intuitive connection to God's will."[34] "Women are not obligated in all of the positive mitzvos. . . .This is because women have a greater tendency toward spiritual growth than the men and therefore do not need these mitzvos to bring that potential to fruition."[35] Again, echoing Victorian notions of female purity, moral intuition, and spiritual nature, Haredi ideology accounts for patriarchal social structure by raising women in the abstract but confining them in actual power.

The retrenchment—the intensified focus on gender separation and distinctiveness—appears not only in theories of gender essentialism but in practices of gender distinctiveness and separatism as well. Haredi men and women study radically separate curricula in gender-separated schools,[36] and outside of the home come in very little contact with one another. Historically unprecedented levels of gender separation have appeared in some Haredi public spaces, with men and women sitting separately not only in synagogues but on buses as well. In some neighborhoods, women are even barred from certain public sidewalks. Most mainstream Haredi publications, even those by and for women, will not publish pictures of females. As Haredi Jews increasingly take up residence in previously non-Haredi neighborhoods, this gender separatism becomes an area of intense conflict. More, an ideology of strong gender essentialism serves as a trope that disallows moves toward egalitarianism that threaten the patriarchal power structure. Female rabbis, prayer leaders, or Knesset members become problematic not because of *halakhic* (Jewish legal) prohibitions against them, but because they violate the separate-but-equal doctrine that has taken on dogmatic weight. Retrenchment, at levels of both ideology and practice, functions as a way of building borders and circling wagons. It sets out maximum contrast between the gender and sexual purity of the Haredi enclave and the supposed sexual decadence and social decay in Western egalitarianism.

## Asymmetry

This retrenchment in ideology and practice represents only part of a much more complex reality, in which the model of separate spheres and the practices of gender separation represent some of the most important themes. But despite the fervency of the rhetoric of separate but equal, we should not assume that it accurately describes the reality of Haredi communities, or even that it serves as a complete model of how Haredi culture talks about gender. For example, the separate-spheres trope does not explain aspects of the actual practice. Haredi women work outside the home, and a woman with good professional prospects is considered a more valuable partner in the competitive *shiddukh* (marriage partner) market. Women's role in the workplace stems, in large part, from the fact that men are encouraged to spend at minimum several years in *kollel*, and in Israel they are sometimes forced to do so by fear of the draft. Female income keeps families afloat. If the ideology of separate but equal were put into practice, women would not serve as primary breadwinners in so many families. Moreover, men are not only permitted but actively encouraged to take on roles within the home. Much Haredi discourse about masculinity holds men responsible for some of the housework as well as the emotional work in domestic life, marital relationships, and childrearing. These rhetorical tropes match some of the reality. Haredi men do take on domestic tasks within the home, and they are thanked and celebrated when they do so.[37]

Men, then, enter feminine space and women enter male space, but the Haredi discourse treats each of these border crossings differently and quite asymmetrically. The separate-but-equal ideology explains restrictions on women's participation in male activities such as Talmud study or political authority, but men who enter the feminine domestic sphere are not condemned. On the contrary, Haredi culture celebrates domesticated men. Men, in much Haredi rhetoric, are not only permitted but encouraged to take an active role in the domestic sphere. When women do go out into the public sphere, particularly in the workforce, their acts are described as fraught with danger, a kind of necessary evil. But—perhaps surprisingly—that is not the case in the other direction. Research and popular writings have taken note of the dual feminine role in the home and workplace in Haredi culture,[38] but almost no research or public attention has focused on the importance of the cultural image of men in domestic roles as part of both Haredi theory and practice.

Haredi prohibitions against women entering the public space are deeply rooted in Jewish culture and religion; for example, women may not create a quorum for public prayer because they do not make up the "public": "A *minyan* is a public unit, expressive of the public functioning of the community. Therefore only men, as the public figures, can legally form a *minyan*."[39] Haredi political parties in Israel defend their practice of excluding women from candidacy on the basis of the claim that "men have one function and women another,"[40] yet as these lines are being written, the news is reporting an underground group of Haredi women in the city of Elad planning on running for municipal office,[41] as well as threats against a Haredi woman running for office in the Jerusalem municipality.[42] Laws of *tzniut* (modesty) and various prohibitions on photographs of women exclude women from the public space. An ideology that insists that women need to move from living with their fathers to living with their husbands, without any role moratorium in between, stands at the center of Haredi attempts to keep women within the domestic sphere and to prevent them from being drafted into the Israeli army and even into National Service. This ideology conceptualizes women who leave the domestic sphere as being in danger.

According to the introduction to one of R. Shlomo Wolbe's works on marital harmony, a wife may assist the husband to fulfill his financial responsibilities, but she does not really belong in the workplace. He should take responsibility for earning a living, and he should make the financial decisions for the family, even when dealing with money that she has earned.[43] Women can and do enter the public sphere to participate in the workforce and earn money, which helps support long-term Torah study among men, but Haredi ideology identifies this as a necessary evil, something dangerous. Work in "office or secretarial jobs" is an "awesome hazard to Tznius."[44]

Two primary dangers are seen to arise when women enter the workforce, both of which explain the Haredi focus on women's domestic role. First, work takes time away from family, and in worst-case scenarios a woman might treat her career as valuable in and of itself rather than as a means to the end of providing income. A fictional but didactic Haredi short story—which featured prominently in Rivka Neriah Ben-Shahar's reception study of Haredi women's attitudes toward the workplace[45]—describes a woman who began working as a secretary and gradually found herself taking on more responsibilities in a public-relations firm. This damaged her relationship with her family, children, and husband. In the end, she went back to a minor role in the firm, which returned her family life to normal.[46] Second, entry into the workforce, particularly one in which men work as well, endangers a woman's modesty, creating a sexually charged atmosphere that could undermine the woman's relationship with her husband. A guide book for young Haredi women in Israel explains: "When working in a mixed-gender workplace, [a woman] must establish boundaries so that she will not develop feelings, not cross an invisible line. A female worker should speak with other workers directly about things necessary to do the job, but she should not call her boss by his first name, and she should not be called by her first name by him! Do not speak of things unrelated to work. Dress modestly with a minimum of jewelry." More, the book compares the atmosphere in a mixed-gender workplace to the trials and tribulations that the biblical Joseph experienced when Potiphar's wife attempted to seduce him: "Remember the 'emergency exit' of the biblical Joseph: 'and he left his clothing and fled outward' when these basic rules are violated. This is not speaking of actual prohibitions, but even of fences built upon fences. When they are violated, abandon everything and run out, even if your seniority or benefits might be hurt."[47]

Despite the fact that Haredi rhetoric treats women who enter the male zone of the workplace as a threat, the same rhetoric celebrates men who enter the female zone of the domestic space. Schwartz, for example, sees this male domesticity as a unique phenomenon, one that distinguishes the Jewish people from both gentiles and from animals. He explains that in the animal kingdom, males are often uninvolved in the raising of offspring. "Among some animal species the male is almost not present. . . ." Among gentiles, men and even women can be cruel to their children rather than loving. But "Jewish women have special motherly feelings. Among gentiles we often find that mothers abandon their children for selfish reasons. . . . But the Jewish family"—both fathers and mothers—"lives for its children."[48] Male animals are uninterested in childrearing. Gentiles, both male and female, may be cruel to their children, but among Jews both parents care, and the man assists the mother in her primary and natural task of childrearing.

The Haredi press and popular literature—which try to find the right balance between didactically teaching families what they ought to be and realistically depicting a more complex reality—speak constantly about men and masculinity. Weekly magazines for women and for a general readership, as well as self-help books, fictional writing, and guidebooks for marriage,[49] constantly envision men as domesticated husbands, fathers, and helpers (though not lovers—that would be too realistic and not didactic enough).[50]

Men are to be involved in both housework and emotional work. Ideal men, for example, help in the kitchen. An article in an Israeli Haredi women's magazine describes a hectic housewife who is a bit jealous of a hostess who served "fish, soup, and chicken which her father had made." This article contrasts that father with other men, who sit at the table waiting to be served.[51]

Men should be emotionally supportive of their wives, similar articles exhort. An American Haredi women's magazine depicts a husband who offers just the kind of emotional support and constructive speech suggested by both general and Haredi self-help books. "I had failed my driving test three times . . . But [my husband] Lavi firmly said, 'Stop counting. It doesn't matter how many times you fail. Just keep going till you pass. Once you have that license, the amount of times you took the driver's test won't matter.' I passed on the next try."[52] At times we learn about the significance of domestic men from the presentation of transgressive men, those who fail in their domestic tasks. An article about taking care of elderly parents contrasts the material inheritance, which should be split evenly among sons and daughters,[53] with the day-to-day work involved in caring for parents, which seems to fall exclusively on the daughter:

> My father, may his memory be a blessing, used to say, "Everything should be divided equally." The children should divide up the things equally. So why is that only true about the property? Why isn't the burden split equally? I'm the only daughter, the only address for every fall or problem. I don't even bother to ask if they called my brothers. Surely not, since they are busy.[54]

At other times, a male is shown to transgress by failing in the emotional work accompanying family and couplehood:

> My husband, Leibel, is a tough man. Not a bad man, but a tough man. . . . His problem is that he has trouble expressing his feelings in a calm, healthy way, and instead of communicating to the people close to him when he's upset or irritated, he either smolders and suppresses anger or explodes in a tempest of rage. I've tried many different ways to help Leibel manage his anger and learn better communication skills, but my efforts have failed dismally.[55]

We could easily find hundreds of examples of depictions of a Haredi ideal of domestically involved men. There is, of course, no suggestion that men take over the domestic sphere. They are not to become househusbands. Men are generally depicted as "compliant helpers" to women, who are described as the "domestic managers."[56] Men choose to help in tasks that come naturally to women.[57] Still, men who help in the domestic sphere are praised. Women, in contrast, certainly should not "help out" the men in the study hall or in the institutions of communal power, and when they do go to work this is depicted as dangerous. One could, then, invert the catchphrase that characterizes much Haredi discussion of gender. Quoting the verse in Psalms, Haredi ideologues explain that "the whole honor of the daughter of the King is inward" (Psalms 45:14). In practice however, some of the honor of Haredi men stems from inwardness, as they too are expected to stand out as helpers to their wives in the domestic sphere. This suggests a measure of disconnect between Orthodoxy's stated ideology, its popular discourse, and the social practices associated with Orthodox gender roles. The ideology of separate but equal is not as separate and not as equal as it seems.

## Making Sense of the Asymmetry

How does one make sense of this asymmetry? At one level, much of the history of feminist thought has revolved around a critique of double standards and asymmetry in cultural treatment of men and women. Some degree of asymmetry is also related to traditions that identify ideal Jewish masculinity as caring, kind, and physically weak.[58] But I think it is important to delve more deeply into these asymmetries in contemporary Haredi discourse. Why adopt a theory of separate but equal when that theory does not explain other aspects of the ideology or the practice? Why, given that both men and women are expected to enter the spheres of the other, is women's entry into the men's sphere perceived as dangerous and men's entrance into the women's sphere celebrated? Is this part of a general pattern where the reality of gender practice does not always match the stated gendered ideology?[59] Is this merely patriarchal sleight-of-hand, an attempt to disguise asymmetrical power relations within the Haredi community?

Part of the asymmetry relates to the phenomenon, mentioned earlier, that Robert Merton has referred to as "sociological ambivalence." For Merton, a society or institution faces a condition of ambivalence when it is pulled in two directions simultaneously. Under certain circumstances, "ambivalence comes to be built into the structure of social statuses and roles."[60] From Merton's functionalist perspective, institutions and individuals find themselves in sociologically ambivalent condition when the society calls upon them to play contradictory or tension-filled roles or when, to do their jobs well, people and institutions must be committed to seemingly contradictory values or actions. He calls this the "functional value of the tension between polarities. Action exclusively in terms of one component in the ambivalent pairs tends to be self-defeating, producing a lopsided development that undercuts the basic objectives of the complex reality."[61] For example, for a company to run well, managers must create an atmosphere of institutional loyalty in which employees feel cared about, even as those managers can afford no personal sympathies when it comes to hiring, firing, and profits.

Sociological ambivalence is central to understanding much of Israeli Haredi culture, particularly regarding its relationship to general culture, the Israeli army, Zionism, and male workforce participation.[62] Thinking about Haredi culture in terms of ambivalence can help explain the violations of the separate-but-equal notion as well as the asymmetry in those violations. There are several ways of describing a push-pull ambivalence in Haredi gender images. First, Haredi Judaism is caught between the perceived purity of the child-centered nuclear family, which encourages female domesticity, and the practical economic need for women to work to support the system of male Torah study. Second, Haredi Judaism is caught between the image of an unchanging, ahistorical ideology of pure Torah and the need to attract adherents by appealing to the concerns of contemporary people. Third, Haredi Judaism is caught between the need for hierarchy that is created by the patriarchy and notions of strong rabbinic authority, and the democratic desire for equality that can make a Haredi life appealing to members.

On the one hand, Haredi Judaism is profoundly committed to the separate-but-equal ideology, which helps solidify patriarchy and maintain nuclear families, both of which are central to the social networks that socialize young people into Haredi norms. On the other hand, economic realities combined with the work involved in maintaining nuclear families push toward violations of the separate-but-equal doctrine. Haredi culture is pushed in two directions: the direction of strengthening nuclear families by emphasizing feminine domesticity, and the direction of pushing women into wage-earning roles to support Torah study. Haredi women must enter the workplace because long-term *kollel* study for men requires it. Haredi men and women believe in the separate-but-equal doctrine, but they make a necessary exception to allow women to work in order to support and pay for male Torah study. Ultimately, male Torah study is more important than keeping women out of the workplace. Haredi culture understands that women at work raises a potential ideological challenge to the neat distinction between spheres but is willing to pay the price for women in the workplace. More, Haredi culture must identify women in the workplace as dangerous to combat the threats to the patriarchy implicit in women's financial power. Yet placing women in the workplace also pushes men into domestic roles, since the redistribution of the wage-earning role leads to a redistribution of the domestic work as well. Men must participate in the emotional work and housework to allow women to work. Thus convincing men to "lower" themselves to do women's work is necessary, requiring that men be celebrated as ideal when they do enter the domestic sphere.

For the women involved, this push-pull ambivalence can be referred to as "bargaining with the patriarchy."[63] Patriarchal structures give women a certain power within the system, and in the Haredi case, part of that power stems from wage earning. The patriarchal system thus maintains itself by offering a bargain: accept the patriarchy and the male power in exchange for a culture that tries to produce dedicated men who are involved in the family and who will support you, both emotionally and with the burdens of housework. Women may have less power within the larger system, but Haredi culture offers them the following image (with the hope that it will actually correspond to the reality): you will not have to deal with a perceived chaotic system of gender roles associated in Haredi rhetoric with general culture. You will not have to deal with constant negotiations about long-term commitment, negotiations associated with the search for relationship-permanence in the serial monogamy of secular society.[64] You will not have to deal with predatory and abusive men. Instead, you will gain the security of a stable family life and support of your husband at home.[65] This bargain can help neutralize the potentially revolutionary implications of women's economic power. It encourages them not to rebel against a system that often gives them the tasks of both wage earning and housework by allowing them to "trade in" that power for kind and helpful husbands, at least in the ideal.

There is another dimension to the ambivalence. Haredi culture is pushed in one direction: it wants to present itself as ahistorical, authentic, and unchanging. But it also is pulled in an opposite direction. To appeal to its existing or potential constituencies, it must present itself as up to date, as satisfying the needs of contemporary people. It must react and respond to cultural and historical change to make itself attractive. Haredi Judaism wants to present itself as beyond time, but to attract adherents in the contemporary world it must make some of its practices compatible with that changing world.

To meet both of these goals, Haredi culture adopts the separate-but-equal rhetoric that it implies something clear-cut, permanent, and unchanging. At the same time, Haredi conceptions of male roles are influenced by changing mores in the general culture. Outside of Haredi Judaism, men in heterosexual nuclear families increasingly spend more time with their kids, they do more housework, and the domestic roles of men and women are becoming more similar over time.[66] The "package deal" of middle-class masculinity today involves not only earning a living but being an active, involved, and domesticated husband and father.[67] Within religious circles, evangelical Christian men have become, in the words of Brad Wilcox, "new men" who are emotionally sensitive and "soft patriarchs" whose role in the family is characterized by compassion and sympathy.[68] Haredi culture drifts in the direction of these trends, even as it presents its gender roles and sex-role ideology as fixed. Supposedly timeless Judaism is profoundly influenced by the general culture that it claims to reject.[69]

In light of this, we might call the centrality of the separate-but-equal concept a kind of "symbolic traditionalism." In analyzing evangelical Christian gender conceptions, Sally Gallagher and Christian Smith explain this concept: an individual or group espouses certain ideals that make them feel traditional, that serve a function in apologetic rhetoric, and that serve to set them apart from others. But the rhetoric is "symbolic" in the sense that people's actual practice differs significantly from the rhetoric they use. According to Gallagher and Smith, Christian families—who, like Haredim, espouse values of divergent gender roles and a masculine public role—talk about gender roles differently than other middle-class families, but they do not act differently. Evangelical men act like other married men in similar socioeconomic situations, and in some cases are more domesticated and child-centered than non-evangelical men.[70] They do not refuse to enter the domestic sphere, but participate along with women in domestic tasks and contribute their share in the home as submissive helpers to their wives' authority in the domestic sphere.[71] The rhetorical need to combat feminism fuels an ideology of strict gender-role separation, but actual practice pushes toward more blurred boundaries.

Mary Douglas's notion of the "enclave" suggests another two-directional pull in Haredi culture, that of hierarchy versus equality.[72] On the one hand, in Douglas's conception, enclave communities protect themselves from the attractive outside culture by focusing on what she calls "group," namely the borders between the in- and out-group. Yet people inside the boundaries of an isolationist enclave may find the outside culture attractive, and enclaves will therefore seek to maintain their adherents by deemphasizing what she calls "grid," the hierarchy within the culture. The enclave culture is deemed attractive because inside each person is seen to be treated as an equal. But Haredi culture pushes against this conception of the enclave, in that it is highly isolationist but also highly hierarchical, high on both group and grid. Submission is a strong value.[73] In theory, this is submission to the Torah and its laws, but in practice this means submission to the generally male representatives of the law. Great rabbis are higher than minor rabbis; men are above women; Ashkenazim take precedence over Sephardim in the hierarchy; and those born into Haredi Jewry are superior to those who enter later as *ba'alei teshuvah*.[74] According to Douglas, "Stronger grid and stronger group will tend to a routinized piety toward authority and its symbols; beliefs in a punishing, moral universe, and the category of rejects."[75] This is a remarkably accurate description of Haredi culture.

Hence, one could describe ambivalence as involving competing drives between hierarchy and equality. Haredi Jewry is pulled in the direction of hierarchy by the logic of authoritarian *halakhah, da'as* Torah (the doctrine that great rabbis should exercise authority over technical halakhic matters as well as other spheres of personal and public life) and the inherently hierarchical patriarchy. At the same time, Haredi culture is pulled in the direction of equality by the need to make the community attractive.

The push-pull toward equality is particularly important for Haredi women, due to their low place on the hierarchy and their centrality in keeping Haredi culture economically and socially viable. The internal logic of the patriarchy would be threatened by women's greater empowerment, but on the other hand too much weakness might make the role of Haredi woman unattractive. They are expected to marry young, raise many children, do the housework, and earn a significant portion of the family income, all while their husbands learn full time and all without being granted a high place in the community's power structure. What keeps them "in"? What makes the many sacrifices worth it? A full answer to this question would require extensive interviews with Haredi women—and such a project is a major desideratum, to my mind[76]—but part of the answer involves easing the burden in ways that don't undermine the fundamental hierarchy. Men who out of the goodness of their hearts contribute to the domestic sphere help even out this burden without fundamentally undermining the basic hierarchical structure.

An article in *Family First*, the women's supplement of the English-language *Mishpacha* magazine, makes this logical most explicit. "I've given everything to my family, all day and all night for three decades," explains a woman. Ideally, other family members would help out: "If family members only knew how powerful and energizing their help and emotional support could be, they would heap it generously upon the woman of the house." But, unfortunately, that does not happen: "I'm really tired of being a one-woman-wonder. I want to retire." The problem stares the woman in the face—she does so much of the work but gets neither the thanks nor the help she deserves. The husband's participation in the domestic sphere would help this woman, but that is simply not available. The magazine cannot quite call for a rejection of the social order, so any solution must leave the basic social order in place. The woman should not despair or abandon the community, but learn to thank herself: "She can put thoughtful little notes to herself in every single room of her house, in her daily agenda and on her wall calendar. Occasionally, she can 'surprise yourself' with small envelope containing cash for a little treat or even a generous gift. . . . She will find her well-deserved acknowledgment for the job well done."[77]

Jewish Orthodoxy has invested a great deal in a "soft patriarchy."[78] In this model, the official ideology of differentiation of gender power serves ideological and apologetic needs in public discourse and guides practice, but on its own does not satisfy either the men or the women involved. Ideological purity and the desire to combat feminist thought pushes Haredi culture toward an official gender ideology with a neat line separating male and female spheres. But a more complex reality pushes Haredi culture to cross that neat line in both directions. The internal logical of the child-centered nuclear family and the companionate marriage requires domesticated and emotionally sensitive men as much as it requires pragmatic, rational, and worldly behavior on the part of women.

## NOTES

1. Jody Myers and Jane Rachel Litman, "The Secret of Jewish Femininity: Hiddenness, Power, and Physicality in the Theology of Orthodox Women in the Contemporary World," in *Gender and Judaism: The Transformation of Tradition*, ed. T. M. Rudavsky (New York: New York University Press, 1995), 51–77.
2. Robert K. Merton, *Sociological Ambivalence and Other Essays* (New York: Free Press, 1976).
3. Naftali Cohn, "Domestic Women: Constructing and Deconstructing a Gender Stereotype in the Mishnah," in *From Antiquity to the Postmodern World: Contemporary Jewish Studies in Canada*, eds. Daniel Maoz and Andrea Gondos (Newcastle: Cambridge Scholars Publishing, 2011), 38–61; Miriam Peskowitz, *Spinning Fantasies: Rabbis, Gender, and History* (Berkeley: University of California Press, 1997).
4. Avraham Grossman, *Pious and Rebellious: Jewish Women in Medieval Europe* (Waltham, MA: Brandeis University Press, 2004).
5. Charlotte Elisheva Fonrobert, "The Semiotics of the Sexed Body in Early Halakhic Discourse," in *How Should Rabbinic Literature Be Read in the Modern World?*, ed. Mathew Krauss (Piscataway, NJ: Gorgias Press, 2006).
6. My father, Eliezer Finkelman, pointed out that, ironically, that very page of the Talmud records the famous story of the "oven of *akhnai*" (the serpentine oven) in which the only female character in the story, Ima Shalom, seems to have the better and more moral grasp of divine providence, the power of prayer, relationships within the family, and the worldly sphere of rabbinic politics. No doubt, the Talmudic editors meant us to identify this irony.
7. Though, as Avraham Grossman has argued, medieval rabbinic treatments of women exemplified a great deal more complexity and nuance than the form-matter distinction. See Avraham Grossman, *Vehu Yimshol Bakh? Haishah Bemishnatam Shel Hakhmei Yisrael*

*Biymei Habeinayim* [And he will rule over you? The woman in the teachings of the sages of Israel in the Middle Ages] (Jerusalem: Zalman Shazar Center, 2011).

8. Ibid.
9. Lawrence Stone, *The Family, Sex and Marriage in England 1500–1800* (New York: Harper and Row, 1977).
10. Christopher Lasch, *Haven in a Heartless World: The Family Besieged* (W. W. Norton, 1995).
11. John Tosh, *A Man's Place: Masculinity and the Middle-Class Home in Victorian England* (New Haven, CT: Yale University Press, 1999).
12. Samson Raphael Hirsch, "The Jewish Woman," in *Judaism Eternal*, ed. Isadore Grunfeld (London: Soncino, 1959), 2:49–96.
13. Ada Rapoport-Albert, "The Emergence of a Female Constituency in Twentieth-Century Habad Hasidism," in *Let the Old Make Way for the New: Studies on Hasidism and Its Opponents, Haskalah and the Musar Movement*, eds. Ada Rapoport-Albert et al. (Jerusalem: Zalman Shazar Center, 2009), 1: 7–68.
14. Shlomo Wolbe and Yoel Schwartz, *Binyan Adei Ad* (Jerusalem: n.p., n.d.), 71–72.
15. Tehilla Abramov and Malka Touger, *The Secret of Jewish Femininity: Insights into the Practice of Taharat HaMishpachah* (Southfield, MI: Targum Press, 1988), 37.
16. Shimon Hurwitz, *Being Jewish* (Jerusalem: Feldheim, 1979), 149–51.
17. Yitzchak Coopersmith, *The Eye of a Needle: Aish HaTorah's Kiruv Primer* (Southfield, MI: Targum Press, 2005), 89.
18. Sarah Shapiro, "Washing Dishes," in *Timeless Parenting: Raising Children in Troubled Times: Understanding, Coping, Succeeding*, ed. Nisson Wolpin (Brooklyn, NY: Mesorah, 2000), 94.
19. Shimshon David Pinkus, *Nefesh Hayyah: Al Tafkidah Shel Haishah Vehaem BeYisrael* [The soul of Eve: On the role of the woman and the mother in Israel] (Jerusalem: Yefeh Nof, 2006), 18.
20. Nisson Wolpin, *Timeless Parenting: Raising Children in Troubled Times: Understanding, Coping, Succeeding* (Brooklyn, NY: Mesorah, 2000), 76.
21. Ibid., 30.
22. Binyamin Brown, "Ve'ein Shiur Rak Hatorah Hazot: Kavei Hayesod Shel Ha'hashkafah' Haharedit," *Eretz Aharet* 41 (October 2007): 56–65.
23. Coopersmith, *Eye of a Needle*, 102.
24. This is based on the Talmud, Sotah 11b, which claims that the backbreaking work of Egypt (*parekh*) involved requiring men to do women's work and vice versa.
25. Hurwitz, *Being Jewish*, 153.
26. Pinkus, *Nefesh Hayyah*, 17.
27. Ibid., 19.
28. Brown, "Ve'ein Shiur Rak Hatorah Hazot."
29. Pinkus, *Nefesh Hayyah*, 15.
30. Wolbe and Schwartz, *Binyan Adei Ad*, 83–84.
31. Coopersmith, *Eye of a Needle*, 92. The focus on perceived equality between genders stems from mainstream Ashkenazic Haredi circles in Israel and the United States. The more extreme Haredim of the Edah Haredit and much Sephardic Haredi rhetoric emphasize more explicitly hierarchical notions of gender relations. See Nurit Novis-Deutsch and Ari Engelberg, "Meaning Making Under the Sacred Canopy: The Role of Orthodox Jewish Guidebooks," *Interdisciplinary Journal of Research on Religion* 8 (2012): 15; Iris Brown (Hausman), "Bein 'Teva Ha'ishah' Le'marut Haba'al': Ha'idiologiah Hahinnukhit Haha-

redit Ugevulot Hahaskalah Hatoranit Lebanot" [Between the "nature of women" and the visage of the husband: The ideology of Haredi education and the limits of Torah enlightenment for girls], *Zehuyot* 3 (2013): 97–123.

32. Yoel Schwartz, *Mahapechat Hinnukh Banot Bedoreinu* [Changes in education for girls in our generation] (Jerusalem: Kest Leibowitz, 1998), 95.
33. Hurwitz, *Being Jewish*, 151.
34. Abramov and Touger, *Secret of Jewish Femininity*, 35.
35. Coopersmith, *Eye of a Needle*, 95.
36. Yoel Finkelman, "Ultra-Orthodox/Haredi Education," in *The International Handbook of Jewish Education*, eds. Helena Miller, Lisa Grant, and Alex Pomson (Dordrecht: Springer, 2011), 1063–80.
37. Nurit Stadler, *Yeshiva Fundamentalism: Piety, Gender, and Resistance in the Ultra-Orthodox World* (New York: New York University Press, 2009); Nurit Stadler, *A Well-Worn Tallis for a New Ceremony: Trends in Israeli Haredi Culture* (Boston: Academic Studies Press, 2012). Stadler sees this trend as a sign of Israelization, as part of a greater influence of general culture on Haredi ideas and practice. She is correct, but as I argue in a recent paper, the Israelization narrative is overstated. See Yoel Finkelman, "The Ambivalent Haredi Jew," *Israel Studies* 19 no. 2 (2014): 264–93. Devorah Wagner is currently working on a dissertation studying the impact of the domestication of men on Haredi male self-image.
38. Tamar El-Or, *Educated and Ignorant: Ultraorthodox Jewish Women and Their World* (Boulder, CO: Lynne Rienner Publishers, 1994); Kimmy Caplan, "The Internal Popular Discourse of Israeli Haredi Women," *Archives de Sciences Sociales Des Religions*, no. 123 (September 2003): 77–101; Menachem Friedman, *The Haredi Woman* [Hebrew] (Jerusalem: Jerusalem Institute for Israel Studies, 1988); Rivka Neriah Ben-Shahar, "Nashim Harediot Vehatikshort Haharedit Hayisraelit: Defusei Hasifah Ve'ofanei Keriah" (PhD thesis, Hebrew University of Jerusalem, 2008).
39. Coopersmith, *Eye of a Needle*, 102.
40. Telem Yahav, "Shas Veyahadut Hatorah: Ein Lanu Nashim Ki 'Tafkidan Aher,'" December 18, 2012, www.ynet.co.il/articles/0,7340,L-4321430,00.html.
41. "Larishonah: Mifleget Imahot Harediot Be'elad," *Ynet*, September 29, 2013, www.ynet.co.il/articles/0,7340,L-4434346,00.html.
42. Yisrael Cohen, "Shuv Iyyumim Al Mitmodedet Haredit," Sept. 11, 2013, www.kikarhashabat.co.il.
43. Shmuel Carlebach, "Introduction," in *Kuntres Hadrakhah Lekalot*, by Shlomo Wolbe (n.p.: n.p., n.d.), 13–15.
44. Pesach Eliyahu Falk, *Oz Vehadar Levushah: Modesty: An Adornment for Life* (Gateshead: Feldheim, 1998), 508.
45. Ben-Shahar, "Nashim Harediot."
46. A. M. Amitz, "Haworkaholic," in *Sippurei A. M. Amitz* (Jerusalem: Mishpacha, 2001), 21–34.
47. S. Simon, *Shalva Be'armenotayikh: Hashkafah Le'olamah Shel Bogeret Seminar* (Bnei Brak, 1997). It is hard to know what to do with the image of clothing here, and it is tempting to assume that the book's authors or editors missed the implications of the clothing images in this passage.
48. Schwartz, *Mahapekhat Hinnukh Banot Bedoreinu*, 102–4.
49. Novis-Deutsch and Engelberg, "Meaning Making Under the Sacred Canopy."

50. Tehilla Abramov and Yirmiyohu Abramov, *Two Halves of a Whole* (Southfield, MI: Targum Press, 1994).
51. Yehudit Sofer, "Orhim Bese'udat Shabbat," *Betokh Hamishpahah*, February 9, 2012, 44.
52. Peshie Needleman, "High Dive: Splashing Debut," *Binah*, March 21, 2011, 93.
53. This assumption is somewhat surprising given that Jewish legal sources do not allow women to inherit. Observant Jews who want to give their inheritance to their daughters must find halakhic loopholes to allow it.
54. Zissel Katz, "Margishah Keru'ah (Geru'ah)" [A bad feeling], *Betokh Hamishpahah*, February 2, 2012, 44.
55. C. Saphir, "Trust Misplaced," *Mishpacha*, July 18, 2012, 70.
56. Andrew Singleton and Jane Maree Maher, "The 'New Man' Is in the House: Young Men, Social Change, and Housework," *Journal of Men's Studies* 12, no. 3 (Spring Spring 2004): 227.
57. Tony Chapman, *Gender and Domestic Life: Changing Practices in Families and Households* (New York: Palgrave Macmillan, 2003), 117.
58. Daniel Boyarin, *Unheroic Conduct: The Rise of Heterosexuality and the Invention of the Jewish Man* (Berkeley: University of California Press, 1997).
59. Chapman, *Gender and Domestic Life*, 35.
60. Merton, *Sociological Ambivalence and Other Essays*, 5.
61. Ibid., 63.
62. Finkelman, "The Ambivalent Haredi Jew."
63. Deniz Kandiyoti, "Bargaining with Patriarchy," *Gender and Society* 2, no. 3 (September 1988): 274–90.
64. Mark Regnerus and Jeremy Uecker, *Premarital Sex in America: How Young Americans Meet, Mate, and Think about Marrying* (Oxford: Oxford University Press, 2011).
65. Lynn Davidman, *Tradition in a Rootless World: Women Turn to Orthodox Judaism* (Berkeley: University of California Press, 1991).
66. Chapman, *Gender and Domestic Life*, chap. 6; Kim Parker and Wendy Wang, *Modern Parenthood: Roles of Moms and Dads Converge as They Balance Work and Family* (Washington, DC: Pew Research Center, March 2013).
67. Nicholas W. Townsend, *The Package Deal: Marriage, Work, and Fatherhood in Men's Lives* (Philadelphia, PA: Temple University Press, 2002). Though, as Townsend argues, it can be very difficult for men to negotiate the contradictory demands of this package deal.
68. William Bradford Wilcox, *Soft Patriarchs, New Men: How Christianity Shapes Fathers and Husbands* (Chicago: University of Chicago Press, 2004); John Bartkowski, *The Promise Keepers: Servants, Soldiers, and Godly Men* (New Brunswick, NJ: Rutgers University Press, 2004).
69. Yoel Finkelman, *Strictly Kosher Reading: Popular Literature and the Condition of Contemporary Orthodoxy* (Boston: Academic Studies Press, 2011).
70. Wilcox, *Soft Patriarchs, New Men.*
71. Sally K. Gallagher and Christian Smith, "Symbolic Traditionalism and Pragmatic Egalitarianism: Contemporary Evangelicals, Families, and Gender," *Gender and Society* 13, no. 2 (1999): 211–33.
72. Mary Douglas, *Natural Symbols: Explorations in Cosmology* (London: Routledge, 2013); Emmanuel Sivan, "The Enclave Culture," in *Fundamentalisms Comprehended*, eds. Martin Marty and R. Scott Appleby (Chicago: University of Chicago Press, 1995), 11–68.

73. Lawrence Kaplan, "Hazon Ish: Haredi Critic of Traditional Orthodoxy," in *The Uses of Tradition: Jewish Continuity in the Modern Era*, ed. Jack Wertheimer (New York: Jewish Theological Seminary, 1992), 145–73.
74. In several recent studies, Yohai Hakak focuses almost exclusively on the importance of egalitarianism and equality, but he largely ignores the contradictory hierarchical impulse. See Yohai Hakak, "Egalitarian Fundamentalism: Preventing Defection in the Israeli Haredi Community," *Journal of Contemporary Religion* 26, no. 2 (2011): 291–310; Yohai Hakak, "Psychology and Democracy in the Name of God? The Invocation of Modern and Secular Discourses on Parenting in the Service of Conservative Religious Aims," *Mental Health, Religion and Culture* 14, no. 5 (2011): 433–58.

    It is possible that the hierarchical structure of Haredi culture is related to the intensity of the discourse on female modesty and chastity. Sherry Ortner and Alice Schlegel have each suggested that hierarchical cultures in which parents conduct marriage transactions to advance socioeconomically are also cultures that emphasize female virginity and chastity. To put it bluntly, the value of the commodity correlates with its rarity. Hence, the woman is kept rare and valuable by being out of sight and virginal. See Sherry B. Ortner, "The Virgin and the State," *Feminist Studies* 4, no. 3 (1978): 19–35; Alice Schlegel, "Status, Property, and the Value on Virginity," *American Ethnologist* 18, no. 4 (1991): 719–34. Haredi culture tends to organize marriage based on *shiddukhim*, in which family and community negotiate with other community members before the couple meets. Often, criteria for determining the appropriateness of the match involve the respective family's location in the internal Haredi hierarchy. I hope to expand on this in a forthcoming article.
75. Douglas, *Natural Symbols*, 66.
76. Lea Taragin's work in this volume is a step in the right direction, and it at the very least hints that some women have internalized aspects of feminine weakness and submission to the male authority and gaze.
77. Sarah Chana Radcliffe, "Thanks for Everything," *Family First*, July 25, 2012.
78. Mary Stewart van Leeuwen, "Servanthood or Soft Patriarchy? A Christian Feminist Looks at the Promise Keepers Movement," *The Journal of Men's Studies* 5, no. 3 (1997): 233–61.

# 13

## Between Modesty and Beauty

*Reinterpreting Female Piety in the Israeli Haredi Community*

Lea Taragin-Zeller

THIS CHAPTER DISCUSSES contemporary understandings of modesty and beauty as understood and experienced by Haredi (ultra-Orthodox) female teenagers in Israel. Examining the words of students and their teachers in personal interviews and analyzing the content of pedagogical materials, I show how the girls juxtapose and transform contradicting ideals drawn from Haredi sociological norms, rabbinical commentaries, and external secular consumer culture. On one hand, these young women aspire to ideals of modest feminine piety rooted in canonical texts and ever-escalating Haredi social control of female dress, but on the other hand, they show a deep desire to fulfill current secular ideals of beauty, materialism, and consumption.

The intersection of these conflicting ideals produce additional—and often unacknowledged—ideological tensions. For example, these young women implicitly criticize rabbinic and social authorities for emphasizing the male gaze as the rationale for female modesty; instead, they understand themselves to be working consistently toward modest dress and deportment as a moral goal and an expression of their devotion to God. At the same time, they are enthusiastic about using makeup, jewelry, and clothing with the goal of being beautiful for their future husbands. Moreover, these women and their teachers articulate differing understandings of the canonical texts, Haredi social norms, and secular ideals. While the teachers mistrust and try to suppress the values of the surrounding culture, the young women are engaged in a process of reinterpreting the texts, the norms, and the surrounding culture to create an integrated world vision that minimizes the tensions that threaten to erupt and disrupt their world.

My findings show how Israeli Haredi women today are rereading canonical texts while incorporating and adapting secular attitudes. They criticize the traditional roles imparted to them through rereading and reinterpreting the texts and creating new ideals of modesty, piety, and beauty. This reinterpretation serves as a useful tool, enabling them to resolve and hold on to both secular and religious ideals. Yet the question remains: Can this reinterpretive and integrative project be regarded as subversive of the Haredi male rabbinic patriarchy—or is it an ameliorative strategy that enables the next generations of young Haredi women to minimize the social psychological discomfort of their own cognitive dissonance?

## Analyzing a Community in Transformation

Many scholars agree that the Haredi societies in Israel have been changing radically since the 1990s.[1] The community's dedication to the Torah, exclusion of women, male yeshiva asceticism, separatism, and withdrawal have been challenged by varying segments of that society, as well as by political, social, and economic trends. The daily threat of suicide bombers together with political instability, war, and the redefinition of sovereignty and state borders during the 1990s can all be seen as factors in this change.[2] Other researchers have highlighted economic factors as explanations for this shift,[3] and some have connected it to changes in the relations between the Haredi community and the general Israeli society.[4] As a result, Haredim have adjusted their views about politics, religion, economics, modern technology, culture, gender, and family. The rash of changes that the ultra-Orthodox society is presently undergoing has also opened up new opportunities for its members to participate in non-Haredi areas of life, such as academic studies, professional careers, and recreation. Hence, current research describes those societies as dynamic, evolving, and diverse, succeeding in their efforts to remain distinctive while adopting some values and patterns from the cities and secular society in which they dwell.[5]

Some research, especially works by Tamar El-Or, emphasizes the power of Haredi women in different domains such as education and literature.[6] However, only a few studies have dealt with the Bais Yaakov Network even though it is the largest network of Haredi female education today.[7] This study focuses on Bais Yaakov and the roles the Bais Yaakov seminaries play in this changing world. The case study of ultra-Orthodox female teenagers is an intriguing chance to understand how the younger generation of the community responds to changes about gender roles and the Jewish family. Bais Yaakov's official aim is to train Haredi women to raise their children and find a job to enable their future husbands to devote themselves solely to the study of Torah.[8] However, as I will show, this ideal is being contested as the feminine ideal for piety is being transformed from the traditional "virtuous mother" model to one in which female piety is achieved through modesty.

Modesty, as Tamar El-Or describes it, has turned into a "vortex moving towards its new targets: tights for girls, gender-separated buses, stitching up *schlitzes* (clothing slits), wig-burning, declaring tricot fabric spawn of the devil, and so on and so forth."[9] Many scholars have tried to explain this escalation in Haredi social control of female dress. Focusing on married women, Berger-Sofer described modesty as a means of protection against men, who are otherwise liable to succumb to their urges. She examined the social functions of women in Mea Shearim, an ultra-Orthodox neighborhood in Jerusalem and discovered that women are classified there under the category of the essence of *tum'ah* (impurity or defilement) and corporeality (nature), as opposed to spiritual man (culture). As a result, women are capable of mediating between man and the external, profane realms. While the Haredi world tries to protect women, women also serve a protective role vis-à-vis Haredi men. Required to come into contact with the outside world, the impure woman serves as a means of protection for male purity.[10]

Jayanti considered modesty an educational tool that, above all, helps men supervise and discipline women.[11] El-Or also referred to modesty, by focusing on the "luxury paradox," to demonstrate its importance in a wider economic context that is tied to the mechanism of making do with little. More specifically, El-Or highlighted the economic hardships in a community that raises the banner of "a society of male scholars," in which the man does not earn a living. These hardships instigated a change in Haredi modesty, altering it from an ideal applied to both men and women alike to one that is specifically emphasized for women. According to this outlook, modesty serves as a mechanism for suppressing one's lust for material wealth. In El-Or's estimation, this sort of frugality is an "ideology" in the Marxist sense of the word. It caters to the patriarchal "society of male scholars" in which the onus of providing for large, low-income households is thrust on the shoulders of the wife.[12]

These researchers argued that, from a Haredi perspective, the main goal of modesty is to regulate and discipline the community's women. Accordingly, their studies have contributed to our understanding of what Oryan termed "the consolidation of the Haredi woman's marginal social standing and inferiority relative to the standing of the Haredi man," for modesty is "an intra-communal and extra-communal parameter by way of which the women are evaluated and supervised."[13]

The second wave of studies about modesty turned to the socialization of gender roles in the ultra-Orthodox community, so that their focus was on girls. While researching elementary schools, Oryan concluded that modesty is a "central cultural ethos, which molds patterns of communication and patterns of socialization among Haredi girls and women in Israel."[14] Yafeh explored the connection between culture, identity, and the integration of psychological processes in ultra-Orthodox society.[15] Examining the socialization of girls in the community's preschools, she considered modesty an example of "a supra-central scheme for the girls in Haredi society that helps organize behavior, judge events, set aspirations, and evaluate the self, other, and the relation between them."[16] Since most of these researchers shared feminist points of departure, most underscore modesty in its capacity as an intra- and extra-communal supervisory tool that intensifies the oppression of the Haredi woman.

Whereas much of the second-wave research considered modesty form of patriarchal oppression of women's body and sexuality,[17] the most current research views modesty as a pathway to female empowerment, highlighting the ways in which modesty enhances women's agency.[18] For example, while describing how the fashion of wearing capes evolved, Zalcberg-Block shows how wearing the cape can be perceived as a way in which women display their "higher spiritual level," which could increase their social status.[19] Following in the footsteps of Nurit Stadler's research on yeshiva students and how they criticize and challenge the meaning of Haredi-masculine devotion by reinterpreting canonical texts,[20] I explore the reassessment processes that ultra-Orthodox seminary girls and their teachers conduct when interpreting canonical texts on the feminine body, modesty, and observance. In light of the "modesty tornado," I also show how modesty touches on topics of body management and religious piety. This paper undertakes to explicate the creativity that Haredi girls and their teachers display while constructing female ideals of modesty and beauty. By exploring their process of reinterpretation and the challenges they present to traditional authorities and texts, current modesty trends can be more deeply understood.

The reconstruction and fusion of body norms in the ultra-Orthodox community coalesce with findings of important anthropologists of Judaism[21] and Islam.[22] It is especially interesting to see how these scholars describe how the fundamentalist processes of deconstructing and reinterpreting venerated texts by women throughout the Islamic world is fomenting change in corporeal practices, especially those that pertain to modesty.[23] I follow the insights of these studies and address the female concepts of modesty and beauty as a creative area in the world of Haredi women. This chapter demonstrates how through rereading and reinterpreting canonical texts the Haredi girls and their teachers create female ideals of piety and beauty that adopt values from the secular community while remaining separate from it. I show how these old-new interpretations function as tools enabling female students and their teachers to live with contradicting ideals.

## Methodology

Determining Haredi women's contemporary understandings about modesty and beauty necessitated a wide-ranging study that combined the following research methods: field observations, interviews, and textual analysis. I conducted twenty in-depth interviews with pupils and teachers at Maayanot seminary in Jerusalem (2008–2011).[24] Maayanot seminary belongs to the Haredi school network Bais Yaakov and is part of the Chinuch Atzmai (independent education system).[25] Maayanot seminary was founded in 1995, currently has six hundred students, most of them Lithuanian-Ashkenazi girls who live in Jerusalem. It is considered a high-level seminary where girls take *chutsim* at the end of their studies, the Haredi equivalent to *bagruyot* (matriculation exams). After high school, the students continue their studies while focusing on a professional program: teaching, accountancy, computers, and graphics, to name a few disciplines. These young ladies finish their studies with a deep religious education together with professional capacities through which they will be able to work in different professions that entail knowledge and skills of both the Haredi and secular communities. Most of the students will end up working to support their families; some will choose to marry Torah scholars and be the sole breadwinners, and others will marry spouses who will work as well.

In addition, I conducted more than fifty field observations at Maayanot in which I was able to observe the values instilled by the seminar teachers as well as the negotiation processes between the teachers and students. Also, I attended "modesty nights," which students organize on their own outside of the seminary setting, with the object of helping each other *le-hitchazek be-tzni'ut* (strengthen ourselves in modesty). A typical evening is organized by one of the older seminary students and attended by approximately sixty students, mostly from the younger classes. One after the other, the students arrive in casual attire, without their ordinary school uniforms, chatting while eating from the snack tables. As the time of the lecture approaches, they settle down on benches or chairs to listen to the "stirring" lecture of the evening. Following the talk, one of the teenage organizers gives a short talk and proposes a specific practice that her schoolmates are supposed to adopt that evening, such as slightly lengthening their skirts. The girls then cap off the evening by breaking out in song and dance.

The final research method employed here was content analysis. I gathered a collection of ultra-Orthodox texts on the topic of modesty that can be divided into two categories. The first consists of published books written by scholarly men that are available in the community's bookstores; the second comprises books and guide pamphlets that are distributed at the seminary. The latter is unique in that both the authors and target audience are exclusively from the Bais Yaakov seminaries. As such, the texts contain rules and express perspectives that are unique to this institution. These works are usually penned by female teachers who feel the need to add to the existing literature on modesty. Consequently, they offer insight on the changes that are transpiring in the area of modesty throughout the ultra-Orthodox sector. It appears as though these in-house publications are designed to establish the rules as well as to forge a new ideology. That said, it is important to note that neither the authors nor readers identify these in-house texts as innovations or additions to the field. On the contrary, they see both themselves and their output as links in an ancient chain.

## Modesty for Heaven's Sake

While in the past, the female ideal of piety was based on the notion of building a home,[26] today its foundation is increasingly based on modesty. Traditionally, the female role entails housework, child education, and creation of a household that enables the husband to devote his life to the study of Torah, a role for which a wife receives a heavenly reward. Women are supposed to send their children and husbands to the *Beit Midrash*,[27] and in the Israeli-Haredi version, they are also supposed to financially support them. This role was accepted among the former generation of Haredi women and was even viewed as a characteristic that attracted non-religious women to ultra-Orthodox Judaism.[28] In contrast to the traditional view, the girls I interviewed aspire to a direct path to God and construct modesty as the ideal for female piety.

During the classes that I attended, I learned how modesty is currently being transformed from a system of *halakhot* (Jewish law), a system of Rabbinic rulings that entail guidelines as to the correct dress code and bodily conduct to a system of *middot* (personal qualities or characteristics) which requires moral improvement. In the realm of middot, modesty is defined as a practice of spiritual improvement that encompasses different parts of the girls' lives: thoughts, speech, body language, and dress. In addition, this process of spiritual improvement is described as an ongoing process, for every person will "always have something to advance towards." The girls that I interviewed embrace this ideal of modesty and create individual systems of body practices and self-improvement that are meant to construct a modest self.[29]

During the interviews with the students, I learned that the girls rejected the Haredi community's primary and well-known discourse, according to which feminine modesty is a set of commandments that are meant to help men.[30] The girls were indeed familiar with this purpose for modesty, but they disagreed with it and refused to accept the responsibilities that it demands of them. As was well explained to me by Rivki, one of the students:

> In principle, we have been prohibited from matters of modesty [i.e., compelled to observe these codes] in order not to lead them [men] astray. Many times they tell us "if a girl walks like this and a man sees it, then he might be punished afterwards because . . . he saw something that is essentially forbidden to him." So, like, do you want to place this on your conscience? You understand? This is something that really discouraged me. Like, it prevented me from going with modest things sometimes. In addition to my own things—things that I have to atone for on my own behalf . . . I am required to go and atone for their [the men's] deeds?!

Though Rivki is evidently well acquainted with what I call the "modesty for the sake of men" discourse, she takes issue with it. In fact, she claims that it dampens her motivation to observe the attendant rules. This discourse, commonly accepted in the Haredi world, views modesty as a system by which female bodies are covered to prevent them from becoming the object of observation and desire in the public domain (and thus causing sin). Rivki is well aware of this ideology but criticizes it. In her words one can almost hear the voices of contemporary feminists who voice similar criticisms.[31] For example, Tova Hartman describes how this ideology burdens women with the responsibility for men's desires and associated sins.[32] I ask Rivki what does inspire her to behave modestly, and she said:

> There is the matter of "behind closed doors." They say about a rabbi's wife [*rabbanit*] that she even went with a head-covering in the bathtub.[33] It turns out that this also has something to do with "behind closed doors." Like, the moment a person does it [observes a modesty stricture] behind closed doors, it points to something specific. Like, why do you have such a burning desire to do it behind closed doors? You understand? Usually, a normal girl . . . has no interest [in behaving modestly in private]—she doesn't feel the need to do it. . . . So a lot of times, I tell myself that "God sees." Like, you're never alone. Behind closed doors never can be called that you're alone.

Rivki explains the importance of observing modesty norms even in the privacy of one's home. In her estimation, "a normal girl" never really wants to be modest. Therefore, behavior of this sort "behind closed doors" attests to the sincerity of one's intentions, for only the eyes of God are upon her. Rivki and other girls I interviewed explain that they are willing to act modestly for a reason I call "modesty for the sake of God." Put differently, the Bais Yaakov girls transform the reason behind modesty from a social-masculine obligation to a divine one.

Marie Griffith describes a similar process that is transpiring in evangelical Christian communities in North America. In Griffith's findings, many evangelical women go on diets. However, unlike most dieters who are driven by social reasons, these women want to lose weight for God. In so doing, they set themselves apart from mainstream American culture and its stress on health and beauty.[34] Put differently, they adopt the same practices as their non-evangelical neighbors, but link their behavior to a different motivation. Replacing social external authority with internal models of self-regulation, these women distance themselves from a "materialistic" emphasis on skinny, normatively beautiful femininity and transform the diet into spiritual work. They discipline themselves by submitting to a Godly authority. In their opinion, this submission begets personal liberty as well.[35]

Similar to their evangelical counterparts, the Bais Yaakov girls transform the reason behind modesty from a social-masculine obligation to a divine one, exchanging one authority for another. They are willing to accept authority, but only one that they interpret as transcendental. As part of their efforts to forge an ideology of modesty, the teachers and students reengage the canonical texts about modesty. A survey of the pertinent sources in historical Jewish texts from the Bible onward indicates that concepts of modesty were continually being reinterpreted. In biblical texts, for example, references to modesty are primarily in the nature of a general call to both sexes for humble and self-effacing behavior.[36] Even though biblical stories mirror ancient female modesty norms—Rivka covers herself when meeting Isaac, and the *sotah* (a women accused of adultery) must unravel her hair as an act of disgrace—these norms are not biblical commandments.[37] Biblical modesty commandments specifically deal with the prohibitions against incest and the exhortation to uphold the purity of sexual relations between spouses. It is within this context that the biblical commandment for both sexes to wear distinct clothing surfaces.[38] Rabbinic commentaries (often referred to as *hazal*) expanded on the notion that feminine modesty was distinct from the masculine variety. Similar to the biblical sources, the rabbinic modesty laws concentrated on the rules of incest. In addition, the Sages also derived practical laws from biblical verses and stories. Their reinterpretations used some of these stories (especially that of the *sotah*) to prove hair covering was necessary for female modesty and to mandate distinctive dress codes for each sex as religious imperatives.[39]

The influence of external cultures on Judaic societies' concepts of appropriate female behavior and rabbinic prescriptions are not new phenomena. Ora Cohen describes how beginning in the eighteenth century, Jewish women dressed and behaved in ways that left almost no distinction between them and their non-Jewish counterparts. In response, rabbinic authorities decided to raise their walls. At the core of the subsequent increased insularity, the supervision of women's dress and activity also increased, a process that has not yet ceased. This has created a paradoxical situation in which practically no facet of the contemporary laws of modesty can be found in the traditional halakhic literature, save for the obligation for female hair covering and the prohibitions against "imitating the ways of the Gentiles," such as wearing red clothes, mixed dancing, and flouting the rules of gender segregation.[40]

How do the teachers deal with the fact that there is little biblical or classical rabbinic authority for contemporary standards of female modesty? Due to the lack of texts on these matters, teachers for teenage girls in Haredi classrooms use creative interpretations while constructing their ideal of modesty and defending contemporary understandings. In the classes I witnessed, creative interpretations were presented especially in connection with existential questions that the girls raised during class discussions. During one of the classes I attended, Mrs. Miller handed out a photocopy of the following Midrash (a homiletical biblical interpretation) on the creation of woman,[41] one of the most cited texts used in Bais Yaakov classrooms. She told the girls that she knew that they were quite familiar with it but asked them to read it while trying to question it:

> R. Joshua of Siknin said in R. Levi's name: WAYYIBEN is written, signifying that He considered well (*hithbonnen*) from what part to create her. Said He: "I will not create her from [Adam's] head, lest she be swelled-headed; nor from the eye, lest she be a coquette; nor from the ear, lest she be an eavesdropper; nor from the mouth, lest she be a gossip; nor from the heart, lest she be prone to jealousy; nor from the hand, lest she be light-fingered; nor from the foot, lest she be a gadabout; but from the modest part of man, for even when he stands naked, that part is covered." And as He created each limb He ordered her, "Be a modest woman, a modest woman."

After fifteen minutes, she asked the girls to share their questions with the class. Some raised textual questions such as, "Why does the Midrash mention all of the things that we were not created from?" Or "The heart is also a concealed place—why were we not created from there?" Others asked questions that came from their own experiences: "It seems that creating woman from a modest part didn't work because there is such difficulty with modesty today." This existential question elicited the following explanation:

> The Holy One Blessed Be He told her, "I am creating you for very important goals and I am helping you by creating you from a specific place. We know that a person has 248 parts and that, at the time of her creation, woman heard from God 248 times: 'Be a modest woman.' One can almost hear . . . the Holy One Blessed Be He's entreaties: 'I beg of you, be modest so that our plan can truly be realized in an unmitigated fashion.'"

The teacher interpreted this Midrash as a personal request of God to woman. According to her, this passage reflects the extreme challenges that observing the laws of modesty entail, for God practically begs Eve to heed His words. While current scholars describe this Midrash as reflecting the traditional subordination of women through bodily covering and confinement to the home,[42] Mrs. Miller interprets it as a special link that exists between God and woman through the practice of modesty. This creative response by the teacher included no reference to an appropriate rabbinic commentator as the source of her interpretation.

During my research I found that teachers as well as booklet authors repeatedly and creatively construed modesty as a way for the students to create a close relationship with God. Another example is found in a booklet *Instilling Modesty in the Students*, which is distributed exclusively within the Bais Yaakov community:[43]

> We must guide girls to walk all of her steps with a feeling of God's sweet closeness (*kirvat elokim neima*). Just like the *passuk* [biblical verse] says: "And to walk modestly with your God" (Michah 6: 8), and "Nearness to God is good" (Tehillim 73:28).

This booklet stresses the importance of creating an inner and individual space for every girl, a space to connect with God anywhere and anytime. While creating this ideal, the author, Mrs. Rosenthal, interprets the verse from Michah "walk modestly with God" as meaning that modesty can "accompany" the girls everywhere. Even though the verse addresses both sexes and even though most of the traditional commentaries explain "walking with God" as a commandment to "walk in God's ways,"[44] Mrs. Rosenthal creatively explains the verse as describing the "feeling" of walking with God. In both cases, the teachers interpret the text creatively while interpreting modesty as a way for females to connect with and feel close to God.

The stress on the inner world, as opposed to the external one, came up in many of the interviews. Furthermore, the internal-external distinction was used for the purpose of separating the Haredi community (the inner realm) from the greater non-Haredi (the outer realm) world. The girls and teachers described the secular world as a world that is very materialistic, one in which "you are what you wear." In contrast to that, the girls describe their inner world as a place where God dwells, a place where God is always with them. In addition, because God is always with them, they do not need social approval from other people to make them feel like they exist. Their existence comes from the inside, from their inner work. As the teacher Mrs. Miller explains: "God knows the depth of my soul—the fact that he knows this is what gives me the strength not to externalize myself for others. I am with God. He knows and that is all I need."

## Sacred Beauty

Haredi classrooms emphasize inward mindfulness as it is projected in female modesty in dress and behavior. But perhaps surprisingly, the construction of modesty as the current ideal for feminine piety is juxtaposed against another ideal—beauty. During the interviews, most girls told me that they aspire to look good and aim to look pretty. Each girl described the different ways in which they try to realize their aspirations, including shopping, makeup, and even working out. However, they also revealed that this aspiration is hard to achieve because it is quite hard to find appropriate clothing; as Yael put it: "Everything looks more beautiful when it is less modest." One after the other, the girls described endless attempts to find clothes and alter clothing at private seamstresses—all so that they can look both pretty and modest. In contrast, the teachers shared with me during interviews how disturbed they are by the girls' aspirations. They see a beauty that reflects an obsession with the physical body and its adornment as problematic because of the secular idealization of materialism and consumption that is at the core of the secular belief system. As Mrs. Schwartz explained:

> The world teaches people to see their bodies as the most important. And, girls are very much influenced by this . . . they won't tell you that they are, their ears are gentle enough, *baruch hashem* [thank god], so they won't say it explicitly—"Yes, I am here for my body." But all of their actions show that they really are . . . how much energy do they put into getting a skirt, makeup, haircuts, and shoes? A girl can walk around for hours for just one item of clothing that she will use for two weeks, maybe two months, and then will never leave her shelf again?

The teachers understood their mission as an attempt to fix these "backward ideals" about materialism, beauty, and consumption. To do so, the teachers create an alternative ideology that they root in canonical texts about beauty. First, they make sure to explain to the girls that body needs and materialism are very important. To strengthen this point, the teachers dress attractively to become role models for the girls. Many of the teachers I interviewed told me how much time they put into dressing nicely so that the girls will want to look like them. They claim that it is not important to them, but it is essential for the girls to have role models who they want to look like. In addition, the teachers use canonical texts to define beauty as a natural inclination for every woman. Mrs. Levy explained to her students:

> There is an important *gemara* about Rav Chisday. One of the Tanaim came to tell him that his wife is beautifying herself in front of her daughter-in-law. To this Rav Chisday answered: "Even your mother, even your grandmother, even a woman who stands upon her grave wishes to beautify herself." What do we learn from this story? We learn that beauty is a female trait. A woman who does not wish to look pretty—something is missing in her femininity.

Even further, the teachers use canonical texts to define the aspiration for beauty as a godly one, as one of the teachers explained:

> There is a Midrash about the creation of Eve that explains that God braided Eve's hair. In the beginning He brought her covered with blood and bodily fluids, and Adam didn't want her, so God decided to beautify her and braided her hair. We can see from this *Hazal* (abbreviation referring to classical rabbinic authorities and commentators) and many others how much importance the Torah attributes to a woman's beauty.

The teachers constructed a positive ideology of religiously motivated and approved materialism, beauty, and consumption. To do so, they reread the canonical texts and showed the girls that the desire to be pretty is important to human beings and God. They built on the girls' aspirations for beauty—which the teachers admit filter in from the secular world—and reconstructed those longings as a Jewish ideal with a goal of inner discipline. Through a creative process of rereading and redefining beauty, they created an ideal that appropriates and transforms secular expectations into religious authority.

I would like to stress how important this is. In the American context, Ayala Fader describes how Hassidic women aim to be able to participle in and transform the material world. Hassidic women hold secular beauty and consumption ideals but elevate them through Judaism. They believe that the desire to consume needs to be "channeled," like the rest of the material world, to serve Hassidic goals of community building and redemption.[45] This, of course, is an ideology that coalesces with the Hassidic views of materialism, with its roots in Luriannic Kabbala and the importance it attributes to raising sparks.[46] In other words, they accept and appropriate the practices, but in their minds they keep the secular and Jewish worlds distinctly apart. However, in the Israeli Haredi milieu I studied, the teachers don't elevate secular ideas through Jewish practices but rather take the secular ideal in itself and make it Jewish.

The girls and their teachers reread the canonical texts in search of a definition of beauty. Interestingly, in a similar way to Douglas's pollution theory in which "dirt is matter out of place,[47] the teachers constructed beauty as dependent on time and place. They derive from a story in the Talmud that the definition of beauty is that it suits the time and place; hence, beauty depends on where and for whom it is used. The teachers introduce two different spheres—outside the house and inside the house. For the eyes of the world, the teachers create a system called respectability, explaining to the girls the importance of looking respectable—a general ideal that must be realized by both men and women. According to the girls and their teachers, every human being has a soul and therefore we must respect it by looking respectable and not unkempt or streetlike. One must honor the soul by dressing it well, for example, buying dignified clothing such as suits and button-down shirts, as well as taking care of the body in which it dwells.

For the eyes of their husbands, the teachers and the girls describe the importance of beauty. Mrs. Cohen said to the girls in class:

> Are cobwebs pretty? Why not?? Because you are thinking about cobwebs in the corner of your living room. It really is gross. But, let's say that we are out in nature, between the rocks, and I am walking with my children and I want to show them how much intelligence there is in nature, how much intelligence God has given to such a small creature. How wonderful it is, how much beauty there is in a cobweb. . . . Beauty is when it is in its natural place. So, when you go outside with loud clothing, with makeup, with perfume. . . . And you attract eyes that are not yours then it is like having a cobweb in your living room. It is only because it is in the wrong place. The torah asks you to look nice, to use makeup and other things—but in the place that [they are] destined for.

The teachers and the girls create a private realm, one in which the young women will be private with their husbands and in which the girls should use beauty. In this realm, a girl should dress nicely, put on makeup, etc. But only here. Thus, when it comes to beauty, there is no rebellion against the emphasis on the male gaze—but there are strict limits on who does the gazing and when.

## Modesty, Beauty, and Female Piety

Concepts of modesty and beauty are currently being reconstructed in the Haredi community, as this chapter has shown. It is intriguing to see how these reconstructions reflect different cultural forces; it is also significant how the Haredi young women's process of redefinition enables them to live with different and at times conflicting aspirations. Rereading and reinterpreting canonical texts serves as a tool by which the girls find a way to mediate different cultural forces, and during this process the teachers step forward to help the students redefine their (secularly influenced) desires as religious feminine ideals. Throughout this process, they find it extremely important to root their emerging ideas in canonical texts, with the consequence that the young women are able to hold on to both secular and religious values.

At the heart of this process of reinterpretation is a redefinition of the motivation to be beautiful and modest. In the case of modesty, the young Haredi women exchange the social-masculine obligation to be modest for a divine path toward communion. In the case of beauty they take secular ideals and turn them into Jewish ones. In both cases, the students and their teachers change the motivating force behind their ideals from external expectations and social dependency to inner modes of self-regulation and discipline. While these redefinitions serve as a way to expand the realms in which the girls may come into touch with sacredness, they also mirror—and transform—modern secular values.

The question remains: Can their reinterpretive and integrative project be regarded as subversive of the Haredi male rabbinic patriarchy, or is it an ameliorative strategy that enables the next generations of young Haredi women to minimize the social psychological discomfort of their own cognitive dissonance? Similar to findings of researchers among other fundamentalist groups,[48] Haredi women are showing discontent with their roles as exclusively wives and mothers and becoming agents of protest and transformation.[49] I propose that the ideals of modesty and beauty presented here represent other realms in which women are reconstructing their religious gender roles. After generations of connecting to God through their husbands and children, Haredi women are constructing a way to connect directly to God through modesty.[50] On the one hand, this practice may be seen as subversive as it creates a distinct and autonomous role for Haredi female piety. In many ways, it informs a creative ideology that empowers femininity insofar as it provides women with a role that entails more than being merely mother and a wife.

However, although they may reinterpret their values and behaviors, they also reinforce many common Haredi principles, especially gendered religious roles, ascetic piety, and suppression of the female body and sexuality through tedious body practice. Thus, there may be some subversive elements in their practice, but as a whole it still functions primarily as a creative way to reinforce the community's traditional ideas. It is for this reason that their ideology remains incomplete, if not incoherent. A close look at the findings reveal that female students criticize authority and dismiss the discourse of modesty for men's sake at the same time that they construct an ideal of beauty founded in part on being beautiful for their future husbands. These contradictions demonstrate the tension created by the opposing social and cultural forces that affect these girls, a tension that cannot be resolved so easily.

This strategy may provide a solution to their cognitive dissonance. Through a creative process of rereading, reinterpreting, and redefining modesty, beauty, and respectability, these women have succeeded in creating new ideals that are implemented in different spheres of their lives. This redefinition enables them to direct apparently competing forces in converging directions and, hence, enables them to become a busy intersection rather than a collision point.[51] These Haredi young women create a crossroads that provides a space for distinct trajectories and generates order between forces and aspirations that otherwise would collide. It is this redefinition of cultural expectations and teachings that enables them to live with seemingly profound contradictions. Will their creativity be enough to prevent collision? Time will tell. For now, they are content with being modest before God, beautiful for their future husbands, and respectable to the eyes of the world.

## NOTES

This article is based on my master's thesis, conducted under the supervision of Nurit Stadler in the Department of Sociology and Anthropology of Hebrew University. This study has benefited from the support of the Shaine Center for Research in the Humanities and the Social Sciences and the Herzl Fellowship Project at the Cherrick Center for the Study of Zionism, the Yishuv, and the State of Israel. I owe a special debt of gratitude to Nurit Stadler and Tamar El-Or for commenting on earlier versions of the manuscript.

1. Gideon Aran, "The Haredi Body" [Hebrew], in *Israeli Haredim: Integration without Assimilation?* eds. Emmanuel Sivan and Kimmy Caplan (Tel Aviv: Van Leer Institute and Hakibutz Hameuhad, 2003); Tamr El-Or, *Educated and Ignorant: On Ultra-Orthodox Jewish Women and Their World* (Boulder: Lynne Rienner, 1994); Yehuda Goodman, "The Exile of the Broken Vessel, Reality Construction and Therapeutic Discourse at Jewish Ultraorthodox Settings for the Mentally Disturbed" [Hebrew] (PhD diss., Hebrew University of Jerusalem, 1997).
2. Yohai Hakak, *Yeshiva Learning and Military Training: An Encounter between Two Cultural Models* [Hebrew] (Jerusalem: Floersheimer Institute for Policy Studies, 2003).

3. Jacob Lupo, *A Shift in Haredi Society: Vocational Training and Academic Studies* [Hebrew] (Jerusalem: Floersheimer Institute for Policy Studies, 2003).
4. Nissim Leon, *Gentle Ultra-Orthodoxy: Religious Renewal in Oriental Jewry in Israel* [Hebrew] (Jerusalem: Ben-Tzvi Institute, 2009); Haim Zicherman and Cahaner Lee, *Modern Ultra-Orthodoxy: The Emergence of a Haredi Middle Class in Israel* [Hebrew] (The Israel Democracy Institute, 2012).
5. Kimmy Caplan and Nurit Stadler, *Leadership and Authority in Israeli Haredi Society* [Hebrew] (Tel Aviv: Hakibutz Hameuhad and the Van Leer Institute, 2009); Yoel Finkelman, *Strictly Kosher Reading: Popular Literature and the Condition of Contemporary Orthodoxy* (Brighton, MA: Academic Studies Press, 2011); Nissim Leon, *Gentle Ultra-Orthodoxy;* Emmanuel Sivan and Kimmy Caplan, *Israeli Haredim: Integration without Assimilation?* [Hebrew] (Tel Aviv: Van Leer Institute and Hakibutz Hameuhad, 2003); Nurit Stadler, *Yeshiva Fundamentalism: Piety, Gender and Resistance in the Ultra-Orthodox World* (New York: New York University Press, 2009).
6. Tamar El-Or, *Reserved Seats: Religion, Gender, and Ethnicity in Contemporary Israel* [Hebrew] (Tel Aviv: Am Oved, 2006); Jody Myers and Jane Rachel Litman, "The Secret of Jewish Femininity: Hiddenness, Power, and Physicality in the Theology of Orthodox Women in the Contemporary World," in *Gender and Judaism: The Transformation of Tradition*, ed. Tamar Rudavsky (New York: New York University Press, 1995); Susan Sered, *Women as Ritual Experts: The Religious Lives of Elderly Jewish Women in Jerusalem* (Oxford: Oxford University Press, 1992); Yael Shenkar, "Haredi Female Writers," in *Authority and Power in the Haredi Community in Israel*, eds. Kimmy Caplan and Nurit Stadler [Hebrew] (Tel Aviv: Hakibbutz Hameuchad, 2009).
7. Adi Finkelstein, "The Preparations of Haredi Girls to their Monthly Period and Sexual Maturity" [Hebrew] (PhD diss., Hebrew University of Jerusalem, 1997); Shulamit Oryan, "None is More Beautiful than the Virtue of Modesty: Communication Patterns in the Socialization of Ultra-Orthodox Girls" [Hebrew] (PhD. diss., Haifa University, 1994).
8. Kimmy Caplan, *Internal Popular Discourse in Israeli Haredi Society* [Hebrew] (Jerusalem: Zalman Shazar Center for Jewish History, 2007); Menachem Friedman, "Back to the Grandmother: The New Ultra-Orthodox Woman," *Israel Studies* 1 (1988): 21–26.
9. Tamar El-Or, " 2007/8: The Winter of the Veiled Women" [Hebrew], *Theory and Criticism* 37 (2010): 52.
10. Rhonda Berger-Sofer, "Pious Women: A Study of the Women's Roles in a Hassidic and Pious Community, Meah She'arim" (PhD diss., Rutgers University, 1979).
11. Vimala Jayanti, "Women in Mea Shearim: A Different Reality" (PhD diss., Hebrew University of Jerusalem, 1982).
12. Tamar El-Or, "Educated and Ignorant: Female Literacy in Chassidut Gur: A Link in a Chain of Paradoxes" [Hebrew] (PhD diss., Bar Ilan University, 1990), 252–61.
13. Oryan, "None is More Beautiful," 3.
14. Ibid., v.
15. Orit Yafeh, "Becoming an Ultra-Orthodox Girl: Socialization Practices, Pedagogical Discourse, and Self- Construction" [Hebrew] (PhD diss., Hebrew University of Jerusalem, 2004).
16. Ibid., 326.
17. El-Or, *Educated and Ignorant*; Tova Hartman, *Feminism Encounters Traditional Judaism: Resistance and Accommodation* (Waltham, MA: Brandeis University Press, 2007); Fatima Mernissi, *Beyond the Veil: Male-Female Dynamics in Modern Muslim Society* (New York:

Schenkman, 1975); Susan Sered, *What Makes Women Sick: Maternity, Modesty and Militarism in Israeli Society* (Hanover, NH: Brandeis University Press, 2000).

18. Lila Abu-Lughod, *Remaking Women: Feminism and Modernity in the Middle East* (Princeton, NJ: Princeton University Press, 1998); El-Or, "2007\8: The Winter of the Veiled Women"; Saba Mahmood, *Politics of Piety, the Islamic Revival and the Feminist Subject* (Princeton, NJ: Princeton University Press, 2005); Sima Zalcberg-Block, "Shouldering the Burden of Redemption: How the Fashion of Wearing Capes Developed in Ultra-Orthodox Society," *Nashim: A Journal of Jewish Women's Studies and Gender Issues* 22 (2011): 32–55.
19. Zalcberg-Block, "Shouldering the Burden of Redemption."
20. Stadler, *Yeshiva Fundamentalism*.
21. Orit Avishai, "'Doing Religion' in a Secular World: Women in Conservative Religions and the Question of Agency," *Gender and Society* 22, no. 4 (2008): 409–33; Lynn Davidman, "The Transformation of Bodily Practices among Religious Defectors," in *Embodied Resistance: Challenging the Norms, Breaking the Rules,* eds. Chris Bobel and Samantha Kwan (Nashville, TN: Vanderbilt University Press, 2011); El-Or, "2007/8: The Winter of the Veiled Women"; Tamar Rapo port, "The Pedagogical Construction of Traditional Woman: An Ethnographic Study of 'Holiness Class'" [Hebrew], *Megamot* 39, no. 4 (1999): 492–517.
22. Lila Abu-Lughod, *Veiled Sentiments: Honor and Poetry in a Bedouin Society* (Berkeley: University of California Press, 1986); Mahmood, *Politics of Piety.*
23. Abu-Lughod, *Remaking Women;* Mahmood, *Politics of Piety.*
24. Fictitious names are used for all the interviewees as well as the name of the institution.
25. This network started as a small school for thirty students founded by Sarah Schneirer in 1917 in Krakow. Schneirer's pioneer idea grew quickly, and her school gradually turned into the "Bais Yaakov Network" and caused a revolution in female education. See Deborah Weissman, "Bais Yaakov as an Innovation in Jewish Women's Education: A Contribution to the Study of Education and Social Change," *Studies in Jewish Education* 7 (1995): 278–99.
26. Jayanti, "Women in Mea Shearim."
27. Stadler, *Yeshiva Fundamentalism*.
28. Lynn Davidman, *Tradition in a Rootless World: Women Turn to Orthodox Judaism* (Berkeley: University of California Press, 1991).
29. Lea Taragin-Zeller, "Modesty for Heaven's Sake: Authority and Creativity among Female Ultra-Orthodox Teenagers in Israel," *Nashim: A Journal of Jewish Women's Studies and Gender Issues* (2013).
30. Rivka Neriya-Ben Shahar, "Modesty Discourse in Female Haredi Newspapers 1960–1989," in *Gender in Israel: New Studies of Gender in the Yeshiva and the State*, eds. Gideon Katz and Margalit Shilo (Beer Sheba: Ben-Gurion Research Institute, 2011); Yafeh, "Becoming and Ultra-Orthodox Girl."
31. For example, see Rachel Elior, "'Present but Absent,' 'Still Life,' and 'A Pretty Maiden Who Has No Eyes': On the Presence and Absence of Women in the Hebrew Language, in the Jewish Religion, and in Israeli Life," *Studies in Spirituality* 20 (2010), 381–455. She explains how this theology enables men to assert control over woman's body and sexuality.
32. Hartman, *Feminism Encounters Traditional Judaism*, 45–61.
33. Rivki seems to be quoting an interpretation of the story about Kimchit, who according to the version in tractate Yoma 47a benefited from her zealous modesty practices by having her seven sons become High Priests. For a detailed discussion of this story and its different

versions see Yaffa Zilke, "Editing Trends in Stories of the Sages in Vayikra Rabba and its Talmudic Parallels" (PhD diss., Bar Ilan University, 2001).

34. In a similar vein, Macleod claims that the Arab head-covering has been transformed from a patriarchal imperative into a religious one. See Arlene Macleod, *Accommodating Protest: Working Women, the New Veiling and Change in Cairo* (New York: Columbia University Press, 1991).
35. Marie Griffith, *God's Daughters: Evangelical Women and the Power of Submission* (University of California Press, 2000), 139–50.
36. For example: "He has told you, O man, what is good, and what the Lord requires of you: only to do justice, and to love goodness, and to walk modestly with God" (Micah 6:8) and "But wisdom is with those who are unassuming" (Proverbs 11:2). However, the verse "All glorious is the princess within her chamber; her gown is interwoven with gold" (Psalms 45:14) is commonly tied to modesty even though its original meaning describes the exact opposite of modest conduct. As we shall see, it may be for this reason that this phrase was not commonly used in the classes about modesty.
37. See note 39, below.
38. "A women must not put on man's apparel, nor shall a man wear women's clothing" (Deuteronomy 22:5).
39. The Talmud (Ketubot 72a-b) argues that a woman must cover her hair from the commandment to "Let the hair of the woman's head go loose" (Numbers, 5:18) as part of the test the *sotah* must perform. In addition, the Sages show from the verse "A women must not put on man's apparel, nor shall a man wear women's clothing" (Deuteronomy 22:5) that men and women should dress and act in distinctive ways. For a detailed discussion, see Getsel Ellinson, *The Modest Way: A Guide to the Rabbinic Sources* (Jerusalem: Eliner Library, 1992). The Sages were Jewish religious leaders from the Second Temple to the late sixth century.
40. Ora Cohen, *Women's Modesty in the Modern Era: Continuation or Halachic Change?* [Hebrew] (Bet-El Press, 1999), 143–45.
41. *Bereshith Rabbah*, 18:2, trans. H. Freedman (London: Soncino Press, 1951).
42. Rachel Elior, "'Present but Absent,' 'Still Life,' and 'a Pretty Maiden Who Has No Eyes': On the Presence and Absence of Women in the Hebrew Language, in the Jewish Religion, and in Israeli Life," *Studies in Spirituality* 20 (2010): 381–455.
43. L. Rosenthal, *Instilling Modesty in the Students* (Beit El: Beit El Publishing, n.d.).
44. See Metsudat David and Ibn Ezra on Michah 6:8. Other commentaries discuss the importance of doing Mitzvot in private—see Rashi and Radak there.
45. Ayala Fader, *Mitzvah Girls: Bringing Up the Next Generation of Hasidic Jews in Brooklyn* (Princeton, NJ: Princeton University Press, 2009).
46. See: Gershom Scholem, *Origins of the Kabbalah* (Philadelphia: Jewish Publication Society, 1987).
47. Mary Douglas, *Purity and Danger: An Analysis of Concepts of Pollution and Taboo* (London: Routledge and K. Paul, 1966), 44.
48. See Abu-Lughod, *Veiled Sentiments*; El-Or, "Educated and Ignorant"; Griffith, *God's Daughters*.
49. Sylvia Barack Fishman, "Reading from Right to Left: Fundamentalism, Feminism, and Women's Changing Roles in Jewish Societies," in *Fundamentalism and the Position of Women in World Religions*, eds. Arvind Sharma and Katherine Young (New York: T. and T. Clark International, 2008).

50. Similarly, scholars have identified new practices through which religious women are expanding the realms in which they may come in contact with holiness. For example: Turning the kitchen into a "Mikdash Miat"(El-Or, *Reserved Seats*), glorification of the rules of Niddah (Avishai, "Doing Religion"), and stringent body covering (El-Or, 2007/8: "The Winter of the Veiled Women"; Sima Zalcberg-Block, "Shouldering the Burden of Redemption") are some examples for these practices.
51. Renato Rosaldo, "Grief and a Headhunter's Rage," in *Violence in War and Peace: An Anthology*, eds. Nancy Scheper-Hughes and Philippe Bourgois (Malden, MA: Blackwell, 2004).

# NOTES ABOUT THE ART

Andi Arnovitz

## Cover Image

*Andi Arnovitz, "A Vest for a Child in these Times," 2009. Mono print on Johonnot paper, machine sewn, threads, Japanese papers, 71 × 46.5 cm.* The Second Intifada was raging, and I felt a peculiar kind of maternal impotence. I could not protect my children; I could not shield them from random acts of violence. All the women I knew, all these mothers had developed a set of private acts, rituals, and superstitions to try to protect their children. Whether it was simply making sure we kissed them before they walked out the door, or more complicated motions of putting prayers or psalms in their pockets or backpacks, we all tried to create these bubbles around the people we loved to protect them. This vest contains various amuletic prayers, charts, and symbols common in traditional Jewish and many other societies. The shape is modeled from ceremonial garments that children wear in Afghanistan, Iraq, and elsewhere.

## Part II: Family Transformations (page 121)

*Andi Arnovitz, "The Commerce of Fertility," 2013. Installation, plastic polymer, stamped metal tags, found ready-made plastic babies. Each baby is 3.5 × 3.5 × 3.5 cm.* There are four hundred little boy and girl babies on "ice," all with a little metal tag wrapped around their ankles. With close examination, one finds each baby has a separate number and no two numbers are the same. The piece was inspired by several events. Two movies—in Canada the movie *Starbuck*, and in America the movie *Delivery Man*—are both based on true stories wherein through human error on the part of sperm banks two men accidentally father hundreds of children. A Montreal man fathered 250 children. In the United Kingdom a man fathered five hundred. In the newspaper in the fall of 2013 was an article about two young women, Mikayla Stern-Ellis and Emily Nappi, freshman at Tulane University, who became friends based on many similar interests and then discovered they shared the same Columbian sperm-donor father. This piece does not at all condemn the progress made in the fertility field. But it does call into question the enormity of the task we have of keeping records, of creating limits, and of keeping greed and finances in check, as this is a very lucrative business. I harbor a suspicion that with all the medical progress and advancements there comes a host of emotional, personal and ethical implications we have not anticipated.

## Part IV: Backlash and Reaction (page 285)

*Andi Arnovitz, "Shut Her Up," 2012. Silkscreen print, edition of 18, 75 × 105 cm.* This is one from a series called "Shut Her Up, Cover Her Up and Cut Her Up," which addresses a series of unfortunate events in Israel with regard to women and their rights. I took Albrecht Durer's classic engraving of Adam and Eve, and I found when I stripped away everything superfluous in the print, Adam's stance toward Eve seemed threatening. I used these two and then played with the image. "Shut Her Up" addresses the issues of women's equal rights to sidewalks and bus seats, being allowed to deliver a eulogy in a cemetery, being allowed to give a paper in a conference of UltraOrthodox men, and on and on. "Cover Her Up" again deals with the fixation of how much of her elbow or collarbone a woman is allowed to show, and "Cut Her Up" deals with the horrifying incident, which has now been rectified, whereby the image of a woman was removed from Israel's organ-donation posters in B'nai Brak and Jerusalem. It suggests that our organs are perfectly fine—just not the vessel that contains them.

# CONTRIBUTORS

SYLVIA BARACK FISHMAN is the Joseph and Esther Foster Professor of Judaic Studies in the Near Eastern and Judaic Studies Department at Brandeis University, and codirector of the Hadassah Brandeis Institute. In addition to *Love, Marriage, and Jewish Families: Paradoxes of a Social Revolution*, she has authored seven other books and numerous articles on the changing Jewish family, intermarriage, transformed gender roles, Jewish education, American Judaism, and Jewish literature, film, and popular culture. She received the 2014 Marshall Sklare Award for distinguished achievement from the Association for the Social Scientific Study of Jewry. She earned her doctorate from Washington University in St. Louis, where she was awarded a Danforth Graduate Fellowship. She won the Samuel Belkin Memorial Award for Distinguished Professional Achievement from Yeshiva University, her undergraduate alma mater.

ANDI ARNOVITZ is an American-born artist living in Jerusalem. A master printmaker, Arnovitz has expanded her artistic lexicon to include multiple media, frequently synthesizing an expansive range of techniques to treat controversial topics of a religious, political, and social nature. Arnovitz continues to produce and exhibit multiple series engaging controversial topics ranging from female fertility to contradictions between contemporary society and traditional Jewish practice. Most recently, Arnovitz embarked on a series that provides novel insight into social challenges created by Israel's political reality. Arnovitz has exhibited in solo and group shows in the United States, Israel, and Europe. Her work can be found in the collections of the US Library of Congress, the Israel National Library, the Israel Museum of Art in Ein Harod, Yeshiva University Museum, and many private collections.

RACHEL S. BERNSTEIN is a doctoral candidate in the Departments of Near Eastern and Judaic Studies and Sociology at Brandeis University, where she received her M.A. in Near Eastern and Judaic Studies and Women's and Gender Studies. Her main research interests include trends in the intersections between gender and Judaism; religious and cultural expression in emerging adulthood; and representations of Jewish women in television and film.

TEHILLA BLUMENTHAL is a clinical and educational psychologist in Jerusalem. She received her doctorate from the Hebrew University of Jerusalem, focusing her research on unwed Orthodox Jewish mothers by choice. In her private practice, she specializes in cultural sensitivity, family issues, and hypnotherapy. She teaches academic courses in gender studies, family dynamics, and psychology, and she also provides psychological emergency services for women who experience domestic abuse and for victims of war trauma.

SERGIO DELLAPERGOLA, born in Italy, has lived in Israel since 1966 and holds a doctorate from the Hebrew University. A professor emeritus of population studies and former chairman of the Hebrew University's Harman Institute of Contemporary Jewry, where he held the Shlomo Argov Chair in Israel-Diaspora Relations, he is an internationally known specialist on the demography of world Jewry, lecturing at over seventy universities and research centers worldwide. His numerous books include *Jewish Demographic Policies: Population Trends and Options* (2011), along with two hundred papers on historical demography, family, international migration, and Jewish identification, in the Diaspora and in Israel. He served as senior policy consultant to the president of Israel, the Israeli government, the Jerusalem municipality, and major national and international organizations. He won the Marshall Sklare Award for distinguished achievement from the Association for the Social Scientific Study of Jewry in 1999, and the Landau Prize by Mifàl HaPayis (the national lottery of Israel) for demography and migration in 2013.

ARI ENGELBERG teaches sociology and Israel studies at the Rothberg School for International Students at the Hebrew University and at the Interdisciplinary Program of the Bar-Ilan University. He received his doctorate in sociology and anthropology at the Hebrew University of Jerusalem, and in 2013 he spent a postdoctoral semester as a Kennedy-Leigh research fellow at Oxford University's Jewish Studies Centre and Oriental Studies Department. He has published articles in Hebrew and English on the subject of Religious-Zionist singles and the subject of Orthodox guidebooks for marriage.

YOEL FINKELMAN is the curator of the Judaica collection at the National Library of Israel. He received his doctorate in Jewish thought from the Hebrew University in Jerusalem. He has taught at Bar-Ilan University and has published widely on the topics of Haredi Judaism, Religious-Zionism, and Jewish education. His book *Strictly Kosher Reading, Popular Literature and the Condition of Contemporary Orthodoxy* appeared in 2011.

LISA FISHBAYN JOFFE directs the Project on Gender, Culture, Religion and the Law at the Hadassah-Brandeis Institute of Brandeis University, edits the Brandeis Press Series on Gender, Culture, Religion and the Law, and cofounded the Boston Agunah Taskforce. She holds a law degree from Osgoode Hall Law School in Canada and an SJD in legal theory from Harvard Law School. With expertise in women's rights under Jewish family law, African customary law, and the intersection between secular and religious law, she edited *Gender, Religion and Family Law: Theorizing Conflicts Between Women's Rights and Cultural Traditions* (2012); *The Polygamy Question* (2015); and *Gender, Religion and Equality* (2015). Her next book, on women's rights and Jewish divorce, is titled *Gender, Justice and Dialogue in Jewish Law.*

IRIT KOREN is a clinical therapist, a writer, and lecturer. She received her doctorate in gender studies from Bar-Ilan University (2007) and an MSW from Wurzweiler School, Yeshiva University. Koren is the author of the book: *You Are Hereby Renewed Unto me: Gender, Religion and Power Relations In the Jewish Wedding Ritual* (2011). In 2003, her first book, *Aron Betoch Aron: Stories of Religious Homosexuals* [Altering the Closet] (Yediot Acharonot), appeared, the first to be published in Israel on religious homosexuals, and has since become a central citation for anyone writing on the subject. In her practice as a clinical therapist in Modi'in her clients include religious gays and lesbians among others.

JONATHAN KRASNER is the Jack, Joseph, and Morton Mandel Associate Professor at the Mandel Center for Studies in Jewish Education and a member of the Department of Near Eastern and Judaic Studies at Brandeis University. His book *The Benderly Boys and American Jewish Education* was the winner of the 2011 National Jewish Book Award in American Jewish Studies and was a finalist for the Sami Rohr Prize for Jewish Literature in 2012. His research interests include the history and sociology of American Jewish education, twentieth-century American Jewish culture, and gender and sexuality. Prior to Brandeis, Jonathan taught for fourteen years at the Hebrew Union College-Jewish Institute of Religion in New York and Cincinnati.

GAIL LABOVITZ is associate professor of Rabbinic literature at the American Jewish University, where she teaches rabbinic texts and Jewish law for the Ziegler School of Rabbinic Studies. Her book *Marriage and Metaphor: Constructions of Gender in Rabbinic Literature* was published in 2009. Prior to joining the faculty of the Ziegler School of Rabbinic Studies, she served as a senior research analyst for the Feminist Sexual Ethics Project at Brandeis University and as the coordinator of the Jewish Feminist Research Group, a project of the Jewish Women's Studies Program at the Jewish Theological Seminary, and was a 2002 recipient of a research award from the Hadassah International Research Institute on Jewish Women at Brandeis University. She is a past chair of the Women's Caucus of the Association for Jewish Studies and is the founder and coordinator of the Dr. Elka Klein Memorial Travel Grant.

DANIEL PARMER, research associate at the Cohen Center for Modern Jewish Studies at Brandeis University and doctoral candidate at the Heller School for Social Policy and Management at Brandeis University, has contributed to several demographic studies including the 2005 Boston Jewish Community Study and the 2008 Berkshire Jewish Community Study. He is one of the principal analysts of the Steinhardt Social Research Institute's American Jewish Population Project (AJPP), leading the project's data synthesis of localized geographic areas. His coauthored studies include *Matrilineal Ascent/Patrilineal Descent: The Gender Imbalance in American Jewish Life* (2008) and *American Jewish Population Estimates: 2012* (2013).

MICHELLE SHAIN is a doctoral candidate at the Heller School for Social Policy and Management writing a dissertation on fertility among American Jews. She is a research associate at the Cohen Center for Modern Jewish Studies at Brandeis University, where she participates in the ongoing evaluation of Taglit-Birthright Israel. She received a bachelor's degree in anthropology and Near Eastern and Judaic studies from Brandeis University and an master's from the Avraham Harman Institute of Contemporary Jewry at the Hebrew University of Jerusalem. Shain has coauthored several articles in the *Journal for the Scientific Study of Religion* and *Contemporary Jewry.*

LEA TARAGIN-ZELLER is a PhD student at the Department of Sociology and Anthropology at the Hebrew University. She is currently writing a dissertation on family planning among Orthodox Jews in Israel, and serves as a research associate at the Israel Democracy Institute, exploring relationships between the Jewish tradition and human rights. Her work has been published in *Megamot* (2014) and *Nashim* (2014).

SUSAN WEISS, an attorney, holds her doctorate in anthropology. She is the founder and executive director of the Center for Women's Justice (CWJ). While at CWJ, she initiated the innovative legal practice of suing recalcitrant Jewish husbands for civil, tort damages if they refuses to deliver a Jewish divorce (*get*) to their wives—a tactic noted as "game-changing" by the prestigious *Ha'aretz* news daily. Weiss is an editor of *The Law and its Decisor*, a journal published by Bar Ilan University Law School, and she coauthored the book *Marriage and Divorce in the Jewish State: Israel's Civil War.* In recognition of her work, she has been honored with several awards.

# INDEX

Note: Page numbers in *italics* indicate figures or tables; page numbers followed by "n" indicate note numbers.